GIANTS DIARY

GIANTS DIARY

A CENTURY OF GIANTS BASEBALL
IN NEW YORK AND SAN FRANCISCO

BY
FRED STEIN

AND
NICK PETERS

NORTH ATLANTIC BOOKS
BERKELEY, CALIFORNIA

Giants Diary

ISBN 0-938190-97-0 (cloth)
ISBN 0-938190-96-2 (paperback)

Published by North Atlantic Books
        2320 Blake Street
        Berkeley, California 94704

Cover photo of 1888 team by J. Hall, as numbered:
1. Stump Weidman, 2. Tim Keefe, 3. Bill George, 4. Sam Crane, 5. Pat Murphy,
6. Cannonball Titcomb 7. Roger Connor, 8. Monte Ward, 9. Elmer Foster, manager
Jim Mutrie (standing), 11. Buck Ewing, 12. Danny Richardson, 13. Willard Brown,
14. Mike Tiernan, 15. Jim O'Rourke, 16. Mickey Welch, 17. Gil Hatfield, 18. George
Gore, 19. Elmer Cleveland, 20. Mike Slattery

Cover photo of 1986 team by Dennis Desprois:
Back Row (L-R): Joel Youngblood, Frank Williams, Jim Gott, Bob Melvin, Bob Brenly,
Mike Krukow, Mark Davis, Roger Mason, Jeff Robinson, Scott Garrelts, Kelly
Downs, Candy Maldonado, Terry Mulholland, Juan Berenguer, Harry Spilman.
Middle Row (L-R): Equipment Manager Mike Murphy, Director of Team Travel Dirk
Smith, Mike LaCoss, Assistant Equipment Manager Lon Lewis, Trainer Mark Le-
tendre, Vida Blue, Dan Gladden, First Base Coach Jose Morales, Third Base Coach
Gordy MacKenzie, Pitching Coach Norm Sherry, Manager Roger Craig, Coach Bob
Lillis, Bullpen Coach Bill Fahey, Randy Kutcher, Greg Minton, Jeffrey Leonard,
Fitness Coach Ken Preminger, Trainer Greg Lynn.
Kneeling (L-R): Batboys Bill Fanara, David Lewis and Jim Mallamo, Steve Carlton,
Mike Aldrete, Robby Thompson, Jose Uribe, Luis Quinones, Will Calrk, Chili Davis,
Chris Brown, Batboy Mike Mullane.

Cover design by Paula Morrison

Giants Diary is sponsored by the Society for the Study of Native Arts and Sciences,
a nonprofit educational corporation whose goals are to develop an ecological and
crosscultural perspective linking various scientific, social, and artistic fields; to
nurture a holistic view of arts, sciences, humanities, and healing; and to publish
and distribute literature on the relationship of mind, body, and nature.

Library of Congress Cataloging-in-Publication Data

Stein, Fred.
        Giants diary.

        Includes index.
        1. New York Giants (Baseball team)—History.
2. San Francisco Giants (Baseball team)—History.
I. Peters, Nick.   II. Title.
GV875.N42S74   1987   796.357'64'0979461   86-33337
ISBN 0-938190-97-0
ISBN 0-938190-96-2 (pbk.)

CONTENTS

ACKNOWLEDGMENTS

The authors wish to thank all those who helped in the preparation of this book.

We particularly wish to thank Pat Gallagher, vice president for operations of the San Francisco Giants, and members of his staff who reviewed the manuscript and provided material for the book.

Members of the Society for American Baseball Research (SABR) were extremely helpful in reviewing the manuscript and providing useful comments, amplifications, and corrections. Special thanks are due SABR founder L. Robert Davids, whose extensive knowledge and zealous attempts to improve the accuracy of descriptions of events are reflected in many of these pages. Other SABR members who took time to improve this book include Mark Gallagher, Bill Mead, and Barry Schweid.

Several books provided much of the descriptive and anecdotal material used. These books include Frank Graham's *McGraw of the Giants,* Arthur Daley's *Times At Bat,* Lawrence S. Ritter's *The Glory of Their Times,* and Arnold Hano's *Greatest Giants of Them All.* Files of the *New York Times* and *The Sporting News* provided other basic sources of event description and date identification. The various baseball encyclopedias were indispensable statistical references.

FOREWORD

Although I presently am working for the crossbay Oakland A's, the Giants always will remain something special in my heart. I grew up in the Bay Area and was involved with the Giants, either as a player or a manager, in four straight decades beginning with the Forties.

I'm proud of the fact that I was one of the few Giants to bridge the New York and San Francisco years, so my memory is filled with good thoughts about an organization which gave me a chance to play in the major leagues and also gave me my first — and last — opportunity to manage in the big leagues.

I played for Oakland before joining the Giants as an infielder after World War 2. I served in the service for three years and didn't reach the majors until I was 26. I was more or less of a regular for three years and have fond memories of being on the team that set the major league home run record (221) in 1947.

The Giants always have been known for the long ball and I was part of some of their best slugging teams as a player and a manager. I was a tall, skinny (6-1, 178) kid, but I contributed 17 home runs to the record, so that 1947 season is most memorable to me.

We didn't play too many 1-0 games in those days, and it was the same story through the Sixties in San Francisco. I remember making the All-Star team in 1948 as a last-minute replacement for the injured Eddie Stanky and serving as a pinch-hitter in four games of the 1951 World Series with the Yankees.

I didn't play much with that '51 club, but how can anyone forget that marvelous comeback and Bobby Thomson's home run against the

Brooklyn Dodgers in the playoffs? I played one more year after that with the Giants before becoming their Triple-A manager at Minneapolis.

We won a pennant in 1955, and the next year I succeeded Leo Durocher as the manager in New York. The 1957 season was a sad one; the club was leaving the Polo Grounds and the fans knew they were about to lose something dear.

I had mixed emotions that year. I was part of the Giants' past in New York, yet I was anxious about returning home to manage the San Francisco club. That 1958 season was a wonderful experience, the Bay Area fans making us feel very welcome.

We also had a great club with which to build our future on the West Coast. In addition to Willie Mays, the greatest player I've ever managed, we had rookies like Orlando Cepeda and Jimmy Davenport. One year later, Willie McCovey joined the group. There were a lot of home runs and lots of excitement.

There was considerable anticipation in 1960, but we were off to a 33-25 start and I was fired by Horace Stoneham. It was a disappointing time for me. A couple of weeks later, Juan Marichal came to the bigs and the Giants continued to field strong teams throughout the Sixties.

I went on to manage the first Angels clubs and the Twins, but I couldn't forget the Giants after being part of the organization since 1946. So, when Bob Lurie purchased the club in 1976 and asked me to manage the Giants again, I agreed because we were friends.

"Giants Diary" captures a lot of pleasant memories from those teams of the past. The franchise has a rich tradition, from New York to San Francisco, and a book like this helps to revive the high points in the first 100-plus years of the franchise.

All the great players and all the magic moments are in this book, one which is filled with wonderful anecdotes, facts, and figures and is ideal for the casual baseball fan as well as the hard-core baseball buff. I feel it's a must for all Giants fans.

Bill Rigney

1

DAY BY DAY HIGHLIGHTS

1882

Sept. 22 — The National League held a special meeting at Philadelphia during which the Troy, New York, and Worcester (Massachusetts) clubs were "invited" to withdraw from the League because they were not being supported adequately. These two franchises were transferred to New York and Philadelphia.

Dec. 7 — The National League awarded franchises vacated by Troy, New York, and Worcester to New York and Philadelphia. John B. Day, who purchased the Troy club, became the New York club's first club president. John Clapp, who had managed at Indianapolis, Buffalo, and Cincinnati, was appointed their first manager.

1883

May 1 — The New York National League club (not yet called the Giants) won its first league game, a 7-5 victory over Philadelphia. The game between the two members of the National League was played at the first Polo Grounds at 110th Street between Fifth and Sixth Avenues in Manhattan. The New Yorkers took the lead in the game early and their future Hall of Fame right-hander, Mickey Welch, held on to win despite the Phillies' five unearned runs. Former U.S. President Ulysses S. Grant was in the fifteen-thousand-plus crowd and, according to the *New York Times'* account, he joined "several times in the applause accorded the players."

May 3 — New York pitcher Monte Ward hit two home runs as the Polo Grounders defeated Boston, 10-9. Player-manager John Clapp drove in the winning run with a one-out single in the bottom of the ninth.

June 9 — New York lost to Buffalo at the Polo Grounds 8-7 despite the valiant efforts of New York catcher Buck Ewing, who had three triples and a single.

Sept. 8 — New York scored thirteen runs in the third inning at Philadelphia en route to a 16-6 win over the Phils. The game was called because of darkness in the eighth inning; an irritated *New York Times* writer attributed the delay to the "baby actions in the box" of the Philadelphia pitchers.

1884

May 24 — New York right fielder Mike Dorgan committed five errors as the Providence club manhandled the Polo Grounders 19-5 in New York. The *New York Times* reported that the home team looked so pathetic that "The Siamese embassy [staff] occupied the [New York club's] stockholder box and showed their knowledge by leaving in the middle of the game." More likely, the embassy staff was late for tea or, like most foreigners, completely baffled by the game.

Aug. 28 — Giant right-hander Mickey Welch defeated the Cleveland Spiders with a remarkable pitching performance, striking out the first nine hitters he faced. In the first inning, "Smiling Mickey" set down, in order, Cleveland first baseman Bill Phillips, right fielder Pete Hotaling, and third baseman George Pinckney. In the second inning, he whiffed consecutively left fielder Ernie Burch, third baseman Mike Muldoon, and right fielder "Bloody Jake" Evans. In the third, he struck out second baseman George "Germany" Smith, but Smith reached first base safely when a fill-in New York catcher misplayed the ball. Welch then rubbed out pitcher John Henry and catcher Jerry Moore on strikes, his eighth and ninth strikeout victims.

Welch's feat went unnoticed because the official scorer did not credit him with striking out Smith, who had reached base safely. Baseball historian Harry Simmons pointed out the error in 1941. Welch's achievement was especially noteworthy because he had been injured in his two preceding starts, first by a line smash through the box (then only 50 feet from the plate), then by a beaning as he batted. Welch's strikeout spree remained the record for consecutive strikeouts until the Mets' Tom Seaver struck out ten straight hitters on April 22, 1970.

1885

May 9 — The Giants won a 1-0 victory over Providence at the Polo Grounds before five thousand fans. New York right-hander Tim Keefe, in his first start for New York, outpitched Providence's star right-hander Charlie "Old Hoss" Radbourn. Keefe gave up only one hit, a single by Providence second baseman Jack Farrell. The Giants scored their run in the bottom of the ninth when catcher Buck Ewing tripled and Radbourn wild-pitched him home.

May 27 — The Giants buried Buffalo 24-0 with a twenty-nine-hit attack led by first baseman Roger Connor, who went 5-for-5. Mickey Welch held Buffalo to five hits. Typical of the era, the one-sided game was completed in a mere one hour and fifty-two minutes.

June 3 — Mickey Welch outpointed the Phillies 8-7 in eleven innings at Philadelphia on some spirited baserunning by Giant third baseman Thomas "Dude" Esterbrook. With two out in the top of the eleventh, Esterbrook singled and came all the way around on a hit-and-run liner to left field by Mike Dorgan. The outfield throw had Esterbrook nailed at the plate, but he kicked the ball out of Philly catcher Charley Ganzel's hand and scored.

   The win gave the New Yorkers nineteen victories in their first twenty-four games and, the story has it, gave rise to the club's famous name. After the game, newly-installed New York manager Jim Mutrie exulted over his team's triumph and great start, proclaiming "My big fellows! My Giants! We are the people!" The name caught on immediately and thereafter the club was always called the Giants.

Sept. 4 — Mickey Welch defeated Boston 6-3 for his seventeenth consecutive win.

Sept. 7 — Giant pitching great Mickey Welch lost to Philly right-hander Charlie Ferguson 3-1 in Philadelphia, breaking Welch's string of seventeen straight wins. It was Welch's first loss in almost two months. The game was highlighted by a Giant triple play in the first inning. Giant first baseman Roger Connor started the play by spearing Ferguson's line smash and stepping on first to double Phil left fielder Ed Andrews. Connor then fired the ball to second baseman Joe Gerhardt to rub out Philadelphia right fielder Jack Manning.

Sept. 29 — With eight games remaining on the schedule for both clubs, the second-place Giants moved into Chicago in a last-ditch effort to stay in the race with the first-place Cubs. Unhappily, Mickey Welch lost 7-4 on a flurry of Cub drives hit into the overflow crowd of five thousand frenzied fans, which included about two hundred Giant buffs who made the train trip from New York. Under the ground rules, a ball hit into the crowd was good for three bases. The Cubs managed five such ersatz triples and the Giants none; the crowd that overflowed the playing field harassed Giant outfielders on long flies but made room to permit Cub fielders to handle fly balls.

Sept. 30 — The Giants lost the second game of their final series to the Cubs in Chicago, and the Cubs clinched the pennant. Chicago's Hall of Fame right-hander John Clarkson outpitched the Giants' Tim Keefe for a 2-1 win in a tight, well-played game. One of the Cub runs came on second baseman Fred Pfeffer's home run. Typical of the highly-partisan sportswriting of the time, the *New York Times'* correspondent wrote, "The defeat can only be attributed to a long fly ball that went over the right field fence and gave the batsman [Pfeffer] a home run. This would have been an easy catch for a right fielder in a fair-sized park."

Oct. 3 — There was a gentlemanly touch to the end of the Giant-Cub season series as the two clubs prepared to play their final game in Chicago. The Cubs had clinched the pennant at the Giants' expense three days earlier. Before the game, Giant captain Monte Ward presented Chicago's manager Cap Anson with a handsome white and maroon satin flag with the inscription "New York to Chicago, 1885." Ward said gamely, "Captain Anson, we came to Chicago hoping and expecting to win this last series of games, but you have beaten us fairly and squarely and we have no complaints." Anson replied with an equally gracious statement.

1886

May 13 — The twelve-man rosters that major league clubs carried in the 1880s left the teams with little margin for putting able-bodied teams on the field at all times. On this date in Chicago, the Giants lost to the locals, 7-3. The Giants were forced to put a makeshift team on the field because of a rash of injuries. Manager Jim Mutrie lamented, "My nine is in bad shape. In fact I have only seven men to depend on."

May 31 — The Giants split two games with Detroit at the Polo Grounds, winning the morning game 6-5 in ten innings and dropping the afternoon game, 4-1. The first game so excited fans in and outside of the Polo Grounds that a great crowd came for the second game. An estimated twenty thousand jammed the park, including a large standing audience on the playing field. After the infield was cleared and the outfield partially cleared, both teams agreed that all fair balls hit into the crowd were to be ruled one-base hits. This accounted for the relatively low-scoring second game.

1887

May 16 — The Giants defeated Indianapolis 11-8 despite five errors by Giant left fielder Mike Tiernan.

May 30 — The Giants lost the morning game of a doubleheader to the Chicago Cubs 12-11 at the Polo Grounds. The Giants led 11-5 going into the top of the ninth, but the Cubs scored seven runs, helped considerably by four walks issued by Giant lefty Bill George. The wild Giant pitcher walked a total of sixteen Cubs in the game, still a tie for the major league record.

June 7 — The Giants scored twelve runs in the third inning at Philadelphia, yet contrived to lose to the Phillies, 15-14. The free-hitting battle was completed in only 2 hours and 15 minutes.

June 11 — The Giants scored eleven runs in the first inning on the way to a 26-2 massacre of Philadelphia at the Polo Grounds. The New Yorkers whacked ten hits in the big inning, including two apiece by outfielder Mike Tiernan, catcher Buck Ewing, and shortstop Monte Ward. Giant second baseman Danny Richardson took top hitting honors with six singles in seven plate appearances.

June 15 — Giant outfielder Mike Tiernan scored six runs in a 29-1 laugher over Philadelphia. This remains a tie for the NL record, which is held by many players.

July 12 — Giant shortstop Monte Ward was replaced as field captain by Buck Ewing because, the Giant management claimed, "it has leaked out that several players are hostile to Ward." There were indications that the Giant front office was even more hostile to Ward; four days later Ward released a letter he had written to National League President N.E. Young detailing a series of abuses to which baseball clubs had been subjecting their players. Ward, a Columbia Law School graduate, was one of the principal figures in the development and operation of the rebel Players League that became active during the 1890 season.

1888

April 19 — Giant shortstop Monte Ward signed to play for $4,000 per year after holding out for several weeks.

May 9 — The Giants belted seven home runs in an 18-4 win at Indianapolis. Roger Connor led the New Yorkers with three homers. Other Giant home runs were hit by outfielders George Gore and Mike Tiernan, second baseman Danny Richardson, and pitcher Mike Welch, who coasted to an easy win.

August 10 — Tim Keefe defeated the Pittsburgh Pirates 2-1 at the Polo Grounds for his nineteenth consecutive win of the season. Keefe's streak began on June 23, 1888. He shares the single-season record with Giant left-hander Rube Marquard, who accomplished the feat in 1912.

August 14 — Tim Keefe lost to Chicago 4-2 at the Polo Grounds, breaking his consecutive game-winning streak at nineteen games. It was a particularly unfortunate loss for Keefe because the Cubs scored two unearned runs on errors by reserve shortstop Gil Hatfield who replaced the ailing regular shortstop, Monte Ward.

August 25 — Mike Tiernan hit for the cycle and drove in four of the Giants' runs. The Polo Grounders defeated the Phillies at Philadelphia, 7-0.

Oct. 4 — The Giants clinched the pennant with a 1-0 win over the Cubs at the Polo Grounds. Giant right-hander Ed "Cannonball" Crane pitched a one-hitter to defeat Chicago right-hander John Tener. Crane struck out four Chicago hitters in the fifth inning; Giant catcher Buck Ewing mishandled a third strike and permitted the hitter to reach first base safely. The only run was scored in the fifth inning on Tener's wild pitch with the bases loaded. Tener would have better days ahead, particularly during the 1913-1918 period when he was president of the National League.

Oct. 13 — The Giants lost to Indianapolis 6-4 in the last regular season game played at the original Polo Grounds at 110th Street and Sixth Avenue in Manhattan.

Oct. 16 — Tim Keefe won the opening game of the championship series against the St. Louis Browns 2-1 at the Polo Grounds. The Giants, the National League winners for the first time, defeated the Browns, who won the American Association pennant.

Oct. 25 — Tim Keefe held the St. Louis Browns in check for an easy 11-3 victory at St. Louis as the Giants won the world championship with a six-games-to-four margin over the American Association winners.

1889

Feb. 4 — The City of New York announced plans to tear down the Polo Grounds stands in order to complete the area known as Douglass Circle at 110th Street and Fifth Avenue in Manhattan. Proving that it meant business, the city rejected an offer from Giant President John B. Day to donate $10,000 to local charities if the city would permit the Giants to use the park in 1889. As a result, Day made plans to use the Manhattan Field site at 155th Street and Eighth Avenue as the Giants' new park. Until the new park was ready for the Giants, the club played at Oakland Park in Jersey City for its first two home games, then moved to St. George Grounds in Staten Island for the next twenty-five home games.

April 24 — The Giants opened their home season at Oakland Park in Jersey City with an 8-7 loss to Boston. They won the following day, 11-10, and completed their brief stay in Jersey City.

June 22 — The Giants lost to Cleveland 8-6 in Cleveland. The game was highlighted by Buck Ewing's grand-slam homer in the third inning over the left-field fence, 478 feet from the plate. This was the longest drive ever hit at the park; the *New York Times* reported that "the ball must have gone 250 yards [on the roll]."

June 25 — Cannonball Crane beat Chicago 12-8 despite yielding eleven walks to the White Stockings (the name "Cubs" would not be adopted by Chicago until 1899).

June 26 — Giant left fielder Jim "Orator Jim" O'Rourke, a future Hall of Famer, had three doubles and a home run as the Giants pummelled the Cubs 12-7 in Chicago.

July 8 — Cannonball Crane outpitched Pirate Hall of Famer Jim "Pud" Galvin to win 7-5. The Giants played their first game at Manhattan Field, located at 155th Street and Eighth Avenue, adjoining the future site of the famous Polo Grounds. Over 10,000 attended the game, and several thousand more fans watched the game from the hilly tract of land just west of the park.

July 14 — John Montgomery "Monte" Ward called a meeting of player representatives to develop plans for obtaining funds from the players to bankroll a new league, the Players League. Ward and others were successful in organizing the new league, and the eight-team Players League operated in 1890.

Sept. 5 — James J. Coogan, whose family owned the Coogan Estate located on a bluff overlooking the Polo Grounds, offered to buy the club for $200,000. Giant President John B. Day astutely turned Coogan down.

Oct. 5 — Tim Keefe defeated Cleveland left-hander Henry Gruber to clinch the Giants' second pennant in a row. Boston finished second, losing to Pittsburgh. Giant manager Jim Mutrie was not on hand to see his club sew up the flag. He was in Pittsburgh, as the *New York Times* darkly put it, "to see that the Bostons do not resort to any underhand work to win the championship." Inexplicably, it had been rumored that Boston, one full game behind the Giants, would make an effort to play two games, instead of the scheduled one game, in order to take the league lead.

Oct. 29 — The Giants defeated Brooklyn, the American Association pennant winner, 3-2 at the Polo Grounds to win their second straight world championship. Giant right-hander Hank O'Day, who would gain greater fame later as an umpire, hurled the win over Brooklyn right-hander William "Adonis" Terry, giving the Giants the series by a 6-3 margin. (Interestingly, this early-day Brooklyn hero — William H. Terry — had almost the identical name as one of Brooklyn's all-time nemeses, Giant manager and first baseman great, William Harold "Memphis Bill" Terry).

1890

Jan. 28 — The U.S. Supreme Court ruled against an injunction that would have prevented Giant shortstop Monte Ward from playing for any other team except the Giants in 1890. As a result, Ward moved to the newly-formed Players League as manager-shortstop of the Brooklyn club. With the collapse of the Players League after the season, Ward returned to the National League to manage Brooklyn in 1891-92 and the Giants in 1893-94.

March 26 — The U.S. Circuit Court denied an injunction sought by the Metropolitan Exhibition Company (the Giants' corporate name at the time) to prevent star Giant catcher Buck Ewing from playing with any other team in 1890. This freed Ewing to move to the Players League and to manage the New York entry. Ewing returned to the Giants as a player in 1891 and 1892. He later returned to manage the Giants for part of the 1900 season.

May 12 — Giant outfielder Mike Tiernan homered in the thirteenth inning, enabling New York right-hander Amos Rusie to defeat Boston's Kid Nichols 1-0. Tiernan's prodigious game-winning blast was especially noteworthy — it cleared the center-field fence at the Polo Grounds and thumped resoundingly against the outside fence of adjoining Brotherhood Park, then the home of New York's entrant in the Players League, where a game was in progress. The triumphant Tiernan was applauded lustily by fans in both ballparks as he trotted around the bases.

May 29 — Giant third baseman Jerry Denny had eleven assists as the Giants lost to Cincinnati, 7-6. This is only one below the major league record.

July 19 — The Giants scored thirteen runs in the second inning of an 18-4 win over Cleveland in the morning game of a doubleheader at the Polo Grounds.

Sept. 23 — The Giants beat Pittsburgh 8-6 despite thirteen walks issued by New York left-hander Jesse Burkett. This was one of only three major league wins registered by Burkett before he was traded to Cleveland to become a full-time outfielder. Burkett's .340 lifetime average led to his election to the Hall of Fame in 1946.

Sept. 27 — Giant shortstop Jack Glasscock had six singles in six trips to the plate as Mickey Welch coasted to a 15-3 Giant win over Cincinnati at the Polo Grounds.

1891

April 22 — The Giants opened the new Polo Grounds before 17,335 with a 4-3 loss to Boston. It was a disappointing defeat for Amos Rusie, who went into the bottom of the tenth inning with a 3-2 lead (the visiting Boston club had last at bats) Boston third baseman Billy Nash opened the inning with a walk, catcher Charlie Bennett singled, and both men scored when Giant center fielder George Gore slipped while moving over to catch Boston shortstop Herman Long's easy fly ball.

   The Giants had purchased Brotherhood Park from the New York club of the Players League after the Players League folded following the 1890 season. Brotherhood Park, renamed New Polo Grounds, was located at 157th Street, a few hundred feet north of the Giants' former home. The Giants remained at the new site until they left New York after the 1957 season.

July 31 — Amos Rusie, who won 33 games during the 1891 season, pitched a no-hit, 6-0 victory over Brooklyn right-hander William "Adonis" Terry at the Polo Grounds.

Nov. 7 — Giant manager Jim Mutrie was replaced by P.T. "Pat" Powers after the New Yorkers finished in third place in 1891, eighteen games behind the pennant-winning Boston Beaneaters.

1892

April 12 — The Giants opened the first twelve-team National League race. Amos Rusie outpointed ex-Giant Tim Keefe in a 5-4 win over the Phillies.

August 17 — Giant center fielder Jack Doyle hit for the cycle as Amos Rusie defeated the Reds 13-7 in Cincinnati.

Oct. 4 — Amos Rusie pitched and won two games against Washington at the Polo Grounds by scores of 6-4 and 9-5.

1893

June 14 — Giant third baseman George Davis hit a home run and a triple in the fourth inning of a 15-11 New York win over Chicago at the Polo Grounds.

Sept. 9 — George Davis hit safely in his thirty-third straight game, and the Giants won the second game of a doubleheader from Cincinnati 10-1 at the Polo Grounds. This remained the longest Giant hitting streak through the 1982 season. The present-day pitching distance of 60 feet, 6 inches had just been put in effect in the 1893 season; thus, Davis' hitting streak is essentially comparable to today's similar hitting feats. Typical of the lack of interest in record performances at the time, newspaper accounts of this game, or the succeeding game, made no mention of the streak.

  Davis, who was on his way to a great season in which he hit .362, had been obtained from Cleveland in an off-season swap for long-time Giant stalwart, Buck Ewing.

Sept. 11 — George Davis' thirty-three game hitting streak ended as Cleveland great Cy Young defeated the Giants 8-6 in Cleveland.

1894

July 4 — Giant right-hander Jouett Meekin was the whole show as the New Yorkers won the morning game of the holiday doubleheader in Cleveland, 4-3. Meekin pitched a solid six-hitter and hit three triples, aided by ground rules permitting three bases on fair balls hit into the overflow crowd.

July 14 — George Davis led the New York attack with three triples in a 9-5 victory at Pittsburgh.

Oct. 8 — The second-place Giants defeated the pennant-winning Baltimore Orioles 16-3, taking the Temple Cup with four straight victories. The Orioles had been odds-on favorites to beat the Giants for the Cup, which had been placed in competition by William Chase Temple, a large stockholder in the Pittsburgh club. It was learned subsequently that several Baltimore players had agreed to split their shares, each worth $564, with Giant players, and the story became public knowledge when the Giant players reneged on the agreement.

1895

Jan. 24 — New York wheeler-dealer Andrew Freedman succeeded C. C. Van Cott as Giant president. Freedman purchased 1,200 shares of Giant stock for $53,000 and took over controlling interest in the club. He also obtained a lease on the Polo Grounds at an annual rental cost of $7,500. A loud, unpopular man but with impressive Tammany Hall contacts, Freedman kept the New York baseball scene in a continual turmoil during the 1895-1902 period. The club fared poorly under Freedman's stewardship, managing only two third-place finishes during the eight seasons.

April 18 — The Giants lost to Brooklyn 7-4 at the Polo Grounds in third baseman George Davis' debut as Giant manager. The twenty-four-year-old Davis, the youngest man to manage a major league team up to that time, lasted only thirty-four games as manager before he was replaced by first baseman Jack Doyle. Davis remained an active player in the ranks until mid-season of 1900, when he again was named manager.

August 15 — The Giants lost to the Phils 23-9 in Philadelphia despite a banner day at the plate by George Davis. Davis had a triple, two doubles, and three singles in six at bats.

August 20 — Giant shortstop Bill "Shorty" Fuller had eleven putouts as the Giants decisioned St. Louis 3-2 at the Polo Grounds. This remained a tie for the fielding record for shortstops through the 1985 season.

1896

Feb. 24 — Former Giant shortstop John Montgomery "Monte" Ward was granted his release by the Giants after the National League Board of Directors adopted a resolution ordering the Giants to release Ward from the club's reserve player list. Ward claimed that the New York club had no right to keep him on their reserve list because he had not been under contract to the Giants in 1894 (the last year he had played for them) nor had he been offered a contract by the Giants in 1895. Ward, a practicing attorney who felt he had in effect played out his option, told the Board of Directors that although he did not intend to play major league baseball again, he did not wish to be tied down for the future by the Giants. Ward did not play or manage again in the big leagues.

June 29 — The National Board of Directors met and decided that a fine imposed upon Amos Rusie by Giant President Andrew Freedman in 1895 was "just and proper." Rusie had sat out the 1896 season, refusing to sign his contract, which included a deduction of $200 reflecting the fine. Rusie brought two suits in November 1895, one asking for $5,000 in damages because ". . . the conduct of the club had prevented him from following his profession," the other enjoining the Giants from reserving his contract for 1897. (There were rumors that Rusie's legal costs had been picked up by another team which hoped to sign him.)

Although a federal court in Chicago refused to rule on Rusie's suits on a technicality, the National League Board of Directors reacted to follow-up suits by Rusie by collecting funds from other National League clubs to meet Rusie's demands for monies owed him. The move was made primarily to eliminate Rusie's attack on the reserve clause of the players' contracts (which would be successfully challenged in 1970).

Rusie returned to the Giants for the 1897 and 1898 seasons after sitting out the 1896 campaign. The big Indiana right-hander was elected to the Hall of Fame in 1977.

1897

May 18 — The Giants defeated the Pirates 11-5 in Pittsburgh with the substantial help of New York third baseman Bill Joyce, who clouted four triples. Only one other major leaguer through the 1986 season has hit four three-baggers in one game —George Strief of the Philadelphia club of the American Association on June 25, 1885.

June 3 — Giant left-hander Cy Seymour pitched two complete game wins over Louisville, winning by scores of 6-1, and 10-6 in the seven-inning nightcap. Seymour held Louisville to three hits in the first game and four hits in the darkness-shortened second game. Seymour, noted for his wildness, pitched .500 ball for the Giants from 1896 through 1900, moved to Cleveland where he became a fine hitter and outfielder, and returned to the Giants for the 1906-1910 seasons.

Sept. 17 — The Giants took a 17-0 shellacking in Boston, their most one-sided loss of the season.

1898

June 11 — The Giants beat Brooklyn 6-2 at the Polo Grounds in the storied Cap Anson's debut as Giant manager. Anson, one of the great figures in Chicago baseball as the Cubs' first baseman from 1876 through 1897, and manager from 1879 to 1897, replaced Bill Joyce as Giant pilot. Joyce, the New Yorkers' field boss for part of 1896 and all of 1897, remained to play first base. But Anson, unhappy to be associated with Giant Owner Andrew Freedman, lasted only twenty-two games before Joyce replaced him.

July 8 — Bill Joyce reclaimed his old job as New York manager, replacing Hall of Famer Cap Anson who had a mediocre 9 and 13 record after taking over for Joyce on June 11, 1898. The Giants celebrated Joyce's return with a 10-1 win over Brooklyn. Joyce's earlier dismissal by Giant owner Andrew Freedman had been unpopular with the players and the New York Times reported that ". . . the release of Anson . . . gave the New Yorks a new lease of life." The improvement in the players' psyches was not reflected in their performance on the field, though; the Giants finished seventh out of twelve clubs.

July 25 — A wild display by Giant owner Andrew Freedman resulted in the Giants' forfeiture of a game to Baltimore and a long, follow-up controversy. In the fourth inning of the game at the Polo Grounds, Baltimore outfielder James "Ducky" Holmes was needled by fans as he returned to the dugout after striking out. A fan shouted at Holmes, who had played for the Giants in 1897, "That's why we got rid of you." According to the New York Times, Holmes (referring to Freedman) fired back, "Well, I'm damn glad that I don't work for a Sheeny any more."

The enraged Freedman, seated in the upper stands behind the plate, raced down to the field and shouted to Baltimore Manager Ned Hanlon, "Get that guy out of the game." Hanlon referred Freedman to Umpire Tom Lynch but Lynch said that he did not hear Holmes' remark. When Freedman refused to leave the field, Lynch forfeited the game to Baltimore.

After the game Freedman insisted on reimbursing the twenty-five hundred spectators' money, proclaiming grandly, "The people have been crying for gentlemanly ball, and they will get it in New York at any cost." With that, Freedman demanded that the Baltimore club return its share of the game receipts to the Giants. When the Orioles understandably refused to do so, Freedman stopped payment on the Giants' check.

On August 15, the National League's Board of Directors agreed that the forfeit should stand, fined the Giants $1,000 to be paid to Baltimore, but also decreed that Holmes be suspended for the rest of the season. Holmes responded by obtaining a court injunction to permit him to play at the Polo Grounds. The upshot of the affair was that the National League hierarchy ate the ball completely — Holmes was reinstated and the $1,000 ultimately was returned to Freedman.

Nov. 15 — Despite a dismal season, during which Andrew Freedman shuffled managers a la George Steinbrenner and lost money in the bargain, Freedman was reelected president at a princely $10,000-a-year salary.

1899

May 24 — Giant left-hander Cy Seymour had a bittersweet day as he pitched and lost to the Reds 7-6 in Cincinnati. On the plus side, Seymour clubbed two doubles and two singles to keep the Giants in the game. But his wildness cost him the game; he walked his thirteenth batter of the game in the ninth inning, forcing in the winning Cincinnati run.

July 5 — Giant Manager John B. Day, the club's president from 1883 through 1892, was replaced by Fred Hoey. The lackluster Giants wallowed in ninth place. Day left with a 30 won and 40 lost record and, as the *New York Times* deadpanned it, ". . . he was very popular with the players and his release is thought to be due to the team's poor showing this season." Hoey, whose chief claim to sporting fame was his earlier prowess as a competing pigeon shooter, had a 30 and 50 record for the remainder of the season, and the club sank to an ignominious tenth place finish.

August 12 — The Giants sold right-hander Jouett Meekin to Boston for $3,500. Meekin averaged twenty-five wins a season during the 1894-98 seasons but the Giants, disappointed with his 5 and 11 record in 1899, traded him in a surprise move.

Sept. 20 — Shortstop George "Zeke" Wrigley left the Giants without notice and played the rest of the season with the pennant-winning Brooklyn club. A messy affair. Wrigley had completed the season with Syracuse, then signed with the Giants and played in four games with them. Meanwhile Brooklyn negotiated with Syracuse for his contract although presumably it had been purchased by the Giants. Wrigley played in fifteen games with Brooklyn. The National League fined Brooklyn $500 and made threatening noises about disallowing the fifteen games in which Wrigley had played for Brooklyn. Apparently, these threats were not carried out; official records indicate that Brooklyn was credited with all of the games it played in 1899. In any event, it amounted to much ado about nothing —Wrigley did not play in another major league game.

Oct. 13 — Cy Seymour walked eleven men in a 6-4 loss to Washington in a game called after seven innings because of darkness.

1900

Feb. 28 — John McGraw and Wilbert Robinson of the Baltimore Orioles signed contracts amid rumors that the Baltimore club would be eliminated and that McGraw and Robinson would be sold to the Giants. When the Orioles disbanded, McGraw and Robinson were ticketed for Brooklyn. Both men refused to report, however, and sat out the first third of the season until St. Louis obtained them. McGraw signed a no-reserve contract for $100 a game, far above-average pay, then jumped to Baltimore in 1901, and moved to the Giants in July, 1902.

June 7 — Cy Seymour beat St. Louis 10-3 at the Polo Grounds despite giving up eleven walks and ten hits. Regardless, the Giants tired of Seymour's wildness (he led the league in bases on balls in 1897-99) and farmed him out to Worcester after the game.

July 13 — Buck Ewing resigned as the club's manager, and the Giants languished in last place with a 21-41 record. Giant shortstop George Davis replaced Ewing and remained as manager through the 1901 season. The Giants responded with a 14-1 win over Brooklyn at the Polo Grounds and managed to play at a .500-plus pace for the rest of the 1900 season, although they finished in last place.

July 17 — Giant immortal Christy Mathewson, just up from Norwalk with a 20 and 2 record, made his first appearance as a Giant. He replaced left-hander Ed Doheny in the fifth inning of a tie game with Brooklyn at Washington Park. The nervous young man, not yet twenty years old, proceeded to hit three batters, walk two men, and strike out only one. The *New York Times* reported that after Mathewson entered the game, "The New Yorks immediately went up in the air and through errors and poor pitching Brooklyn won as it pleased." Joe "Iron Man" McGinnity, Mathewson's future comrade-in-arms, pitched and won the game for Brooklyn, 13-7.

Mathewson had an 0 and 3 record for the Giants before they sent him back to Norfolk. Matty was drafted by Cincinnati after the season and the Giants regained him shortly thereafter in a trade in which another Giant Hall of Fame right-hander, Amos Rusie, moved to the Reds.

1901

June 9 — The three Giant outfielders had sixteen of the club's thirty-one hits as the New Yorkers blasted Cincinnati, 25-13. An overflow crowd in excess of 17,000 packed League Park in Cincinnati and saw Giant left fielder Albert "Kip" Selbach obtain four singles and two doubles in seven trips. Giant right fielder Charles "Piano Legs" Hickman and center fielder George Van Haltren had five hits apiece.

July 15 — Christy Mathewson pitched a no-hitter against the Cardinals in St. Louis, winning 5-0. This was the first of two no-hitters pitched by Mathewson in his brilliant career.

1902

June 2 — The Giants replaced Manager Horace Fogel with second baseman George "Heinie" Smith. But Smith was a figurehead; the discredited Fogel continued to direct the last-place club's moves behind the scenes. Within six weeks the Giants replaced Smith with John McGraw.

July 16 — John McGraw left the managership of the Baltimore Orioles and moved to the Giants as player-manager for a four-year, $6,500 a year contract. He brought with him from the Orioles pitchers Joe "Iron Man" McGinnity and Jack Cronin, catcher Roger Bresnahan, first baseman Dan McGann, and outfielder Steve Brodie. On this date the Giants were in last place, a cool 33 1/2 games behind first-place Pittsburgh and six games behind seventh-place Cincinnati. Under McGraw the Giants won twenty-five and lost thirty-eight games to finish in last place, 53 1/2 games behind the pennant-winning Pirates.

July 19 — Pitcher Joe McGinnity and the Giants lost 4-3 to Philadelphia at the Polo Grounds in John McGraw's first game as Giant manager. Despite the loss, the *New York Times* reported that the crowd ". . . had nothing but encouragement for the home players." A third baseman in his prime, McGraw played shortstop and had one putout and two assists in the field, and one hit in three at bats.

July 23 — The Giants defeated Brooklyn 4-1 before 7,000 to record John McGraw's first win as Giant manager.

Sept. 9 — John T. Brush, a wealthy clothier from Indianapolis, sold the Cincinnati Reds for $200,000 and bought controlling interest in the Giants from controversial Giant president Andrew Freedman. It was a great break for John McGraw, who had chafed under Freedman's tight-fisted regime and who was given a free hand in buying players under Brush.

1903

May 7 — Giant first baseman Dan McGann stole four bases in an 8-4 New York victory in St. Louis.

May 16 — The largest crowd in New York City baseball to that time, 31,500, watched Christy Mathewson beat Brooklyn 7-3 at the Polo Grounds.

June 3 — Symptomatic of the fevered pace of John McGraw's first full season as Giant manager, gentlemanly Christy Mathewson was ejected from the third base coaching box for protesting a decision in the Giants' 5-0 loss to Pittsburgh.

June 26 — Giant catcher Frank Bowerman and Pittsburgh manager Fred Clarke brawled in the Giant office. The fight was reported to League President Harry Pulliam by Pittsburgh owner Barney Dreyfuss. The reason for the fight was far less clear than the tangible results. There was no report as to the cause, but Pulliam fined Bowerman $100 (a significant amount in 1903) and Clarke, who escaped a fine, wound up with a black eye.

July 16 — Roger Bresnahan, later to become a Hall of Famer as a catcher, started a triple play as a center fielder. In a 5-1 win over St. Louis, Bresnahan caught a fly ball with the bases loaded. His throw to catcher John Warner held the runner at third, and Warner's throw to shortstop George Davis nailed the runner trying to advance from first base. Davis then quickly threw back to Warner to catch the runner belatedly coming home from third base for the third out.

August 1 — Joe McGinnity pitched two solid games to win a double-header at Boston by scores of 4-1 and 5-2.

August 8 — One week after pitching a doubleheader win over Boston, Joe McGinnity repeated the feat against Brooklyn, winning 6-1 and 4-3 before 31,647 in Brooklyn. In the third inning of his second-game victory, the rubber-armed McGinnity singled, went to second on a sacrifice, and slid safely into third base on a hotly-disputed play. The Superbas (the Brooklyn club's nickname at the time) failed to call time before protesting the call, and McGinnity raced home safely.

August 12 — Giant outfielder Sam Mertes walked five times as the Giants defeated the St. Louis Cardinals, 14-4.

August 31 — Joe McGinnity won two complete games in one day for the third time in August, 1903. This time he defeated the Philadelphia Phils twice, winning the first game 4-1 and the second game 9-2. The Iron Man had the remarkable stamina to strike out nine Philly hitters in his second-game win.

Sept. 8 — In an early version of the New York-Brooklyn donnybrooks to follow, the clubs split a turbulent twin bill. New York won the morning game in Brooklyn 6-4, but lost the afternoon game at the Polo Grounds, 3-0. A riot appeared imminent in the morning game when Brooklyn's Jimmy Sheckard flagrantly interfered with New York catcher Frank Bowerman. As Bowerman threw to cut down a

Brooklyn runner, Sheckard raised his bat and the throw hit the bat. Umpire Tim Hurst refused to call interference. Meanwhile, the Brooklyn runner raced around the bases with the tying run and the Giants, completely ignoring the runner, stormed frantically around Hurst. The understandably aggrieved Bowerman was ejected from the game but, in poetic justice, the Giants scored two more runs to win the game.

Sept. 19 — The Giants purchased third baseman Art Devlin from Newark and outfielder Harry "Moose" McCormick from Jersey City.

Dec. 13 — The Giants traded pitcher Jack Cronin and shortstop Charlie Babb to Brooklyn for shortstop "Bad Bill" Dahlen. It was a fine trade for the Giants; Dahlen anchored McGraw's infield for the next four seasons.

1904

May 27 — Dan McGann stole five bases in a 3-1 Giant victory over Brooklyn.

June 11 — Joe McGinnity lost to Chicago 1-0 in twelve innings, his first loss of the season after fourteen straight wins.

July 4 — The Giants won a doubleheader from the Phillies at the Polo Grounds 4-1 and 11-3, running their winning streak to eighteen games. Christy Mathewson's victory in the second game tied the then-existing team consecutive-game winning record of the 1894 Baltimore Orioles. The 1916 Giants broke this record with their twenty-six-game string.

July 5 — The Giants lost to the Phillies 6-5 in ten innings at Philadelphia to end their eighteen-game winning streak.

August 7 — The Giants obtained outfielder Mike "Turkey Mike" Donlin from Cincinnati for outfielder Moose McCormick and cash. The high-living Donlin contributed several key hits to help the Giants win the 1904 pennant. Turkey Mike played superbly in the Giants' pennant win in 1905 and near-pennant year of 1908.

August 31 — Giant catcher Frank Bowerman slugged a fan who had been riding him during a Giant 3-2 win in Cincinnati. Bowerman was escorted from the field despite the threat of Giant players to drag him away from the gendarmes. The aggrieved fan, holding his badly cut jaw, claimed that John McGraw had "ordered the assault" but decided the next day not to press charges, and Bowerman was released.

Sept. 6 — Overenthusiastic Giant fans celebrated an exciting 6-1 and 4-3 doubleheader win over the Boston Braves by nearly trampling John McGraw as he left the field for the Polo Grounds clubhouse. Several fans tried to carry the Giant manager off the field in triumph, but they dropped him and exuberant fans walked over the prostrate McGraw. Fortunately, he sustained only a badly sprained ankle and was in the dugout the following game.

Sept. 15 — Giant left-hander George "Hooks" Wiltse rolled to his twelfth straight win of the season, defeating Boston 3-2 at the Polo Grounds.

Sept. 22 — The Giants clinched John McGraw's first pennant as Joe "Iron Man" McGinnity decisioned Cincinnati, 7-5. Catcher Jim O'Rourke, a fifty-two-year-old veteran who had last played in the major leagues with Washington in 1893, was given the honor of catching for the Giants. This was the only game of the season for O'Rourke, who was elected to the Hall of Fame in 1945.

Oct. 3 — Christy Mathewson struck out sixteen Cardinals as the Giants won in St. Louis, 3-1. Mathewson's feat broke the then-existing record of fifteen strikeouts in pitching his masterpiece in a brisk one hour and 15 minutes.

Oct. 4 — Sam Mertes hit for the cycle in a 7-3 Giant loss to St. Louis at the Polo Grounds.

1905

May 19 — John McGraw and Pittsburgh manager Fred Clarke almost came to blows during a game at the Polo Grounds. McGraw had been riding Pittsburgh pitcher Mike Lynch unmercifully and when Clarke came to his pitcher's defense, McGraw and Clarke squared off. Umpire James Johnstone separated the would-be combatants and ejected McGraw. Ever defiant, McGraw retreated to the toilet adjoining the Giant dugout where, surprisingly, Johnstone allowed him to remain despite loud Pirate complaints.

May 21 — John McGraw continued his feud with the Pittsburgh Pirates, complaining after an adverse call that the umpires and the National League office were under the influence of Pittsburgh owner Barney Dreyfuss. McGraw followed this up by sassing Dreyfuss, a Polo Grounds spectator that day, in the famous "Hey, Barney" episode. Dreyfuss complained of McGraw's behavior in a letter to League President Pulliam, which included a formal protest against McGraw for using foul language in public, shouting with unwonted familiarity "Hey, Barney" to the irate Pittsburgh owner from the field, and offering publicly to wager $10,000 that the Giants would win that day's game.

McGraw responded to Dreyfuss' complaints with the statement that President Pulliam could not "forget his former role as the secretary to Dreyfuss at both Louisville and Pittsburgh." With that, Pulliam called a meeting of the League's board of directors to "try" McGraw. McGraw responded by rebuking Pulliam over the phone. The League President countered with a $150 fine and a fifteen-day suspension. Twelve thousand Giant fans then signed a petition calling on the League directors to reject the charges against McGraw. Before the directors could meet to consider the matter further, Dreyfuss went public with a description of arguments he had engaged in with McGraw on their betting activities. This so concerned the directors that they exonerated McGraw and blasted Dreyfuss for his undignified conduct of engaging in a public altercation with a manager.

McGraw and Giant President John Brush applied for and were granted a Superior Court injunction permitting McGraw to manage the Giants immediately. Eventually the case petered out, with McGraw ignoring the fine and suspension and getting away with it. For years after, Dreyfuss was greeted by fans in all parks with derisive shouts of "Hey, Barney!"

June 13 — Christy Mathewson pitched his second career no-hitter, defeating Chicago, 1-0.

July 24 — Giant left fielder Sam Mertes made an unassisted double play as the New Yorkers defeated Cincinnati 4-3 at the Polo Grounds. In the top of the second inning, with one out and Cincinnati outfielder Cy Seymour on third, Mertes raced in from left field to grab Reds catcher George "Admiral" Schlei's short fly ball. Mertes sprinted to touch third base before Seymour returned to the bag.

Oct. 1 — The Giants clinched their second pennant in a row with a ten-inning victory over Cincinnati.

Oct. 14 — The Giants won the World Championship by defeating Connie Mack's Philadelphia Athletics four games to one as Christy Mathewson outpitched the A's Chief Bender for a 2-0 victory. This was Mathewson's third shutout of the Series. A sign of the times: a winning share was worth $1,142 and a losing share $832.

Nov. 10 — John McGraw signed to manage the Giants through 1908 for an undisclosed salary.

1906

Feb. 8 — Several Giants terrified passengers on a train en route from New York City to Troy, New York, where the players were to be honored. The chief offender was outfielder Mike Donlin, who was charged with assaulting a conductor and drawing a pistol on a porter. The *New York Times* reported that the trouble started when several players became drunk and "very soon balls were flying and suitcases were used to help along the disturbance."

May 15 — Giant left-hander George "Hooks" Wiltse defeated Cincinnati 4-1 with a sensational pitching performance. Wiltse struck out twelve Reds but, more spectacularly, he struck out seven hitters in two innings. In the fourth inning, Wiltse struck out outfielders Joe Kelley, Cy Seymour, and Bill Hinchman. Wiltse struck out Red third baseman Jim Delehanty to open the fifth, but Delehanty took first base when Giant catcher Roger Bresnahan mishandled the third strike. Unruffled, Wiltse rubbed out on strikes shortstop Tommy Corcoran, catcher George "Admiral" Schlei, and pitcher Chick Fraser to complete his unusual feat.

June 7 — The Giants lost to the Cubs in Chicago by a whopping 19-0 score, one of the most overwhelming defeats in manager John McGraw's tenure.

July 24 — Joe McGinnity and Pittsburgh catcher Heinie Peitz brawled in Pittsburgh after needling each other continuously from the start of the game. In the fourth inning, Peitz, coaching at first base, cussed the Iron Man with special fervor. McGinnity raced over from the mound and the players rolled on the ground, pummeling each other furiously. An especially interesting twist was supplied by Pittsburgh Mayor Charles F. Kirschler, who shouted from his box (referring to McGinnity), "Arrest that man, I will appear against him myself." The following day, however, cooler political heads prevailed and the case was dropped at the behest of Allegheny County political boss Frank Torrance.

Subsequently, League President Pulliam fined McGinnity $100 and suspended him for ten days for "attempting to make the ball park a slaughterhouse." Peitz was fined $50 and suspended for five days. And Umpire Hank O'Day was fined $50 for not stopping the "disgraceful affair."

August 6 — John McGraw and Giant third baseman Art Devlin were ejected for arguing too strenuously with Umpire James Johnstone in a game against the Cubs. McGraw was suspended by League President Pulliam after the game. The next day the Giants refused to admit Johnstone to the Polo Grounds, claiming that the New

York City Police Department had forbidden his entrance because it "might precipitate a riot." (This was denied by the Police Department.) As a result, the game was forfeited to the Cubs who were ahead of the Giants in the standings and who refused to play unless Johnstone was allowed to officiate. The Giants protested Pulliam's support of Johnstone and later filed a civil suit to recover $8,500 in damages for the Cubs' refusal to play the game. The Giants lost the case.

After the season, a *New York Times* editorial referred to the forfeited game as the fruit of McGraw's "piratical tactics" and pinpointed that loss and two other losses in the same series with the Cubs as the Giants' "Waterloo" for the season.

Oct. 1 — The Giants won a doubleheader shutout over St. Louis as Leon "Red" Ames pitched a 3-0 first-game win and George Ferguson hurled the 2-0 second-game victory.

Oct. 5 — Right-hander Henry Mathewson, the great Christy's younger brother, lost his only major league decision to Boston. In the process of losing his career game, 7-1, Henry proved to John McGraw that he was not ready for the major leagues, issuing fourteen walks and hitting a batter.

1907

Jan. 10 — John McGraw climbed out of a careening carriage as it was being pulled through crowded Los Angeles streets by a runaway horse, seized the reins, and brought the horse to a halt after being dragged for two blocks. The Giant manager was credited with preventing serious injury to his wife and another woman who was riding with the McGraws.

April 11 — Giant catcher Roger Bresnahan wore shin guards in the season opener against Philadelphia, the first use of such equipment in major league history. Six weeks later, National League President Pulliam ruled against Pittsburgh manager Fred Clarke's protest of a loss to the Giants on grounds that the new equipment was illegal.

May 18 — The Giants won their seventeenth straight game as Hooks Wiltse hurled a 6-2 victory over the St. Louis Cardinals at the Polo Grounds. After the game, the first-place Giants had a phenomenal 24 and 3 record. The Chicago Cubs, the eventual pennant winner, were only one game behind John McGraw's high-riding club.

May 20 — The St. Louis Cardinals ended the Giants' seventeen-game winning streak with a 6-4 victory over McGraw's club at the Polo Grounds.

May 21 — More than 10,000 fans raced onto the Polo Grounds playing field after a 3-2 loss to the Cubs to protest a series of adverse calls against the Giants. Aided by private police with drawn revolvers, umpires Hank O'Day and Bob Emslie managed to leave the field unharmed.

July 12 — The practice of permitting spectators to keep baseballs hit into the stands had not yet caught on at the Polo Grounds. During a Giant game on this date a fan insisted on retaining a foul ball which landed in his lap. Giant team secretary Fred Knowles, although deciding not to prosecute the fan, warned ominously, "In the future I will not be so lenient and any person deliberately trying to steal a ball will be arrested and the complaint pushed."

July 22 — Giant second baseman Larry Doyle played his first major league game as the Giants lost 2-0 to the Cubs at the Polo Grounds. Despite a lackluster start (only one scratch hit and an error in the field), "Laughing Larry" had an excellent career and was a long-time New York favorite.

July 25 — Recovering from a beaning sustained earlier in the season, Roger Bresnahan became the first major leaguer to wear a pneumatic head protector while batting.

August 29 — The Giants purchased first baseman Fred Merkle from Tecumseh in the Southern Michigan League for $2,500. Merkle went on to have a fine major league career despite his historic "boner" in a 1908 tie game with the Chicago Cubs.

1908

April 13 — Giant outfielder Mike Donlin returned to the club after taking the 1907 season off to perform on the stage. However, Turkey Mike was reinstated by League President Pulliam only after paying a $100 fine for playing with "outlaw" teams in 1907; that is, teams which harbored players ineligible to play in organized baseball.

July 4 — Hooks Wiltse pitched a ten-inning no-hitter against the Phillies.

Sept. 18 — The largest crowd in major league history up to that point, almost 35,000, saw the Giants slug out a doubleheader win over Pittsburgh at the Polo Grounds. For the first time during the season a large contingent of police was at the game, and it was fortunate for Mike Donlin that they were there. The crowd began needling Donlin for an errant play in the field and he responded by rushing foolishly into the overflow crowd and smashing a fan in the face. Infuriated, the suddenly ugly crowd closed menacingly around

Donlin. Just before he disappeared from sight, a number of policemen raced to Donlin, dragged him out by his heels, and escorted him to the Giant dugout. For the remainder of the game, a large number of officers patrolled the outfield to prevent the hot-tempered Donlin from serious harm.

Sept. 19 — The Giants' pennant stretch drive of eleven straight victories ended with a 6-2 loss to the Pirates. The loss left the Giants with a 3½ game lead, which disappeared completely on September 30.

Sept. 23 — Fred Merkle's historic "boner" caused the Giants to lose an apparent game-winning hit against the Cubs at the Polo Grounds. Merkle, on first base as a teammate drove in the game-winning run, failed to touch second base and the game was ruled a tie. In the resulting playoff game, the Giants lost and the Cubs took the pennant. (See "Famous Polo Grounds Games.")

Sept. 25 — Giant left-hander Richard "Rube" Marquard made his first big league start and lost to Cincinnati, 7-1. Marquard was blasted for six hits and five runs in four innings, walking two hitters, hitting another, and throwing a wild pitch. The urbane, Cleveland-born "Rube," (a misnomer if ever there were one) was referred to as the "$11,000 lemon" in part because of this first and only outing of 1908. But he eventually outgrew the nickname and went on to a great career with the Giants, Dodgers, Reds, and Braves, which led to his election to the Hall of Fame in 1971.

Sept. 29 — The Giants split a doubleheader with Philadelphia and lost first place to the onrushing Cubs. Christy Mathewson won the first game 6-2, but virtually unknown Philly right-hander Harry Coveleski pitched a masterful 7-0 victory to upset the Giants. Coveleski became known as "The Giant Killer" because his surprise win eventually forced the Giants into a pennant playoff game with the Cubs on October 8 that the Giants lost.

Oct. 8 — The Giants lost to the Cubs 4-2 in a pennant playoff game made necessary by Fred Merkle's "boner" on September 23, which converted an apparent Giant win into a tie game. Christy Mathewson lost to Chicago's great right-hander Mordecai "Three Finger" Brown. The Cubs won with a four-run third inning, during which shortstop Joe Tinker tripled, catcher Johnny Kling singled, second baseman Johnny Evers walked, and outfielder Frank Schulte and manager-first baseman Frank Chance each doubled.

Dec. 11 — Under questioning by National League President Harry Pulliam, umpires Bill Klem and James Johnstone testified that Dr. William "Doc" Creamer, a part-time trainer and osteopath with the

Giants, had attempted to bribe them before Klem and Johnstone umpired in the pennant playoff game of October 8, 1908. Creamer was barred from all ballparks in organized baseball. (A good question: How was such an edict enforced?)

Dec. 13 — The Giants traded Roger Bresnahan to the St. Louis Cardinals for outfielder Jack "Red" Murray, catcher Admiral Schlei, and right-hander Arthur "Bugs" Raymond. Bresnahan was appointed to manage the Cards. Murray was a regular outfielder during the 1909-1913 campaigns, and Raymond had an 18 and 12 year for the Giants in 1909, although his nonstop drinking ruined his career within a few years.

1909

April 15 — A tough outing for Giant right-hander Leon "Red" Ames. He held Brooklyn hitless for nine innings, gave up a hit in the tenth, but lost 3-0 in thirteen innings.

August 8 — Giant outfielder Bill O'Hara stole second, third, and home in the eighth inning of a 3-0 Giant win over St. Louis.

Sept. 16 — President William Howard Taft attended the Giant-Cub game in Chicago, and Christy Mathewson outpitched Chicago's Three Finger Brown 1-0 in one of their classic pitching duels.

1910

May 7 — Wee Willie Keeler, of "Hit 'em where they ain't" fame, signed with the Giants after being released by the New York Highlanders (not yet known as "Yankees"). McGraw used his old Baltimore teammate almost exclusively as a pinch hitter. Keeler hit .300 (three hits in ten trips) for his last major league club.

June 23 — There was a near-riot at Brooklyn's Washington Park as the Giants defeated the home club, 8-2. A group of Brooklyn fans in a field box rode Giant third baseman Art Devlin unmercifully. His patience exhausted, Devlin hustled over to the box and hit one Bernard J. Roesler squarely on the chin, knocking him out cold. Roesler's companions retaliated and in no time Giants second baseman Larry Doyle and outfielder Josh Devore joined Devlin in the brawl. Devlin was taken to the Bergen Street police station where he was charged. Although the case eventually was dropped, League President Lynch suspended Devlin for five days and fined Doyle and Devore $50 each.

July 14 — Even the great Christy Mathewson had his trying days. On this date he went into the bottom of the ninth, leading the Pirates 3-0 in Pittsburgh. But he yielded two runs in the inning, then uncharacteristically walked in the tying run. After Matty threw two wide pitches to Pirate outfielder Tommy Leach, John McGraw brought in Red Ames, who completed the walk and forced in the winning Pittsburgh run.

Oct. 10 — In a pregame field day at Cincinnati, Giant third baseman Hans Lobert set records by running from home to first base in his baseball uniform in 3.4 seconds and circling the bases in 13.8 seconds.

Oct. 21 — The Giants defeated the New York Highlanders in an exhibition World Series, four games to two. Christy Mathewson won the Series almost single-handedly, with three wins, and saving the fourth win. This series between the second-place Giants and the second-place Highlanders proved to be a reasonable facsimile of a real World Series, featuring exciting games, Mathewson's brilliant pitching, and McGraw's ouster from the first game for arguing too vociferously. Each of the winning Giants received $1,100, but the difference between the "shadow" World Series and the real thing was reflected in the poor attendance — a mere one-hundred-and-three thousand for an average of less than fifteen thousand per game.

1911

April 14 — A destructive fire of undetermined origin ravaged the Polo Grounds on the third day of the season. All the wooden stands except the left-field seats were destroyed by the fire, which began shortly after midnight. Within an hour the entire park resembled a huge bonfire, with flames rising 100 feet in the air and extending to the train storage yards that adjoined the park to the north. Damages were estimated at $250,000 to the park, and food caterer Harry M. Stevens estimated losses of food, supplies, and equipment at $25,000.

   The Giants immediately accepted an offer by the Yankees to use their home, Hilltop Park, located at 168th Street and Broadway in Manhattan. The Giants returned to the rebuilt Polo Grounds on June 28, 1911.

April 15 — With the Polo Grounds stands largely destroyed by fire, the Giants played their first "home game" at the Yankees' Hilltop Park and defeated Brooklyn, 6-3.

May 3 — Giant President John. T. Brush announced that he had obtained a long-term lease ("for the life of the National League") from Mrs. Harriet G. Coogan, the owner of the Polo Grounds site.

May 9 — The Giants filed plans for building a new Polo Grounds grandstand to replace the structure which was destroyed by fire. The new doubledeck, reinforced concrete and steel-supported stands were designed to accommodate 50,000.

May 13 — The Giants won a 19-5 laugher over the St. Louis Cardinals. John McGraw's club scored thirteen runs in the bottom of the first inning. He removed his ace, Christy Mathewson, after the inning and permitted Rube Marquard to pitch the rest of the game. Marquard gave up twelve hits but struck out fourteen batters, a record for relief pitchers. First baseman Fred Merkle drove in six runs in the Giants' big first inning with a home run and a triple.

June 5 — Fred Merkle hit a double and triple to lead the Giants' seven-run outburst in the top of the ninth as the New Yorkers won 7-1 in Chicago.

June 28 — The Giants celebrated their first game at the partially rebuilt Polo Grounds with a 3-1 win over the Boston Braves. Although 16,000 seats were available, the crowd numbered a disappointingly small 6,000.

The game also marked the return of Giant outfielder Mike Donlin after a two-year absence from the game. Donlin had long been interested in a stage career and, following his marriage to stage star Mabel Hite in 1906, he went into vaudeville, winding up in Hollywood making movies. Donlin's return to the Giants was short-lived; he was traded to Boston after appearing in only twelve games. McGraw brought him back for a final encore in 1914 in Donlin's last major league season.

July 12 — Rube Marquard struck out six straight Pirate hitters en route to a 4-3 New York win at Pittsburgh. Marquard's victims were second baseman Dots Miller, first baseman Newt Hunter, and right fielder Owen Wilson in the second inning, and pitcher Elmer Steele, third baseman Bobby Byrne, and center fielder Tommy Leach in the third inning.

August 11 — Christy Mathewson gave up eleven hits to the Phillies, yet pitched a 6-0 shutout.

Sept. 4 — Rube Marquard struck out fourteen Boston Brave hitters in the first seven innings, but blew up in the eighth and lost the game, 8-7.

Oct. 26 — The Giants lost the World Series 4 games to 2 to Connie Mack's Philadelphia Athletics. A's right-hander Chief Bender won a decisive 13-2 victory over Red Ames as the A's wiped out the New Yorkers with a seven-run seventh inning.

Nov. 30 — The Giants topped off a barnstorming trip to Cuba with a Thanksgiving Day shutout win over the Havana Almendares. Christy Mathewson outpitched the Almendares' ace right-hander, Jose Mendez, who was called the "Black Matty" because of the similarity of his style and performance to that of Mathewson. That night after the game, the not-very-sober duo of John McGraw and National League Umpire Cy Rigler became involved in a fight with Cuban fans and both men wound up being arrested and reprimanded by the Havana police.

1912

April 11 — Brooklyn's Washington Park was the setting for a riotous scene as the Giants slaughtered the home club, 18-3. The overflow opening day crowd was so much in excess of tho park's capacity that the game became a travesty, a large number of fights broke out and several normally catchable balls fell into the crowd for ground-rule doubles. Umpire Bill Klem halted the game after six innings to prevent injuries to the fans and damages to the ball park.

April 19 — The Giants formally dedicated an enlarged and redesigned Polo Grounds and celebrated with a 6-2 win over Brooklyn.

May 26 — An exhibition game in Paterson, New Jersey, between the Giants and the Smart Sets, a local black team, broke up in the tenth inning when player disputes with the umpires led the Giants to leave the field with the score tied. The Giants escaped to their bus through a hail of sticks and pebbles thrown by fans unhappy with the unsatisfactory conclusion of the game.

June 10 — Giant catcher Chief Meyers hit for the cycle, but the Giants lost to Chicago 9-8 at the Polo Grounds on Cub third baseman Heinie Zimmerman's home run in the top of the tenth inning.

June 20 — The Giants annihilated the Braves 21-12 in Boston in a farce of a game in which both clubs totalled thirty-four hits, nineteen for New York and fifteen for Boston. Giant outfielder Josh Devore stole second and third base twice each as the Giants scored seven runs in the top of the ninth. But the kicker came in the home ninth when, with the Giants leading 21-2, John McGraw brought in twenty-one-year-old rookie right-hander Ernie Shore to make his major league debut. Shore nearly succeeded in putting some suspense back into the game. Almost everything he served was hammered solidly, and he faced thirteen Brave hitters and gave up ten runs before retiring the side. Understandably, this was the only appearance Shore ever made for the Giants. He had a much better outing for the Boston Red Sox on June 23, 1917, when he relieved left-hander Babe Ruth (ejected for protesting after walking the first hitter), saw the runner cut down stealing, then retired the next twenty-six hitters in order.

July 3 — Rube Marquard won his nineteenth straight game of the season without a loss, defeating Brooklyn 2-1 in the first game of a doubleheader. His victory tied the major league record set by Giant pitcher Tim Keefe in 1888. Actually, under present scoring rules Marquard would have been credited with twenty consecutive wins. On April 20, 1912, he replaced pitcher Jeff Tesreau in the ninth inning and retired the Dodgers, but not before they had gained a 3-2 lead. The Giants pulled out a 4-3 win, but Marquard did not receive credit for it under then-existing scoring rules.

Tesreau won the second game, a 10-9 slugfest, which stretched the Giant winning streak to sixteen games. This win moved the first-place Giants into a 14½ game lead over the second-place Cubs.

July 4 — The Giants' sixteen-game winning streak ended with a 10-4 loss to Pittsburgh.

July 8 — Rube Marquard's record-tying nineteen-game winning streak ended as the Cubs defeated the Giants, 7-2.

Sept. 6 — Jeff Tesreau threw a 3-0 no-hitter against the Phillies.

Sept. 26 — The Giants clinched John McGraw's fourth pennant win by taking a doubleheader from Boston. Right-hander Al Demaree, making his major league debut in the second game, pitched a 4-0 shutout.

Oct. 16 — The Giants lost the World Series to the Boston Red Sox 4 games to 3 as the Sox's right-hander Smokey Joe Wood won in relief over Christy Mathewson, 3-2. The Giants went ahead in the top of the tenth, but Giant outfielder Fred Snodgrass committed his famous muff of a fly ball and the Red Sox went on to win.

Nov. 26 — Giant President John T. Brush died in St. Charles, Missouri, after becoming ill on a train trip from New York to California. Brush was succeeded by his son-in-law, Harry N. Hempstead, who knew nothing about baseball. Hempstead's resulting reliance on Giant club secretary John B. Foster caused many internal front office problems over the next few years until John McGraw reestablished his dominance over the Giants' overall operation.

Dec. 16 — John McGraw was honored by Cincinnati fans in a tribute spearheaded by Cincinnati Reds President August Herrmann. The unexpected honor to the volatile Giant manager, who had more than his share of rows in Cincinnati, was part of a local theater program.

1913

April 23 — Christy Mathewson pitched a machine-like 3-1 decision over the Phillies. Exhibiting remarkable control, Matty required only sixty-seven pitches, an average of less than eight pitches an inning, in the one hour and 25 minute game.

May 22 — The Giants obtained veteran right-hander Art Fromme from Cincinnati for pitcher Red Ames, outfielder Josh Devore, and infielder Heinie Groh. Fromme won ten games for the Giants in 1913 and nine games in 1914 before departing the major leagues in 1915. Ames pitched for the Reds, Cardinals, and Phillies through 1919. Devore's major league career ended in 1914. Groh developed into a fine third baseman, returned to the Giants in 1922 and remained through the 1922-1924 pennant-winning years before leaving the club in 1926.

June 30 — John McGraw was knocked down, beaten, and kicked by a partisan crowd in Philadelphia after the Giants won an exciting 11-10, ten-inning slugfest with the Phillies. There had been intense needling between McGraw, coaching at third base, and several of the Phils during the game. As the game ended, McGraw and Philadelphia pitcher Ad Brennan began scuffling and the crowd piled on McGraw. National League President Thomas J. Lynch suspended both McGraw and Brennan and fined Brennan $100. McGraw escaped without a fine, presumably because he had suffered enough at the hands of the irate mob.

July 18 — Christy Mathewson completed an astounding sixty-eight complete innings without issuing a walk in an 8-0 victory over St. Louis at the Polo Grounds. Mathewson walked first baseman Ed Konetchy in the eighth inning, breaking the streak.

Sept. 1 — The Giants swept a doubleheader from Boston and moved into a commanding eleven-game lead over the second-place Phillies. Right-hander Al Demaree won the morning game 3-2 in ten innings and Rube Marquard took the afternoon game 2-1 in fourteen innings.

Sept. 27 — The Giants lost to Brooklyn's star left-hander Nap Rucker 4-0, but backed into the pennant when Philadelphia lost to Boston. This was the Giants' third pennant in a row and their fifth since John McGraw took over as manager in 1902.

Oct. 2 — The Giants played in three separate games against Philadelphia. The two clubs split the originally-scheduled doubleheader at the Polo Grounds, the Giants winning the first game 8-3 and losing the second game 4-3. Before the twinbill, the clubs completed a transferred game that had been halted on August 30 in Philadelphia, the Giants batting with one out in the top of the ninth and losing, 8-6. That was the final score as the last two Giants went out without a struggle. This was hardly a blow to the Giants, who had clinched the pennant five days earlier and were interested only in gearing up for the upcoming World Series with the Philadelphia Athletics.

Oct. 11 — The Giants lost their third straight World Series, this time 4 games to 1 to the Philadelphia Athletics. The A's star left-hander Eddie Plank beat Christy Mathewson 3-1 and allowed the Giants only two hits.

Oct. 18 — The Giants and the Chicago White Sox embarked upon a forty-four-game world tour. The tour took them to Japan, China, the Philippines, Australia, Ceylon, Egypt, Italy, France, and England where King George V (in complete bewilderment with the goings-on) saw the game. The trip ended in London in February just in time for the clubs to begin training for the 1914 season.

Oct. 30 — Giant pitching coach Wilbert Robinson was released. After his long friendship with McGraw, which went back to the 1890s with the Baltimore Orioles, relations between Robinson and McGraw cooled as the 1913 season wore on. Within a few months, Robinson was hired to manage Brooklyn and the traditional Giant-Dodger (the Dodgers became known as the "Robins" as a reflection of the fans' affection for Robinson) rivalry became even more intense.

Nov. 10 — Harry Hempstead, who had succeeded John T. Brush as the Giants' president in November 1912, was reelected to the position.

1914

May 16 — Jeff Tesreau won 2-0 over Pittsburgh, but lost a no-hitter with two out in the ninth on Pirate outfielder Joe Kelly's hit.

July 17 — The Giants defeated Pittsburgh 3-1 in a twenty-one-inning game, the longest game in major league history up to that point. Rube Marquard went the distance and outpitched Pirate right-hander Babe Adams.

Sept. 7 — The Giants split a Labor Day doubleheader with the Boston Braves and both clubs remained tied for first place. Christy Mathewson lost the morning game 5-4 but Jeff Tesreau coasted to an easy 10-1 victory in the afternoon game before thirty-four thousand, the largest crowd in Boston baseball history up to that point.

Giant outfielder Fred Snodgrass and Braves' pitcher Lefty Tyler almost came to blows in the afternoon game when Tyler walked Snodgrass on four pitches aimed close to Snodgrass' head. Snodgrass went to first base after a detour through the pitcher's box to tell Tyler not to repeat his headhunting act. In retaliation, Tyler did an imitation of Snodgrass' famous muff of a fly ball in the deciding game of the 1912 World Series game with the Red Sox. The crowd got into the act, showering Snodgrass with pop bottles until Boston Mayor Curley rushed from his box seat onto the field and coaxed the crowd to desist. Umpire Bill Klem, aware that Curley was up for election, did not chase him off the field until Curley took bows for his effectiveness in halting the rowdyism.

Sept. 26 — Rube Marquard staggered to a 13-6 win over Pittsburgh after having lost twelve straight decisions.

Sept. 30 — The "miracle" Boston Braves clinched the pennant with a 3-2 win over Chicago while the second-place Giants were losing to Pittsburgh, 5-2. The remarkable Braves were in last place on July 4, fifteen games behind the Giants who led the league on that date.

Oct. 1 — Umpire Bill Klem banished twenty-four Giants from the dugout in the seventh inning of a meaningless 7-6 loss to the Braves, who had clinched the pennant the previous day. The Giants were ejected en masse for referring to Klem as "Catfish," a nickname that he hated. Most of the ousted players were rookies just brought up from the minors.

1915

April 15 — Rube Marquard pitched a 2-0 no-hitter against Brooklyn.

August 19 — The Giants released outfielder Fred Snodgrass, who was picked up by the Boston Braves.

August 20 — The Giants purchased first baseman George "Highpockets" Kelly for $1,200 from the Victoria, British Columbia club. After a slow start and trade to Pittsburgh during the 1917 season, the San Francisco native returned to the Giants in 1919 and starred from 1920 through 1929. Kelly was elected to the Hall of Fame in 1973.

August 26 — The Giants released Rube Marquard. The future Hall of Famer was picked up by Brooklyn and his 13 and 6 performance in 1916 was an important factor in Brooklyn's pennant win.

Sept. 1 — Outfielder Jim Thorpe, just recalled from Harrisburg, led the Giants to a 6-5 win over the Phillies with a 3-for-3 day at the plate. The great all-around Indian athlete had failed with the Giants in 1914 and earlier in 1915, and his inability to hit curveball pitching prevented him from becoming a regular performer with the Giants, or with Cincinnati or the Boston Braves in subsequent seasons.

Oct. 7 — The Giants finished the season in last place, twenty-one games behind the pennant-winning Phillies although only 3½ games behind the fourth-place Cubs. This was the Giants' only last place finish during the thirty years that John McGraw managed the club.

1916

Jan. 17 — The Giants purchased outfielder Benny Kauff, catcher Bill Rariden, and right-hander Fred "Spitball" Anderson from the Newark club of the Federal League. McGraw paid $30,000 for Kauff who demanded and obtained $5,000 from the Giants and $5,000 from multimillionaire Newark club owner Harry Sinclair before agreeing to come to the Giants' spring training camp.

Jan. 20 — The Giants bought outfielder Edd Roush from Newark of the Federal League for $7,500. Roush batted a meager .188 for the Giants before being traded to Cincinnati on July 20. Within a year, he showed the form that made him a lifetime .323 hitter and a Hall of Fame electee in 1962.

April 11 — Giant third baseman Hans Lobert snapped cartilage in his left knee while sliding in a preseason exhibition game against Yale University in New Haven and missed most of the season. He came back later in 1916 and in 1917 but was only a part-time player during those seasons and he retired after the 1917 season.

April 12—The Giants lost the Opening Day game 5-4 to the Phillies' great right-hander, Grover Cleveland Alexander, then in his prime. Benny Kauff, the widely heralded "Ty Cobb" of the Federal League, went hitless in his Giant debut.

April 14—The Giants obtained third baseman Bill McKechnie from Newark of the just-defunct Federal League. McKechnie, only a journeyman player, became a Hall of Famer after a fine career as a National League manager at Pittsburgh, St. Louis, Boston, and Cincinnati.

May 2—The Giants snapped an eight-game losing streak as Jeff Tesreau hurled a three-hit, 2-1 win over Brooklyn.

May 9 — The Giants, opening a western trip with a 2 and 13 record and in last place, defeated Pittsburgh, 13-5. This was the first win in a seventeen-game winning streak that catapulted the Giants into second place, only 1 1/2 games behind league-leading Pittsburgh.

May 26—The Giants beat the Braves handily in Boston, 12-1, a victory margin that probably would have been larger had Benny Kauff not been picked off first base three times during the game.

May 29—The Giants won their seventeenth straight victory, all on the road, as Christy Mathewson pitched a four-hit, 3-0 win over Boston.

May 30—The Giants' seventeen-game winning streak ended as ex-Giant right-hander Al Demaree and the Phillies defeated McGraw's club 5-1. Giant third baseman Bill McKechnie was caught stealing three times in the game.

July 19—Giant center fielder Benny Kauff tagged out two baserunners at second base in an unusual play as the Giants defeated the Cubs 8-6 in Chicago. The Cubs loaded the bases with one out, center fielder Cy Williams on first, left fielder Les Mann on second, and second baseman Otto Knabe, the runner at third. Giant catcher Bill Rariden snapped a throw to shortstop Mickey Doolan, trapping Mann off second base. Knabe broke for home and a rundown ensued between third and home as the Giants switched their attention from Mann to Knabe. But Doolan dropped the ball and Knabe scored. Doolan recovered the ball and threw it to Kauff who had come in from center field to help out at second base. Kauff tagged out Mann coming back to second base and then tagged out Williams coming from first base to complete the double play.

July 20—The Giants traded Christy Mathewson, third baseman Bill McKechnie, and outfielder Edd Roush to Cincinnati for third baseman Buck Herzog and outfielder Wade Killefer. McGraw made the trade to permit his good friend Mathewson to become manager of the lowly Reds. Herzog, the Reds' playing manager, had been traded from the Giants twice before because he and McGraw disliked each other intensely. Regardless, the Giants needed a stabilizing influence on the field and McGraw felt the peppery Herzog would steady his erratic club.

July 26—In his first meeting with the Giants since they traded him a week before, Christy Mathewson's Cincinnati Reds defeated the Giants at the Polo Grounds, 4-2. Lefty Slim Sallee, just obtained from the Cardinals, was hit hard in his Giant debut.

July 31—The Giants won a doubleheader shutout over the Pittsburgh Pirates by 7-0 scores. Slim Sallee pitched the first victory and Jeff Tesreau the second.

August 26—The Giants traded Fred Merkle to Brooklyn for catcher Lew McCarty.

August 28—The Giants traded second baseman Larry Doyle and infielder Herb Hunter to the Cubs for third baseman Heinie Zimmerman. Doyle had slowed down perceptibly and the deal permitted McGraw to strengthen his infield by shifting Buck Herzog to second base and installing Zimmerman at third base.

Sept. 7—Giant left-hander Ferdie Schupp stopped Brooklyn 4-1, the first of twenty-six consecutive Giant wins. The record-breaking streak, which is still the record, ended on September 30.

Sept. 9—Giant right-hander William "Pol" Perritt defeated the Phillies twice by scores of 3-1 and 3-0.

Sept. 15—The Giants' winning streak of nine games was barely maintained as a game with Cincinnati was halted by rain after four innings, with the Giants losing 2-0.

Sept. 18—The Giants extended their winning streak to eleven by defeating the Pirates in the first game of a doubleheader. The second game was called because of rain after eight innings with the score tied, 1-1.

Sept. 25—The Giants stretched their winning streak to twenty-one as they defeated the Cardinals twice by scores of 1-0 and 6-2. This broke the old twenty-game winning streak of Providence in 1884.

Sept. 28—For the second time in the 1916 season, the Giants won a doubleheader shutout. Jeff Tesreau won the first game over the

Boston Braves 2-0 and Ferdie Schupp followed with a 6-0 win. Schupp was en route to a remarkable 0.90 earned run average for the season.

Sept. 30—The Giants' incredible twenty-six game winning streak ended with an 8-3 loss to Boston's Lefty Tyler. Jeff Tesreau was unable to stop the Braves in relief of Slim Sallee. The Giants' twenty-sixth win came in the day's first game as Rube Benton shut out the Braves, 4-0.

Oct. 3—The Giants lost to Brooklyn 9-6 in a sloppily-played game that clinched the pennant for Brooklyn. McGraw left the bench in disgust after the fifth inning, stating: "I do not say that my players did not try to win but they simply disobeyed my orders." The next day's headlines, "McGraw Charges Players with Throwing Game to Robins," caused Manager Pat Moran of the contending Phillies, to demand an investigation, but McGraw refused to amplify his charge and the matter was dropped.

1917

March 25—John McGraw signed a five-year contract for a record $40,000 per year plus bonuses. This made him the highest salaried figure in the game.

March 30—In an exhibition game in Dallas, Detroit's Ty Cobb slid into Giant second baseman Buck Herzog and ripped Herzog's leg. The pair fought furiously until they were separated. In his book, *McGraw of the Giants*, Frank Graham reported that Herzog challenged Cobb to a fight to be held in Cobb's room that evening. They agreed to be accompanied by one teammate and to have Tiger trainer Harry Tuttle act as referee. At 10 p.m., Herzog and Giant third baseman Heinie Zimmerman entered Cobb's room and found that Cobb was accompanied by eight other Detroit players. Graham reported that it wasn't much of a fight. Herzog knocked Cobb to his knees with the first punch. But Cobb got up and beat Herzog unmercifully until Tuttle stepped in. Tuttle said later, "They fought like a couple of washerwomen." But both men were satisfied. Herzog felt that he had avenged himself for the spiking by knocking Cobb down. Cobb figured he had squared accounts by giving Herzog a bad beating.

The Giants and Tigers played the rest of the week despite the fact that Cobb refused to play in the remaining games because he had been ejected after his fight on the field with Herzog. After the last game of the series, the Giants sent Cobb a postcard. Signed by all the Giants the card read, "It's safe to rejoin your club; we've left."

June 8—John McGraw smashed Umpire Bill Byron in the face under the grandstand after a tempestuous Giant loss in Cincinnati. McGraw claimed that he had struck Byron because of personal remarks Byron had made, matters unrelated to the contentious game. League President John K. Tener fined McGraw $500 and suspended him for two weeks. McGraw responded by accusing Tener of being a tool of the Phillies and the umpires of being the poorest he had ever seen. McGraw told highly respected New York writer Sid Mercer that he wanted to see his accusation of Tener quoted in "every newspaper in New York." The writers took him at his word and quoted him.

However, McGraw denied having made his remarks about Tener in a hearing before the league directors a month later, even signing a statement to that effect. The New York writers demanded a second hearing during which Tener became convinced that McGraw had been quoted accurately and Tener fined McGraw an additional $1,000. After that Mercer never spoke to McGraw again or covered another Giant game. As another writer summed it up, "It cost McGraw $500 for writing and $1,000 for talking about it."

July 31—The Giants traded infielder Pete Kilduff to the Cubs for Al Demaree, who had pitched for the Giants from 1912 to 1914.

August 14—The Giants and the Brooklyn Robins split a typically hectic doubleheader at the Polo Grounds, the Giants' Ferdie Schupp winning the first game 5-4 and ex-Giant pitcher Rube Marquard holding the Giants in check 3-1 in the second game. The second game ws highlighted by a wild brawl at second base between Brooklyn's Casey Stengel and Giant shortstop Art Fletcher.

August 21—Slim Sallee's ten-game winning streak ended as Christy Mathewson's Cincinnati club defeated the Giants, 7-5.

Sept. 18—The Giants suspended Buck Herzog, the team captain, for refusing to accompany the team when it left on a western trip. After a few days, Herzog returned to the team without explanation. Herzog was traded after the season, the usual fate of players who got on the wrong side of McGraw. However, the Herzog case was notable because McGraw had brought him back twice after having traded him.

Sept. 25—The Giants clinched their sixth pennant under John McGraw's leadership as left-hander Slim Sallee beat the Cardinals 2-1 in the first game of a doubleheader. In the second game, Giant outfielder Ross "Pep" Youngs made his major league debut in a 5-3 loss. The future Hall of Famer went hitless in four trips.

Oct. 15—The Giants lost the World Series to the Chicago White Sox 4 games to 2 as Chicago right-hander Red Faber outpitched Rube Benton for a 4-2 win.

1918

Jan. 8—The Giants obtained old favorite Larry Doyle and right-hander Jesse Barnes from the Cubs in exchange for Buck Herzog. Doyle, no more the ball of fire that he had been for the Giants in earlier years, played through the 1920 season for the Giants before retiring.

   The strong mutual dislike between McGraw and Herzog made it inevitable that Herzog would leave the Giants for the third time. Also, Herzog had been suspended for a time for refusing to accompany the Giants on their final western trip of 1917 and he tried vainly to recover $830 that had been deducted from his pay during his suspension.

May 23—Giant outfielder Benny Kauff struck out five times as the Giants won 6-4 in St. Louis.

July 18—Giant third baseman Heinie Zimmerman left the ballpark in a huff during an 8-5 win in St. Louis after a tongue-lashing from John McGraw for failing to run out a fly ball. Zimmerman returned to the Giants a few days later after paying a stiff fine.

July 22—The Giants purchased right-hander Fred Toney from Cincinnati.

Oct. 5—Giant infielder Eddie Grant was killed while leading his infantry unit in the Argonne Forest near Verdun, France. A memorial to Grant, the first major leaguer killed in World War I, was erected in deepest center field at the Polo Grounds.

Dec. 31—Giant pitcher Fred Toney was sentenced to four months in jail after pleading guilty to violating the Mann Act (prohibiting the interstate transportation of women for immoral purposes).

1919

Jan. 3—The Giants obtained catcher Earl Smith from Rochester for outfielders Joe Wilhoit and Bill Kelly, right-handers Waite Hoyt and Jack Ogden, first baseman Joe Rodriguez, plus cash. Smith gave the Giants four years of aggressive play but the real story was the loss of Hoyt, who developed into a great Hall of Fame pitcher.

Jan. 14—A syndicate headed by stockbroker Charles A. Stoneham, John McGraw, and New York City Magistrate Francis X. McQuade bought the Giants from the John T. Brush estate for an amount in excess of $1 million. Stoneham was elected president and McGraw became the vice president and continued as manager.

Feb. 19—The Giants obtained fancy-fielding first baseman Hal Chase from Cincinnati in exchange for first baseman Walter Holke and catcher Bill Rariden. Chase had been suspended by the Reds on August 9, 1918, for "indifferent playing." The Reds also charged him with attempting to throw games, but the National League's board of directors threw the charges out because of insufficient evidence.

During September, 1919, both Chase and Heinie Zimmerman failed to play in a number of games and McGraw sent them home without public explanation. A year later, during the investigation of the Black Sox scandal, McGraw testified that he had dismissed both players because they had thrown games and had attempted unsuccessfully to bribe Fred Toney and Benny Kauff to do the same.

March 7—Christy Mathewson, back from World War I service and no longer associated with the Cincinnati Reds, rejoined the Giants as McGraw's pitching coach and heir apparent as manager.

May 4—The Giants lost to the Phils 4-3 in the first Sunday game at the Polo Grounds. (Sunday baseball had just been legalized in New York City). A crowd of thirty-five thousand attended, the largest turnout for any game in New York up to that time except for World Series games.

Casey Stengel, then with the Phils, told an amusing story about the game. He said that before the game, Giant captain Art Fletcher walked over to the Phils' dugout and said, "McGraw doesn't want any trouble today because the Sabbath Society people (violently opposed to Sunday baseball) are looking for something to complain about. So let's have a peaceful game." But, to the Phils' amazement, after the fifth inning of the game Giant teammates Fletcher and Rube Benton got into a dispute over an infield play and soon were brawling over the bats in front of the dugout in full view of the crowd. As Stengel described it, the umpires deliberately ignored the combatants, who were separated by their teammates as the "peaceful" game continued.

May 19—The Giants purchased catcher Mike Gonzalez from St. Louis. The pidgin English spoken by the Havana, Cuba, native gained wide circulation years later when Gonzalez scouted a smooth-fielding minor league player and described him pithily as: "Good field, no hit."

May 21—The Giants sent outfielder Jim Thorpe to the Boston Braves on waivers.

June 17—Second baseman Frank Frisch, who had been signed after graduating from Fordham, played in his first major league game. Frisch pinch hit unsuccessfully for Hal Chase as the Giants lost 7-2 in Chicago.

July 4—Giant right-hander Jesse Barnes, on his way to a brilliant 25 and 9 season, won the morning game of the holiday doubleheader, pitching a one hit, 3-1 victory over the Phillies in Philadelphia.

July 16—The Giants traded Ferdie Schupp to the St. Louis Cardinals for catcher Frank "Pancho" Snyder. Snyder, who did most of the catching for the Giants as they won pennants in 1921-1924, coached several years under Bill Terry in the 1930s.

August 17—In one of their best trades, the Giants obtained star left-hander Art Nehf from the Boston Braves for right-handers Joe Oeschger and Cecil "Red" Causey and an estimated $55,000. Nehf, the premier Giant pitcher during their 1921-1924 pennant wins, won one hundred seven games and lost only sixty during his seven years with the Giants.

Sept. 24—The Giants obtained right-hander Phil "Shufflin' Phil" Douglas from the Cubs for outfielder Dave Robertson.

Sept. 28—The Giants beat the Phillies 6-1 in 51 minutes, the fastest nine-inning major league game ever.

1920

March 9—Giant President Charles Stoneham denied the Giants were for sale, indicating that he had purchased the club primarily to turn it over to his son. This proved to be the case as his son, Horace, ran the club after the death of the elder Stoneham on January 6, 1936, until Horace sold the club to a group headed by Robert A. Lurie on March 2, 1976.

May 11—The Giants had five triples in a 9-4 loss to the Reds in Cincinnati. Outfielder Ross Youngs had three of the triples, connecting in the first, third, and seventh innings.

May 14—The Giants informed the Yankees that the American Leaguers' lease to use the Polo Grounds would not be renewed after the 1920 season. No reason was given although it was obvious that the wide acclaim for the Yanks' recently-acquired Babe Ruth had been a great irritant. Yankee Owner Jacob Ruppert responded angrily that the Giants "had gone back on their word," the understanding that had been in effect since the Yanks had begun using the Polo Grounds in 1912. The Giants' eviction order was rescinded a week later, but the Yankees began immediate efforts to obtain a site for their own ballpark.

May 19—League President John Heydler suspended John McGraw for five days for a game-long harangue with umpires Bill Klem and Charley Moran during a hectic 8-6, twelve-inning Giant win in Chicago.

June 8—The Giants obtained shortstop Dave "Beauty" Bancroft from the Philadelphia Phillies for veteran shortstop Art Fletcher, pitcher Wilbur Hubbell, and an estimated $100,000. Considered one of the best shortstops in the game, Bancroft gave the Giants three superb years in their 1921-1923 pennant-winning seasons, then moved to the Boston Braves as their player-manager from 1924 to 1927. Bancroft was elected to the Hall of Fame in 1971.

June 28—Dave Bancroft stroked six singles in six trips as the Giants smothered the Phillies 18-3 in Philadelphia. Despite twenty Giant hits, the game was played in less than two hours — one hour and 58 minutes to be exact.

July 3—The Giants traded Benny Kauff to Toronto for outfielder Vernon Spencer. Kauff had averaged over .300 in five years with the Giants, but he never lived up to his reputation as the Federal League's "Ty Cobb." After leaving the Giants, Kauff was accused of stealing an automobile and receiving stolen goods in New York, but he was acquitted. Regardless, after reviewing the record of the trial, newly-appointed Baseball Commissioner Kenesaw Mountain Landis barred Kauff from organized baseball. Kauff later obtained an injunction against Landis and National League President Heydler, but he subsequently withdrew the action. Only thirty years old when the Giants traded him, Kauff never played in the majors again.

July 16—Giant Rube Benton threw a sparkling 7-0, seventeen-inning shutout against Pittsburgh. After going scoreless for sixteen innings, the Giants exploded for eight hits and seven runs in the top of the seventeenth inning. The big inning included three straight triples by second baseman Frank Frisch (with the bases loaded), first baseman George Kelly, and outfielder Lee King.

August 8—Actor John Slavin, a friend of John McGraw's was found badly beaten in front of McGraw's New York City apartment. Although there were indications that McGraw had fought with Slavin, McGraw denied that he had and he was not officially contradicted. However, prohibition agents obtained a federal grand jury indictment against McGraw, charging him with violating

the Volstead Act by "unlawfully possessing a bottle of whiskey."
The upshot was that McGraw settled with Slavin out of court and
the Lambs Club (where McGraw had reportedly been drinking
before the incident) expelled McGraw as a member.

In a related incident on September 18, 1920, another Lambs
Club member visited McGraw to "give him some friendly advice"
and wound up with a broken ankle after the Giant manager
admitted punching him. On September 21, McGraw retaliated
against the Lambs Club by withdrawing some members' passes to
attend games at the Polo Grounds.

The Lambs Club affair ended happily for McGraw. In May
1921, a jury acquitted him of the liquor possession charge and
three years later the Lambs Club reinstated him.

August 28—Ross Youngs punched teammate Jesse "Tex"
Winters in the nose as both men returned to the Giant bench after
pregame batting practice in Cincinnati. Youngs objected to close
pitches which Winters had thrown to him. (This apparently was a
practice of Winters, who had fought with Benny Kauff in a similar
incident earlier in the season in Dallas.) In the game that followed,
Rube Benton gave up twelve hits to the Reds, yet won a 4-0
shutout.

Sept. 6— The Giants reacquired left-hander Slim Sallee
from Cincinnati. Sallee, who had won 134 games for the Giants
during the 1908 through 1918 period, had little left and he left the
major leagues after pitching for the Giants in 1921.

Sept. 17—Giant left fielder George Burns hit for the
cycle and added a double for good measure as the Giants beat
Pittsburgh 4-3 in ten innings at the Polo Grounds. Ross Youngs
drove in the winning run with a bases-loaded single in the bottom of
the tenth inning.

Sept. 18—The Giants obtained catcher Walter "Butch" Henline
from Indianapolis for third baseman Doug Baird, second baseman
Fred "King" Lear, and cash. Henline played in only one game for
the Giants in 1921, then moved to the Phillies in July 1921 in an
important deal in which the Giants obtained outfielder Emil "Irish"
Meusel.

Oct. 6—Former Giants Hal Chase and Heinie Zimmerman were
indicted on bribery charges as an aftermath of the investigation of
the crooked Cincinnati Reds/Chicago White Sox World Series in
1919. John McGraw testified that he had dropped Chase and
Zimmerman after the 1919 season for throwing games and for
attempting to bribe Giants Fred Toney and Benny Kauff to do the

same. Zimmerman angrily denied the charge and filed a court suit in March 1921. Chase characteristically ignored the charge.

Oct. 29—Hughie Jennings, John McGraw's old Baltimore teammate, joined the Giants as a coach.

Dec. 15—The Giants released veteran second baseman Larry Doyle in order for him to become manager of the Toronto club.

1921

March 4—Ex-Giant Heinie Zimmerman, banned from organized baseball, filed an affidavit that accused John McGraw of making Zimmerman "the goat" in Zimmerman's alleged participation in attempting to bribe three Giant teammates (Fred Toney, Rube Benton, and Benny Kauff) to throw games in the final Giant-Cub series of 1919. Zimmerman claimed that he had carried the bribe offer to the players from a Chicago gambler but that otherwise he was innocent. McGraw responded that Zimmerman's statement amounted to a "confession" of guilt.

April 2—Giant coach Cozy Dolan and first baseman George Kelly were sued for $1,000 for assaulting umpire Ed Lauzon. In the third inning of the previous day's game in Mobile, Alabama, Lauzon reacted to violent complaints by Dolan and Kelly by swinging wildly at the Giant coach. Dolan responded more effectively with a punch that landed squarely in Lauzon's eye. Both Dolan and Lauzon were arrested for disorderly conduct. On July 29, 1921, a Mobile judge ordered Dolan and Kelly to pay $600 each to Lauzon who was then umpiring in a minor league.

June 1—Dave Bancroft hit for the cycle as the Giants defeated the Phillies 8-3 in the first game of a doubleheader at the Polo Grounds.

June 30—The Giants traded third baseman Goldie Rapp, outfielder Lee King, and infielder Lance Richbourg to the Phillies for second baseman Johnny Rawlings and outfielder Casey Stengel. Rawlings waited until the next day before joining the Giants, but the overjoyed Stengel grabbed the next train to New York "before McGraw changes his mind."

July 5—The Giants bought brilliant outfield prospect Bill Cunningham from Seattle for an estimated $75,000, the highest price for a minor league player up to that time.

July 25—The Giants obtained outfielder Emil "Irish" Meusel (hitting a cool .354) from the Phillies for catcher Butch Henline and outfielder Curtis Walker. A brother of Yankee outfielder Bob

Meusel, Irish played key roles in the Giant pennant wins of 1921-1924.

August 24—Trailing the confident, visiting first-place Pirates by 7 1/2 games, the Giants reared up and took a doubleheader 10-2 and 7-0. A midweek throng of almost thirty-five thousand watched Art Nehf handily win the first game, supported by home runs from George Kelly and Irish Meusel. Phil Douglas won the second game behind the slugging of Meusel and George Burns.

August 25—The Giants defeated the league-leading Pirates for the third straight game as Fred Toney pitched a 5-2 win and hit a three-run homer.

August 26   The Giants took their fourth straight game from the league-leading Pirates at the Polo Grounds to draw to within 3½ games of Pittsburgh. Phil Douglas, pitching with only one day of rest, gave up ten hits but struggled to a 2-1 decision.

August 27—The Giants captured their fifth straight game from the league-leading Pirates as Art Nehf, pitching with only two days' rest, won 3-1. The Giants' sweep at the Polo Grounds left them only 2 1/2 games behind Pittsburgh.

Sept. 11—The Giants took over first place from Pittsburgh with an 11-3 thumping of Wilbert Robinson's Brooklyn Robins. Fred Toney relieved a faltering Phil Douglas and stopped Brooklyn cold for seven innings.

Sept. 29—The idle Giants clinched their seventh pennant under McGraw as the Pirates lost a doubleheader to the Cardinals.

Sept. 30—The Giants were scheduled to play a benefit game for Christy Mathewson who was at Saranac Lake, New York, fighting a lengthy bout with tuberculosis, a holdover from his World War I service. The game was rained out but, as a result of a rain postponement insurance policy, the club was able to pay Mathewson about $45,000.

Oct. 13—The Giants defeated the Yankees 5 games to 3 in the World Series as Art Nehf pitched a brilliant four hit, 1-0 win over Yankee right-hander Waite Hoyt.

Dec. 7—The Giants obtained third baseman Heinie Groh from the Reds for outfielder George Burns, catcher Mike Gonzalez, and an estimated $100,000.

1922

Jan. 20—John McGraw signed a five-year contract to manage the Giants through the 1926 season.

April 25—Giant rookie outfielder Ralph Shinners, off to a great start, was beaned by Phillies' right-hander George Smith as the Giants won 9-3 in Philadelphia. An infuriated John McGraw accused Smith of deliberately beaning Shinners, but the cocky Smith laughed in his face. Shinners returned to the lineup in a few days, but he was not the same hitter and McGraw had to remove him from the lineup and, on August 3, option him to Toledo.

Before Shinners was optioned out, he obtained some slight measure of revenge. Smith was knocked out of the box by the Giants in a subsequent game at the Polo Grounds. As he took the long walk to the clubhouse in center field, Shinners approached him from the Giant bullpen in right field and asked him whether the beaning had been deliberate. McGraw, seeing Shinners approach Smith, raced from the dugout directly to Smith. Before McGraw could reach them, Shinners spun Smith around with a punch to the jaw and the two men began to wrestle violently. McGraw tried to help Shinners out with assorted kicks at Smith until the combatants were separated and escorted to the clubhouses. Shinners returned to the Giants in 1923 and 1925, but he never regained his form of early 1922.

April 29—The Giants overwhelmed the Braves 15-4 with a twenty-hit performance in Boston as Phil Douglas coasted to the win. The Giant attack included two inside-the-park home runs by George Kelly and a five-hit spree by Ross Youngs, who hit for the cycle.

May 7—Giant pitcher Jesse Barnes hurled a 6-0, near-perfect, no-hit win over the Phillies at the Polo Grounds. Barnes faced twenty-seven men, allowing only outfielder Cy Williams to reach base. Williams drew a walk in the fourth but he was rubbed out in a double play.

May 19—The Giants signed sixteen-year-old Fred Lindstrom from Loyola Academy in Chicago and announced plans to send him to Toledo for seasoning. Lindstrom, brought up to the Giants in 1924, went on to a brilliant career that led to his election to the Hall of Fame in 1976.

May 26—Heinie Groh walked five times as the Giants manhandled Boston 10-2 in the second game of a doubleheader at the Polo Grounds.

May 28—The Giants defeated the Phillies easily, 8-1, despite four errors by Giant second baseman Frank Frisch.

July 7—The Giants defeated the Pirates 9-8 in eighteen innings despite the heroics of Pittsburgh outfielder Max Carey, who went 6-for-6 plus three walks.

July 30—The Giants obtained right-hander Hugh McQuillan from the Boston Braves for experienced pitchers Fred Toney and Larry Benton, untried left-hander Walter Houlighan, plus an estimated $100,000.

August 16—Left fielder Casey Stengel saved a 7-6 Giant win with a sparkling catch in Pittsburgh. In the last of the ninth, the Pirates filled the bases with two out. Pirate catcher Walter Schmidt drove a long clout to deep left center. Stengel raced over to his left on the dead run and pulled the ball in with his arm outstretched, ending the game dramatically.

August 17—Giant right-hander "Shufflin' Phil" Douglas, who had been drinking with special gusto after a tongue-lashing from John McGraw, wrote a letter to St. Louis Cardinal outfielder Les Mann suggesting that he (Douglas) would "go fishing" for the rest of the season if the price was right and thereby help St. Louis win the pennant. Mann gave the letter to Card Manager Branch Rickey. Rickey notified the Giants and Commissioner Landis and Landis immediately banned Douglas from organized baseball for life. Tragically, it was learned later that after Douglas sobered up he called Mann to ask him to destroy the letter but Mann already had passed it on to Rickey.

Sept. 3—The Giants won an exciting 8-7 victory over the Phillies in the bottom of the ninth and pulled a triple play earlier in the game. With the score tied 7-7 in the last of the ninth and Frank Frisch on second base, Irish Meusel drove a hot smash down the first base line. Philadelphia first baseman Roy Leslie came up with the ball and threw to pitcher Jimmy Ring, covering the bag in time to nail Meusel. But Ring muffed the ball and Frisch, with characteristically aggressive base running, scored from second base.

The second-inning triple play was unusual. With the Phils' Roy Leslie on first, Cliff Lee on second, and none out, Jimmy Smith popped deep to second base and the infield fly rule was called. However, Giant second baseman Frisch failed to field the ball and many of the players did not realize that Smith had been called out. Ross Youngs raced in from right field and threw to Dave Bancroft covering second base. Bancroft relayed the ball to third baseman Heinie Groh to nail Lee for the second out. Groh rifled the ball to first baseman George Kelly to get the confused Leslie sliding back into first base for the third out.

Sept. 25—The Giants defeated the Cardinals 5-4 in ten innings at the Polo Grounds to clinch their eighth pennant under John McGraw. George Kelly and Frank Frisch starred as right-hander Wilfred "Rosy" Ryan relieved starter Hugh McQuillan to win the game.

Sept. 27—Giant shortstop Travis "Stonewall" Jackson made his debut, relieving Dave Bancroft and going 0-for-2 in a 3-2 win over the Phillies. A fine player with a great arm, the popular Jackson spent all his fifteen playing seasons with the Giants. He was elected to the Hall of Fame in 1982.

Oct. 5—The second game of the World Series between the Giants and the Yankees was called "on account of darkness" with the score tied at three-all and the sun high in the sky. There was such an uproar at the decision of umpire George Hildebrand to call the game that Commissioner Kenesaw M. Landis ordered the receipts of more than $120,000 divided between New York City charities and disabled veterans groups.

Oct. 8—Art Nehf beat the Yankees 5-3 in the final game of the World Series. The Giants won 4 games to none plus a tie in the second game to defeat the Yankees two Series in a row for John McGraw's third Series victory.

1923

March 21—Colorful Jack Bentley, a hard-hitting pitcher/first baseman/outfielder purchased from Baltimore for $65,000 during the offseason, reported belatedly to the Giants' spring training camp at San Antonio, Texas. Bentley had announced that he would not report unless he received $5,000 of the purchase price either from the Giants or from Baltimore owner Jack Dunn. Bentley, who reported 20 pounds overweight, did not receive any of the purchase price. The big left-hander had a 40 and 22 career record with the Giants during the 1923-1925 seasons.

April 14—The Giants announced that an expansion of the Polo Grounds to bring its capacity to 54,555 was nearly completed. The original fifteen thousand bleacher seats were reduced to five thousand-five hundred as many of the old bleacher seats in left center and right center were converted to covered, double-decked grandstands. This was the last significant addition to the Polo Grounds' seating capacity.

May 20—The Giants crushed the St. Louis Cardinals 14-4 with twenty hits. The game was played before more than forty-two thousand at the expanded Polo Grounds, a new National League attendance mark.

June 1—The Giants slaughtered the Phillies 22-8 at Baker Bowl, the Phils' closet-sized home park at the time. Three Giants (Heinie Groh, Ross Youngs, and Jimmy O'Connell) had five hits apiece as the Giants banged out a total of twenty-three hits. O'Connell's hits included a single, three doubles, and a home run. McGraw's club set a modern record by scoring at least one run in each of the nine innings. The feat had last been accomplished by Boston against Cleveland in an American League game in 1903.

June 7—The Giants traded pitcher Jesse Barnes and catcher Earl Smith to the Boston Braves for right-hander John Wilson and catcher Hank Gowdy.

August 4—Giant shortstop Travis "Stonewall" Jackson drove in eight runs with a home run, a double, and two singles as the Giants beat the Reds 14-4 in Cincinnati.

Sept. 17—George Kelly went 5-for-5, including three consecutive home runs, as the Giants defeated the Cubs in Chicago.

Sept. 28—The Giants clinched their third straight pennant, the ninth under John McGraw, as Art Nehf shut out Brooklyn, 3-0.

Sept. 30—Future Giant manager and Hall of Famer Bill Terry played his first major league game. The big first baseman singled in three at bats as the Giants edged the Boston Braves 4-3 in ten innings at the Polo Grounds.

Oct. 3—The Giants, with Babe Ruth in their lineup, defeated the Baltimore Orioles 9-0 in an exhibition game. Ruth, wearing an ill-fitting Giant uniform, hit a mammoth home run over the Polo Grounds right-field roof. The game was played as a benefit affair for destitute, former Giant owner and manager John B. Day as the Giants and Yankees awaited the start of their third consecutive "subway series."

Oct. 15—The Giants lost the World Series to the Yankees, 4 games to 2, as Art Nehf lost to Yankee left-hander Herb Pennock 6-4.

Nov. 12—The Giants traded Dave "Beauty" Bancroft, Casey Stengel, and Bill Cunningham to the Boston Braves for pitcher Joe Oeschger and outfielder Billy Southworth. Bancroft was installed as the Braves' new manager. McGraw told the writers that although he considered Bancroft to be the best shortstop in the game, he had made the trade to help out his good friend Christy Mathewson, then the Braves' president.

1924

April 8—The Giants "lost" a tied game in an exhibition with the Chicago White Sox at Nashville, Tennessee. The Sox scored eight runs in an early inning, but the keeper of the scoreboard hung up a big "9." Several writers noted the error but it went unreported because there was no communication between the press box and the scorekeeper. Thus, when the Giants pecked away to even the score at eight runs, the scoreboard indicated the Sox were leading 9-8. After the Giants were retired in the ninth, the teams rushed off the field, apparently not realizing that the game was actually tied.

McGraw and White Sox manager Johnny Evers missed the game because of illness, but both men were furious when they learned of the oversight. A young reporter said to McGraw, "Well, after all, it was only an exhibition so why get excited?" The enraged McGraw put the matter in neat perspective. He shouted, "What difference does it make? I don't care whether it was an exhibition game or a World Series! These people down here look up to the major league clubs. What do you think they are going to say when they read the papers tomorrow morning and see what a lot of incompetents I have traveling around with me?"

April 15—Eighteen-year-old Freddy Lindstrom, a future Hall of Famer, made his first major league appearance. He went in to run for Giant catcher Hank Gowdy in the ninth inning as the Giants beat Brooklyn 3-2 in the season opener. Lindstrom got his first major league hit on April 27, 1924, as a pinch hitter for Bill Terry in a 9-5 win over Brooklyn.

June 14—George Kelly batted in all of the Giant runs in an 8-4 Giant win at Cincinnati. Kelly hit three home runs in the game, the second time he had accomplished the feat.

July 16—George Kelly's seventh home run in the Giants' last six games carried the club to an 8-7 victory over the Pirates in Pittsburgh.

July 29—Art Nehf decisioned the St. Louis Cardinals 5-2 at the Polo Grounds and hit two homers in the process.

Sept. 10—The Giants mauled the Boston Braves with twenty-seven hits in a 22-1 rout at the Polo Grounds in the first game of a doubleheader. Frankie Frisch had five singles and a home run before going out on his seventh at bat.

Sept. 27—The Giants clinched their fourth straight pennant as left-hander Jack Bentley pitched a four hit, 5-1 win over Philadelphia. This was John McGraw's tenth and last pennant as Giant manager.

Oct. 1—Philadelphia Philly shortstop Heinie Sand told his manager, Art Fletcher, that Giant outfielder Jimmy O'Connell had offered him $500 not to bear down against the Giants in a series at the Polo Grounds. O'Connell, readily admitting his involvement to Commissioner Kenesaw M. Landis, accused Giant coach Cozy Dolan, Frank Frisch, George Kelly, and Ross Youngs of having induced him to make the offer. After questioning all of the parties concerned, Landis expelled the impressionable O'Connell and Dolan (who kept repeating unconvincingly, "I don't remember") from organized baseball and cleared Frisch, Kelly, and Youngs.

Oct. 10—The Giants dropped a seven-game World Series to the Washington Senators. Giant reliever Jack Bentley lost to the great Walter Johnson 4-3 in the bottom of the ninth when the Senators' Earl McNeely's bouncer hit a pebble and hopped over Giant third baseman Freddy Lindstrom's head.

   Bentley put the tough-luck loss in perspective after the game. Walter Johnson had lost the first game of the Series to Art Nehf in a twelve-inning heartbreaker and had lost to Bentley in the fifth game. Bentley looked around the somber Giant clubhouse and said, "Cheer up, boys. It just looks as though the Good Lord couldn't stand seeing Walter Johnson get beat again."

Oct. 11—The Giants and the Chicago White Sox left on a European tour. The most publicized game of the tour was played at Stamford Bridge, England, with King George V in attendance. The game, won by the Giants 8-5, drew little reaction from the crowd except for a moment in the fifth inning when Washington catcher Muddy Ruel, who caught for the American Leaguers, hit a foul ball that narrowly missed entering the Royal Box.

1925

July 1—Giant outfielder Lewis "Hack" Wilson hit two home runs in the third inning of a 16-7 slugfest won by the Giants in Philadelphia. Wilson played unspectacularly with the Giants during the 1923-1925 seasons, then moved to the Chicago Cubs where his powerhitting eventually led to his election to the Hall of Fame.

August 8—With the Giants struggling to stay close to the league-leading Pirates, John McGraw made two moves. He traded Hack Wilson to Toledo for outfielder Earl Webb plus $5,000. The deal was a bummer; Webb went hitless in three at bats with the Giants before moving back to the minors and Wilson had a wild, wooly, but sensational career.

   McGraw also obtained right-hander "Fat Freddy" Fitz-simmons from Indianapolis for two players to be named later and an undisclosed amount of cash. Fitzsimmons went on to a fine career with the Giants and the Dodgers.

August 11—The Giants released catcher Hank Gowdy to permit him to manage the Columbus, Ohio, club.

August 12—Freddy Fitzsimmons made his Giant debut in relief of Virgil "Zeke" Barnes in a 5-3 loss at Pittsburgh. Fitzsimmons held the Pirates scoreless in the last four innings.

    The game was enlivened by a brawl between George Kelly and the Pirates' great (and usually mild-mannered) third baseman Pie Traynor. With Irish Meusel on second and Kelly at first, Bill Terry lined a single to center. Meusel was cut down at the plate and Kelly crashed heavily into Traynor, who was waiting to make the tag at third base. The collision knocked Traynor's glove off but the infuriated Traynor, instead of chasing down his glove and the ball, rushed at Kelly and rammed both fists into the towering Kelly's chest. Umpire Hank O'Day and other peacemakers stopped the fight quickly and Traynor won a victory of sorts—Kelly was called out for interference and Traynor was permitted to remain in the game.

August 22—A record Polo Grounds crowd of nearly fifty-five thousand saw the Giants lose a doubleheader to the league-leading Pirates by scores of 8-1 and 2-1. Another thirty thousand fans tried in vain to get into the park. With the loss, the second-place Giants fell five games behind the Pirates, a lead they never overcame.

August 23—A Polo Grounds gathering of nearly fifty-eight thousand, breaking the National League attendance record, watched the Giants split a doubleheader with the Pirates to remain five games behind Pittsburgh. Giant right-hander Kent Greenfield, relieved by Jack Scott, won the first game, 7-4. Freddy Fitzsimmons lost the second game 3-2 as Stuffy McInnis (one of Connie Mack's former stars) and ex-Giant second baseman Johnny Rawlings delivered run-scoring hits.

Oct. 7—Giant pitching great Christy Mathewson died of tuberculosis, after fighting the ailment for several years, at Saranac Lake, New York. At the time of his death, Mathewson was president and part owner of the Boston Braves.

Dec. 19—The Giants bought twenty-two-year-old Andy Cohen from the Waco, Texas club for an unannounced price. The highly-touted second baseman remained with the Giants during the 1926-1929 period, hitting .281 but never living up to his early promise.

Dec. 30—The Giants obtained pitcher Jimmy Ring from the Phillies in a trade for pitchers Jack Bentley and Wayland Dean.

1926

Feb. 28—John McGraw arrived at the Giants' Sarasota, Florida, spring training camp and announced he would spend no more time on schemes to sell real estate in the Sarasota area. He had spent the off-season shuttling between New York City and Florida, working with a land speculation group. Within a year the real estate venture failed and evidently McGraw lost a lot of money in settling claims to buyers of oversold lots of land.

April 27—Seventeen-year-old Mel Ott appeared in his first major league game as a pinch hitter for Giant pitcher Jimmy Ring. The scared youngster struck out against Philadelphia pitcher Wayland Dean in a 9-8 Giant victory. Ott had joined the Giants in September, 1925, fresh from his native suburban New Orleans home and, in one of the game's great stories, McGraw decided to keep Ott with the Giants rather than "have him spoiled by one of those minor league managers."

May 2—Mel Ott got his first major league hit in his third pinch-hitting attempt. The stocky little "boy wonder" batted for Giant pitcher Tim McNamara and, facing Philly pitcher Dutch Ulrich, bounced a hot smash off the glove of third baseman Clarence "Gilly" Huber and beat the throw to first. The future Hall of Famer and Giant manager did not play regularly until well into the 1927 season.

May 11—The Giants sold sore-armed Art Nehf to the Cincinnati Reds. Unpleasantness developed between Nehf and John McGraw when the high-principled Nehf learned that McGraw had made the trade without informing Reds' manager Jack Hendricks of Nehf's arm problem. Nehf and McGraw did not speak to each other again until Nehf visited the Giants' spring training camp in 1932. He came with Hank Leiber, a husky young outfielder who had played for him when he coached baseball at the University of Arizona. Nehf, answering questions as to why he had brought the promising player to McGraw, said, "It's curious, the grip that McGraw gets on you. My other managers were fine men who treated me well but when I had a ballplayer that I knew could make the big leagues, I had to give him to McGraw although I hadn't spoken to Mac for six years."

August 2—Giant center fielder Ty Tyson had an unassisted double play as the Giants defeated the St. Louis Cardinals 4-2 at the Polo Grounds. In the top of the eighth with two Cardinals on base and one out, Tyson raced in from center field to spear second baseman

George "Specs" Topercer's low liner and ran to touch second base to double Card shortstop Tommy Thevenow for the final out. Two innings before, Tyson had been beaned by Cardinal right-hander Vic Keen, but Tyson remained in the game to pull off his unusual play.

August 8—The Giants obtained highly-touted outfielder De Witt "Bevo" Lebourveau from Toledo. Despite his imposing publicity (and marvelous name), Lebourveau never played a game for the Giants.

August 21—Giant captain Frank Frisch jumped the club in St. Louis after receiving a tongue-lashing from McGraw. The Giants had been going poorly and, as was McGraw's custom, he took out his frustration on the team captain. Frisch and McGraw met when the team returned to New York, and Frisch rejoined the Giants shortly after. However, it was clear that McGraw had not forgiven him and that Frisch would be gone as soon as McGraw could arrange it.

Sept. 16—With the Giants slipping into the second division (they finished in fifth place) they began to clean house. Heinie Groh was released and Irish Meusel was permitted to buy out his release so that he could make a deal for himself.

Dec. 20—Frank Frisch and Jimmy Ring were traded to the St. Louis Cardinals for manager-second baseman Rogers Hornsby. Frisch's departure had been expected after he left the Giants when they were in St. Louis in August, 1926. The Cardinals got the better of the deal; Frisch performed beautifully for them, first as a player and then as manager of the famed "Gas House Gang." Hornsby had a great season for the Giants in 1927 but his arrogance alienated the Giants and their front office and Giant owner Charles Stoneham personally arranged for Hornsby's departure.

1927

Jan. 8—Rogers Hornsby signed a $40,000 a year, two-year Giant contract. His contract made Hornsby the second highest paid player in the game behind Babe Ruth, who was being paid $55,000 a year. Hornsby was appointed team captain, replacing Frank Frisch.

Jan. 10—Right-handed spitballer (and future Hall of Famer) Burleigh Grimes was obtained from Brooklyn and outfielder George Harper came to the Giants from the Philadelphia Phillies in a complicated four-team deal that involved the Giants, the

Brooklyn Robins, the Phils, and Buffalo of the International League. The Giants gave up infielder Fresco Thompson and pitcher Jack Scott in the deal.

Jan. 27—Rogers Hornsby was sued for $70,075 by Frank Moore, a Kentucky betting commissioner. Moore filed suit for Hornsby's alleged unpaid betting debts on horses, a well-known Hornsby preoccupation. Hornsby ultimately won the case.

Feb. 1—National League President John Heydler ordered Rogers Hornsby to sell his St. Louis Cardinal stock before playing with the Giants. Cardinal owner Sam Breadon made an offer to Hornsby who responded, "I want $116 a share." Breadon shouted, "You only paid $45 a share." Hornsby, who had managed the Cardinals to a World Championship in 1926, shot back, "Hell, that was before I won the whole thing for you last year!" The upshot was that all National League club owners paid Hornsby equally for the stock and he was in the opening day lineup for the Giants.

Feb. 9—The Giants traded George Kelly to Cincinnati for outfielder Edd Roush. Roush had been traded by the Giants to the Reds in 1916 and he became one of the best hitters in the league. Roush had a good year for the Giants in 1927, a miserable 1928 season, but came back with an adequate year in 1929. The future Hall of Famer held out for the entire 1930 season and returned to Cincinnati in 1931 to complete his career.

March 9—The Giants announced that Ross Youngs, ill with a serious kidney ailment, would be out for the 1927 season.

May 17—The Giants completed a working agreement with the Newark Bears of the International League under which the Giants received an option to purchase Newark players in exchange for sending Giant players to the Bears for seasoning.

July 18—Eighteen-year-old Mel Ott, a future National League home run king, hit his first major league homer in a 6-4 loss to the Cubs at the Polo Grounds. Ott cracked a low liner to center field on which Chicago outfielder Hack Wilson made a futile shoestring catch attempt. The ball rolled all the way to the distant center field clubhouse as McGraw's stocky little "boy wonder" circled the bases.

July 19—The Giants lost to the Cubs 8-5, dampening a Polo Grounds celebration of John McGraw's twenty-fifth year as Giant manager.

August 29—Giant outfielder Clarence "Heinie" Mueller had a great day and the Giants beat the Cubs twice at the Polo Grounds, 8-7 and 4-1. In the first game, Mueller led the Giants in a seven-run third inning, opening with a pinch-hit home run and hitting a two-run single later in the same inning. In the second game, with the score tied in the eighth and the bases loaded, Mueller singled in two runs to put the game away for the Giants. This was his best day with the Polo Grounders. Mueller's other claim to Giant fame was that he was an uncle of Don Mueller, the Giants' right fielder during the 1948-1957 period.

Sept. 5—The Giants pulled to within one game of the league-leading Pirates after splitting a Labor Day doubleheader with the Boston Braves before a record Polo Grounds crowd of well over fifty-eight thousand. Brave right-hander Charlie Robertson outpitched Giant right-hander Virgil Barnes for a 6-1 Giant loss, ending a ten-game winning streak for the Polo Grounders. In the second game, Giant left-hander Dutch Henry relieved Fred Fitzsimmons and won a 9-8 come-from-behind victory on catcher Jack Cummings' double in the last of the ninth that scored Bill Terry. This was the high point of the Giant campaign as McGraw's club finished in third place, two games behind the pennant-winning Pirates.

Sept. 26—Giant right-hander Burleigh Grimes lost to the Phillies 9-2, his first loss after thirteen straight wins.

Oct. 22—Ross Youngs died of Brights' Disease in San Antonio. He was elected to the Hall of Fame in 1972.

1928

Jan. 10—"After due deliberation and in the best interests of the club," the Giants traded Rogers Hornsby to the Boston Braves for catcher Frank "Shanty" Hogan and outfielder Jim Welsh. Hornsby had been a success on the field for the Giants in 1927, hitting .361 (second to Paul Waner's league-leading .380) but he had feuded with Giant President Charles Stoneham and several of the Giants when he had managed in McGraw's absence. The deal was made at Stoneham's insistence.

Hogan was an indulgent eater with a resulting weight problem. He devised elaborate schemes with waitresses to disguise his eating excesses from McGraw, who routinely inspected Hogan's written meal checks. A written Hogan order for a salad, for example, meant that he was really ordering a serving of mashed potatoes, and so on. Until McGraw had the situation investigated closely he could not understand how such a sparse eater could continue to gain weight. Despite his twin weaknesses — a knife and a fork — the 240-pound Hogan had a .295 career batting average.

Feb. 11—The Giants traded Burleigh Grimes to Pittsburgh for another veteran pitcher, Vic Aldridge. The deal turned out poorly for the Giants; Grimes was 25 and 14 for the 1928 Pirates while Aldridge held out until May 3, then won only four games for the Giants in his final major league season.

April 11—Second baseman Andy Cohen, who replaced the traded Rogers Hornsby, starred as the Giants beat the Braves 5-2 in the season opener at the Polo Grounds. The twenty-four-year-old youngster scored two runs and drove in the tying and winning runs with a double, outshining (for a day) the Braves' Hornsby, who was held to a single. A natural favorite of the Giants' many Jewish fans, Cohen was carried off the field in triumph and, because Cohen hit well over the next several days, the *New York World* began printing a box in its daily sports page showing how Cohen was making the slower-starting Hornsby look bad. Predictably, the great Hornsby eventually left Cohen far behind.

The Giant opener was broadcast over the radio for the first time. New York City Stations WOR and WEAF, with the renowned Graham McNamee at the mike, carried the game.

May 2—Judge Francis X. McQuade, the Giants' third largest stockholder who purchased the club in 1919 with Charles Stoneham and John McGraw, was replaced as club treasurer "in the interests of harmony on the ball club." This led to a vicious legal action that dragged on for several years.

May 10—The Giants traded outfielder George Harper to the Cardinals for veteran catcher Bob O'Farrell. The move paved the way for nineteen-year-old Mel Ott's installation as the Giants' regular right fielder, a position he held for the next eighteen years.

May 14—John McGraw was knocked down and painfully injured by a Chicago motorist as McGraw crossed a street outside Wrigley Field after the Giants lost to the Cubs, dropping the Giants into fourth place. The preoccupied McGraw accepted blame for the accident, which laid him low for a few weeks.

May 26—The Giants lost to the Phillies 6-5 at the Polo Grounds despite Freddy Lindstrom's four extra-base hits—two homers, and two doubles.

May 27—Bill Terry hit for the cycle and batted in six runs as the Giants beat the Dodgers 12-5 at Ebbets Field.

June 25—Freddy Lindstrom tied the major league record with nine hits in a 12-4 and 8-2 doubleheader win over the Phillies at Philadelphia. In the first game, Freddy clubbed five singles in six trips. In the second game he went 4-for-5, including a double.

July 12—Twenty-five-year-old left-hander Carl Hubbell was purchased from Beaumont by the Giants for a large, unspecified price that was said to be the highest ever paid for a Texas League player. The future Hall of Famer had been sent to the minors by Detroit Tiger manager Ty Cobb, who felt that Hubbell's screwball pitch would ruin his arm. Dick Kinsella, a McGraw acquaintance and a delegate to the 1928 Democratic Party convention in Houston, saw Hubbell pitch and recommended his purchase to McGraw.

July 26—Carl Hubbell made his debut with the Giants and lost 7-5 to Pittsburgh at the Polo Grounds. After a scoreless first inning, Hubbell was knocked out of the box in the second inning on hits by Pie Traynor, George Grantham, Glenn Wright, Sparky Adams, Lloyd and Paul Waner, and a parting shot by Traynor.

July 31—Carl Hubbell won his first Giant victory in a come-from-behind 8-7 win over the Cubs at the Polo Grounds before 30,000 fans. Freddy Fitzsimmons was losing 7-3 after eight full innings and Hubbell held the Cubs scoreless in relief in the top of the ninth. The Giants came back with five runs in the bottom of the ninth with two men out and a runner on first base. Base hits by Mel Ott, Freddy Lindstrom, Bill Terry, Andy Reese, and Andy Cohen brought in three runs against Cub pitcher Sheriff Blake. Right-hander Guy Bush relieved Blake and Giant catcher Shanty Hogan greeted him with a double to deep right center to bring in Reese and Cohen with the tying and winning runs.

Sept. 11—The Giants beat the Boston Braves twice at the Polo Grounds, 11-6 and 7-6, with right-hander Jack Scott winning the first game and Carl Hubbell the second. Freddy Lindstrom went 8-for-10 on the day with three singles and a double in the first game and three singles and a homer in the nightcap. The sweep moved the Giants into second place, 2½ games behind St. Louis, the eventual pennant-winner.

Sept. 27—The Giants, only half a game behind the league-leading Cardinals, lost a controversial first game of a doubleheader to the Cubs 3-2. In the bottom of the sixth inning with the Cubs leading 3-2, the Giants had Andy Reese on third base and Les Mann on second. Shanty Hogan hit back to Cub pitcher Art Nehf in the box and Reese was hung up at third. Nehf threw to third and Reese darted for home, smashing into Cub catcher Gabby Hartnett on the baseline. Gabby, knocked back by the impact, threw his arms around Reese to keep from falling. While they remained tangled, Cub third baseman Clyde Beck tagged Reese and plate umpire Bill Klem called Reese out.

McGraw was nearly hysterical as the Giants swarmed around Klem, claiming that Hartnett had interfered with Reese and that the run should be allowed. But Klem would not change his call. McGraw protested the game but League President Heydler, who was at the game, disallowed the protest. The Giant loss, combined with another loss the following day, permitted the Cardinals to clinch the pennant. McGraw was said to hold a grudge against Heydler for the rest of his life because of Heydler's failure to side with the Giants.

Oct. 29—The Giants obtained outfielder Fred Leach from the Philadelphia Phillies for outfielder Frank "Lefty" O'Doul and $25,000. Although Leach had three respectable years with the Giants, the Phils came out well ahead; the colorful O'Doul had his greatest season in 1929, cracking out a phenomenal 254 hits and hitting .398. Lefty followed with a resplendent .383 season in 1930.

1929

May 8—Carl Hubbell pitched an 11-0, no-hitter against Pittsburgh at the Polo Grounds. Hubbell's only difficult inning came in the ninth when Pirate pinch hitter Harry Riconda lined directly to Giant left fielder Chuck Fullis, who dropped the ball for an error. Sparky Adams followed with a ground ball to shortstop Travis Jackson, who fumbled it for another error. Hubbell then struck out Lloyd Waner and started a game-ending double play on Paul Waner's smash back to the box. Hubbell's good friend and long-time collaborator, Mel Ott, supported the great left-hander with two home runs.

May 16—Mel Ott hit for the cycle as the Giants lost 5-4 in the second game of a doubleheader at Boston. Ott's seventh-inning home run landed halfway up the right-field bleacher section, the longest drive hit into that sector since Braves Field opened in 1915.

June 15—The Giants slugged out a 20-15 win over the Pirates in a fourteen-inning, 4 hour and 17 minute marathon in Pittsburgh. The teams had a total of fifty-two hits, twenty-eight by the Giants. Edd Roush had five hits and teammates Freddy Lindstrom, Travis Jackson, and Fred Leach had four apiece. Jackson's four blows included two homers, a triple, and a single.

June 18—Bill Terry had nine hits in a doubleheader loss to Brooklyn. Memphis Bill went 5-for-5, including a home run, as the Giants lost the first game, 8-7. In the 7-6 loss that followed, Terry whacked out four singles in four trips, tying Freddy Lindstrom's nine-hit performance of June 25, 1928.

June 19—Some heavy hitting by Mel Ott as the Giants took a doubleheader from the Phillies at Baker Bowl by scores of 15-14, in eleven innings, and 12-6. In the first game, Ott crashed two homers and two doubles and in the second game the little twenty-year-old slugger was "held" to two doubles. Edd Roush went 8-for-12 on the day.

June 20—Mel Ott batted in three runs as the Giants defeated the Phils, 11-6. This marked the eleventh straight game in which Master Melvin had batted in at least one run. (Ray Grimes holds the National League record with 17 consecutive games.) Ott batted in a total of twenty-seven runs during the streak.

August 9—The Giants batted out of order and got away with it in a 7-1 win over Cincinnati. McGraw had switched the usual batting order, spotting Mel Ott in the third slot ahead of Bill Terry and moving Terry to Ott's normal cleanup spot. In the Giants' half of the first, by force of habit, Terry batted before Ott and the Reds did not catch the error. In the third inning, the Giants got it straight and Ott marched to the plate first, to the confusion of the fans and to the chagrin of Reds' manager Jack Hendricks when he realized his earlier lack of alertness.

Sept. 24—Mel Ott hit his forty-first and forty-second home runs of the season, one in each game, as the Giants won a doubleheader from the Boston Braves, 5-4 and 6-5. The mighty little Giant's second homer tied the then-existing National League record set by Rogers Hornsby in 1922.

Oct. 5—Mel Ott and the Phillies' Chuck Klein began the day's meaningless (the Cubs had clinched the pennant) doubleheader in Philadelphia on the next-to-last day of the season tied with forty-two home runs apiece. Klein homered in his first at bat, breaking Rogers Hornsby's old National League record set in 1922. Ott obtained a single and a walk in the first game and singled in his first trip in the second game. Then, in a remarkable display of poor sportsmanship by Philly manager Burt Shotton and his club, Ott was walked intentionally in his remaining five trips to the plate in order to protect Klein's lead, the last time with the bases filled, forcing in a run. In the final game of the season the following day against the Braves in Boston, Ott was held to two singles and lost the home-run title to Klein, 43-42. With today's greater emphasis on records, it would be inconceivable that a contender for a record title would be so unfairly treated, particularly if the game were televised.

Oct. 16—The Giants sold Andy Cohen to Newark. This ended the noble effort begun in 1928 to replace the great Rogers Hornsby with the unproven Cohen.

Dec. 14—Officers of the Giants filed a $200,000 damage suit against New York City Magistrate Francis X. McQuade, a major stockholder who had been rejected as club treasurer on May 2, 1928, after serving in that post for nine years. The Giants' suit charged McQuade with seeking to "wreck and destroy" the National Exhibition Company (the Giants' corporate name). In response McQuade brought suit against President Charles Stoneham and Vice-President John McGraw, charging that he had been removed by a dummy board of directors at Stoneham's direction in violation of the 1919 contract entered into by Stoneham, McGraw, and McQuade when they had purchased controlling interest in the Giants.

After long and arduous litigation, New York Supreme Court Justice McCook ordered the Giants to pay McQuade back salary as club treasurer but refused to order his reinstatement as treasurer. As *New York Daily News* sportswriter Marshall Hunt put it, "The Judge gave McQuade a divorce and $30,000 alimony." The Giants protested the payment to McQuade and subsequently were upheld by the Court of Appeals, leaving McQuade completely out in the cold.

1930

April 6—The Giants played their first game under the lights, an exhibition game with their Bridgeport, Connecticut, farm team in Bridgeport that the Giants won, 9-1. It was not until ten years later, on May 24, 1940, that the Giants played their first league night game at the Polo Grounds.

May 8—Freddy Lindstrom hit for the cycle and added an additional single as the Giants defeated the Pirates 13-10 in Pittsburgh.

May 12—A hitters' wind was blowing out of Wrigley Field as the Giants won a 14-12 slugfest from the Cubs. Giant right-hander Larry Benton, the winning pitcher, and outfielders Freddy Leach and Mel Ott hit homers for the Giants. But the Cubs put on a flashier hitting display with four homers in the seventh inning. In the bottom of that inning, Cliff Heathcote opened with his second home run of the game. Kiki Cuyler grounded out, but Hack Wilson hammered a drive into the right-field bleachers and Charlie Grimm smoked one into the same sector. Les Bell flied out and Benton appeared out of the inning as Gabby Hartnett missed a two-strike pitch. But Giant catcher Shanty Hogan dropped the third strike and the slow-moving Hartnett rumbled into second when Hogan threw past first baseman Bill Terry. With that reprieve, Clyde Beck walloped a lofty shot into the center-field bleachers, making the score 14-9 and finishing off the shell-shocked Benton for the day. The four Cub homers in one inning tied the existing major league record and stood until June 6, 1939, when the Giants hit five home runs in the fourth inning against Cincinnati.

May 21—The Giants traded Larry Benton to Cincinnati for second baseman Hughie Critz. The little infielder from Greenwood, Mississippi, gave the Giants four solid seasons before retiring after the 1935 season.

July 3—The Giants announced plans to have regular Ladies' Days each Friday in an effort to draw more women to the Giants' games. Women were to be given free admission, an attendance enhancement plan that had succeeded in several National League cities.

July 21—On the first Ladies' Day game at the Polo Grounds (with women allowed in free), about 3,500 women attended the game. But they failed to inspire the Giants, who were steamrollered by two Hack Wilson home runs in a 6-0 loss to the Chicago Cubs.

August 23—Freddy Lindstrom hit safely in his twenty-fourth consecutive game, obtaining a single in three at bats as Cubs right-hander Pat Malone decisioned Carl Hubbell 4-2 in Chicago.

August 24—Freddy Lindstrom's twenty-four-game hitting streak ended as the Giants lost to the Cubs 3-2 in Chicago. The defeat stunned the Giants, who were struggling to get back in the race. With the game tied at two-all, the Cubs loaded the bases with two out in the bottom of the ninth. Giant reliever Joe Heving appeared to have the situation under control as he went ahead 0 and 2 to the next batter, Chicago right-hander Guy Bush. On the next pitch the runner at third base, Cub left fielder Danny Taylor, raced for the plate and slid in safely with the winning run as Heving, taken completely by surprise, went through a deliberate warmup and threw a pitch that was wide of the plate. For years after, the *New York World-Telegram*'s famed writer, Daniel M. Daniel, who covered the game, would sigh regretfully when talking about it and say, "All I can see is Heving holding that damn ball."

August 30—Carl Hubbell lost a tough one to Brooklyn, his career-long nemesis team. Hub went into the bottom of the ninth in a scoreless tie with the Robins' Dazzy Vance at Ebbets Field. Brooklyn right fielder Babe Herman opened the inning with a double and he was sacrificed to third. Giant manager John

McGraw ordered the next two batters walked intentionally but Hubbell, who had held Brooklyn to four hits, walked second baseman Jake Flowers and forced in the winning run. The Giants complained so bitterly over the fourth ball call by plate umpire Lou Jorda that Jorda had to be escorted off the field by policemen. Giant coach Dave Bancroft argued so vociferously that he was suspended for three games.

August 31—Mel Ott hit three successive home runs before more than forty thousand Polo Grounds fans as the Giants lost the second game of a doubleheader to the Braves, 11-10. Ott, who also had a double and six RBI, blasted his final home run completely over the right-field roof and out of the park.

Sept. 3—John McGraw signed a five-year contract to manage the Giants through the 1935 season. The signing was announced while the season was still under way because of persistent rumors that McGraw was on the verge of leaving the Giants for a managing job in the American League.

Sept. 27—Bill Terry tied Lefty O'Doul's National League record for hits in a season at 254 with a single off pitcher Phil Collins as the Giants defeated the Phils 5-3 at the Polo Grounds. Terry went hitless the following day as the Giants closed out the season with a 7-6 win over Philadelphia. Memphis Bill wound up the season at .401; he remains the last National Leaguer to hit over .400.

1931

March 26—The Giants sold Edd Roush back to Cincinnati. Roush, who was elected to the Hall of Fame in 1962, sat out the entire 1930 season, refusing to play for the $15,000 contract offered him.

April 15—Giant right-hander Hal Schumacher, in his major league debut, gave up seven hits and seven runs in 1 1/3 innings and was charged with the loss as the Giants lost to the Phillies, 10-7.

May 26—The Giants shut out the Boston Braves twice. Carl Hubbell pitched a 3-0 victory and left-hander Bill Walker hurled the 6-0 win that followed.

July 11—The Giants overwhelmed the Phillies 23-5 in the first game of a doubleheader at Baker Bowl. John McGraw's club pounded out twenty-eight hits, including two homers by Freddy Leach, one each by Bill Terry, Mel Ott, and reserve first baseman Sam Leslie, and seven doubles. Spitballer Clarence Mitchell was the beneficiary of the Giants' heavy hitting.

July 18—John McGraw was ejected following a violent argument after Giant outfielder Chuck Fullis was called out on a close play in a 4-0 Giant victory in St. Louis. McGraw exploded in a rage in public view before the next day's game when he received a telegram from League President John Heydler notifying him that he had been fined $150 and suspended for three days. When Heydler arrived at the game that day, McGraw angrily upbraided him and expressed his special objection at not having had a chance to present his case to Heydler, who arrived in St. Louis that morning. This was the first time the fiery McGraw had been suspended since 1921.

August 12—The Giants obtained highly-touted outfielder Len Koenecke from Indianapolis for outfielder Harry Rosenberg and pitchers Joe Heving and John Berly. Koenecke had a mediocre season for the Giants in 1932 and McGraw sent him to Brooklyn where he showed promise before tragically dying in 1935.

Sept. 5—The second-place Giants pulled to within 5½ games of the league-leading Cardinals after capturing a doubleheader from Brooklyn by scores of 5-1 and 10-1. Freddy Fitzsimmons, who won the first game, pitched only seven innings but during that time almost everything possible happened to the stout right-hander. He gave up only three hits and he whacked a home run. In the top of the seventh inning, Brooklyn's Fred Heimach slashed a sharp grounder to the box that struck Fat Freddy in the stomach, knocking him flat. Then, in the bottom of the seventh, Fitzsimmons was hit in the head by a pitch from Austin Moore. Again he went down in a heap although after a few minutes he managed to walk slowly off the field. Freddy collapsed again in the clubhouse, where it was found that he had a ruptured blood vessel in his head. Amazingly, the rotund knuckleballer missed only one turn on the mound.

Sept. 13—Giant first baseman Bill Terry had two doubles and two triples as Freddy Fitzsimmons beat the Reds 9-4 in Cincinnati.

Sept. 18—Mel Ott was beaned by St. Louis Cardinal right-hander Burleigh Grimes in the fifth inning of a 4-3 Giant loss in St. Louis. Ott suffered a brain concussion and, with the Cardinals having clinched the pennant, Master Melvin sat out the rest of the season.

Sept. 21—Hal Schumacher defeated the Cubs in Chicago 15-7 in his first Giant start. He allowed the Cubs ten hits as he easily won behind a game-long lead. A superb competitor, Prince Hal was a standout clutch pitcher in his thirteen seasons with the Giants.

Sept. 28—Bill Terry went 1-for-4 as the Giants closed out the season with a 12-3 loss to Brooklyn at Ebbets Field. Terry wound up with a .3486 average and lost the batting title to the St. Louis Cardinals' Chick Hafey, who hit .3489.

1932

Jan. 11 — Bill Terry sent his 1932 contract back to the Giants with a verbal blast, refusing to accept a $9,000 cut from his 1931 salary of $22,500 after narrowly missing the 1931 batting championship with a .3486 average, compared with winner Chick Hafey's .3489 average. Terry told the writers that he was "thoroughly disgusted" because the club had promised him that he "would be taken care of" despite the Depression that was gripping the country. Giant President Charles Stoneham angrily responded that Terry had been difficult to sign every year since he was a rookie and that his 1931 salary was within $1,500 of the combined salaries paid by the St. Louis Cardinals to Terry's main competitors for the 1931 batting title, Hafey and Jim Bottomley. After all the fuss, Terry signed for a compromise figure.

Jan. 15—Giant right-hander Joe Genewich, who held out for the 1931 season, was reinstated by Commissioner Landis. However, Genewich showed little in spring training and was released without appearing in a regular season game.

April 12—John McGraw received a congratulatory telegram from President Herbert Hoover as he began his thirtieth campaign as Giant manager. McGraw undoubtedly would have traded the telegram for a different result as the Giants lost their home opener to the Phillies, 13-5. (Hoover, like McGraw, was in for a difficult year.)

April 21—Bill Terry clubbed his sixth home run in four games as the Giants bombarded the helpless and hopeless Phillies in Philadelphia, 13-8.

June 3—Bill Terry succeeded John McGraw as Giant manager. Dave Bancroft resigned immediately as head coach in order to permit Terry to set up his coaching staff as he wished. The story broke as a complete surprise.

   The Giants' doubleheader with the Philadelphia Phils at the Polo Grounds had been rained out. The New York World-Telegram's Tom Meany headed aimlessly for the Giant clubhouse in search of a story or interview with no idea that he was falling into the biggest exclusive a New York sportswriter had obtained in many years. As Meany neared the Polo Grounds clubhouse steps, a hot dog vendor asked him, "Did you know that McGraw is out and Terry is the new manager?" Meany then ran into Giant coach Tom Clarke who confirmed the story, pointing to a note on the clubhouse bulletin board. Meany read the full statement, which described McGraw's lengthy consideration of resigning as manager because of his declining health.

An interesting note — Terry told sports broadcaster Red Barber years later that he (Terry) had not been on speaking terms with McGraw during the two years before his appointment.

June 4—Bill Terry's debut as Giant manager was a smashing success as the Giants took two games from the Phillies, 10-4 and 6-4, and moved out of last place. An ailing, white-haired John McGraw watched the proceedings from the Giant offices atop the Polo Grounds center-field clubhouse.

June 23 — The Giants signed veteran right-hander Waite Hoyt who had been released by Brooklyn. Hoyt, whom John McGraw had failed to keep as a teenager in 1919, had a mere 5 and 7 record with the Giants before being released after the 1932 season. Hoyt continued as a major league pitcher with the Pirates and Dodgers before becoming a successful broadcaster at Cincinnati. He was elected to the Hall of Fame in 1969.

August 13—Bill Terry, Mel Ott, and Freddy Lindstrom hit home runs on three consecutive pitches in the fourth inning of an 18-9 Giant loss to Brooklyn in the first game. Player-manager Terry had three homers in the game and Ott hit two. In the first inning of the second game, which the pitching-poor Giants lost 5-4, the Dodgers returned the favor as third baseman Joe Stripp, left fielder Lefty O'Doul, and second baseman Tony Cuccinello homered off Giant right-hander Waite Hoyt.

Sept. 12—Bill Terry signed a two-year contract as manager-first baseman that ran through the 1934 season.

Sept. 20 — Although eliminated from the pennant race, the Giants put on an impressive hitting performance as Freddy Fitzsimmons won a 13-3 "laugher" over the Braves at the Polo Grounds. Mel Ott led the attack with his thirty-seventh and thirty-eighth home runs, a double, a single, and six RBI. Bill·Terry chipped in with a monstrous inside-the-park home run that landed on the fly in the runway between the right and left center-field bleachers only a few feet in front of the Eddie Grant Memorial, which stood 483 feet from the plate.

Oct. 10—The Giants obtained catcher Gus Mancuso and right-hander Ray Starr from the Cardinals for pitchers Bill Walker and Jim Mooney, outfielder Ethan Allen, and catcher Bob O'Farrell. The acquisition of the steady Mancuso was one of the key Giant deals during the Bill Terry managerial years.

Dec. 12—In a three-club deal with the Pirates and the Phillies, the Giants traded Freddy Lindstrom to the Pirates and outfielder Chick Fullis to the Phils, obtaining pitcher Glenn Spencer and outfielder George "Kiddo" Davis. Lindstrom had not attempted to conceal his disappointment at not being named to replace John McGraw, and his departure had been expected.

Dec. 21—The Giants signed their former outfielder Billy Southworth as a coach. After leaving the Giants in 1926, Southworth had finished his playing career as player-manager of the St. Louis Cardinals for most of the 1929 season. Southworth developed into a successful manager for the Cardinals and Braves during the 1940-1951 period.

Dec. 29—The Giants sold veteran catcher Shanty Hogan to the Boston Braves.

1933

March 11—A major earthquake struck during an exhibition game between the Giants and the Cubs at Los Angeles. The terrified players huddled around second base as the ground trembled and the steel stands swayed. Fortunately, none of the players were injured.

April 1—Typical of the bland reporting style of the day, the *New York Times* reported that Giant coach Billy Southworth had suffered a knee injury that would force him out "indefinitely" and that manager Terry would ". . . engage a new coach in a day or two." There were rumors that Southworth's quick replacement was the result of a violent disagreement the day before in Galveston, Texas, with Terry, Southworth's old comrade-in-arms in the rollicking 1920s. Memphis Bill turned up with an unexplained black eye, which the *New York World-Telegram*'s Tom Meany subsequently attributed to Southworth. The story, which would have been headline news in today's more candid reporting style, stuck despite denials by both Southworth and Terry.

April 26—Giant right-hander LeRoy "Tarzan" Parmelee pitched a one hit, 3-1 win over the Phillies. Infielder Mike Finn got the only Philadelphia hit.

May 7—The Giants shut out the Cincinnati Reds twice. Carl Hubbell won the first game 1-0 and Hal Schumacher pitched the second victory, winning 5-0.

June 10—The Giants took over first place for good as Freddy Fitzsimmons defeated the Phillies, 5-2.

June 12—On a day off, the entire Giant squad accompanied Hal Schumacher to St. Lawrence University where he received his diploma. Relatively few professional baseball players were seen on college campuses, either as students or visitors, during this era.

June 15—The Giants traded first baseman Sam Leslie to Brooklyn for left-hander Watson Clark and former Giant outfielder Frank "Lefty" O'Doul.

June 20—The Giants sold outfielder Len Koenecke to the Dodgers. The talented Koenecke died in September, 1935, when he went berserk on an airplane flight; he was knocked out while being subdued in flight and never came to.

July 2—The Giants won an epic doubleheader from the Cardinals at the Polo Grounds. Carl Hubbell pitched an incredible eighteen scoreless innings to win the first game 1-0 after Tex Carleton had pitched sixteen brilliant scoreless innings for the Cards and had been relieved by Jesse Haines. Hubbell pitched perfect ball in twelve innings, allowing only six hits with no more than one coming in any inning. He struck out twelve batters and walked none. The Giants scored the game's only run in the bottom of the eighteenth when Joe Moore walked, went to second on Gus Mancuso's sacrifice, took third on Hubbell's groundout, and scored on Hughie Critz's single. The first scoreless seventeen innings came close to tying the then-existing major league record of twenty scoreless innings in a 1918 game between the Pittsburgh Pirates and the Boston Braves. (The 1918 record was broken in 1968 when the Houston Astros edged the New York Mets 1-0 in twenty-four innings.)

In the second game, Roy Parmelee, pitching in semidarkness (the Polo Grounds was not yet equipped with lights) and a steady drizzle, shut out the Cards and the Giants won 1-0 on a fourth-inning home run by third baseman Johnny Vergez. This game was completed in a snappy one hour and twenty-five minutes, hastened no doubt by the Cards' reluctance to stand up to the plate against Parmelee, who was nicknamed "Tarzan" because of his extreme wildness. In this game, however, he walked none and struck out thirteen.

July 8—The Giants brought up catcher Harry "The Horse" Danning from Buffalo. After understudying Gus Mancuso for several years, the popular Danning became the regular catcher in 1937. He starred through the 1942 season, after which he went into service.

Foot ailments, worsened by military service, prevented Danning from playing after World War II.

July 11—After a 2-1 loss to the St. Louis Cardinals' Dizzy Dean, the Giants' seventh loss in a row, the Polo Grounders received a telegram from their injured shortstop, Blondy Ryan. It read, "They cannot beat us. Am en route." That telegram remained posted on the bulletin board in the Giants' clubhouse and was to become the team watchword for the remainder of the season as the underdog Giants took the pennant and World Series. Ryan was a peppery, rangy Lynn, Massachusetts, native who had played briefly for the White Sox in 1930 and who had his best season in a mediocre career as the Giants' sparkplug shortstop.

July 20—John McGraw came out of retirement to manage the National League squad in the first All-Star Game at Comiskey Park in Chicago against Connie Mack's American Leaguers. The American League won 4-2 on Babe Ruth's third-inning home run. This was McGraw's last appearance in a major league dugout in an official capacity.

August 1—Carl Hubbell lost to the Boston Braves 3-1 at the Polo Grounds and, in the bargain, saw his National League record-breaking skein of consecutive scoreless innings end at 46 1/3 innings. (Actually, the great left-hander's streak ended at 45 consecutive innings in games that he had started. League President John Heydler ruled that an additional 1 1/3 outs that Hubbell recorded in relief of other Giant starters after his streak began also should be considered as part of his streak.) King Carl's streak, which broke the National League record held by the Chicago Cubs' Ed Ruelbach in 1908, was broken when Braves' right fielder Randy Moore singled in two runs in the sixth inning. The major league record at the time of fifty-six consecutive innings was held by Washington Senator pitching great, Walter Johnson.

August 27—Mel Ott, a notably gentle person, was thrown out of the second game of a doubleheader with the Cardinals at the Polo Grounds along with coach Tom Clarke. But there was an amusing story behind it. Umpire Ted McGrew called a play against the Giants and manager-first baseman Bill Terry went completely "bananas," firing his cap and glove to the ground and stamping on them as though they were an extension of McGrew. Eventually, McGrew lost patience and thumbed Terry out of the game with a classic thumb-jerking "heave ho" move. As the argument continued, McGrew caused even greater consternation by thumbing peacemakers Ott and Clarke off the field but permitting Terry to continue in the game. After the game, Ott reported the following dialogue to the inquiring press:

McGrew: "Terry, you're out of here, I've had enough."

Terry: "You can't throw me out, I'm the only first baseman we've got."

McGrew: (turning to Ott and Clarke who were trying to placate the raging Terry) "O.K., then you guys are out."

Sept. 1—Carl Hubbell exhibited amazing control in a ten inning, 2-0 Giant win over the Boston Braves in the first game of a doubleheader. He not only did not walk a batter but was never behind a hitter in the count, not even going to a 3 and 2 count in the game. Famed columnist Heywood Broun, watching the game from the press box, commented, "Such control in a left-hander is incredible. There must be a skeleton in Hubbell's closet somewhere, perhaps a *right-handed* maternal grandmother."

Sept. 19—The Giants clinched their first pennant under Bill Terry's leadership when the second-place Pirates lost to the Phillies.

Oct. 3—The Giants defeated the Washington Senators 4-2 in the first game of the World Series at the Polo Grounds. Carl Hubbell struck out ten Senators and did not allow an earned run, and Mel Ott went 4-for-4 including a first-inning home run.

Oct. 7—The Giants won the World Series against the Washington Senators 4 games to 1. The Giant heroes in the 4-3 victory were Mel Ott, who won the game with a tenth-inning home run, and veteran right-hander Dolf Luque, who relieved Giant starter Hal Schumacher.

Oct. 9—Bill Terry, fresh from winning the World Series from the Washington Senators in his first full year as Giant manager, signed a five year, $40,000 a year contract as player-manager.

1934

Jan. 15—John McGraw made his last public appearance at a birthday party at Leone's Restaurant in New York.

Feb. 6—At the National League meetings in New York, Bill Terry was asked by New York Times writer, Roscoe McGowen, "how do you figure Brooklyn to do this year?" Referring to the Dodgers' inability to make any off-season deals, Terry responded offhandedly, "Is Brooklyn still in the league? I haven't heard from them." This unintentional "snub" raised the ire of Brooklyn rooters who took their wrath out on Terry for the remainder of his managerial career but most significantly during the 1934 season when the sixth-place Dodgers knocked the Giants out of the race over the last weekend of the season.

Feb. 23—John McGraw died of uremia in New Rochelle, New York. His death cast a pall over the Giants who had just begun spring training at Miami Beach. Bill Terry was visibly shaken, commenting softly, "I owe everything I have to him. He made me a first baseman and then he put me in as manager. At times he appeared to be pretty harsh and severe and I had my differences with him. But all he wanted was to get the best out of us." Henry Fabian, the veteran Polo Grounds groundskeeper, wept. He had been a rookie with McGraw in 1891 in Cedar Rapids, Iowa. Coaches Pancho Snyder and Tom Clarke said that McGraw would be remembered particularly by the older players for his loyalty and unpublicized handouts to many of them after they had left the game. Hal Schumacher spoke of McGraw's support of his younger players despite his outbursts at their mistakes.

April 18—Some unintentional comedy at the Polo Grounds. In the second game of the season against the Phils, the Giants were leading 2-0 in the seventh inning with a Philadelphia runner on first. The next batter rifled a smash off the right-field wall. Mel Ott played the ball smartly and winged it to cutoff man Travis Jackson, holding the hit to a single and keeping the lead runner at third. But the action didn't stop there. The alert Jackson, seeing that the batter had strayed far off first base, threw quickly to Bill Terry. The throw hit the surprised Terry smack between the eyes, knocking him down, and the runner scrambling back to first base trampled all over Terry to complete the demolition job. The action continued with half the Giants rushing to the assistance of their fallen leader while the other half did what they could to keep the runners from advancing. Both groups were successful; the Giants came out of the inning with only one Phil run scoring and Terry survived to play the following day.

May 21—The Giants defeated the Cardinals in St. Louis 5-2, but lost one of their starting pitchers before the game in an unusual accident. Freddy Fitzsimmons was warming up to start the game when he was struck in the back by an errant fungo bat 10 minutes before the game. The injury forced him to miss several starts.

June 7—Giant third baseman Johnny Vergez had a home run and a double in a six-run eighth inning, and the Giants defeated the Boston Braves 14-5 at the Polo Grounds.

July 4—Carl Hubbell "eked out" a 15-0 win over the Boston Braves in the second game of the holiday doubleheader 14-5.

July 10—The National League lost to the American League 9-7 in the second All-Star Game that was played at the Polo Grounds. The big story of the game was Carl Hubbell's feat in striking out consecutively future Hall of Famers Babe Ruth, Lou Gehrig, Jimmy Foxx, Al Simmons, and Joe Cronin.

August 4—Ott tied the modern major league record by scoring six runs in a 21-4 Giant victory at Philadelphia in the second game of a doubleheader. The Giants scored eleven runs on eleven hits in the ninth inning.

Sept. 29—With two games left to play and the Giants and the Cardinals in a first-place tie, the Dodger fans got their revenge for Bill Terry's preseason query, "Is Brooklyn still in the league?" Dodger fireballer Van Lingle Mungo started against the Giant's LeRoy "Tarzan" Parmelee at the Polo Grounds. The Dodgers took a 2-0 lead after six innings, with Mungo driving in both runs. They increased their lead to 5-0 in the ninth and the Giants got their only run on George Watkins' home run. Meanwhile, out in St. Louis, Paul Dean beat the Cincinnati Reds easily and the Cards were one up with only one game to go.

Sept. 30—The Giants lost to the Dodgers 8-5 in the season finale at the Polo Grounds before forty-five thousand fans (a sizable portion of whom had stormed over from Brooklyn) and lost any chance for the pennant. Brooklyn right-hander Ray Benge, opening against Freddy Fitzsimmons, was routed in a four-run first as Terry, Gus Mancuso, and Blondy Ryan drove in the runs. But the fired-up Dodgers fought back to tie the game at five-all and the game moved into the tenth inning. In the top of the tenth, with darkness settling over the Polo Grounds, the Dodgers drove out Hal Schumacher, who had relieved Fitzsimmons, and scored three unearned runs off Carl Hubbell, who replaced Schumacher. The Giants went down meekly in the bottom of the tenth and the Dodgers won, 8-5. With Dizzy Dean shutting out the Reds for his thirtieth victory, the Cardinals won the pennant race by two games.

Oct. 31—The Giants obtained shortstop Dick Bartell from the Phillies for third baseman Johnny Vergez, pitcher John "Pretzels" Pezzulo, outfielder George Watkins, and cash. Bartell, an aggressive little fellow, was one of the key figures in Giant pennant wins in 1936 and 1937.

1935

April 16—The Giants opened in Boston before a freezing crowd that came out to see forty-one-year-old Babe Ruth play his first National League game. The Babe rewarded their fortitude by leading the Braves to a 4-2 win over Carl Hubbell, driving in the first run with a blistering single and blasting a 430-foot homer to drive in the other runs. To top it off, Ruth chipped in with the game's fielding gem when he raced in from deep left field to pick off a fly ball.

April 23—The Giants beat the Babe Ruth-led Braves in eleven innings before 47,000 Polo Grounds fans, at that time the largest crowd to watch a National League opener in New York. Mel Ott stole the big guy's thunder with the game-winning hit, giving the Giants a 6-5 victory. The Babe went hitless, forerunning the career-end disappointment that would bring him to leave the Braves before the season was half over.

April 28—Hal Schumacher pitched a one-hit game in defeating the Phillies 3-0 at the Polo Grounds. On a day when Schumacher faced only twenty-nine batters, Philadelphia's only safety was a scratch hit past the box by Phil pitcher Orville Jorgens in the third inning. Dick Bartell fielded Jorgens' bouncer near second base and his off-line throw to Bill Terry arrived at first base almost simultaneously with Jorgens' arrival. The throw eluded Terry and Jorgens took second base. At that time, close scorers' decisions were not flashed on the scoreboard and it was erroneously assumed by many onlookers that the play had been scored as a two-base error on Bartell. It was not until after the game that these fans learned that Schumacher had not pitched a no-hitter.

June 7—Roy Parmelee defeated the Braves' Ben Cantwell 3-2 in an exciting game at the Polo Grounds. With the Giants behind 2-1 in the ninth, Mel Ott homered to tie the game and Bill Terry won it in the bottom of the tenth with a run-scoring hit. Giant left fielder Joe Moore hit safely in his seventh straight game.

July 3—Giant shortstop Dick Bartell did not have a fielding chance as Carl Hubbell lost to the Phillies 4-3 in ten innings.

July 10—Hal Schumacher won his eleventh straight game, defeating the Pirates 10-3. Hank Leiber, who was having the best season of his career, led the Giant attack with three hits.

July 15—The Giants lost to Cincinnati 13-6, Hal Schumacher's first loss after eleven straight wins. This was the first time the Reds defeated Prince Hal since he joined the Giants in 1931.

July 25—Hal Schumacher, relieved by Allyn Stout, beat the Cardinals and Paul Dean 3-1 in the first game of a doubleheader as the Giants took a three-game, first-place lead. Schumacher gave the Giants a bad scare when he collapsed on the mound in the sixth inning in the broiling 95-degree heat. To the relief of the frightened Giant players, Doctor Hyland, the Cards' team physician, packed Schumacher in ice and "brought him back from the dead" as Giant shortstop Blondy Ryan dramatically described it.

July 28—The Giants took two shutout victories from the Dodgers. Carl Hubbell pitched the 6-0 first game win over Brooklyn's knuckleballing Emil "Dutch" Leonard, and New York right-hander Clydell Castleman beat the Dodgers' George Earnshaw 1-0, the only run scoring on Mel Ott's homer.

August 18—The Giants moved into a two-game, first-place lead over St. Louis as Carl Hubbell defeated Cincinnati 8-4 at the Polo Grounds. King Carl helped himself with a home run, but center fielder Hank Leiber wielded the big stick with a homer, triple, and two doubles.

August 24—Hank Leiber had two home runs in an eight-run second inning as the Giants beat the Cubs 9-4 at the Polo Grounds. Carl Hubbell relieved a very wild Roy Parmelee and pitched steady ball in winning his nineteenth game of the year.

August 30—The Giants purchased right-hander Harry Gumbert from Baltimore. The lanky curveball specialist contributed to the Giants' pennant wins in 1936 and 1937, had his best year with an 18 and 11 record in 1939, then moved to the Cardinals in 1941.

Sept. 15—Carl Hubbell outpitched Dizzy Dean for a 7-3 Giant win over the Cardinals before 41,284 fans who overflowed Sportsmans Park at St. Louis. The victory, the Giant's fourteenth in twenty-two games, pulled them to within 1 1/2 games of the league-leading Cardinals. This was the Giants' last gasp of the season; they lost four straight to the Cubs, who were then in the middle of a twenty-one-game winning streak that steamrolled them to the pennant. The Giants, who had led the league from the start of the season until August 25, finished third behind the Cards.

Oct. 10—The Giants, who had long resisted broadcasting their games on radio, filed suit to restrain bootleg broadcasts of all sporting events from the Polo Grounds. The suit was brought against several communications companies although the Giants admitted "the method of acquiring the simultaneous description of baseball games is unknown."

Nov. 23—The Giants purchased veteran right-hander Dick Coffman from the St. Louis Browns. Coffman, a well-traveled journeyman, gave the Giants four years of solid relief pitching.

Dec. 9—The Giants obtained infielder Burgess Whitehead from the Cardinals for pitchers Roy Parmelee and Allyn Stout, infielder Al Cuccinello, and first baseman Phil Weintraub. Whitehead proved to be a brilliant, acrobatic second baseman whose presence was indispensable to the Giants' pennant wins in 1936 and 1937.

1936

Jan. 6—Giant President Charles A. Stoneham died. He had been the only survivor of the triumvirate that purchased controlling interest in the Giants in 1919. The other two members were John McGraw and New York City Magistrate Francis X. McQuade.

Jan. 15—Horace C. Stoneham succeeded his father, Charles A. Stoneham, as the Giants' president. Horace, then only thirty-two, remained in that position for forty years until the Giants were sold to a group headed by Robert Lurie and Bud Herseth on March 2, 1976.

Feb. 15—Eddie Brannick, a Giants employee since the early McGraw days, succeeded Jim Tierney as the club's secretary. A popular figure around town, the affable Brannick was the subject of many columns by New York baseball writers with whom he was a particular favorite.

Feb. 20—The Giants acquired first baseman Sam Leslie from Brooklyn. A good hitter but a mediocre fielder, Leslie had been with the Giants from 1931 until being traded to Brooklyn in 1933. The round-faced native of Moss Point, Mississippi, alternated at first base with Bill Terry as the Giants won the pennant in 1936. He had a lifetime major league batting average of .304.

April 15—Giant right-hander Harry Gumbert defeated Van Lingle Mungo and the Dodgers 5-3 in a game featured by a violent brawl between Mungo and Dick Bartell. Rowdy Richard grounded out to first base for what appeared to be a routine, unassisted putout by Dodger first baseman Buddy Hassett. Mungo, coming over to cover the bag, sent Bartell sprawling with a hard jolt as he raced by. Bartell took a couple of somersaults, landed flat, and then bounced to his feet, screaming at Mungo. With that the two men charged at each other and began flailing away, with the much larger Mungo falling on top of the bantamweight Bartell. Umpire Beans Reardon raced over and, knee-deep in ballplayers, finally managed to pry the two men apart. They were immediately ejected and fined the next day by League President Ford Frick.

April 16—The Giants pulled out a come-from-behind 7-6 win over Brooklyn as the Dodgers kicked the game away. Winning 6-5 with two men out in the bottom of the ninth, Dodger pitcher Van Lingle Mungo walked Burgess Whitehead and gave up a single to Mel Ott. Hank Leiber popped a fly into short left, apparently an easy game-ending out. Ex-Giant Freddy Lindstrom trotted in easily to make the catch. Uncharacteristically, he crashed head-on into Dodger shortstop Jimmy Jordan as Jordan reached for the ball. The ball bounced out of Jordan's glove and both men tumbled to the ground, dazed. Whitehead and Ott, running with two out, scored the tying and winning runs. Later, Lindstrom said unbelievingly, "I've been in the league for twelve years and that never happened to me until I became a Dodger."

May 11—Mel Ott starred in a 13-12 slugfest in Philadelphia. The little Giant right fielder drove in eight runs with a single, a double, and a three-run homer with two men out in the ninth that pulled out the game.

July 15—After losing the first game of a doubleheader 5-4 at Pittsburgh when Carl Hubbell walked in the losing run in relief of Freddy Fitzsimmons, the Giants hit their low point of the season as they fell eleven games behind the league-leading Cubs. But the club rebounded to win the second game as Bill Terry, playing on a crippled knee against his doctor's advice, led the club to a 14-4 win with a single, double, and triple. With that boost, the Giants won thirty-nine of their next forty-seven games, moving into first place to stay.

July 17—King Carl Hubbell beat the Pirates 6-0, supported by four Giant triples in the first inning. The three-baggers were hit by Joe Moore, Mel Ott, Hank Leiber, and third baseman Eddie Mayo.

July 26—The Giants came from behind with three runs in the bottom of the ninth to defeat Cincinnati, 5-4. The game was featured by a triple play by the Giants that took the Reds out of a fourth-inning scoring threat. Cincinnati outfielder Kiki Cuyler was on second base with first baseman Les Scarsella on first when catcher Ernie Lombardi walloped a soaring 450-foot clout off Carl Hubbell that nearly reached the Polo Grounds' left-center-field bleacher wall on the fly. Hank Leiber raced back and made a brilliant catch for the first out. Cuyler, not thinking that Leiber had a chance for the catch, ran almost to third base before returning to second base to tag up while Scarsella, running with his head down, raced past Cuyler. Kiki set sail for third base again and was rubbed out on a close play as Leiber's throw was relayed to third baseman Eddie Mayo. Scarsella meanwhile recrossed second base on his way back to first base, saw the mountainous Lombardi in his way and wavered uncertainly near second base as Mayo threw to first baseman Sam Leslie for the third out.

July 27—The Giants purchased left-hander Cliff "Mountain Music" Melton from Baltimore. The 6-foot 5-inch, jug-eared Melton reported in 1937 and had a great 20 and 9 season to help the Giants win the pennant.

August 28—Bill Terry, coaching at first base, inserted himself as a pinch hitter in the fourteenth inning and cracked a bases-loaded single to break a 1-1 tie in Pittsburgh and precipitate a six-run outburst. The resulting 7-2 Giant win was the Giants' fifteenth in a row, their longest winning streak since 1916.

August 30—Mel Ott clubbed seven hits as the Giants took a doubleheader from the Cubs in Chicago. Carl Hubbell won his twentieth game in the first game, defeating right-hander Bill Lee, 6-1. Dick Coffman relieved Hal Schumacher in the second game and held on to decision Cub lefty Larry French.

Sept. 23—In his last game of the regular season, Carl Hubbell defeated the Phillies 5-4 for his sixteenth straight win of the season. Hub extended his winning streak to twenty-four during the 1937 season before losing to the Dodgers. This excludes the fourth game of the 1936 World Series with the Yankees, which Hubbell lost 5-2. The screwballer was brilliant during the 1936 campaign, leading the league in wins (twenty-six), winning percentage (.813), and earned run average (2.31).

Sept. 24—The Giants clinched their second pennant under Bill Terry's leadership with a 2-1, ten-inning win over the Boston (new name) Bees. Hal Schumacher was the hero, pitching a solid game and singling in the winning run in the tenth inning.

Oct. 6—The Yankees defeated the Giants in the World Series 4 games to 2 with a 13-5 win over the outclassed Polo Grounders.

Dec. 18—The Giants purchased the Albany, New York, (International League) club for $60,000 and transferred it to Jersey City for the 1937 season. Plans were made for the club to play in Roosevelt Stadium, a modern park that had just been completed courtesy of the political clout of Jersey City's famed political leader, Frank "Boss" Hague. Giant infield star Travis Jackson, who had just retired, was named to manage the club.

1937

Jan. 8—Bill Terry, his playing career over, signed his first Giant contract as a manager only for an estimated $27,500 a year.

Feb. 19—The Giants opened their spring training camp in Havana, Cuba. They remained in Cuba until March 13 when they took a boat to Miami, played a few exhibition games there, then moved to Gulfport, Mississippi, to complete the training season.

April 4—Hank Leiber was beaned by hard-throwing Cleveland right-hander Bob Feller in an exhibition game in New Orleans. The beaning ruined Leiber's 1937 season and probably his promising career. The big Arizonan suffered severe headaches for a long period, playing in only fifty-one games in 1937.

April 20—The Giants and Dodgers opened the season at Ebbets Field in a typically tense game as Hal Schumacher outpointed Dodger fireballer Van Lingle Munto, 4-3. Dick Bartell, particularly unpopular in Brooklyn since he spiked Dodger infielder Lonny Frey a few years before, took the first pitch thrown to him across the letters for a strike. As Bartell turned to protest the call to umpire Beans Reardon, the little shortstop was hit squarely in the chest with an overripe tomato that came flying out of the stands behind first base. Bartell took the splattering with commendable calmness and the game continued after an extended toweling-off period.

May 19—In one of the epic Giant-Cardinal battles of the era, Carl Hubbell outpitched Dizzy Dean for a 4-1 Giant win in St. Louis. Trouble started when umpire George Barr called a balk on Dean in the sixth inning, which led to three Giant runs and raised Dean's temper to the boiling point. The Great One took out his frustration on the Giants, knocking down batter after batter and precipitating an angry shouting match with the Giants that lasted through the next few innings.

The climax came in the top of the ninth when Dean sent Giant outfielder Jimmy Ripple sprawling to avoid a pitch headed for his chin. On the next pitch, Ripple bunted toward first base in a classic baseball maneuver to get the pitcher to come within reach of the batter on the first base line. But the ball bounded to Cardinal second baseman Jimmy Brown, who prepared to throw it to Johnny Mize at first base. Brown held the ball as Dean, who no longer had any business in the play, raced over to first base, determined to block the stocky Ripple's path to the bag. The two men crashed right on the base. Almost simultaneously, the Giants poured out to the mound where they were joined by the entire Cardinal team. Fists flew wildly, and for a time it was difficult to tell the fighters from the peacemakers. Off to one side near the backstop, Giant catcher Gus Mancuso fought it out in a private slugfest with fellow catcher Mickey Owen of the Cardinals.

Eventually, umpires Barr, Dolly Stark, and Bill Stewart, and a squad of policemen managed to separate the battlers.

Surprisingly, only Mancuso and Owen were ejected, presumably because they had started a private fight. The ruffled but otherwise uninjured Dean and Ripple were allowed to remain in the game, and Ripple was credited with a single as, in all the excitement, he had not been put out at first. Equally surprising, the only reported injury was a magnificent black eye administered to Cardinal third baseman Don Gutteridge by Giant coach Dolph Luque. Through it all the serene Hubbell, the only player to remain quietly on the sidelines, moved along imperturbably to win his sixth straight victory of the campaign and his twenty-second regular-season decision in a row.

May 27—Carl Hubbell won his twenty-fourth straight game (his last regular season loss had come on July 13, 1936) as Mel Ott's ninth-inning home run defeated the Reds, 3-2.

May 31—Carl Hubbell's winning streak ended at twenty-four games as the Dodgers defeated him 10-3 in the first game of the Memorial Day doubleheader. The second largest crowd in Polo Grounds history, 61,756, watched as King Carl was routed in the fourth inning after retiring only one batter. But it was not the great left-hander's last appearance of the day. Between games of the double header, he was presented with the 1936 National League's Most Valuable Player Award by Babe Ruth.

June 11—In a shocker of a trade, the Giants sent long-time favorite Freddy Fitzsimmons to the hated Brooklyn Dodgers for young right-hander Tom Baker. This was perhaps Bill Terry's worst deal; Baker won only two games for the Giants before they gave up on him in 1938 whereas Fitzsimmons, who dreaded the move at the time, found a new home at Ebbets Field and pitched effectively for the Dodgers for several years.

June 15—The Giants obtained outfielder Wally Berger from the Boston Bees for right-hander Frank "Gabby" Gabler and $25,000.

June 27—Aided by two home runs by Mel Ott, Carl Hubbell outpitched Dizzy Dean for an 8-1 Giant win at St. Louis. This was the last of the eleven head-to-head games between the two Hall of Fame pitchers, eight of which were won by Hubbell.

July 12—The Giants lost to the Phillies in Philadelphia 6-3 as the last-place Phils knocked Hal Schumacher out of the box with a six-run seventh inning. But the game was notable, nevertheless. Bill Terry was ejected from the field for the first time in his fifteen-year Giant career after an argument with veteran umpire Bill Klem. And the Giants pulled a triple play in the bottom of the first inning.

Second baseman Leo Norris and outfielders Herschel Martin

and Johnny Moore opened the Philadelphia first inning with consecutive singles to load the bases. Outfielder Morrie Arnovich followed with a low liner to short right field that appeared to be a sure hit. But Mel Ott raced in and snared the ball just off the grass, juggled it, and finally brought it under control before it hit the turf. Ott gunned the ball to catcher Gus Mancuso to nail Norris at the plate and Martin was out trying for third base, completing the play.

August 3—Hal Schumacher lost to the first-place Cubs 3-2 in ten innings. But, more noteworthy, Bill Terry shook up the lineup as the Giants fell seven games behind the Cubs. He benched weak-hitting third baseman Lou Chiozza and replaced him with Mel Ott. Jimmy Ripple left the bench to take over for Ott in right field. With Ott rebounding at the plate from his slump-ridden first half of the season and Ripple playing brilliantly, the Giants stormed back to take over first place on August 30. They fought off a determined challenge by the Cubs in a great September stretch drive and won the pennant.

Sept. 7—Bill Terry signed a five-year $40,000 per year contract as Giant general manager/field manager. The move to increase Terry's responsibilities was made in response to speculation that the Cleveland Indians had offered Terry an attractive contract.

Sept. 29—Giant rookie left-hander Cliff Melton won his twentieth game of the year, defeating the Phillies, 6-3. Melton, who did not enter the starting rotation until late June, had a 20 and 9 record, by far his best season in eight years with the Giants.

Sept. 30—The Giants clinched their second straight pennant and their third under the managership of Bill Terry as Carl Hubbell decisioned Philly right-hander Hugh "Losing Pitcher" Mulcahy, 2-1. This was a typical 1937 Giant win—Hubbell's airtight pitching, good defense, and a one-run victory.

Oct. 10—The outgunned Giants lost the five-game World Series to the Yanks, their second Series loss to the Yanks in two years. The Yanks' Lefty Gomez outpitched Cliff Melton to win 4-2 at the Polo Grounds.

1938

April 24—The Giants' Hal Schumacher pitched a masterful one-hit, 1-0 win over Van Lingle Mungo of the Dodgers. Brooklyn outfielder Goody Rosen opened the game with a single for the Dodgers' only hit. Mel Ott homered for the Giant run.

May 28—Carl Hubbell pitched a one-hit, 11-0 win over the Phillies, allowing only a walk and a single to outfielder George "Tuck" Stainback.

June 24—The Giants purchased outfielder Bob Seeds from Newark for $25,000. The veteran Seeds, who had been burning up the International League, reported to the Giants immediately and hit a creditable .291 in eighty-one games.

June 26—Carl Hubbell outpitched Cubs' left-hander Larry French as the Giants won 5-1 at the Polo Grounds. The game was featured by newly-acquired Giant outfielder Bob Seeds' 470-foot inside-the-park home run to the Eddie Grant Memorial in dead center.

July 10—Perhaps you thought Brooklyn Dodger rooters confined their team support to verbal expressions of admiration, disgust, pride, and annoyance. Well, you can add murder to the list. On this day, Dodger fan Robert Joyce killed Giant rooter Frank Krug after Krug teased Joyce about the Dodgers' futility in a game against the Giants.

July 15—Giant catcher Harry Danning was suspended for refusing to play after missing several games with a kidney ailment. Danning, then hitting .317, rejoined the club a week later but the disagreement with Bill Terry reflected his uneasy relationship with the Giant manager.

July 23—Hal Schumacher lost to the Cubs' Dizzy Dean 3-1 in Chicago in a game enlivened by a violent brawl between Dick Bartell and Cub shortstop Billy Jurges. It started when Jurges crashed hard into Bartell on a rundown play. The two veteran infielders rolled around the base path, kicking and punching, and it took a number of players to pry them apart. As the Giants returned to their dugout, Giant outfielder Jimmy Ripple commented, "Well, the season is official now—Bartell finally got into a scrap."

August 12—Harry Gumbert defeated the Phillies 1-0 in Philadelphia. This was the Giants' first game at Shibe Park in twenty-five years (renamed Connie Mack Stadium in 1953), the Phils having abandoned Baker Bowl a month before.

August 18—Carl Hubbell was forced out of a 5-3 loss to the Dodgers by sharp pains in his pitching elbow. A few days later, Hubbell underwent surgery for the removal of bone chips and he was out for the rest of the season. Hubbell told the writers that he had suffered from severe pains in his elbow, caused by the unnatural reverse twist required to throw his famous screwball, for several years before the loosened bone chips required surgery.

Before the game, Mel Ott received tangible evidence of his

popularity with the fans. Ott had alternated between right field and third base all season as Terry struggled to get some additional punch in the lineup. A cereal company announced the results of a contest to determine the most popular major league player at each position. Master Mel received the most votes of all third basemen and of all right fielders and was rewarded with a resplendent, robins-egg-blue sedan. Ott accepted the prize as a right fielder and asked the company to award his other prize to well-liked Chicago Cub third baseman Stan Hack.

Sept. 15—Ott was hit by pitches in three different times at bat by Pirate right-hander Jim Tobin as Tobin outpitched Cliff Melton in a 7-2 Giant loss.

Dec. 6—The Giants traded Dick Bartell, Hank Leiber, and Gus Mancuso to Chicago for their opposite numbers on the Cubs: shortstop Billy Jurges, outfielder Frank Demaree, and catcher Ken O'Dea. After the deal was announced, a writer asked Giant manager Bill Terry, "What do you think of the trade?" Never one to suffer fools or foolish questions gladly, Terry snapped, "What the hell do *you* think I think of it? I just made the trade!"

Dec. 11—The Giants obtained first baseman Henry "Zeke" Bonura from the Washington Senators for minor league first baseman Jim Carlin and $25,000. The powerful Bonura had been one of the American League's hardest hitters in four years with the Chicago White Sox and in 1938 with the Senators. His fielding, which would limit his tenure as a Giant to one year, was something else. One of the Washington writers, having observed Bonura's still life, wooden-Indian style at first base for a full season, commented, "I hope Mel Ott hasn't signed his contract yet. The extra chasing he'll be doing in right field in back of Zeke ought to be worth at least a few extra thousand dollars."

Dec. 16—The Giants, along with the Yankees, bowed to the inevitable and announced they had made arrangements to broadcast all home games except Sunday dates over Station WABC. Mel Allen and Arch McDonald were named to announce the games. The agreement to broadcast was forced by an earlier decision of the Dodgers' Larry MacPhail to broadcast all of the Dodgers' home and away games in 1939. The Giants and Yankees claimed that MacPhail had broken a long-standing agreement not to broadcast games, although broadcasting was already an established practice in many big league cities.

1939

May 2—Mel Ott's three-run homer with two out in the bottom of the ninth inning off Cincinnati right-hander Gene Thompson pulled out an 8-7 Giant win.

May 14—Carl Hubbell made his first pitching appearance for the Giants since an elbow operation in August 1938. The great left-hander made it a successful one, defeating the Phils 2-1 on a tenth-inning pinch-hit home run by catcher Ken O'Dea.

Before the game, the Giants picked up ex-Yankee Tony Lazzeri from the Chicago Cubs. But Lazzeri was too far over the hill and he was released a few weeks later after a poor fielding performance.

June 6—The Giants hit seven homers in a 17-3 massacre of the Cincinnati Reds at the Polo Grounds. The Polo Grounders set a record (since tied by the Phillies in 1949 and by the San Francisco Giants in 1961) with five home runs in one inning. In that inning, Harry Danning and Frank Demaree homered and, with two out, Burgess Whitehead, pitcher Manuel Salvo, and Joe Moore hit consecutive home runs. The other two homers were hit by Moore and Mel Ott.

July 2—The Giants and Dodgers split an exciting doubleheader at the Polo Grounds before 51,000. Leo Durocher's Dodgers won the opener 3-2 by routing Giant starter Bill Lohrman and weathering a Giant threat on Mel Ott's two-run homer off right-hander Luke Hamlin. In the second game, Leo Durocher ended the fourth inning by banging into a double play. As Lippy Leo crossed the bag and ran down the baseline there was an astonishing sight. Bonura, after taking the inning-ending throw at first, wheeled and chased Durocher. On the way, Zeke fired the ball at Leo's head, barely missing, and then threw his glove at Durocher. Bonura closed in on the Dodger manager and delivered a series of uppercuts while Leo returned fire with an assortment of body blows. Both men were ejected and the Giants went on to win as Harry Danning broke an eighth-inning tie with a homer.

Later, in the Giant clubhouse, Bonura claimed that Durocher had spiked him on purpose. Durocher's only comment was, "If that big clown hadn't got his foot in my way, I wouldn't have been close to him." Actually, Leo felt that Giant starter Hal Schumacher had been throwing at the Dodgers and, with Schumacher out of the game by the time Durocher hit into the double play, Bonura became the fall guy for Leo's retaliation.

July 9—Zeke Bonura grounded into a record-breaking fifth double play in two consecutive games as the Giants defeated the Dodgers 3-2 at Ebbets Field.

July 15—The Giants lost 8-4 to the Reds at the Polo Grounds, beginning a disastrous nine-game losing streak that ended any chance for the Giants to compete for the pennant. The game caused the eventual construction of nets along foul poles in major league parks to help umpires determine whether balls hit into the stands near the foul poles were fair or foul.

The Giants' Harry Gumbert held a 4-3 lead as the Reds came to bat in the top of the eighth. With a runner on, the Reds' Harry Craft lined a low, curving drive into the lower left-field stands at the foul pole. Plate umpire Lee Ballanfant ruled it a fair ball, pulling the Reds into a 5-4 lead. Harry Danning stormed around Ballanfant, shoving the official, and was ejected from the game.

The Giants then took their case to Ziggy Sears, the second base umpire. After a long harangue, easygoing Joe Moore, who presumably had the best view of the ball when it passed the foul pole, was thrown out of the game. But the Giants still had plenty of fire power left and they continued their verbal assault until big George Magerkurth, the first base umpire, trotted up to home plate to try to terminate the argument. As he moved toward the center of the debate, he began to talk animatedly with Giant shortstop Billy Jurges. Suddenly, according to Magerkurth's account, Jurges shouted at him, "Don't you spit in my face." Magerkurth, his big face reddening, bellowed back, "Don't get your face so near mine and it won't get spit on." Jurges roared, "I'll spit on yours." The Major responded, "I'd like to see you do that." Billy obliged. With that, Magerkurth belted Jurges in the ribs, and Billy responded with a punch to the umpire's cheek.

The fisticuffs brought the protest to an abrupt end as Ballanfant ordered Jurges off the field. The Giants, suddenly realizing the seriousness of the situation, had to put in a patchwork lineup after the game continued. Lou Chiozza moved from third base to shortstop. Mel Ott came in to play third. First baseman Johnny McCarthy went to right field and Hal Schumacher took over center field. The crippled Giants lost the game. They also lost the valuable services of Jurges who, along with Magerkurth, was suspended for ten days.

Within a few days, nets were installed along the lengths of the Polo Grounds' foul poles and within a few years most major league parks were so equipped.

August 13—The Giants hit seven homers in a game for the second time during the season as Bill Lohrman defeated the

Phillies 11-2 in the first game of a doubleheader at the Polo Grounds. Frank Demaree had two home runs and Zeke Bonura, second baseman Alex Kampouris, Lohrman, Joe Moore, and Bob Seeds had one apiece. Kampouris, Lohrman, and Moore hit their homers consecutively in the fourth inning.

August 16—Giant second baseman Burgess Whitehead was suspended indefinitely. He turned up the next day at Yankee Stadium in full uniform and asked Yankee manager Joe McCarthy for permission to work out with the Yanks. McCarthy, of course, turned him down. Whitehead rejoined the Giants a few days later, but he left the team in mid-September and was suspended by the Giants for the remainder of the year.

Sept. 11—The Giants bought left-hander Tom Gorman from their Clinton, Iowa, farm club. Gorman, a native New Yorker, appeared in four games without a decision during the 1939 season. He subsequently injured his arm and did not return to the majors until several years later when he began a fine career as a National League umpire.

Nov. 14—The Giants announced plans to equip the Polo Grounds for night games at a projected construction cost of $150,000.

Dec. 27—The Giants obtained promising infielder Mickey Witek from the Newark Bears for $40,000 plus infielder Alex Kampouris and catcher Tommy Padden. Witek had been the International League's MVP for the 1939 season.

1940

March 19—The Giants signed right-hander Paul Dean (Dizzy's little brother), who had been released by the Cardinals. Dean, who had done little with the Cards since winning nineteen games in 1935, had a 4-and-4 record with the Giants in 1940 before his release in 1941.

April 26—The Giants traded Zeke Bonura back to the Washington Senators for left-hander Rene Monteagudo plus $10,000. Monteagudo did not pan out and the Giants released their option on him without using him in a regular season game.

May 24—Harry Gumbert pitched and won the first night game at the Polo Grounds, defeating Casey Stengel's Boston Bees, 8-1. He was aided by homers by Joe Moore, Billy Jurges, and Harry Danning.

May 30—The Giants took a Memorial Day doubleheader at Ebbets Field from the Dodgers and knocked Leo Durocher's club out of first place. Carl Hubbell won the first game 7-0, allowing only one hit (to infielder Johnny Hudson) and facing only twenty-seven men as Hudson was erased in a double play. No other Dodger reached base. Bill Lohrman won the second game 12-5 in twelve innings.

June 7—Mel Ott, having a sub-par year and moved from the fourth-place hitting spot down to sixth, wore glasses for the first time in a game. (There were still relatively few big league hitters who used them on the field at the time.) Ott's experiment with glasses ended a few weeks later and he played through the 1945 season as a Giant regular without wearing glasses.

June 15—Harry Danning hit for the cycle as the Giants belabored Pittsburgh 12-1 at the Polo Grounds. Danning's home run was a tremendous inside-the-park clout that landed 460 feet on the fly in front of the Giant clubhouse and lodged behind the Eddie Grant Memorial 483 feet from the plate. The slow-footed Danning scored easily as Pirate center fielder Vince DiMaggio was slow in extricating the ball from behind the memorial tablet.

June 23—Giant shortstop Billy Jurges was beaned by the Reds' Bucky Walters. Although Jurges did not suffer a skull fracture, he was out of the lineup for a long period and he suffered from severe headaches for some time later.

August 7—The Giants lost to the Dodgers 8-4 as Mel Ott Night Night was celebrated at the Polo Grounds before almost 54,000. Cash gifts from fans supplied Ott with a sterling silver set of 208 pieces and a sterling silver tea service; the *New York Times'* John Drebinger presented the Giant captain with the first life membership card of the New York Baseball Writers Association to be given to a ballplayer. Fighting back tears, Ott thanked the fans "not only for these gifts but for the loyalty you have shown me in all these years."

Sept. 19—Bill Lohrman lost an 8-2 game to the Cubs' Claude Passeau. This was the Giants' eleventh straight loss, their longest drought during the Bill Terry managerial years from 1932 through 1941.

Sept. 29—Giant center fielder Johnny Rucker, not known for his power hitting, batted in seven runs in two consecutive innings in a 14-0 Giant win over the Boston Bees at the Polo Grounds. The RBI came on Rucker's grand-slam homer off Boston right-hander Al Piechota in the second inning and his three-run home run off right-hander Nick Strincevich in the third inning. This two-inning splurge accounted for almost one-third of Rucker's total of 23 RBI for the entire 1940 season.

Nov. 13—The Giants signed Cub catching great Gabby Hartnett, who had been released as Chicago manager. Hartnett hit .300 as a player-coach for the Giants in 1941, then became a minor league manager, including a stint as manager of the Giants' Jersey City club in 1943.

1941

March 5—Veteran Giant catcher Harry Danning ended his holdout and signed a $16,500 contract. Bill Terry surprised the Giant writers and fans with the announcement that the heavy-footed catcher would be the club's new left fielder. The "noble experiment," as some of the more cynical writers referred to it, ended in failure and within a few weeks Danning was back behind the plate to stay.

May 10—Bill Lohrman's no-hitter against the Braves for 8 1/3 innings was broken when outfielder Johnny Cooney singled cleanly to center field. Lohrman held on to win the game, 4-2.

May 14—In an unpopular deal, the Giants obtained right-hander "Fiddler Bill" McGee from the Cardinals for Harry Gumbert plus cash. McGee came to the Giants far overweight, which showed in the disappointing 2-and-9 record he compiled with the Giants for the remainder of the season. McGee had an overall Giant record of 8-and-12 when he left the major leagues for good after the 1942 season. By comparison, Gumbert won eleven and lost five for the Cardinals in 1941, and he remained in the majors until 1950.

May 15—The Giants reacquired shortstop Dick Bartell from the Detroit Tigers. Bartell had left the Giants for the Cubs after the 1938 season; he subsequently moved to the Tigers and sparked them to the 1940 American League pennant.

May 27—The serious nature of the war in Europe was driven home to the fans during a night game with the Braves at the Polo Grounds. President Franklin D. Roosevelt delivered one of his famous "fireside chats," proclaiming an "unlimited emergency" and the U.S.'s intention of resisting further German attempts to stop or destroy Allied vessels. With Hal Schumacher facing the Braves' Manuel Salvo and the game tied at one-all, umpire Jocko Conlan called "Time!" For 45 minutes the crowd and the players sat in engrossed silence and listened to the President's solemn voice booming out of the loudspeakers atop the center-field clubhouse.

June 1—Hal Schumacher decisioned Reds' right-hander Monte Pearson 3-2 in the first game of a doubleheader at the Polo Grounds. Mel Ott drove in the winning runs with a two-run homer, accounting for the 400th home run and 1,500 RBI of his career.

June 6—The Giants used plastic batting helmets for the first time in the regular season as they took on the Pirates in a doubleheader at the Polo Grounds. The helmets may have given the Giant hitters added security but it did not add to their clutch-hitting capabilities—they lost twice, 5-4 and 4-3.

June 18—The Giants played to an eleven-inning tie at Pittsburgh in a game held up temporarily in the fourth inning while the fans listened to the famous title fight between Joe Louis and local favorite Billy Conn. The game had to be called because of local regulations requiring that no inning could be started after 11:50 P.M. After the game, an angry Bill Terry snapped, "I can see holding up a game so we can hear a presidential speech but, hell, not for a prize fight. They might as well hold up the game to listen to a Jack Benny or Bob Hope radio show."

August 30—The Giants, floundering in fifth place and twenty-two games behind Brooklyn, knocked the Dodgers out of first place with a doubleheader win over Leo Durocher's club at the Polo Grounds. Giant right-hander Bob Bowman defeated the Dodgers' Kirby Higbe 4-3 on Mel Ott's home run in the first game and Fiddler Bill McGee decisioned Hugh Casey 5-1 in the second game.

Sept. 1—The Giants purchased left-hander Dave Koslo from Milwaukee. Koslo, a steady if unspectacular worker, won 91 and lost 104 with the Giants.

Sept. 9—The Giants bought left-hander Tom Sunkel from Syracuse of the International League. The ex-Cardinal is remembered best, not for his mediocre 4-and-8 career record with the Giants, but because he pitched in the majors with sight in only one eye.

Sept. 20—Outfielder Babe Barna homered in his first at bat as Giant right-hander Rube Fischer defeated the Boston Braves, 7-3. Barna had played earlier for the Philadelphia Athletics. Outfielder Sid Gordon made his Giant debut in the game. The solidly built Brooklyn native singled in his first at bat, then was unceremoniously picked off first.

Dec. 2—The Giants named Mel Ott to replace Bill Terry as Giant manager. Terry was given a two-year contract as general manager in charge of the club's farm and scouting operations at a $30,000 per year salary. Ott was given a two-year player-manager pact paying $25,000 a year. There had been speculation for some time that Terry wanted to leave his playing field position, but there had been no indication that Ott would succeed him. Ott had been visiting at the major league meetings in Jacksonville and his appointment came as a complete surprise to him. Giant players, fans, and writers greeted his promotion with enthusiasm.

Dec. 3—The Giants reacquired outfielder Hank Leiber from the Chicago Cubs for right-hander Bob Bowman and $25,000. Leiber hit a mere .218 for the Giants in 1942, his last year in the major leagues.

Dec. 11—The Giants obtained first baseman Johnny Mize from the St. Louis Cardinals for right-hander Bill Lohrman, first baseman Johnny McCarthy, catcher Ken O'Dea, and $50,000. A great player with the Cardinals, Mize hit powerfully for the Giants from 1942 through most of the 1949 season (with time out for service in World War II). Traded to the Yankees in 1949 as part of Giant manager Leo Durocher's drive for "my kind of player." Mize was a deluxe pinch hitter and reserve first baseman with the Yanks through the 1953 season, after which he retired. Mize was voted into the Hall of Fame in 1981.

1942

Feb. 1—Newly appointed Giant manager Mel Ott was presented with the Bill Slocum Award by the New York chapter of the Baseball Writers of America for "distinguished service to baseball over a period of years."

April 14—Mel Ott's debut as Giant manager was unsuccessful. His old friend Carl Hubbell lost the opener at the Polo Grounds to the Dodgers, 7-5.

April 17—Mel Ott, captain-shortstop Billy Jurges, and Hal Schumacher were ejected by umpire Ziggy Sears from the game during a 4-3 loss to the Braves at Boston. Schumacher was suspended for five days and fined $50 for pushing the umpire after Sears' delayed call on a play on the bases. The next day, Giant President Horace Stoneham sat in a box seat behind the Giant dugout to see for himself whether his players received any more "pushing around."

May 8—The Giants lost to the Dodgers 7-6 at Ebbets Field. All proceeds went to the Navy Relief Society. The game, which raised almost $60,000 for servicemen, was the first twilight major league game played in twenty-four years. Everybody at the game, including the players, paid to get into the ballpark.

May 12—Cliff Melton defeated Pittsburgh left-hander Ken Heintzelman 7-3 in a game highlighted by a Giant triple play. In the seventh inning, Pirate pitcher Johnny Lanning was the runner at second and shortstop Pete Coscarart was on first. Frank Gustine lined to Giant second baseman Connie Ryan, who was playing in his first major league game. Ryan threw quickly to Billy Jurges, who stepped on second to erase Lanning, then tagged out Coscarart coming down from first base. Ryan could have made the triple play unassisted, an unusual feat, had he not been so excited in his first game. The inexperienced Ryan was optioned to Jersey City within three weeks after playing only eleven games for the Giants.

May 14—Giant pinch hitter Babe Young had a double and a triple in the ten-run eighth inning of a 12-6 Giant win over Cincinnati at the Polo Grounds.

May 23—The Giants reacquired thirty-seven-year-old catcher Gus Mancuso from the Cardinals for the $7,500 waiver price. With this purchase, the Giants now had back on their roster all three players traded to the Cubs on December 6, 1938—Mancuso, Hank Leiber, and Dick Bartell.

June 4—Mel Ott set a National League career with his 1,583d RBI in a 4-3 Giant win over the Cubs in Chicago.

July 26—It was a tempestuous scene at the Polo Grounds as the Giants, in third place half a game ahead of Cincinnati, took on the Reds in a doubleheader. Mel Ott, who was on a home-run hitting tear, came to the plate in the bottom of the Giant first and the near-capacity crowd buzzed with anticipation. Plate umpire Jocko Conlon called two questionable strikes on the Giant manager. The 0-and-2 pitch was a curve from Reds right-hander Elmer Riddle that appeared to shave Ott's chin. Conlon surprised everyone with a booming "Stee-rike—you're out!" Ott immediately turned on Conlon, shouting his disapproval and emphasizing his complaints by pounding his bat on the plate in an unusual display of temper. Conlon ejected Master Mel from the game.

After a few more minutes of impassioned protest, Ott slammed his bat down and began the long walk to the clubhouse in deep center field, banished from the second game as well as the first under the rules then in effect. As the stocky little manager walked past second base, the fans barraged the home-plate area with fruits and vegetables. A tomato intended for Conlon struck Babe Young, the next hitter, squarely in the back. As Ott stomped up the steps to the clubhouse and slammed the door, a shower of beer bottles descended, the fans belatedly realizing that he was out of the second game as well. After that violent episode, the loss of two important games was almost an anticlimax for the disappointed throng.

August 3—The Giants lost to the Dodgers in the Army Emergency Relief Fund twilight game before 57,305, the largest crowd in Polo Grounds history. Losing 7-4 in the bottom of the ninth, the Giants had Bill Werber and Mel Ott on base with none out, but the game was abruptly called because it was 9:10 P.M. and a government order mandated that the lights be turned out. The furious Giant fans did not quiet down until the opening bars of "The Star-Spangled Banner" were played while a solitary spotlight was shined on an American flag on top of the center-field clubhouse.

After the game, Giant President Horace Stoneham said that the twilight games would have to be terminated because "playing against the clock was too tough." As if to emphasize Stoneham's point, the following night's game with the Dodgers ended in a 1-1 tie as Pee Wee Reese's grand-slam homer in the top of the ninth was wiped out by the time deadline. This was the last regular season twilight game played at the Polo Grounds.

August 9—An amusing story came out of Bill Lohrman's 3-2 win over Philadelphia's Johnny Podgajny. The Giants won in the tenth inning when Mel Ott deftly squeezed in Lohrman, who was the baserunner at third base. A few days later at Toots Shor's restaurant, comedian Jay C. Flippen, Shor, and several habitues were sitting around when Ott walked in for dinner. Flippen greeted Ott with: "Congratulations on that beautiful squeeze play, Mel." Ott grinned sheepishly and drawled, "Thanks, Jay, but I'm not bragging about it. Remember when Dolph Luque came in from the third base coaching box? It was one out with the bases loaded. Dolph suggested that it would be a good spot for a squeeze play but I told him no, that I would hit away. So I tap my bat on the plate like I always do and get ready for Podgajny's pitch. But, just as he delivers the ball, to my complete surprise here comes Lohrman in from third. I made a last-minute stab at the ball and luckily it was a good bunt and he scored. I had forgotten that by tapping the plate I had given the squeeze bunt sign. And yet everybody's been congratulating me since on the play."

August 18—Thirty-nine-year-old Carl Hubbell defeated the Boston Braves 10-2 for his eighth straight win. Mel Ott led the Giant attack with his twenty-first home run of the year (one of the few he hit into the left field stands at the Polo Grounds), a double, and a single.

August 30—Mel Ott collected his twenty-five hundredth career hit in a 5-5 tie game with the Cubs in Chicago.

Sept. 25—Hank Leiber pitched a complete-game 9-1 loss to the Phillies at the Polo Grounds. The big outfielder yielded nine hits, five walks, and had five strikeouts in his only pitching appearance in the major leagues. Leiber was used as a pitcher because the Giants already had clinched third place but had been eliminated from the first- and second-place slots.

Sept. 26—The Giants were forced to forfeit the second game of a doubleheader against the Boston Braves at the Polo Grounds with the Giants leading 5-2 in the eighth inning. Youngsters admitted to the Polo Grounds free for contributing scrap metal to the war effort swarmed onto the field, making it impossible to complete the game.

Nov. 30—Bill Terry, who supervised the Giant farm system in 1942 after being replaced by Mel Ott as field manager, resigned to go into private business. Terry cited the reduced number of Giant farm clubs (from nine at the start of 1942 to only the Jersey City and Ft. Smith, Arkansas, clubs) as the chief reason for his resignation.

1943

March 14—With all major league teams' spring training sites restricted by World War II government regulations, the Giants opened their 1943 training season at Lakewood, New Jersey, the little town in which the Giants had trained during the Spanish-American War. The Giants and their Jersey City farm club shared an old, pine-tree covered estate owned formerly by John D. Rockefeller.

When the Giants gathered together on their cold, snow-fringed practice field, several of their more prominent players were either in the service or scheduled for induction. Other players expected to hear from their draft boards at any time.

April 22—Bill Lohrman lost the season opener 5-2 to the Dodgers' right-hander Ed Head at Ebbets Field. The big story of the game was the seriously flawed new baseball being used in the major leagues. Mel Ott, despite having gone 4-for-4 in a losing effort, reported that the new ball had the resiliency of an overripe grapefruit and the unpredictable airborne characteristics of a flying saucer. A few days later the manufacturer, A.G. Spalding Company, admitted that the balls had a rubber cement of inferior quality. Instead of providing resiliency, the cement had hardened between the wool layers and had deadened the ball. The problem was solved when all teams agreed to use the remaining balls left over from the 1942 season until a new stock of higher quality baseballs were available.

April 28—The Giants obtained veteran catcher Ernie "Schnozz" Lombardi from the Boston Braves for catcher Hugh Poland and infielder Connie Ryan. The following day, Giant right-hander Van Lingle Mungo lost to the Braves on Ryan's ninth inning homer. Lombardi, in unhappy contrast, ended the game by striking out as a pinch hitter with the tying run on base.

June 5—Carl Hubbell broke a string of seven straight Giant losses by pitching his final masterpiece, a brilliant one-hitter against Pittsburgh. Pirate first baseman Elbie Fletcher's home run accounted for the only Pittsburgh hit and run, and the Giants won, 5-1. This was Hubbell's 250th career win.

June 17—Mel Ott received five walks as Giant right-hander Harry Feldman decisioned the Dodgers' Kirby Higbe, 8-5.

June 18—Mel Ott walked in his first two trips to the plate as the Giants lost the first game of a doubleheader to Boston, 8-6. This gave Ott seven walks in his last seven at bats over two games.

July 6—The Giants obtained outfielder Joe Medwick from the Dodgers for $50,000. Medwick, although only a shadow of the powerhouse he had been in his heyday with the Cardinals, had several good games and managed to hit a respectable .281 with the Giants. Medwick was elected to the Hall of Fame in 1968.

July 31—The Giants obtained (or thought they had obtained) first baseman Dolph Camilli and fiery right-hander Johnny Allen from the Dodgers for right-handers Bill Lohrman and Bill Sayles, and first baseman Joe Orengo. The deal turned sour when Camilli unexpectedly announced that he was quitting the game, feeling that he had not helped the Dodgers and could not help the Giants. The disappointed Giants wound up with Allen and $7,500 (the waiver price) since the Dodgers had made the deal in good faith.

August 7—On their way to a last-place finish, the Giants tied an old record for futility. They left eighteen men on base in a nine-inning 9-6 loss to the Phillies.

August 18—Carl Hubbell won his 253d and final Giant game, a 3-2 decision over the Pirates.

Sept. 8—Giant shortstop John "Buddy" Kerr made his major league debut and homered in his first at bat as the Giants lost to the Phils at the Polo Grounds.

Sept. 9—With the Giants mired irretrievably in last place, beleaguered manager Mel Ott got a vote of confidence from the Giants in the form of a three-year contract to manage the club through the 1946 season.

Nov. 30—Carl Hubbell announced his retirement as a player and the Giants announced his appointment as farm system director, succeeding Bill Terry. At the time, the Giant farm system consisted of the Jersey City club, the Class D Bristol team of the Appalachian League, and a small scouting system.

1944

Jan. 8—Ex-Giant manager Bill Terry, who had been essentially inactive during the 1943 season, announced he was quitting baseball for good to become a partner in a business firm.

April 30—The Giants crushed the Dodgers by an incredible 26-8 score before more than 58,000 at the Polo Grounds. First baseman Phil Weintraub batted in eleven runs with a homer, triple, and two doubles. Ernie Lombardi batted in seven runs. Mel Ott equaled his own records by walking five straight times and scoring six runs. And the Giants received seventeen walks, six of them in a row, from the dismal Dodger pitching staff.

May 21—The Giants split a doubleheader with the Cardinals in St. Louis, losing 10-3 then winning 7-5. Mel Ott, recovering from an injury, returned to the lineup prematurely in an attempt to instill some life into his listless club. Giant right-hander Rube Fischer was soundly thumped in the first game as Ott played right field and contributed a triple and a single. In the second game Ott shook up his lineup. Shortstop Buddy Kerr was benched and replaced by Billy Jurges, who had been playing third base. Ott replaced Jurges at third and the little manager, in his nineteenth major league campaign, proceeded to beat the Cardinals almost single-handedly with a long home run and two ringing doubles.

May 23—With the World War II situation improving and Nazi submarines no longer prowling the North Atlantic, wartime restrictions on night baseball in New York were lifted and the Giants played their first night game in New York since 1941. Giant right-hander Bill Voiselle was well on the way to a 2-1 win over the Dodgers at Ebbets Field in the last of the ninth. With two out and two on, ex-Pirate Lloyd Waner lifted an easy fly to right center for what appeared to be the last out. Just as the ball landed in center fielder Johnny Rucker's glove, Charley Mead, inserted in right field for defensive purposes, bumped into Rucker and jarred the ball loose. Both Dodger runners scored and Brooklyn won, 3-2. Ott rushed out to the mound to console the stunned Voiselle as he walked tearfully to the Giant dugout. The incident reminded older fans of the Giant-Dodger game of April 16, 1936, that Van Mungo lost in identical fashion when Dodgers Freddy Lindstrom and Jimmy Jordan collided.

June 12—The Giants purchased 6'9" left-hander Johnny Gee from Pittsburgh. Gee's chief virtue, based upon his lackluster major league record at the time (five wins, eight losses), was that he didn't qualify for the military draft because of his height. Gee compiled a 2 and 4 record with the Giants before being released after the 1946 season.

June 21—Mel Ott passed Honus Wagner's National League record for runs scored with his career 1,741st as Bill Voiselle beat the Dodgers, 11-2.

August 15—With the Giants in the midst of a horrendous losing streak, Mel Ott was particularly disturbed at his team's play in a 6-3 loss at Cincinnati. The Giants were leading 3-2 going into the bottom of the seventh. With Redlegs on first and second, Buddy Kerr was slow in returning to his shortstop position after a pickoff attempt at second, and the next hitter drove a bouncer through the vacated area to send in the tying run. With two runners on later in the inning, the Reds' Frank McCormick blooped a fly ball to left that umpire Dusty Boggess ruled Joe Medwick had trapped. While the winning runs came around, Medwick foolishly held the ball aloft and raced in to protest to Boggess. Ott fined both Kerr and Medwick $100 for "inexcusable mental errors." Kerr took the fine without complaint but Medwick, who had a weaker case, objected loudly to the disciplinary action. Joe later admitted that he had pulled a boner and deserved the penalty.

August 20—The Giants lost the first game of a doubleheader to the Cardinals in St. Louis 7-4 for their thirteenth straight loss, the longest Giant losing streak since 1902. Bill Voiselle won the second game 3-1 to end the streak.

Sept. 1—The Giants lost to the Dodgers 8-1 at Ebbets Field as baseball rules were relaxed to give the wartime spectators a better run for their money. The Giants' Joe Medwick was hit on the elbow by a pitched ball. He sank to the ground, apparently out of the game. In deference to the Giants' shortage of outfielders, the low standings of both clubs in the race, and the desire to display all remaining resources of authentic major league talent, managers Ott and Durocher conferred as to what could be done to get Medwick back in the game after he had received treatment. Finally,

Durocher agreed that Medwick could reenter the game later so long as Leo could select a pinch runner for him. Durocher picked the lead-footed Gus Mancuso only because the even slower Ernie Lombardi was in the game. Big Lom, the next hitter, obliged Leo by thumping resoundingly into a double play.

1945

May 20—A Polo Grounds crowd of 51,340 watched as the Giants split a doubleheader with Pittsburgh. In the opener, Bill Voiselle won his eighth straight game, 5-1. Off to a good start, the Giants finished the day leading the league by 3 1/2 games.

May 24—Giant relief right-hander Ace Adams beat the Reds 7-6 on colorful Danny Gardella's pinch home run. Gardella also enlivened the Giants' stay in Cincinnati with a spectacular off-the-field antic. First baseman Nap Reyes was Gardella's roommate. Nap went up to his hotel room late in the morning to pick up Gardella and head for the ballpark. As Reyes entered his room he noticed the window was wide open and there was a note on the bed from Gardella. "Dauntless Dan" had written that he was committing suicide because "life is too much for me." A horrified Reyes leaped to the open window. As he approached it, he nearly jumped out of his skin when Gardella's grinning countenance rose up over the window sill. Gardella had been hanging onto the window by his arms, several stories above the street, "just for a laugh." Reyes was still shaking when he arrived at Crosley Field for the game.

May 30—Mel Ott passed Honus Wagner's National League career record of 4,888 total bases as the Giants defeated the Cubs 8-6 in the first game of a holiday doubleheader in Chicago.

June 1—Mel Ott fined Bill Voiselle $500 for an errant pitch to Cardinal outfielder Johnny Hopp. Voiselle went into the bottom of the Cardinal ninth with a 3-1 lead, one out, and a runner on base. Then, with a no-ball and two-strike count, Hopp tripled to run the score to 3-2 as Ott looked on angrily from his right-field post. Hopp held at third as the next hitter bounced out. Suddenly, a tremendous rainstorm came up and held up play for an hour. When play resumed, a cooled-off Vioselle gave up a single to Ray Sanders to tie the game and a triple to Whitey Kurowski to lose it.

After the game, Ott surprised the writers with the announcement that Voiselle had been fined for "disobeying pitching instructions" (for not wasting the 0 and 2 pitch). Voiselle's only reaction was to comment lamely that the pitch had gotten away from him. The general feeling among the players and writers was that the fine was unduly severe, although Ott had repeatedly warned his pitchers to avoid such a mistake. But much of the criticism of Ott also was directed at his failure to replace Voiselle after the long rain delay, particularly since Voiselle had pitched almost an entire game. Ott later rescinded the fine, but the sensitive Voiselle never seemed to get over the incident.

June 14—The Giants traded outfielder Joe Medwick and left-hander Ewald Pyle to the Boston Braves for catcher Clyde Kluttz.

June 19—The Giants lost to the Braves 9-2 at the Polo Grounds. But the big story was that Allied Commander Dwight D. Eisenhower, just back from Europe after the Allied forces' victory on the Continent, attended the game. Ike was given a tremendous roar of approval by the large crowd as his automobile circled the field before the game.

July 5—The Giants' Whitey Lockman homered in his first major league at bat in a 7-5 loss to the Cardinals at the Polo Grounds.

August 1—Mel Ott hit his five-hundredth career home run in a 9-2 Giant win over the Boston Braves at the Polo Grounds. Hit off Braves right-hander Johnny Hutchings, it was a typical Ott home run, a sharply-pulled smash into the upper-right-field stands. Later that night there was a big party at Toots Shor's restaurant to celebrate Ott's milestone. (At the time, the only players with more career home runs were Babe Ruth with 714 and Jimmy Foxx with 527.)

Sept. 23—National League President Ford Frick presented Mel Ott with a lifetime pass to league games in honor of Ott's twentieth year with the Giants. Still, it was an unhappy day for the Giant manager—his charges lost a doubleheader to the Braves, 4-1 and 7-3.

Sept. 26—The Giants passed the one million home-attendance mark for the first time. The event was not an artistic success, though; the Dodgers' Ralph Branca decisioned Giant right-hander Jack Brewer, 8-1.

Sept. 27—Mel Ott signed a five-year contract at a "substantial boost" to continue managing the Giants through the 1950 season.

Dec. 11—The Giants obtained pitcher-outfielder Clint "Hondo" Hartung from the Minneapolis Millers for $20,000 and three players to be named later. The purported feats of the "Pheenom," as he was referred to, were unreal. After a continuing string of stories of the deeds of this latter-day Paul Bunyan, *New York World-Telegram* writer Tom Meany commented caustically, "Hartung's a sucker if he reports to the Giants. All he has to do is sit at home, wait until he's eligible, and he's a cinch to make the Hall of Fame."

1946

Jan 5—The Giants bought catcher Walker Cooper from the Cardinals for $175,000, by far the largest sum the Giants had paid for a player. Big Coop, still in the navy when the deal was made, was widely considered the best catcher in the game before going into service early in the 1945 season.

The Giants also signed Carl Hubbell to a new five-year contract as farm-system director. When Hubbell took over in 1944, the Giants had only a few clubs and scouts. Now, with the war over, the Giants owned franchises in Jersey City, Trenton, and Fort Smith, and soon would purchase the Triple A Minneapolis Millers. The club also had working agreements with eight minor league teams and had a dozen scouts.

Feb. 19—Giant outfielder Danny Gardella became the first major league player to announce that he was jumping to the new, "outlaw" Mexican League operated by Mexican customs broker, Jorge Pasquel. Gardella's futile attempt to return to the major leagues a few years later triggered his major court suit against organized baseball and its reserve clause contract provision.

April 9—Wild, young Giant right-hander Mike Budnick beaned Mel Ott in batting practice before a Giant-Indian exhibition game in Danville, Virginia, forcing the Giant skipper to remain in a local hospital overnight for observation. Ott rejoined his club the next day.

April 12—The Giants purchased the Minneapolis Millers of the American Association for an unannounced price.

April 16—The Giants defeated the Phillies 8-4 in the season opener at the Polo Grounds. Mel Ott hit his 511th, and last, career home run in the first inning off Philadelphia left-hander Oscar Judd, a looping fly that barely reached the right-field seats. The following day, Ott dove futilely for a fly ball, injured his knee, and played only sporadically and ineffectively for the rest of the season.

April 26—The Giants bought outfielder Goody Rosen and first baseman Jack Graham from Brooklyn for $25,000. Two days later, Rosen was the Giants' hitting star as the Giants won a doubleheader from the Dodgers. Because the Dodgers wound up the 1946 regular season schedule tied with the Cardinals and then lost the ensuing playoff, fans and writers speculated that the Dodgers may well have lost the pennant by trading Rosen two days too soon.

Giant right-handers Ace Adams and Harry Feldman unexpectedly jumped to the newly formed Mexican League, joining ex-Giants Danny Gardella, infielder George Hausmann, first basemen Nap Reyes and Roy Zimmerman, and pitcher Adrian Zabala, who had joined it in preceding weeks.

May 1—This was a busy day on the trading block for Giant catcher Clyde Kluttz, who was the property of three clubs within four hours. Kluttz, and the Giants, were in St. Louis; Mel Ott called Kluttz during breakfast and told him that he had been traded to the Phillies for outfielder Vince DiMaggio. Ott added, "You'd better stay near the phone, Clyde, because the Phils' people will be calling you very soon." Philadelphia General Manager Herb Pennock called Kluttz two hours later to tell him to report to the Phils in Cincinnati the next day. At lunch two hours later, Cardinal manager Eddie Dyer called Kluttz and told him he had been traded to St. Louis by the Phils. Kluttz returned to his cooled-off lunch, reasonably confident that he would not be traded again—before dinner.

June 8—The Giants gave up on veteran outfielder Vince DiMaggio, obtained from the Phillies a month before, and sold him to the San Francisco Seals.

June 9—Mel Ott's frustration with his inept Giants surfaced as he was thrown out of each game of a doubleheader loss in Pittsburgh. In the first game, a 2-1 loss, umpire Tom Dunn ejected Ott for complaining about a call on the bases. In the 5-1 loss in the second game, umpire George Magerkurth bounced Ott for protesting too vigorously on a tipped-bat call against catcher Ernie Lombardi. Giant fans, hearing the game on radio or reading about it the next day, could hardly believe it. Their mild-mannered idol Mel Ott had set a major league record unmatched even by *his* idol John McGraw—Ott was the first manager to be thrown out of two games on the same day!

July 5—Dodger manager Leo Durocher made his contribution to the American idiom before a game at the Polo Grounds. The day before, the last-place Giants had hit five home runs during the holiday doubleheader with the Dodgers. Broadcaster Red Barber sat on the Dodger bench before the game, kidding Durocher. "Leo," Barber said, "your guys were lucky to split yesterday the way the Giants were hitting, especially those home runs." Durocher scoffed, "Hell, they were nothing, just cheap Polo Grounds specials." Barber continued to needle, "Come on, Leo, be a nice guy and give credit where it's due." Durocher snapped back, "Nice guys! Do you know a nicer guy than Mel Ott? Or any of the other Giants? And where are they? The nice guys over there are in last place!" That was the way Frank Graham of the *New York Sun* reported the dialogue in his column, and that was the origin of the familiar tough-guy phrase, "Nice guys finish last."

August 11—The Giants purchased right-hander Larry Jansen from the San Francisco Seals.

August 31—Young Giant left-hander Montia Kennedy outpitched Kirby Higbe and won 2-1 on Buddy Kerr's home run. (Kerr atoned for hitting into three double plays in the game.) The game was enlivened by a rousing fistfight between the Giants' Goody Rosen and the Dodgers' Eddie Stanky after Rosen slid into second base with spikes high. Stanky took the throw, tagged Rosen squarely in the face, and the two little gamecocks went at it with a vengeance. After several vicious, if ineffectual, blows were exchanged, both combatants were ejected. In the earlier McGraw-Terry-MacPhail days, this would have called for a special squad of police at the park for the next day's doubleheader. But these were different times, and Stanky and the Dodgers got their revenge peaceably enough by easily beating Bill Voiselle and Ken Trinkle before 53,000 at the Polo Grounds, en route to a regular season first-place tie with the Cardinals.

Sept. 2—For the first time in the memory of Giant fans, a pinch hitter batted in place of Mel Ott. Manager Ott called on right-hand hitting Sid Gordon to replace him as the Boston Braves brought in left-hander Ernie White in relief in the seventh inning of an 8-3 Giant win in Boston. (Gordon bounced out to third base.)

Sept. 9—Bobby Thomson played in his first game for the Giants as they lost to the Phillies 5-4 in Philadelphia. Thomson, who would gain baseball-immortal status with his "miracle" homer to win the 1951 pennant playoff for the Giants, had a single and a double in four trips.

Sept. 26—Buddy Kerr broke Eddie Miller's National League record for consecutive chances by a shortstop without error when Kerr handled his 252d chance flawlessly in an 8-0 Giant loss to the Braves.

Sept. 29—Buddy Kerr played in his 52d consecutive errorless game at shortstop as the Giants defeated the Phils 3-1, breaking Leo Durocher's old National League record of fifty-one games set with the 1931 Cincinnati Reds.

1947

Jan. 21—Giant pitching great Carl Hubbell was elected to the Hall of Fame.

April 8—Youthful Giant outfielder Whitey Lockman, who appeared headed for a great season, broke his right leg sliding into second base in an exhibition with the Cleveland Indians at Sheffield, Alabama. Lockman missed virtually all of the 1947 season.

April 24—Johnny Mize hit three consecutive home runs in a 14-5 loss to the Braves in Boston. This was the fifth time Mize hit three home runs in a game, the first four coming in his earlier years with the Cardinals. The big Georgian accomplished the feat for a sixth time with the Yankees in 1950.

May 9—After flopping as an outfielder, Clint "Hondo" Hartung pitched six shutout innings as a reliever against the Braves. Thereafter, Hartung started twenty games for the 1947 Giants and compiled a pitching record of 9 and 7. Despite this promising start, Hartung never developed into a reliable starter; he wound up his Giant career in 1952 without ever realizing his great promise.

May 25—Giant shortstop Buddy Kerr committed his first error after sixty-eight consecutive games, during which he handled 383 chances flawlessly (still the National League record). Kerr's error came on a hard ground ball drilled directly at him by the Braves' Bob Elliott in a 9-3 Giant victory.

June 4—The Giants defeated the Cincinnati Reds 9-3 at the Polo Grounds in a game highlighted by consecutive sixth inning homers by Whitey Lockman, Sid Gordon, and Willard Marshall.

June 7—The Giants obtained veteran right-hander Joe Beggs from Cincinnati for Babe Young. Babe had two decent years with the Giants in 1940 and 1941, but the Giants' trade for Johnny Mize knocked him out of the regular first baseman job and he never found a regular spot with the Giants after that.

June 9—Walker Cooper hit a two-run homer in the eighth inning to cap an eight-run splurge, then hit a three-run homer in the ninth to propel the Giants to a 13-10 win over the Pirates at the Polo Grounds. Pinch hitter Sid Gordon had a single and a double in the Giants' big eighth inning.

June 11—Mel Ott made his last appearance as a player when he batted for pitcher Ken Trinkle and popped to short in an 8-7 Giant loss at Pittsburgh.

June 13—The Giants obtained veteran right-hander Mort Cooper from the Boston Braves for Bill Voiselle plus cash. Voiselle had never been the same since being fined $500 by manager Mel Ott in June 1945 for an errant 0 and 2 pitch that led to a Giant loss to the

Cardinals. Ott was blamed by many for Voiselle's failure to win after the incident. However, in fairness to Ott, Voiselle did not regain his earlier form after leaving the Giants.

June 28—Walker Cooper homered in his sixth straight game to help his brother Mort win a 14-6 slugfest against the Phillies. Cooper's seventh homer of the streak enabled him to tie George Kelly's feat with the 1924 Giants. Willie Mays tied the record in 1955 and the Washington Senators' Frank Howard broke it in 1968 with ten home runs in six consecutive games.

July 5—The Giants set a still-standing record with a total of thirty-seven homers in sixteen straight games. Big Johnny Mize hit two home runs as Clint Hartung shut out the Phils 4-0 to account for the thirty-sixth and thirty-seventh homers in the Giant streak.

July 18—Willard Marshall hit three consecutive homers as Larry Jansen decisioned the Cincinnati Reds at the Polo Grounds.

July 31—Walker Cooper hit the Giants' fifty-fifth home run in the month of July in an 8-7 loss to the Reds at Cincinnati. This monthly home run total remains the National League record, since tied by the American League's Minnesota Twins in May 1964.

August 24—The Giants broke the Chicago Cubs' National League record for homers in a season with their 172d in a 4-0 whitewash of the Cubs by Larry Jansen.

August 31—The Giants broke the 1936 Yankees' record of 182 home runs as infielder Jack "Lucky" Lohrke homered in a 10-4 Giant loss to the Dodgers. The Giants wound up the season with 221 homers, a National League record since tied by the Cincinnati Reds in 1956.

Sept. 21—The Giants ended their 1947 home season as rookie Larry Jansen won his twentieth game of the season, defeating the Phillies' veteran righthander Schoolboy Rowe, 6-4. Mel Ott's club ran off a record-breaking string of eighteen consecutive games with at least one home run (a record since broken) and the Giants' home attendance rose to 1,599,784, almost 380,000 more than the 1946 record.

Sept. 25—Larry Jansen defeated Boston Brave right-hander Red Barrett 2-1 for Jansen's tenth straight win, all of them complete games.

Oct. 2—Ex-Giant outfielder Danny Gardella, under a five-year suspension from major league play for jumping to the Mexican League in February 1946, filed suit for $300,000 in damages. He charged that the major league players' agreement, particularly the reserve clause, was "monopolistic and tended to restrain trade and commerce" in violation of federal antitrust laws. The suit was filed against Baseball Commissioner Happy Chandler, National League President Ford Frick, American League President Will Harridge, the National Association of Baseball Leagues, and the Giants.

1948

April 10—The Giants, hard pressed for pitching help, signed well-traveled right-hander Louis "Buck" Newsom, who had been released by the Yankees. Newsom was too far over the hill to help the Giants and he was released by the Polo Grounders after compiling an 0-and-4 record in eleven appearances.

May 21—In his first trip to the plate in the major leagues, Giant outfielder Les Layton hit a pinch-hit home run in the ninth inning of an 8-3 loss to the Cubs at the Polo Grounds.

June 20—Johnny Mize, Willard Marshall, and Sid Gordon hit consecutive home runs in the eighth inning of a 6-4 Giant win over the Cardinals.

July 16—In a move that surprised the baseball world and infuriated many Giant fans, Dodger manager Leo Durocher replaced Mel Ott as Giant skipper. Ott became an assistant to Farm System Director Carl Hubbell.

Bill Corum dropped the bombshell in an exclusive story in the *New York Journal-American.* He reported that Ott had been fired, Durocher had been named to replace him, and Burt Shotton had been called out of semi-retirement to take over the Dodgers. Beginning with a Giant slump in June, there had been a resurgence of old rumors that Ott was on the way out, but they were not taken seriously. With the Dodgers also floundering, there had been rumors of Durocher's dismissal but, here too, very little credence given to the stories. Even then, if either manager had been let out in unrelated moves, this would have been accepted as part of the game. But Durocher the new boss at the Polo Grounds! To most Giant fans this was unthinkable. As Ken Smith wrote in the *Daily Mirror,* "Giant fans hated Durocher because he was a Dodger. To drop him suddenly in the Polo Grounds, where the feats of McGraw, Terry, Ott, Matty, and the others are a sacred memory, was a shock too abrupt for acceptance." Interestingly, Stoneham told the writers the next day that Ott had suggested to Stoneham that he try to obtain Durocher if it were possible.

How Corum got the exclusive story was a story in itself. Dodger General Manager Branch Rickey and Stoneham had agreed to release the story simultaneously on July 16 from New

York and from Pittsburgh, where the Giants were scheduled to play. Rickey was enraged when Corum's scoop appeared in advance of the agreed-upon announcement time. Although both the Giants and the Dodgers had taken precautions to guard against a news leak, Giant Publicity Director Garry Schumacher, who knew Durocher well, was positive that the story would come out prematurely. According to Giant announcer Russ Hodges' account, Schumacher deliberately spent the night of July 15 with Stoneham to make sure that he (Schumacher) would not be held responsible for any leak. Just as Schumacher anticipated, Durocher called Corum as soon as the deal was set with Stoneham to ask Corum what he thought of it. Presumably, Corum expressed his opinion and then immediately filed the story. The net result—a big scoop for Corum and, most important, a new manager at the Polo Grounds.

Dec. 1—Leo Durocher and newly signed Giant coach Freddy Fitzsimmons had a hearing before Baseball Commissioner Happy Chandler on charges that the Giants had been guilty of tampering with Fitzsimmons while he was still a coach with the Boston Braves. On January 12, 1949, Chandler fined Durocher and Fitzsimmons $500 apiece and suspended Fitzsimmons from March 1 to April 1, 1949 (which did not prevent Fitz from coaching during the regular season). The Giants also were slapped on their corporate wrist for "failing to satisfy themselves of Fitzsimmons' status." Baseball officials were in universal agreement that the Giants had gotten off very lightly.

1949

Jan. 28—Belatedly following the Brooklyn Dodgers' lead, the Giants signed their first black players, outfielder Monte Irvin and pitcher Ford Smith, and assigned them to Jersey City. Irvin moved up to the Giants in July 1949, but Smith never played in the major leagues.

April 28—Leo Durocher was accused of kicking and slugging a fan, Fred Boysen, after a 13-2 Giant loss at the Polo Grounds. The alleged attack by Durocher occurred as the Giants were walking to their clubhouse in center field. Boysen accused Durocher of knocking him to the ground as Boysen ran out on the field to shake hands with Dodger second baseman Jackie Robinson. After reviewing more than one hundred affidavits from others who attended the game, Baseball Commissioner Happy Chandler concluded that there was insufficient evidence that Durocher had deliberately assaulted Boysen, who reportedly had been heckling Durocher during the game. As a result of the incident, the Giants announced that fans would no longer be permitted on the Polo Grounds playing field after games until all of the players and umpires had left the field.

May 13—Leo Durocher signed a two-year contract to continue to manage the Giants through the 1951 season.

June 4—Whitey Lockman, Sid Gordon, and Willard Marshall hit consecutive home runs in the sixth inning as the Giants lost 6-3 to the Cincinnati Reds at the Polo Grounds.

June 13—The Giants traded Walker Cooper to Cincinnati in exchange for catcher Ray Mueller.

June 26—Leo Durocher was suspended for five days and fined $150 by National League President Ford Frick for protesting too vigorously and profanely an adverse call at second base by umpire Lee Ballanfant. The Giants beat the Cubs 6-2 in Chicago.

July 3—The Giants' Montia Kennedy showed the Dodgers no mercy; he shut them out 16-0 and contributed a grand-slam homer.

July 5—The Giants brought up their first two black players, outfielder Monte Irvin and infielder Hank Thompson, both from the Jersey City club. Irvin, who was hitting .385, was no stranger to the Polo Grounds; he had played there several times as a member of the Newark Eagles of the Negro National League.

July 7—Dave Koslo hit two homers and drove in five runs as he won an 11-3 decision over the Phillies at the Polo Grounds. The two home runs were the first of Koslo's career.

July 8—Monte Irvin and Hank Thompson became the first black players to play for the Giants as the Dodgers beat the Giants 4-3 in Brooklyn. Irvin, who would be elected to the Hall of Fame in 1973, pinch-hit for Clint Hartung in the eighth inning and drew a walk. Thompson started at second base in place of Bill Rigney and went 0-for-3, scored a run, and handled nine chances flawlessly.

July 31—The Giants shut out the Reds twice as Larry Jansen won the first game 10-0 and left-hander Adrian Zabala won the second game, 9-0. Giant third baseman Sid Gordon hit two home runs in the second inning of the second game. This duplicated a feat accomplished by Giants Hack Wilson (in 1925) and Hank Leiber (in 1935).

August 21—The Giants won the second game of a doubleheader in Philadelphia by forfeit when fans showered debris on the field after umpire George Barr ruled that Phils outfielder Richie Ashburn had trapped a drive off the bat of the Giants' Joe Lafata.

August 22—The Giants sold Johnny Mize to the Yankees for $40,000.

Oct. 7—Ex-Giant Danny Gardella withdrew his $300,000 suit against organized baseball and said he was returning to the major leagues as a member of the St. Louis Cardinals. He told writers several months later that he had "been paid something" to drop his suit, but he would not reveal the amount involved although he admitted that he had paid his attorneys "more than half."

Dec. 14—In a major trade, the Giants obtained shortstop Alvin Dark and second baseman Eddie Stanky from the Boston Braves for Sid Gordon, Willard Marshall, and Buddy Kerr.

1950

May 17—The Giants sold catcher Ray Mueller to Pittsburgh and bought third baseman Johnny "Spider" Jorgensen from Brooklyn.

June 22—The Giants shut out the Cardinals twice as Larry Jansen won the first game 3-0 and Dave Koslo the second contest, 5-0.

June 24—Wes Westrum hit three home runs and a triple in a 12-2 Giant win over Cincinnati. The Giants had seven homers in the game as Alvin Dark, Monte Irvin, Whitey Lockman, and Hank Thompson contributed the other four homers.

July 10—The Giants obtained right-hander Jim Hearn from the Cardinals on waivers. Hearn contributed heavily during the Giants' 1951 pennant win and he remained with the Giants through 1956.

July 20—The Giants blasted the Cardinals for a 13-3 win in St. Louis with every Giant getting at least one hit. In an eight-run third inning, Giants' left fielder Roy "Stormy" Weatherly opened with a double and closed the scoring with a three-run triple.

August 12—The Giants lost a tumultuous, eleven-inning 5-4 decision to the Phillies in Philadelphia. Leo Durocher protested the game after Eddie Stanky was ejected in the fourth inning for waving his arms to distract Phillie batter Andy Seminick. Stanky had pulled his arm-waving act several times while Seminick was at bat in the previous night's game. Durocher had agreed before the game to have Stanky desist until League President Ford Frick ruled on the legality of the tactic. But after Seminick knocked out Giant third baseman Hank Thompson with a rough slide early in the game, Durocher annulled the agreement. So when Seminick came to bat in the fourth, Stanky went into his arm-waving routine. Seminick responded by throwing his bat in the infield and umpire Lon Warneke thumbed out Stanky. Durocher immediately protested the game.

But that was not the end of the day's acrimony. Bill Rigney moved to second base to replace the ousted Stanky. Seminick, on base on an error, crashed violently into Rigney on a force play and the slightly built Rigney swung at him in retaliation. Both benches emptied and police had to help the umpires restore order. Rigney and Seminick were ejected from the game.

After the Giants had lost the game in the eleventh on Phil catcher Stan Lopata's triple and Eddie Waitkus' sacrifice fly, a still-livid Durocher insisted there was no rule against Stanky's arm gyrations. Durocher claimed, "Smart ballplayers have been pulling stuff like that for all of the twenty-five years I've been in the game and it's perfectly legal as far as I'm concerned." Predictably, Durocher's unconvincing protest was denied by Ford Frick and arm-waving tactics had to be removed from Durocher's strategic arsenal.

August 30—Eddie Stanky drew his seventh straight walk (over two games) as Sal Maglie shut out the Pirates 4-0 in Pittsburgh. Stanky tied the record held jointly by the Tigers' Bill Rogell and by Mel Ott.

Sept. 9—Sal Maglie, supported by two solo home runs by shortstop Alvin Dark, pitched his fourth consecutive shutout, defeating the Dodgers 2-0 at the Polo Grounds. The major league record is six, held by the Dodgers' Don Drysdale.

Sept. 13—Sal Maglie defeated the Pirates, 3-1. He had a forty-five-inning runless streak broken (only four outs short of Carl Hubbell's Giant record of 46 1/3 consecutive innings in 1933) when Pittsburgh outfielder Gus Bell hit a 257-foot fly ball that barely cleared the Polo Grounds right-field wall at its closest point to the plate. Maglie's rain-shortened, seven-inning win was his eleventh victory in a row.

1951

Jan. 21—Giant great Mel Ott was elected to the Hall of Fame.

April 30—Sal Maglie beat the Dodgers 8-5 at Ebbets Field in a game that typified the bitter season of Giant-Dodger struggles that lay ahead. Maglie erased Jackie Robinson on called strikes in the first inning after knocking Robby down with a pitch headed directly for his skull. In Robinson's next turn at bat, he bunted down the first-base line in an attempt to trample Maglie on the line. Robinson did manage to whack Maglie soundly on the rear end to send him sprawling as Robby beat out a hit. Maglie raced over to first base to challenge Robinson, but the two men were separated before any blows were struck. After a tense 10 minutes, the game continued with neither man being ejected.

May 25—Willie Mays, hitting .477 with the Giants' Minneapolis farm club, played in his first Giant game. The twenty-year-old youngster took a third called strike in his first at bat against Philadelphia right-hander Bubba Church, then went out four more times for an 0-for-5 debut. The Giants won the game, 8-5.

May 28—After going hitless in his first twelve times at bat for the Giants, Willie Mays blasted a towering home run against Boston off the left-field grandstand roof at the Polo Grounds. Mays' first major league hit was stroked off the Braves' great left-hander, Warren Spahn, in a 4-1 Giant loss.

June 22—Willie Mays hit a three-run homer in the tenth inning off knuckleballer Emil "Dutch" Leonard of the Chicago Cubs, propelling the Giants to a 9-6 win. This was the first of Mays' twenty-two career extra-inning home runs, a major league record.

July 13—The Giants regained second place with a 14-4 rout of the Cardinals at the Polo Grounds. In the process, the Giants had two grand-slam homers, one by catcher Wes Westrum in the third inning and the other by rookie second baseman Davey Williams in the eighth.

July 20—Leo Durocher put outfielder Bobby Thomson at third base because none of the other players tried there—Hank Thompson, Bill Rigney, Hank Schenz—had hit. This proved to be an inspired move; Thomson's hitting improved dramatically, his fielding was adequate, and the change seemed to spark the club. Durocher's move was reminiscent of Bill Terry's midseason shift of Mel Ott from right field to third base, which was largely instrumental in the Giants' 1937 pennant win.

Before the game, Leo Durocher signed a contract to manage the Giants in 1952.

August 12—The Giants began the day at their lowest point of the season, 13 1/2 games behind the first-place Dodgers. But Leo Durocher's club snapped back with a doubleheader win over the Phillies at the Polo Grounds. Sal Maglie won the first game 3-2 and rookie right-hander Al Corwin, just up from the Giants' Ottawa farm club, took the second game, 2-1. This began a streak during which the Giants won thirty-nine of their remaining forty-seven games to force a playoff.

August 15—Jim Hearn defeated the Dodgers 3-1 in a game remembered best for a miraculous play by Willie Mays. The game was tied at one-all with one out in the Dodgers' top of the eighth with Billy Cox the runner at third. Carl Furillo flied deep to right center and the speedy Cox prepared to tag up and score the go-ahead Dodger run.

Mays raced to his left from left center and made a fine catch while running at full speed. Amazingly, he made no attempt to reduce his momentum to his left before throwing, but instead he allowed his momentum to spin him around completely. As he whirled counterclockwise, he rifled the ball past cutoff man Whitey Lockman and the ball carried on a line about 325 feet to catcher Wes Westrum, who tagged out the astonished Cox as he slid in. Before the wild cheering had died down, Mays opened the Giant eighth with a ringing single to left and Westrum came through with a homer for the Giants' 3-1 win.

After the game, veteran players and writers were still marvelling over Mays' amazing instinctive play and his great throw. Westrum said, "Hell, I was so sure that Willie wouldn't bother to make the throw that I didn't even take my mask off." But Dodger manager Charley Dressen paid the ultimate tribute with the comment, "I won't believe that play can be made until I see it *again.*"

August 27—The Giants won a doubleheader from the Cubs at the Polo Grounds, by scores of 5-4 in twelve innings and 6-3, to run their winning streak to sixteen games, their longest string of wins since 1916. In the process, the second-place Giants moved to within five games of the league-leading Dodgers. The Giants were losing 4-3 going into the bottom of the twelfth inning, but they scored two runs on a walk to Alvin Dark, singles by Monte Irvin and Whitey Lockman, and a sacrifice fly by Bill Rigney. Larry Jansen pitched all twelve innings for his seventeenth win of the season.

August 28—Pittsburgh Pirate left-hander Howie Pollet shut out the Giants 2-0 at the Polo Grounds to end their sixteen-game winning streak.

Sept. 1—Giant right fielder Don "Mandrake the Magician" Mueller hit three home runs (the third just after learning that he had become a father) to carry the Giants' Sal Maglie to an 8-1 victory over the Dodgers at the Polo Grounds. In addition to Mueller's heavy hitting, the game was marked by repetitive close pitches by Maglie and Dodger retaliatory measures on the bases, and a triple play executed by the Giants' Eddie Stanky and Alvin Dark.

Sept. 2—Jim Hearn beat Brooklyn 11-2 at the Polo Grounds to pull the Giants to within five games of the league-leading Dodgers. Don

Mueller, who had three homers the previous day, had two more homers. Mueller's five home runs in two consecutive games set the National League record, since tied by Stan Musial of the Cardinals and Nate Colbert of the San Diego Padres.

Sept. 30—The Giants and Dodgers won their last games of the regular 1951 season, forcing a three-game playoff to decide the pennant winner. The Giants assured themselves of a tie as Larry Jansen pitched a gritty 3-2 win over the Braves in Boston. In their game at Philadelphia, the Dodgers pulled out a dramatic fourteen-inning, 9-8 victory as second baseman Jackie Robinson held off the Phillies in the thirteenth inning with a great catch of Eddie Waitkus' line drive and then won the game with a home run that won the pennant two days later.

Oct. 2—Dodger rookie right-hander Clem Labine defeated the Giants' Sheldon Jones 10-0 at the Polo Grounds, tying the pennant playoff series at one-all. Labine's mastery over the Giants was best exemplified by the experience of Willie Mays, who hit into three double plays.

Oct. 3—The Giants won the best-of-three playoff series and the pennant on Bobby Thomson's come-from-behind, three-run homer in the bottom of the ninth, which gave the Giants an unforgettable 5-4 victory. (See page 292 for details.)

Oct. 10—The Yankees defeated the Giants in the World Series 4 games to 2 with a 4-3 win at Yankee Stadium. Yankee right-hander Vic Rashi, supported by outfielder Hank Bauer's three-run triple in the sixth inning, prevailed over the Giants' Dave Koslo to win.

   Just before the game, Giant manager Leo Durocher turned over a letter he had received to National League President Ford Frick offering Durocher a $15,000 bribe if the Giants "manage to lose the next three games." The letter also contained a threat against Durocher's wife, actress Laraine Day.

Oct. 18—Leo Durocher was voted Manager of the Year in an Associated Press poll.

Nov. 15—Willie Mays was voted 1951 Rookie of the Year honors by the Baseball Writers Association of America.

Dec. 10—The Giants traded Eddie Stanky to St. Louis for left-hander Max Lanier and outfielder Chuck Diering. The Cardinals signed Stanky to a player-manager contract for 1952.

1952

April 2—The Giants lost Monte Irvin for most of the season when he suffered a compound fracture of his right ankle sliding into third base in an exhibition game against the Cleveland Indians at Denver. Irvin returned to play in only forty-six games for the 1952 Giants.

April 9—The Giants obtained infielder-outfielder Bob Elliott from the Boston Braves for right-hander Sheldon Jones plus $75,000. Elliott, nearing the end of a fine career, batted a mere .228 in ninety-eight games with the Giants in 1952, his only year with the club.

April 25—In his first major league at bat, Giant knuckleballer Hoyt Wilhelm dropped a homer into the right-field seats at the Polo Grounds against Boston Braves' left-hander Dick Hoover. This was the only homer Wilhelm hit in his twenty-one year major league career. Wilhelm also pitched five solid relief innings as he won his first big league victory, 9-5.

May 29—Willie Mays entered the army, effectively ending the Giants' chances to win a second successive league title. Although Mays was hitting a mere .236 when he left, the Giants led the league by 2 1/2 games at the time. The Giants lost eight of their next ten games and never regained the lead, finishing the season in second place, 4 1/2 games behind the Dodgers.

June 29—Leo Durocher was suspended for four days after a violent scene with plate umpire Bill Stewart when Stewart ruled that Philadelphia outfielder Del Ennis had caught a low line drive hit by Don Mueller. Durocher earned his suspension for kicking dirt on the plate, the umpire, and kicking Stewart in the shins.

August 18—Leo Durocher was suspended for five days and fined $100 for getting into an overly-spirited debate with umpire Augie Donatelli. More specifically, Leo the Lip drew back his arm as if to strike Donatelli. Durocher's players and other umpires successfully dissuaded him.

August 23—The records indicate that Giant third baseman Bob Elliott was out on strikes in the seventh inning of a Giant loss to the Cardinals at the Polo Grounds, but there was more to the story than that. Elliott complained so loudly and kicked so much dirt on the plate in protesting a second-strike call by umpire Augie Donatelli that Elliott was ejected from the game. Bobby Hofman came in to complete Elliott's at bat and he was thrown out of the game for complaining and kicking dirt after the third-strike call.

Sept. 9—Leo Durocher was suspended (his third suspension of the year) and fined $100 following a beanball incident in a 10-2 Giant loss to the Dodgers the day before. In addition, Montia Kennedy was fined $50 and Larry Jansen $25 (remitted because of the mild-mannered Jansen's "excellent conduct record"). Kennedy had ignored a warning by the plate umpire when he knocked down Gil Hodges at the plate and narrowly missed hitting Dodger pitcher Joe Black. Jansen had been banished for hitting Dodger third baseman Billy Cox with a pitch.

1953

April 29—Hoyt Wilhelm lost to Milwaukee Braves left-hander Warren Spahn 3-2 on a ninth-inning wild pitch at the Polo Grounds. The game was highlighted by Braves first baseman Joe Adcock's two-run, 475-foot home run into the distant left center-field bleachers in the third inning. Adcock's drive landed about ten rows up in the stands after clearing the five-foot wall that enclosed the bleachers. This was the first home run hit into the Polo Grounds center-field bleachers in a regular season game. The feat had been accomplished by pitcher Schoolboy Rowe in batting practice before an exhibition game in 1933 and by Luke Easter (later a first baseman with the Cleveland Indians) in a Negro League game in 1948. Chicago Cub outfielder Lou Brock duplicated the feat on June 17, 1962 in a game against the New York Mets.

July 1—The Giants purchased right-hander Marv Grissom from the Boston Red Sox. Grissom had his best year with the Giants with his 10 and 7 contribution as a reliever in the club's World Championship year in 1954. He remained with the Giants through the 1958 campaign in San Francisco.

July 6—In his first Giant start, right-hander Al Worthington shut out the Pittsburgh Pirates 6-0 at the Polo Grounds.

July 11—Al Worthington shut out the Dodgers 6-0 at Ebbets Field in his second Giant start.

July 18—The Giants moved into the first division (fourth place) for the first time in the season with a 12-7 win over the Cubs at the Polo Grounds. The New Yorkers hit five home runs during the game, including three in the first inning. Whitey Lockman opened the Giant first with a homer and Hank Thompson and Bobby Thomson followed suit.

July 19—For the second game in a row, Whitey Lockman opened the first inning with a homer as the Giants defeated the Milwaukee Braves, 7-5.

July 30—Giant outfielder Monte Irvin hit into three double plays as the Giants lost 5-0 to the Milwaukee Braves.

August 13—Leo Durocher signed a two-year contract to manage the Giants through 1955.

August 26—Hitting only .167 before the game, part-time Giant outfielder Dusty Rhodes hit three consecutive home runs and drove in five runs as the Giants overpowered the Cardinals 13-4 at the Polo Grounds. Alvin Dark was another hitting standout, going 5-for-5, including a homer and batting in five runs.

Sept. 4—The Giants lost to the Dodgers 8-6 at the Polo Grounds in a game marked by umpire baiting, beanball incidents,and home runs. Plate umpire Bill Stewart ejected Leo Durocher and Wes Westrum in the sixth inning after Westrum challenged a fourth-ball call on Pee Wee Reese with the bases loaded.

The beanball episode started in the Giant seventh when Giant third baseman Bobby Hofman had to duck to avoid a Clem Labine pitch. In the eighth inning, the Giants' Larry Jansen low-bridged Duke Snider. The Duke responded with a safe bunt down the first-base line but he failed to make contact with Jansen, who fielded the ball. Jackie Robinson sacrificed Snider along with a bunt to the same area, but again Jansen avoided the baserunner easily as he fielded the ball and threw to first. In reprisal, Jansen knocked down Roy Campanella, the next Dodger hitter. Umpire Bill Stewart called acting Giant manager Bill Rigney and Dodger manager Charley Dressen out and succeeded in ending the macho behavior.

The home run pyrotechnics came in the Giant third when successive homers by Westrum, pitcher Al Corwin, and Whitey Lockman drove out Dodger starter Russ Meyer.

Sept. 6—Two days after the Giants and Dodgers exchanged beanballs in a game at the Polo Grounds, the Giants lost to the Dodgers 6-3 in a game remembered for an historic brawl between Dodger right fielder Carl Furillo and Leo Durocher. In the second inning, Giant right-hander Ruben Gomez hit Furillo on the wrist. Carl walked out to the mound, exchanged angry words with Gomez, but went on to first after the umpires intervened. The count went to 3 and 2 on Billy Cox, the next hitter, when Furillo began pointing at someone in the Giant dugout. Suddenly, after apparently calling time, Furillo left first base and raced to the Giant dugout, where he was met by Durocher. The two men exchanged punches as both teams raced to separate them. During the melee, someone stepped on Furillo's left hand and broke one of his fingers. Durocher and Furillo were separated after considerable effort and both men were ordered off the field.

After the game, Furillo claimed that Durocher had motioned him to come to the dugout — by signalling with his index finger. Predictably, Durocher said that he had done nothing to provoke

Furillo. The injured Dodger right fielder was out for the rest of the season, but this was hardly a problem because the Dodgers had the pennant cinched and Furillo, with his batting average frozen at .344, led the league in hitting.

The bad feeling between Durocher and Furillo was nothing new. It went back at least as far as 1949 when Furillo was hospitalized after being hit by a pitch from Giant right-hander Sheldon Jones, which Jones said had been ordered by Durocher. Furillo blamed Durocher for other Giant-Dodger beanball episodes since then. (Durocher's reputation as a beanball instigator extended back to the early 1940s, when his stewardship of the Dodgers was marked by continuing involvement in beanball feuds with a number of clubs.)

Oct. 18—The Giants left on a one-month tour of Japan, Korea, and the Philippines, during which they played All-Star teams and entertained American servicemen.

1954

Jan. 20—Bill Terry was elected to the Hall of Fame. Terry, who had been miffed over his long-delayed entrance to the Hall, responded with an icy "I have nothing to say" when informed of his election. But Memphis Bill later became a familiar figure at Hall of Fame functions and, reportedly, a champion of needy former players.

Feb. 1—The Giants traded Bobby Thomson and catcher Sam Calderone to the Milwaukee Braves for left-handers Johnny Antonelli and Don Liddle, infielder Billy Klaus, and catcher Ebba St. Claire. The key men in the deal were Thomson and Antonelli and the exchange clearly was advantageous to the Giants. Thomson had 3 1/2 lackluster seasons with the Braves before returning to the Giants in midseason of 1957. By contrast, Antonelli had a brilliant 21-and-7 season in 1954 as the Giants became World Champions, and he had six more seasons with the Giants, winning at least fourteen games in five of these seasons before slipping in 1960.

March 2—Willie Mays was released from the army. He immediately rejoined the Giants and led them to the pennant and a World Series win over the Cleveland Indians.

April 8—The Giants sold veteran left-hander Dave Koslo to the Baltimore Orioles.

April 25—The Giants shut out the Phillies twice. Sal Maglie hurled the first game 3-0 win and Johnny Antonelli followed with a 5-0 performance.

April 30—Willie Mays homered in the fourteenth inning at Chicago off Cub left-hander Warren Hacker to win a 4-2 decision for Maglie.

May 28—The Giants crushed the Dodgers 17-6 at the Polo Grounds with a six-home-run barrage. The Polo Grounders warmed up with a home run by Whitey Lockman in the first inning and a 447-foot blast by Willie Mays in the second inning. The Giants went into high gear in the eighth when second baseman Davey Williams, Alvin Dark, Monte Irvin, and third baseman Bill Gardner homered.

June 3—The Giants outslugged the Cardinals 13-8 in St. Louis. Hank Thompson and Willie Mays supplied the punch, batting in all the Giant runs between them. Thompson hit three straight homers and batted in eight runs. Mays had two home runs and 5 RBI.

June 20—The Giants won an exciting 7-6 contest with the Cardinals at the Polo Grounds. The highlight of the game came in the sixth inning when the Giants hit three successive homers, two by pinch hitters. Bobby Hofman, pinch-hitting for Bill Gardner, hit the first; he was followed by Wes Westrum, who belted a long smash into the upper left-field stands. Dusty Rhodes pinch-hit for pitcher Marv Grissom and topped off the outburst with a long smash into the right-field stands.

July 11—The Giants hit six home runs in a game for the second time during the season as they polished off the Pirates 13-7 at the Polo Grounds. Monte Irvin, Whitey Lockman, and Alvin Dark homered in the second inning. The other circuit drives were hit by Hank Thompson, Willie Mays, and Don Mueller who hit for the cycle.

July 28—Giant left-hander Johnny Antonelli won his tenth straight game with an easy 10-0 win over the Cardinals at the Polo Grounds. Left fielder Dusty Rhodes led the Giant attack with three consecutive home runs. Willie Mays hit his thirty-sixth home run to move ahead of Babe Ruth's 1927 pace when Ruth hit sixty round-trippers. Mays's drive was a well-crushed clout that landed in the upper left-field stands above the 447-foot marker.

August 2—Johnny Antonelli won his eleventh consecutive game, running his season's record to 16 and 2 as the Giants beat the Reds 9-4 in the first game of a doubleheader at the Polo Grounds.

August 6—Johnny Antonelli's eleven-game winning streak ended as he was knocked out of the box in the fourth inning of a 6-5 Giant loss to Cincinnati.

August 20—Giant left-hander Don Liddle shut out the Pirates 4-0 at the Polo Grounds, all the runs scoring on Don Mueller's grand-slam home run in the fifth inning. Willie Mays hit safely in his twenty-first straight game, leaving him three behind Freddy Lindstrom (of the 1930 Giants) and Mike Donlin (of the 1908 club) for the modern Giant record.

August 29—The Giants split a doubleheader with the Cardinals in St. Louis, losing the first game 5-4 and winning the second, 7-4. Dusty Rhodes had six extra-base hits on the day. In the first game, he hit two triples in two at bats in a losing cause. Rhodes dominated the second-game victory with two home runs and two doubles in five trips.

Sept. 8—The Giants purchased catcher Joe Garagiola from the Cubs. Garagiola hit .273 in five games,then retired to pursue his successful TV career.

Sept. 10—The Giants lost to Cincinnati Reds' right-hander Art Fowler 8-1 at the Polo Grounds. Trying unsuccessfully to handle Hoyt Wilhelm's knuckleball, Giant catcher Ray Katt was charged with a record-breaking four passed balls in the eighth inning. Wilhelm faced only five hitters in that inning despite yielding a single and two walks as the Reds scored twice on Katt's passed balls. With two men out, the inning ended oddly when the Reds' Bobby Adams, confident that Katt would commit a fifth passed ball, raced for the plate when Wilhelm prepared to throw a knuckler to Red shortstop Roy McMillan. But Katt hung on to the pitch after McMillan missed it and Adams was tagged out at home to end a long, unhappy experience for one embarrassed Katt.

Sept. 11—The Giants beat Cincinnati 7-5 at the Polo Grounds. The decisive blow was a grand-slam home run by Whitey Lockman. Willie Mays's double in the seventh inning was his eighty-first extra-base hit of the season, tying the club record set by Mel Ott in 1929. Don Mueller hit in his twenty-first consecutive game, duplicating Mays's feat of August 20, 1954; like Mays, Mueller's streak was broken in his next game.

Sept. 14—Willie Mays cracked a first-inning double, his eighty-second extra-base hit of the season, to break Mel Ott's old Giant record set in 1929. Of more immediate significance, Mays's double enabled him to score the only run as Johnny Antonelli defeated the Cardinals 1-0 at the Polo Grounds.

Sept. 20—The Giants clinched their second pennant under Leo Durocher's stewardship with a 7-1 victory over the Dodgers at Ebbets Field. Willie Mays took over the batting lead for the first time in the season with three hits in five trips to move ahead of the Dodgers' Duke Snider.

Sept. 26—Willie Mays won the National League batting title, just beating out teammate Don Mueller and Duke Snider as the pennant-winning Giants closed out the regular season with a 3-2, eleven-inning win over the Phillies' Robin Roberts. Before the game, Mueller led with an average of .3426, Snider was second with .3425, and Mays was hitting .3422. Wondrous Willie had a single, double, and triple in four at bats to finish with a .345 average. Mueller was second at .341.

Sept. 29—The Giants took the World Series in four straight with a 7-4 win over the Indians in Cleveland. Giant starter Don Liddle, with relief help from Hoyt Wilhelm and Johnny Antonelli, prevailed over the Indians' Bob Lemon.

Dec. 16—Willie Mays was voted the Most Valuable Player in the National League for 1954.

1955

Jan. 11—Willie Mays and Ruben Gomez brawled as a result of a dispute in batting practice before an exhibition game in San Juan, Puerto Rico. According to the *New York Times,* the fracas started when Gomez slipped into the batters' box just as Mays prepared for his turn to hit. When the batting practice pitcher, Milton Ralat, refused to pitch to Gomez, the Giant pitcher sat down in a sulk at home plate. Mays directed Ralat to pitch to him just off the plate and when Ralat threw Mays an insultingly slow pitch, Mays grabbed it barehand and fired it back hard to Ralat, striking him on the shoulder. Ralat shouted an unkind word to Mays and Willie walked out to the mound in anger. Gomez got up and apparently tried to stop Mays. Willie, believing that the bat-carrying Gomez was out to protect his fellow Puerto Rican at Mays's expense, dropped Gomez with a right-hand punch. Giant coach Herman Franks and Milwaukee Braves first baseman George Crowe separated the two men before the fight could continue. Although Mays and Gomez apologized to each other in the dressing room shortly after, Mays returned to the States within a few days. Mays, Gomez, and Franks made light of the incident when they got together in spring training.

May 23—Old Giant favorite Sid Gordon was obtained from Pittsburgh. The sturdy Brooklyn native hit .243 in sixty-six games with the Giants in 1955, his last year in the major leagues.

July 31—The Giants sold Sal Maglie to Cleveland. The Indians dealt Maglie to Brooklyn in May 1956; Sal, thought to be washed up, contributed thirteen wins to the Dodger effort as they won the 1956 National League pennant.

August 18—Giant President Horace Stoneham asked for aid from New York City in obtaining a new home for his ballclub. He suggested that the city consider building a stadium in the Bronx near the Whitestone Bridge to house both the Giants and the Yankees. The Yankees' General Manager George Weiss reacted with the brief statement, "We're very happy with Yankee Stadium." Reading this, many older fans must have recalled the baseball scene of the 1903-1920 period when the situation was reversed — John McGraw ruled the New York City baseball roost unchallenged from the Polo Grounds while the downtrodden, pre-Babe Ruth Yankees sought to gain a baseball home to call their own.

August 24—Alarmed by a downward trend in attendance, the Giants and Yankees admitted they were considering a TV blackout of home night games in 1956. But the proposal was not carried out largely because of fears that such might be in violation of antitrust statutes.

August 28—Giant Secretary Eddie Brannick was given a dinner at the posh Waldorf-Astoria to commemorate his fiftieth year with the club. More than a thousand attended the affair for the popular Brannick, who joined the Giant organization in 1905 as John McGraw's personal jack-of-all-trades.

Sept. 20—Willie Mays homered in each game as the Giants routed the Pirates twice at the Polo Grounds by scores of 11-1 and 14-8. Mays's fiftieth homer of the season in the second game tied the major league record of seven home runs in six consecutive games. The other holders of the record also were Giant players, George Kelly of the 1924 Giants and Walker Cooper of the 1947 club.

Sept. 24—Leo Durocher resigned as Giant manager and Bill Rigney, who managed the Giant's Minneapolis farm club in 1955, was named to replace him. Durocher, whose 1955 club finished in third place eighteen games behind the Dodgers, told skeptical writers that he had planned to leave the Giants regardless of where they finished the season. A significant number of Giant fans were glad to see Durocher leave despite the pennant he had won in 1951 and the World Championship season in 1954.

Sept. 25—The Giants split a doubleheader with the Phillies at the Polo Grounds in Leo Durocher's finale as Giant manager. The Polo Grounders won the first game 5-2 as Willie Mays belted his fifty-first home run to tie Johnny Mize's club record set with the 1947 Giants. The Phils took the second game 3-1 with a flourish as they wiped out a budding ninth-inning Giant rally with a triple play. With Joe Amalfitano on second base, Whitey Lockman on first, and none out, Bobby Hofmann lined to Philadelphia shortstop Ted Kazanski. He flipped the ball to Bobby Morgan at second and the throw to first baseman Marv Blaylock ended the inning, game, season, and Durocher regime.

Sept. 28—Bill Terry told writers that he was ready to buy the Giants and have them play their games at Yankee Stadium. Horace Stoneham killed the story the next day by stating that the Giants were not for sale. Putting Terry completely in his place, Stoneham added, "If the Giants are ever for sale, the negotiations will be done with one of several New York individuals or groups who from time to time have expressed interest in the Giants."

Oct. 6—Bill Rigney signed a contract to manage the Giants for the 1956 and 1957 seasons.

1956

March 3—The Giants and Cleveland Indians cancelled their exhibition game scheduled in Meridian, Mississippi, for April 10 because of racial outbursts in nearby Alabama. The action was considered necessary because both clubs' rosters included several black players.

April 10—Horace Stoneham expressed "great interest" in a proposal by Manhattan Borough President Hulan E. Jack for the construction of a stadium on Manhattan's west side. The proposed 110,000-seat stadium, to be available to the Giants by 1962 (when their Polo Grounds lease was due to expire), was to be a triple-decked structure built on stilts over the open tracks of the New York Central Railroad yards. It would have extended from 60th Street to 72nd Street and encompassed the area from West End Avenue to the West Side Highway with parking facilities for twenty thousand cars and a subway station under the stadium. The projected $75 million cost eventually torpedoed the project. Presumably, this was one of the factors in Stoneham's decision to move the club to San Francisco for the 1958 season.

May 2—The Giants beat the Cubs 6-5 in seventeen innings in Chicago as Giant second baseman Daryl Spencer drove in Alvin Dark with a sacrifice fly in the top of the seventeenth. The two teams set a major league record by using forty-eight players between them. The Giants used twenty-five players, including eight pitchers, to break the old record held by the 1940 Pirates and the 1948 Dodgers. Whitey Lockman began the game in left field, switched to first base, went back to left, and returned to first as

Giant manager Bill Rigney pulled out all stops in maneuvering his players during the marathon affair.

May 6—Willie Mays stole four bases as the Giants defeated the St. Louis Cardinals, 5-4.

May 7—Giant first baseman Bill White homered in his first major league at bat, then added a double and a single as the Giants lost to the Cardinals 6-3 at the Polo Grounds.

June 14—The Giants traded Whitey Lockman, Alvin Dark, catcher Ray Katt, and left-hander Don Liddle to the St. Louis Cardinals for second baseman Red Schoendienst, catcher Bill Sarni, outfielder Jackie Brandt, and left-hander Dick Littlefield.

July 8—The Giants hit seven homers in administering an 11-1 pasting to the Pirates at the Polo Grounds. Willie Mays, Daryl Spencer, and Wes Westrum each hit two home runs and Hank Thompson added another. Three of the round-trippers — by Thompson, Spencer, and Westrum — were hit consecutively in the fourth inning.

July 10—Willie Mays hit a pinch-hit, two-run homer off the Yankees' Whitey Ford as the National League All-Stars beat the American Leaguers 7-3 in Washington, D.C. Dodger manager Walt Alston, who managed the National League squad, named Mays to his team after the fans failed to vote Willie to the starting lineup. Mays's homer was his seventh straight hit off Ford.

July 17—There was an astounding scene as the last-place Giants beat the league-leading Braves 8-6 in Milwaukee. In the bottom of the second inning, Ruben Gomez hit Braves first baseman Joe Adcock on the wrist with his first pitch. Adcock took a few steps toward first base, stopped to shout something out to Gomez, then charged the mound. With the menacing figure of the 6'4", 220-pound Adcock coming at him, Gomez fired the ball at Adcock, hitting him on the left thigh — very likely the shortest time interval within which a batter was hit twice by the same pitcher in baseball history.

A panic-stricken Gomez ran full speed to the Giant dugout with the enraged Adcock in hot pursuit. Milwaukee third base coach Johnny Riddle tried to tackle Gomez, but missed. In a flash, the entire Braves squad stormed the Giant dugout and the Giants took appropriate defensive positions. Meanwhile, Gomez raced to the Giant clubhouse, grabbed an ice pick, and started to return to the field before he was restrained and pinned on the clubhouse floor.

When order was restored, Gomez and Adcock were ejected

from the game. Gomez, showing no remorse, said with disarming
simplicity, "I saw him coming at me so I threw the ball at him. I ran
away because I didn't want him to break my ribs." Adcock's only
printable comment was "I've never been so mad in all my life."
The penalties assessed the players by National League president
Warren Giles seemed appropriate —Gomez was suspended for
three days and fined $250 while Adcock was fined $100 with no
suspension.

Oct. 11—The Giants traded Jim Hearn to the Phillies for right-hander
Stu Miller.

Dec. 13—The Giants obtained Jackie Robinson from the Dodgers
for left-hander Dick Littlefield and $35,000. But the deal was
cancelled in January 1957 when Robinson announced his
retirement. In an article in *Look* magazine, Robinson wrote, "The
Giants don't need me. It would be unfair to the Giant owners to take
their money." Horace Stoneham wrote Robby graciously, "All of us
wish you well, success and happiness, but I can't help thinking it
would've been nice to have had you on our side for a year or two."

1957

Jan. 6—Dodger star Jackie Robinson, scooping his own article in *Look*
magazine due out the following day, announced his retirement
from baseball. This cancelled his trade from the Dodgers to the
Giants, which was announced on December 13, 1956. The thirty-
eight-year-old Robinson took a position with the Chock Full O'
Nuts restaurant chain in New York City at a salary that was
believed to match the one paid to him by the Dodgers.

Feb. 26—The Giants reacquired Whitey Lockman from the
Cardinals eight months after having traded him to St. Louis.

May 28—The Giants and the Dodgers received unanimous
approval from all National League clubs to move to San Francisco
and Los Angeles, respectively.

July 12—St. Louis Cardinal right-hander "Toothpick Sam" Jones
held the Giants to two hits and defeated them 5-1 at the Polo
Grounds. The game was marked by an unusual beanball-throwing
contest between the pitchers, Jones and Ruben Gomez. In the top
of the third inning, Jones took exception to a close pitch by Gomez
that was headed for Jones's neck. Toothpick Sam retaliated in the
bottom of the inning by sending Gomez spinning away from a pitch
that was zeroing in on his jaw. When Gomez subsequently missed
the third strike, his bat suspiciously flew out of his hands and
landed between the pitching mound and third base. Jones gave

Gomez a long, accusing stare. Gomez continued the headhunting expedition when Jones batted in the fifth inning, forcing the big Cardinal pitcher to duck under another knockdown pitch. The battle ended there when plate umpire Tom Gorman summoned Giant manager Bill Rigney and Cardinal skipper Fred Hutchinson and threatened them with immediate expulsion unless the pitchers ceased target practice.

July 17—Horace Stoneham announced that his club would not play at the antiquated, limited-parking-access Polo Grounds in 1958 and that the Giants would move to San Francisco unless either of two unlikely alternatives panned out. One alternative was the construction of a new city-owned stadium near the Bronx-Whitestone Bridge. The other alternative was satisfactory terms for the Giants to share Yankee Stadium with the Yanks. Neither of the possibilities materialized.

August 19—The Giants' Board of Directors voted 8-1 to move the club to San Francisco for the 1958 season. The only dissenting vote came from the minority stockholder, M. Donald Grant, who later would be the Chairman of the Board of the New York Mets, the Giants' successors in New York. Horace Stoneham's most telling point during the press conference that followed the announcement came when a reporter asked him, "How do you feel about taking the Giants from the kids in New York?" Stoneham replied, "I feel bad about the kids, but I haven't seen many of their fathers [attending games] lately!" Stoneham's reference was to the attendance at the Polo Grounds, which had fallen from almost 1.2 million in 1954 to less than 630,000 in 1956.

San Francisco offered the Giants a deal that the National Exhibition Company (the Giants' corporate name) calculated would yield annual profits of $200,000 to $300,000. This was based upon construction of a new stadium seating nearly fifty thousand and providing parking facilities for twelve thousand automobiles, favorable concession terms, exclusive occupancy and liberal rental arrangements.

August 23—The Giants defeated the Cubs 3-2 in sixteen innings at the Polo Grounds. Willie Mays started the last inning with a single off Cub starter Bob Rush and Giant third baseman Ray "Jabbo" Yablonski ended the 4-hour, 14-minute contest with a line drive double off the right-field wall to score Mays.

Sept. 17—The Giants signed nineteen-year-old right-hander Juan Marichal and sent him to Michigan City, Indiana, for seasoning.

Sept. 27—Paul I. Fagan, owner of the San Francisco Seals, agreed to lease his club's ballpark to the Giants for the 1958 season.

Sept. 29—The Giants were defeated by the Pirates before 11,606 in their last game at the Polo Grounds.

Oct. 15—The Giants traded their Minneapolis (American Association) club to the Boston Red Sox for Boston's San Francisco club of the Pacific Coast League. The trade involved the transfer of franchises but not players.

Oct. 16—Bill Rigney signed a two-year contract for an estimated $30,000 a year to manage the Giants in 1958 and 1959. Rigney told writers that any of the Giants could be traded except Willie Mays.

Oct. 21—The Giants purchased the Class A Phoenix, Arizona, team and took steps to have the Pacific Coast League accept the Phoenix franchise as a replacement for the San Francisco club, a casualty of the Giants' move into the Bay Area.

Nov. 25—Horace Stoneham confirmed a report that the Giants had turned down a million-dollar deal in June 1957 that would have involved the trade of Willie Mays to the St. Louis Cardinals for $750,000 in cash plus several Cardinal-owned players.

Dec. 2—The Giants agreed to pay the Pacific Coast League $300,000 in indemnities over a three-year period for the right to move the old San Francisco franchise to Phoenix.

1958

April 15—A capacity crowd of 23,449 jammed Seals Stadium for the Giants' historic West Coast opener. Ruben Gomez responded with a six-hit, 8-0 victory over the Los Angeles Dodgers. Daryl Spencer hit the first major league home run at Seals Stadium, and rookie Orlando Cepeda homered in an eleven-hit attack.

April 16—The first night game at the Giants' park found the Dodgers spoiling the party with a 13-1 romp behind Johnny Podres. Duke Snider hit one of the longest home runs in Seals Stadium history, a 425-foot shot over the right-field wall.

April 18—Hank Sauer hit two home runs, including the first at the L.A. Coliseum, but the Giants' first road game was a 6-5 loss to the Dodgers before 78,682. Rookie Jim Davenport collected three hits, but failed to tag third base in the ninth, costing San Francisco a run.

April 20—Two home runs by Danny O'Connell powered a 12-2 victory at Los Angeles. Willie Mays had three hits, including a home run, in three at bats, scoring thrice and collecting three RBI.

April 23—The Giants began their first of a series of comeback victories, scoring four times in the bottom of the ninth for an 8-7 triumph over the Cardinals. Davenport singled, Mays was safe on an error, Cepeda hit a two-run triple with two outs, and Spencer hit a game-winning homer.

April 24—Sauer's two homers, including a two-run shot in the ninth, downed the Cardinals, 6-5. Hank became the first National League slugger to homer in twelve parks.

April 26—Mays hit his first home run in a San Francisco uniform, a solo shot off the Cubs' Glen Hobbie. It was his 188th career homer and it helped Johnny Antonelli down Chicago 3-1 for his first victory.

April 30—The Giants vaunted power erupted for five home runs in a 10-1 rout of the Phillies behind Antonelli's six-hitter. Davenport belted two homers and Cepeda, Spencer, and Bob Schmidt hit one apiece.

May 4—Unheralded Roman Mejias hit three homers to lead the Pirates to a 6-2 victory in the opener, but the Giants gained a split of the doubleheader when Eddie Bressoud's run-scoring single in the tenth won the nightcap, 4-3. Cepeda had two homers and a double in the twin bill.

May 5—This was the greatest comeback in S.F. history, even though it fell short by one run. The Pirates entered the bottom of the ninth leading 11-1, but had to survive a nine-run Giants rally before emerging 11-10 winners. The eruption featured two-run pinch doubles by Jim King and Antonelli, a three-run homer by Ray Jablonski, and a solo homer by Cepeda for the final run. The game ended when pinch hitter Don Taussig popped to second with the bases loaded.

May 6—Left-hander Mike McCormick, 19 years old, scattered three infield singles in a three-hit, 7-0 victory at Pittsburgh. Schmidt cracked a three-run double in the five-run first and Cepeda homered.

May 12—Mays hit two home runs, including a grand slam off Ed Roebuck, pacing a 12-3 victory at L.A. Mays finished with five RBI.

May 13—Mays hit two more homers in a 16-9 crunching of the Dodgers, the Giants setting a major league record with fifty total bases. Mays totaled fifteen total bases, also belting two triples among his five hits. Spencer was overshadowed, but he had two homers, a triple, a double, six RBI, and thirteen total bases in the offensive orgy.

May 21—Mays hit a home run in the tenth at Cincinnati, handing Hal Jeffcoat a 5-4 defeat.

May 25—The "new" Giants were embroiled in their first brawl during a 5-2, 6-1 sweep before 35,797 partisan Pittsburghers. The fight broke out in the opener and was triggered by a beanball battle between Gomez and Vernon Law. Mays tackled Cepeda to prevent The Baby Bull from possibly striking someone with a bat.

June 5—The Giants beat Milwaukee 5-4 in the twelfth. Mays led off the final inning with a single and Jim Finigan doubled, but Hank Aaron threw Mays out at the plate. Cepeda then hit Gene Conley's first pitch for a game-winning homer. Cepeda had four hits.

June 22—Willie Kirkland's fourteenth-inning homer edged the Phillies 5-4 in the opener of a doubleheader, Antonelli firing six shutout innings for the win. Gomez had a 1-0 lead in the sixth inning of the second game, but a curfew rule halted the game at Philadelphia. When it was resumed on July 23, the Phillies won, 3-2.

July 4—The Giants trailed the Cubs 5-1 entering the bottom of the ninth in the opener of a doubleheader, but scored five runs to win, 6-5. Pinch hitter Spencer's bases-loaded walk opened the scoring and Kirkland followed with a two-run pinch single. With two away, Mays belted a two-run, game-winning single off Dick Drott. The Cubs won the second game, 6-1.

July 6—Lightning struck twice for Larry Jackson and the Cardinals. On July 5, Jackson walked Willie Kirkland with the bases full in the bottom of the ninth for a 5-4 Giant victory; the next day, there were two outs and the bases loaded in the ninth again. This time, Jackson hit Jim Davenport with a pitch for another 5-4 triumph.

July 11—Cepeda's three-run homer off Jeffcoat in the twelfth produced a 7-4 victory. The Giants were ahead 4-0 when a two-run homer by Frank Robinson helped create a 4-4 tie.

July 12—Cepeda's 420-foot, three-run homer beat Warren Spahn and the Braves 5-3, pulling the Giants to within one-half game of Milwaukee.

July 13—Felipe Alou's run-scoring single in the bottom of the ninth edged the Braves 6-5 and gave the Giants the league lead. Cepeda hit his third homer in three days.

July 28—The blazing Giants swept a doubleheader at Philadelphia 3-2 and 2-1 to tie for first. Alou's two-run homer won the opener for McCormick, and Kirkland had the game-winning RBI in Gomez' four-hitter in the nightcap.

July 29—Robinson's homer in the eighth gave the host Reds a

3-2 lead, but Mays' single and Jablonski's two-run homer lifted the Giants to a 4-3 victory in the ninth. It was San Francisco's eighteenth win on its last at bats.

August 10—Davenport walloped two of the Giants' five home runs in a 12-8 victory at L.A. Pinch-hitter Bob Speake, O'Connell, and Spencer hit the other homers. Davenport belted five hits and scored four runs, giving him eight hits and three homers in two games.

August 19—Antonelli hit the first home run by a pitcher at Seals Stadium and pitched a ten-inning five-hitter in a 4-3 victory. Kirkland belted a run-scoring triple.

August 27—Cepeda's bases-loaded walk off Bob Trowbridge in the twelfth shaded Milwaukee 4-3 and snapped the Braves' eight-game win string over the Giants. Spencer stroked a two-run homer.

August 30—The Giants swept a day-night doubleheader over the Dodgers, 3-2 and 3-1. Davenport hit two homers in support of Gomez in the first game and Mays had a two-run homer and three RBI behind McCormick's five-hitter in the finale. The crowd was cleared from the stadium after 16,905 attended the day game; then 9,865 watched the night game.

August 31—Bob Schmidt's grand slam off Sandy Koufax in the first inning started a 14-2 drubbing of the Dodgers. Schmidt finished with six RBI and Mays had three of the Giants' fifteen hits, including a two-run homer.

Sept. 1—A crowd of 19,800 attended the memorable second game of a morning-afternoon doubleheader with the Dodgers. The Giants won the four-hour, 35-minute contest with two runs in the sixteenth, taking five of the six games in the Labor Day weekend series. Schmidt's homer in the ninth forced extra innings. S.F. Police Chief Frank Ahern died of a heart attack in the fifteenth inning. Carl Furillo's RBI gave L.A. a 5-4 lead in the sixteenth, but Whitey Lockman's homer tied it in the bottom of the inning. Then Jablonski beat out a bunt single and scored on errors by John Roseboro and Furillo following a bunt by Gomez. Mays went 5-for-5 with two doubles and a homer as the Giants won the opener 3-2, and was 11-for-20 in the series with four homers.

Sept. 4—The Giants clobbered the Dodgers 13-3 at the Coliseum to take a final 16-6 edge in the season series. Podres was routed in an eight-run first, Stu Miller pitched a five hitter, Mays and Cepeda homered, and Alou and Bressoud each totaled three RBI.

Sept. 12—The host Phillies were swamped 5-2 and 19-2 in a twin bill, Mays raising his average to .333 with six hits. Davenport homered to lead the opening win for Gomez. He added a three-run, inside-the-park homer in an eight-run first inning of the second game, finishing the day with seven hits and seven runs scored.

Sept. 20—Ruben Gomez fired a three-hitter, all by Bobby Gene Smith, in a 5-1 victory at St. Louis. Mays' three hits give him the batting lead at .340. He also stole his thirtieth base, becoming the first man to do it three times since Kiki Cuyler in 1930.

Sept. 28—The Giants concluded their first S.F. season with a 7-2 victory over the Cardinals. Mays belted three hits, including a homer, to finish with a .347 average (highest of his career), but Richie Ashburn won the batting title at .349.

Oct. 8—Ernie Broglio and Marv Grissom were traded to St. Louis for Billy Muffett, Hobie Landrith, and Ben Valenzuela, a costly move because Broglio blossomed into a Cardinals star.

Dec. 3—Gomez and catcher Valmy Thomas were swapped to the Phillies for Jack Sanford, who eventually pitched S.F. to its only pennant in 1962.

1959
March 25—The Giants acquired pitcher Sam Jones from St. Louis in exchange for first baseman Bill White and third baseman Ray Jablonski.

April 10—The Giants opened the season at St. Louis with a 6-5 victory on Jackie Brandt's RBI double in the ninth. Johnny Antonelli was the winner, backed by home runs from Bob Schmidt and Willie Kirkland.

April 11—Jones made his San Francisco debut against his former teammates at St. Louis, striking out seven in a 5-2 victory. Orlando Cepeda belted two doubles and had four RBI. White, for whom Jones was traded, was hitless in four trips, striking out thrice.

April 12—The Giants swept the Cardinals when Cepeda's two-out, 400-foot, ninth-inning triple cracked a 3-3 tie in a 6-3 victory. Felipe Alou added a two-run homer.

April 18—Jack Sanford pitched a one-hitter against the Cardinals at Seals Stadium and Cepeda belted his fifth homer in four games. Sanford had a no-hitter until pinch hitter Stan Musial led off the seventh with a bloop single. St. Louis scored in the first inning when Sanford issued three walks, hit a batter, and uncorked a wild pitch.

May 2—The Giants took the league lead with a seventeen-hit attack and an 8-5 victory at Milwaukee. Willie Mays had four singles and scored four runs, and Willie Kirkland supplied the power with two home runs. Catcher Hobie Landrith also homered, while Sanford raised his record to 4-1.

May 11—A twenty-hit splurge buried the Pirates, 14-4. Sanford, Kirkland, Brandt, and Schmidt each had three hits, including two doubles and four RBI by Schmidt. A six-run sixth broke open the game.

May 13—Jones pitched a two-hitter and struck out a league-high twelve Phillies in a 6-0 victory. Jones had a no-hitter until Willie "Puddinhead" Jones singled with two down in the seventh. Mays hit a three-run homer in a five-run first; outfielder Leon Wagner also homered.

May 14—The Giants got a well-pitched gem for the second straight day when Mike McCormick fired a three-hitter and struck out nine in an 8-0 romp over the Phillies. McCormick had a no-hitter until Granny Hamner hit a pinch double in the eighth. Mays hit a three-run homer for the second day in a row; Daryl Spencer and Wagner also homered.

May 26—Sandy Koufax had a 4-2 lead entering the ninth inning at Los Angeles, but the Giants rallied for a 6-4 victory on a dramatic, pinch-hit grand-slam by Wagner. Brandt walked, Alou singled, and Spencer walked, loading the bases. Wags then smacked Art Fowler's second pitch for the game-winning homer.

June 4—Lew Burdette, who had beaten the Giants thirteen straight times since 1954, had a 5-1 lead entering the fourth inning at Milwaukee. But two home runs and a double by Cepeda drove in seven runs and powered an 11-5 victory. Cepeda started his splurge with a two-run homer in the fourth. One inning later, he ripped a 500-foot, three-run homer, the first blast to clear the left field bleachers at County Stadium. He added a two-run double in the eighth.

June 12—Mike McCormick pitched an abbreviated five-inning no-hitter while downing the Phillies 3-0 at Philadelphia. Richie Ashburn singled in the sixth, but the game was rained out and the final outcome was based on the last completed inning. Hobie Landrith hit a two-run homer and National League President Warren Giles ruled that it wasn't an official no-hitter.

June 19—Brandt's two-run single in the bottom of the tenth gave the Giants a 4-3 victory over Milwaukee before 22,934 at Seals Stadium and lifted them into first place over the Braves. It was 2-2 after nine innings, but Billy Bruton's homer off Jones pushed the Braves ahead. In the bottom of the inning, Mays walked and raced to third on Cepeda's single off Bob Buhl. Don McMahon walked Spencer and Brandt struck the game-winning blow.

June 21—Hank Aaron belted two-run homers off Antonelli, Miller, and Gordon Jones to power the Braves to victory at Seals Stadium. "It's a good park for right-handed hitters," Aaron said following the only three-homer game of his career.

June 26—McCormick three-hit the Phillies 8-0, with Brandt belting a grand slam in the five-run seventh and Mays cracking a 420-foot homer.

June 29—Davenport and Mays hit back-to-back home runs off Stan Williams in the thirteenth, giving the Giants a 6-4 victory at Los Angeles and snapping the Dodgers' seven-game win string. It was Davvy's second homer of the game.

June 30—Official scorer Charlie Park of the L.A. *Mirror* deprived Sam Jones of a no-hitter against the Dodgers. Jim Gilliam grounded to Andre Rodgers with two down in the eighth and the Giants shortstop had difficulty picking the ball up. It was ruled a controversial hit and Sad Sam finished with a one-hitter and ten strikeouts. Mays' two-run homer off Don Drysdale in the third produced a 2-0 victory.

July 30—Willie McCovey, batting .372 with twenty-nine homers and ninety-two RBI at Phoenix, made a sensational major league debut against Robin Roberts in a 7-2 victory over the Phillies at Seals Stadium. McCovey had four hits in as many trips, including two triples, to begin a brilliant career. Willie became the first player to collect four hits in his first major league game since Casey Stengel of the Dodgers, September 17, 1912.

August 2—McCovey hit his first of 521 major league homers, a two-run shot off the Pirates' Ron Kline, in a 5-3 victory. McCovey boosted his average to .500 (9-18) and Antonelli won his fifteenth game.

August 5—McCovey continued to tear the cover off the ball, blasting two homers off Bob Buhl in a 4-1 victory over the Braves. Mays added a home run and Sanford was the winner as San Francisco climbed into first place.

August 7—Mays' two-out, ninth-inning single beat the Reds 3-2, giving him two singles and a double in support of Antonelli's sixteenth victory.

August 9—Don Newcombe was 4-0 against the Giants in '59 until Cepeda's tenth-inning home run produced a 4-3 victory over the Reds for Sanford.

August 10—The Giants trailed 2-0 entering the ninth at St. Louis, but rallied off Larry Jackson to post a 3-2 victory. Wagner started the surge with a one-out pinch single, and singles by Davenport and Mays ruined the shutout bid. McCovey's infield single made it 2-2 and, after Cepeda struck out, Kirkland cracked a run-scoring double.

August 11—Willie Kirkland was the hero again with four RBI, including a game-winning single in the tenth for a 5-4 victory at St. Louis. Kirkland belted a three-run homer in the first and scored a run in the fourth, but it was 4-4 after nine. Mays doubled and scored on Kirkland's hit in the tenth.

August 13—The Cubs and the Giants set a National League record when their regulation game consumed 3 hours and 50 minutes. Chicago hit five home runs and belted nineteen hits at Wrigley Field, winning 20-9. Mays and Kirkland homered for the Giants. George Altman hit two for the winners.

August 25—Antonelli became the league's first eighteen-game winner and hit a two-run homer in a 12-5 runaway at Pittsburgh. Spencer also homered for the Giants.

August 31—Sandy Koufax struck out eighteen Giants for a new National League record, erasing Dizzy Dean's seventeen, but needed Wally Moon's three-run homer in the ninth to win 5-2 before a crowd of 82,974.

Sept. 11—The Giants lost to the Phillies 1-0 on a three-hitter by Robin Roberts, who gained revenge for McCovey's blockbuster debut. The Phillies ace held the rookie first baseman hitless this time, snapping his twenty-two-game hitting streak which fell one short of the National League record for a rookie held by Richie Ashburn.

Sept. 12—Jones became a twenty-game winner by downing the Phillies 9-1 and vaulting the Giants into the league lead by one game. Cepeda backed the four-hitter with a home run.

Sept. 17—The Giants enjoyed their final moment of glory for the season when Mays' four hits and five RBIs pounded Warren Spahn and the Braves 13-6 for a two-game lead with eight games to go. Sanford was the winner and Eddie Bressoud and Davenport hit homers to neutralize a pair by third baseman Eddie Mathews.

Sept. 20—The final game at Seals Stadium attracted 22,923, but wasn't a joyous occasion. The Dodgers won 8-2 behind Johnny Podres, sweeping the series and knocking S.F. from first to third.

Sept. 22—Outfielder George Altman landed a telling blow to the Giants' pennant hopes with a two-run, ninth-inning homer for a 5-4 Cubs victory at Wrigley. The Giants had taken the lead with two runs in the eighth, but ex-Giant Alvin Dark triggered the winning rally off Jones and Altman came through with two away.

Sept. 23—Mays belted two homers and Cepeda one, and Antonelli had a 3-0 lead while bidding for victory number twenty, but Cal Neeman's homer in the tenth off Eddie Fisher gave the Giant-killing Cubs a 9-8 decision.

Sept. 26—Hard-luck Sam Jones pitched a seven-inning no-hitter at St. Louis, but League President Giles ruled it unofficial. Rain wiped the last two innings out, but Jones won his twenty-first game 4-0 on home runs by Mays and McCovey. It was the first no-hitter, official or not, against the Cardinals since 1919.

Oct. 5—Demolition began at Seals Stadium, a sad day for Bay Area baseball lovers.

Nov. 30—The Giants traded outfielder Jackie Brandt and pitcher Gordon Jones to the Orioles for pitchers Billy O'Dell and Billy Loes.

Dec. 15—Don Blasingame, who batted .289 for the Cardinals, was acquired by the Giants in exchange for Spencer and Wagner. The deal was made because the Giants desperately needed a leadoff batter, but it was a bust because The Blazer fizzled.

1960

April 12—The historic opener at Candlestick Park attracted 42,269 and a host of dignitaries, including Vice President Richard Nixon. Sam Jones fired a three-hitter for a 3-1 victory and Mays started a sixteen-game batting streak. The distinction of hitting the first home run at Candlestick went to ex-Giant Leon Wagner.

April 16—Jones retired seventeen straight batters and had a no-hitter until pinch hitter Walt Moryn homered with two outs in the eighth. Sad Sam settled for a one-hitter and a 6-1 victory.

April 30—Willie McCovey clouted two home runs off "cousin" Don Drysdale and the Giants posted a 6-3 victory at Los Angeles.

May 7—The Giants trailed the Pirates 5-0 entering the seventh before erupting for six runs in a 6-5 victory. The six-run seventh featured a 397-foot, inside-the-park grand slam by shortstop Eddie Bressoud off Harvey Haddix.

May 13—Mike McCormick fired a six-hit, 3-0 victory over the Dodgers to give the Giants their seventh straight victory and an 18-7 record. It also was the club's third consecutive shutout, following successive 1-0 two-hitters over the Phillies by Jones and Sanford. A bases-loaded walk won for Jones and Landrith hit an RBI single in behalf of Sanford.

May 15—Johnny Antonelli blanked the Dodgers 2-0, and Orlando Cepeda blasted a 420-foot triple to center. L.A. manager Walter Alston said it was the hardest-hit ball into the teeth of a wind he had ever seen.

June 12—As a pinch hitter, McCovey blasted his first major league grand slam, and Cepeda bashed a three-run double in a 16-7 romp over the Braves. The game consumed three hours and fifty-two minutes, equaling the major league record for nine innings.

June 18—Manager Bill Rigney was fired by Horace Stoneham despite three straight wins over the Phillies and a 33-25 record. Tom "Clancy" Sheehan took over and the Giants beat the Phillies 7-4 before losing five in a row. Sheehan finished the season with a 46-50 record.

June 24—Mays enjoyed one of his finest all-around performances in a 5-3 victory at Cincinnati. Wondrous Willie belted two home runs, singled, stole home, scored thrice, knocked in three runs, and made ten putouts.

June 30—Jack Sanford needed only ninety-one pitches to dispatch the Pirates 11-0 in the first game of a doubleheader. Mays was the hitting hero with two doubles and a home run. In the second game, Dick Stuart slugged the Bucs to an 11-6 victory with three home runs and a two-run single.

July 15—This was the famous fog game against the Dodgers. Shortly after McCovey's triple was lost in a thick mist, umpire Frank Dascoli halted the game for 24 minutes in the third inning. Three balls were dropped in the eerie conditions and the Giants were beaten, 5-3.

July 17—McCovey, batting .214 and fielding poorly, was optioned to Tacoma.

July 19—Juan Marichal's debut was as sensational as McCovey's the previous season. The Dominican right-hander hurled a no-hitter until the Phillies' Clay Dalrymple hit a pinch single with two outs in the seventh. Marichal struck out twelve and won 2-0. Two days later, Robin Roberts returned the favor, allowing the Giants only one hit, by Felipe Alou.

August 25—Mays hit an inside-the-park grand slam in a seven-run rally against the Reds, giving the Giants an 8-5 victory.

August 27—Felipe Alou ended Lew Burdette's scoreless innings streak at 32 2/3 innings with a fourth-inning homer in a 3-1 victory over the Braves. Alou's hit protected the National League record of 46 1/3 scoreless frames by the Giants' Carl Hubbell in 1933.

August 28—A 15-2 Giants victory capped a three-game series with the Braves that drew 94,047 to Candlestick Park. That raised the season total to 1,605,871, an all-time Giants record. The previous high was 1,600,793 by the 1947 New York club.

Sept. 3 — McCormick won a 1-0 pitchers' battle from Koufax at Los Angeles. Felipe Alou provided the offense with a home run.

Sept. 7—During a 6-5 loss at Milwaukee, manager Tom Sheehan emerged from the dugout to yank Jack Sanford, but the veteran right-hander beat him to the punch. Before Clancy could get to the infield, Sanford stalked past him. Sanford was fined $200 for showing up the skipper.

Sept. 15—Mays walloped three triples and a double, including a 420-foot three bagger off Turk Farrell in the eleventh inning for an 8-6 victory over the Phillies.

Sept. 19—The Giants registered their first doubleheader sweep of the year, 11-4 and 4-1 over the Cubs. Willie Kirkland cracked two homers in the opener and Bob Schmidt hit a grand slam in the nightcap.

Oct. 20—The Giants landed in Japan for the start of a sixteen-game goodwill tour headed by President Horace Stoneham and Lefty O'Doul. McCovey hit eight home runs and Mays added seven to dazzle the Japanese fans and power the Giants to an 11-4-1 record.

Oct. 31—Andre Rodgers was swapped to the Braves for Alvin Dark, who was named manager while the Giants were in Japan.

Dec. 14—Johnny Antonelli, who frequently complained about the San Francisco wind currents, and Willie Kirkland were traded to Cleveland for Harvey Kuenn during the winter meetings at St. Louis.

1961

April 12—Catcher Tom Haller's first major league hit, a seventh-inning homer, cracked a 1-1 tie and lifted the Giants to a 2-1 victory over the Pirates' Vern Law. Haller, a $50,000 bonus baby, had a second chance after right fielder Roberto Clemente dropped his foul fly. Billy Loes, making his first start since 1958, was the winner.

April 25—Willie Mays made what many regard as his finest fielding play as a San Francisco Giant in a 3-1 victory over the Dodgers. With the fleet Maury Wills on third base, Wally Moon hit a sinking liner to left center. Mays made a one-handed catch and rifled a 300-foot throw to the plate to double up Wills, who tagged at third after the catch.

April 27—The Giants swapped Don Blasingame, Bob Schmidt, and Sheldon Jones to Cincinnati for slugging catcher Ed Bailey.

April 28—Warren Spahn fired a no-hitter against the Giants in the opener of a remarkable three-game series at County Stadium in Milwaukee. Sam Jones was a 1-0 loser, yielding an unearned run in the first and pitching a five-hitter.

April 30—The incomparable Mays belted four home runs and drove in eight runs to power a 14-4 victory at Milwaukee. Jose Pagan added two homers, and Felipe Alou and Orlando Cepeda contributed one apiece as the club tied a major league record with eight home runs. The Giants also hit five homers in a 7-3 victory April 29, equaling the major league mark of thirteen homers in two games.

May 7—Cepeda's tape-measure home run helped to clobber the Phillies 7-0 at Connie Mack Stadium. The three-run homer off Robin Roberts cleared the roof of the second deck, a drive of more than 500 feet.

June 22—Mays hammered two home runs off Bob Buhl in an 8-6 loss at Milwaukee. It marked the second time in six weeks that Mays had belted a pair off Buhl, having turned the trick at Candlestick Park on May 13 with a grand slam and a two-run shot in an 8-5 victory.

June 28—The Giants and the Phillies played the longest night game in major league history. They went at it for five hours and 11 minutes before a curfew halted the proceedings with the game tied at 7-7 after fifteen innings at Philadelphia.

June 29—Mays blasted three home runs in the first game of a doubleheader at Philadelphia, the Giants winning, 8-7. He hit a pair of two-run shots off Dallas Green and a solo off Frank Sullivan.

July 4 — Orlando Cepeda accumulated eight RBI in a 19-3 debacle against the Cubs at Wrigley Field in Chicago.

July 11—San Francisco hosted the All-Star Game and 44,115 showed up on a blustery day at Candlestick. Mays doubled home the tying run in the tenth and scored the winner on Roberto Clemente's single for a 5-4 National League victory. Stu Miller gained lasting fame by being blown off the mound in the ninth and being charged with a balk.

July 29—Phillies manager Gene Mauch ordered Mays to be intentionally walked in the first inning and Cepeda followed with his first major league grand slam, giving the Giants a 4-3 victory.

August 2—Juan Marichal pitched a one-hitter against the Dodgers, winning 6-0. Tommy Davis' single in the fifth inning ruined the no-hit bid.

August 23—The Giants erupted for five home runs in the ninth inning at Cincinnati, demolishing the Reds, 14-0. The outburst tied the major league record for homers in an inning. The Giants who took part in the outburst were Cepeda, Felipe Alou, John Orsino, Mays, and Davenport. Davvy's was an inside-the-park job. The ninth inning included eleven hits by the Giants. Cepeda homered and singled in the prodigious rally, while McCovey doubled and singled.

Sept. 25—Cepeda had four RBI and catcher John Orsino had two homers in a 10-2 rout at Philadelphia. Cepeda's binge gave him 140 RBI, the most ever for a Giant first baseman. Johnny Mize had the previous high mark with 138 in 1947.

Oct. 10—The Giants lost four players to the expansion draft, stocking the New York and Houston franchises. Sam Jones and Joe Amalfitano were selected by the Colt .45s, and Hobie Landrith and Ray Daviault went to the Mets.

Nov. 30—In a trade that was to pay huge dividends for the Giants in 1962, pitchers Billy Pierce and Don Larsen joined the club in exchange for Ed Fisher, Dom Zanni, Bob Farley, and Verle Tiefenthaler. The foursome went to the White Sox in two separate deals on the same day at the winter meetings in Miami.

1962

April 10—Juan Marichal hurled a three-hitter and Willie Mays hit the first pitch Warren Spahn threw to him for a home run in a 6-0, Opening Day victory over the Braves. A crowd of 39,811 watched Juan strike out Hank Aaron three times.

April 14—Orlando Cepeda and Felipe Alou each hit two home runs in a 13-6 blasting of the Reds. The Giants were off to a 5-0 start, outscoring opponents, 37-13.

April 16—Giants showed the Dodgers what kind of a year it was going to be by clobbering L.A. 19-8 in their first Candlestick Park meeting as Mays, Alou, and Jim Davenport homered.

April 21—The Comeback Kids were at it again. Behind Cincinnati 6-1, the Giants rallied on home runs by Alou and Ed Bailey for an 8-6 victory.

April 29—The finest pitching of a championship season found Jack Sanford and Billy Pierce each firing three-hit shutouts in a 7-0, 6-0 sweep of the Cubs before 40,398. Mays' two-run homer provided the punch in the opener and Bailey homered in the nightcap.

April 30—Right-hander Gaylord Perry, a $90,000 bonus baby, made his first major league complete game a four-hit, 4-1 victory over Pittsburgh. It was his third start and it placed the Giants in first place with their sixth straight win.

May 4—Plane trouble forced a landing at Salt Lake City and the Giants did not arrive at Chicago until 6 A.M., yet they mustered enough energy for an 11-6 pounding of the Cubs. The victory was the club's tenth in a row, increasing its league lead to 2 1/2 games.

May 10—Billy O'Dell blanked Bob Gibson and the Cardinals, 6-0. Willie McCovey, substituting in left field, cracked a three-run homer to support the four-hitter.

May 26—Mays was the slugging hero with two homers, a triple, and four RBI in a 7-6 conquest of the Mets. Willie's homer in the eighth tied the game, and he won it with a two-run homer off Jay Hook in the tenth.

May 27—Manager Casey Stengel made his first Candlestick Park visit with the Mets, but a brawl and the Giants' 7-1, 6-5 sweep spoiled the show for the venerable skipper. Cepeda and pitcher Roger Craig went at it, as did Mays and Mets' infielder Elio Chacon.

June 1—Giants made their first regular-season return to New York since 1957 and thrilled many of their old fans among the 43,742 in attendance with a 9-6 victory over the Mets. McCovey hammered two homers off Craig, Mays added number seventeen, and Davenport notched his first major league grand slam.

June 12—Billy O'Dell struck out twelve batters at Philadelphia and went the distance for a 4-3 victory as Ed Bailey belted a home run in the top of the twelfth to break a tie.

July 4—The Giants treated their fans to plenty of fireworks in an 11-4, 10-3 sweep of the Mets. McCovey drove in seven runs in the opener with a pair of homers and two sacrifice flies. Mays registered five RBI with a pair of homers in the second game. It still was a "costly" day for the home team, though, because the Giants gave $150,000 to sign Santa Clara pitcher Bob Garibaldi.

July 6—Marichal struck out thirteen Dodgers, a season high for the Giants, in a 12-3 romp over L.A. The victory squared the series and S.F. won it 10-3 the next day on homers by Mays and Davenport.

August 6—Mays belted five hits in as many trips, blasting two home runs and registering five RBI in a 9-2 rout of the Phillies. Lefty Billy Pierce won his tenth game of the season.

August 10—Mays' first-inning homer and four RBI powered the Giants to an 11-2 rout of the Dodgers in the opener of a three-game series with the Dodgers, pulling S.F. to within 4 1/2 games of first-place L.A.

August 11—Willie McCovey's three-run, pinch homer off Don Drysdale with two outs in the sixth inning produced a 5-4 victory over the Dodgers. The blow snapped Drysdale's eleven-game win string, gave Billy Pierce his two-hundredth major league victory, and slashed the L.A. lead to 3 1/2 games.

August 12—The Dodgers were furious because excessive water between first and second in the first two games of the series at Candlestick Park hampered their running game. Umpire Bill Jackowski ordered sand to be placed in the area prior to the final game of the series, but it didn't matter. Marichal's four-hitter and Jose Pagan's hitting produced a 5-1 victory, cutting the lead to 2 1/2 games.

August 23—Reserve infielder Ernie Bowman almost single-handedly beat the Mets 2-1 at New York, ending a tailspin that had the Giants drop six out of seven. Bowman homered in the fifth and added the game-winning single in the tenth.

August 24—Orlando Cepeda belted five hits, including two homers, and totaled four RBI in a 6-0 romp at Philadelphia. Billy O'Dell pitched the shutout.

Sept. 3—The opener of a crucial, four-game series found the Giants winning their first game ever at Dodger Stadium, 7-3, after losing ten in a row at Los Angeles. Jack Sanford registered his twentieth victory of the season and his fourteenth in a row, and Mays and Haller homered.

Sept. 5—After the Dodgers squared the series with a 5-4 victory the previous day, Marichal and Bob Bolin collaborated on a 3-0 shutout. Juan suffered a leg injury in the sixth while beating fleet Willie Davis to first base, and Bolin mopped up.

Sept. 6—The Giants rallied with four runs in the ninth to down the Dodgers 9-6 and climb within 1 1/2 games of the lead. Drysdale was behind 4-0 after three, but Frank Howard's two-run homer off O'Dell created a 4-4 tie in the fourth. Harvey Kuenn's RBI-hit in the eighth was neutralized by Tommy Davis' homer, and it was 5-5 entering the ninth. Cepeda's bases-loaded walk cracked the tie and Harvey Kuenn followed with a three-run double off Ron Perranoski.

Sept. 11—Jack Sanford blanked the Pirates 2-0 for his sixteenth consecutive victory and a 22-6 record. Felipe Alou belted a home run. Sanford, unbeaten since June 17, had his string snapped on September 15 in a 5-1 loss at Pittsburgh.

Sept. 12—Mays collapsed in the dugout at Cincinnati, suffering from fatigue, during a 4-1 loss to the Reds. The Giants went on to drop six in a row, seemingly dropping out of the race.

Sept. 19—Haller's two home runs helped to snap the losing streak in a 7-4 victory at St. Louis.

Sept. 21—Gaylord Perry, recalled from Tacoma, gave the Giants a lift with an 11-5 victory at Houston. Mays collected four hits.

Sept. 26—Billy Pierce raised his record at Candlestick to 11-0 and Haller knocked in four runs with a home run and a double to defeat St. Louis 6-3 and keep Giant flag hopes alive.

Sept. 29—The Giants had a chance to tie for the lead with a makeup doubleheader against Houston. Spirits were high when Sanford's twenty-fourth victory downed the Colt .45s in the opener, 12-5. But Bob Bruce defeated the Giants 4-2 in the second game, keeping them one game behind with one game remaining.

Sept. 30—One of the most tension-filled days in San Francisco baseball history found Mays' eighth inning homer off right-hander Turk Farrell edging the Astros, 2-1. The Giants then huddled around clubhouse radios and reacted deliriously when Gene Oliver of the Cardinals hit a home run to down the Dodgers 1-0 and force a playoff.

Oct. 1—Pierce's three-hit pitching and two home runs by Mays guided the Giants to a decisive 8-0 victory in the opening playoff game before 32,660 at Candlestick. Mays's forty-eighth and forty-ninth homers gave him the major league lead and Pierce completed a 12-0 season at home. Cepeda and Davenport also homered for the Giants, but the issue was decided in the first inning when Felipe Alou doubled with two away and Mays bashed a home run to right center off Sandy Koufax.

Oct. 2—The playoffs shifted to Los Angeles and the Giants jumped to a 5-0 lead. But the Dodgers, shut out for 35 innings, erupted for seven runs in the sixth and won it in the ninth, 8-7 on Maury Wills's running and poor fielding by Gaylord Perry.

Oct. 3—The Giants won their only San Francisco pennant in dramatic fashion at Dodger Stadium, rallying with four runs in an improbable ninth for a 6-4 victory. The Dodgers went ahead, 3-2 in the sixth on Duke Snider's single and Tommy Davis' homer, and made it 4-2 in the seventh with the help of Wills' record 103d and 104th stolen bases. With Ed Roebuck pitching, Matty Alou triggered the winning rally in the ninth with a pinch single. Kuenn forced him, but McCovey and Felipe Alou walked, loading the bases. Mays singled off Roebuck's glove for 4-3, leaving the bases loaded. Stan Williams took over and Cepeda's sacrifice fly produced a tie. A wild pitch sent Mays to second and Ed Bailey was walked intentionally, again filling the sacks. Davenport then walked, forcing home the go-ahead run. Pierce, in relief, retired the

Dodgers in order in the bottom of the ninth and the jubilant Giants headed for the World Series.

Oct. 4—The World Series seemed anticlimactic as Whitey Ford downed the Giants 6-2 in Game 1 before 43,852 gloomy fans at Candlestick. Clete Boyer's seventh-inning homer cracked a 2-2 tie.

Oct. 5—Sanford pitched a three-hitter and McCovey blasted a home run to give the Giants a Series-squaring, 2-0 victory in Game 2. A crowd of 43,910 watched at Candlestick.

Oct. 7—The Series shifted to New York and 71,434 saw Yankee right-hander Bill Stafford prevail over Pierce, 3-2. Stafford had the Giants blanked until Bailey hit a two-run homer in the ninth.

Oct. 8—Second baseman Chuck Hiller became the first National Leaguer to hit a grand-slam homer in the World Series, powering a 7-3 Giants victory in Game 4. Hiller's blow off Marshall Bridges snapped a 2-2 tie in the seventh. Ex-Yankee Don Larsen was the winner in relief; Haller also homered for the Giants.

Oct. 10—The Yankees took a 3-2 edge in the Series when Tom Tresh's three-run homer in the eighth inning erased a 2-2 tie and gave New York a 5-2 victory. Jose Pagan homered for the Giants.

Oct. 15—After three days of rain, the Giants once again tied the Series when Pierce's 5-2 victory shackled the Yankees before 43,948 at Candlestick. Cepeda, hitless in twelve previous Series at bats, had three hits and two RBI.

Oct. 16—The moment of truth, with 43,948 at the edge of their seats, came with two on and two out in the bottom of the ninth. McCovey lined sharply to second baseman Bobby Richardson and the Yankees won the Series, 1-0. Ralph Terry pitched a four-hitter and had a perfect game until Sanford's two-out single in the sixth. The Yankees scored on Tony Kubek's double-play grounder in the fifth.

Nov. 30—Pitcher Dick LeMay and utility outfielder Manny Mota were traded to Houston for Joe Amalfitano, a former Giants bonus baby. It wasn't a good move because Mota went on to become the National League's career pinch-hit leader.

Dec. 15—Another questionable deal sent pitchers Mike McCormick and Stu Miller and catcher John Orsino to the Orioles in exchange for pitchers Jack Fisher and Billy Hoeft and catcher Jim Coker.

1963

April 9—The defending National League champions opened the season with a 9-2 romp at Houston. Home runs by Willie Mays, Willie McCovey, Orlando Cepeda, and Felipe Alou powered a seventeen-hit attack. It was the first time four homers were smacked against the Colt .45s.

April 10—Giant catcher Ed Bailey's pinch-hit grand slam off Don McMahon defeated the Colt .45s, 8-7.

April 16—Opening Day at Candlestick resulted in Juan Marichal's six-hit, 7-0 victory over the Dodgers. It was the great right-hander's fourteenth consecutive victory at home.

May 3—It was Willie Mays Day at the Polo Grounds and 49,431 paid to honor the Giants superstar. He received a telegram from President John Kennedy. Wondrous Willie doubled and knocked in a run in a 5-3 victory. Duke Snider hit two homers for the Mets and, as usual, was overshadowed by Mays.

May 11—Sandy Koufax pitched a no-hitter and downed the Giants 8-0 at Los Angeles. The Dodgers lefty had a perfect game until Bailey walked with one out in the eighth.

June 2—Mays belted three home runs in a 6-4 victory at St. Louis. The victims were Ernie Broglio, Bob Humphreys, and Bobby Shantz. Mays was hitless in eighteen trips before connecting off Broglio in the first. The blast off Humphreys carried an estimated 480 feet.

June 11—Juan Marichal scattered seven hits and Willie McCovey took care of the offense with a three-run homer in the sixth for a 3-0 victory at Dodger Stadium.

June 12—Right-hander Bobby Bolin set a San Francisco Giants record with fourteen strikeouts in a 3-1 victory over the Cubs. McCovey supplied the pop by belting two home runs off Bob Buhl for the third time in his career.

June 15—Juan Marichal pitched the first Giants no-hitter in thirty-four years, a 1-0 victory over Houston before a crowd of 18,869 at Candlestick. The Giants collected only three hits off Dick Drott, scoring in the eighth on a leadoff double by Davenport and a two-out two-bagger by Chuck Hiller. The no-hitter was the first for the franchise since Carl Hubbell smothered the Pirates 11-0 on May 8, 1929.

June 22—Billy O'Dell, an avid golfer, said he wanted to work quickly so he could get home to watch the U.S. Open on television. He took only one hour and 58 minutes in a two-hit, 3-0 triumph at

Milwaukee. But this wasn't the Giants' fastest game. Jack Sanford won in one hour and 36 minutes on June 14.

July 2—Marichal defeated Warren Spahn 1-0 on Mays' one-out homer in the sixteenth inning in what is regarded as the finest game in S.F. history. It was a classic pitching duel because Spahn, forty-two years old, was 11-3 with five straight victories and Marichal was 12-3 with eight in a row entering the game. A crowd of 15,921 witnessed the gem, which concluded at 12:31 A.M. in Candlestick.

July 7—The Giants' top regular-season crowd (42,787) watched Jim Ray Hart make a sensational major league debut in the opener of a doubleheader with the Cardinals. Hart doubled, walked with the bases loaded, singled, and scored the tying run on Bailey's double in the thirteenth. He was intentionally walked in the fifteenth as S.F. pulled out a 4-3 victory. In the second game, Bob Gibson hit Hart with a pitch in the first inning, cracking the rookie's shoulder blade.

July 12—Willie McCovey hit a pair of two-run homers off Art Mahaffey in a 7-5 loss at Philadelphia. The blasts made Stretch the number one home-run hitter among Giants left fielders with twenty-five. Monte Irvin held the record with twenty-four in 1951.

July 19—McCovey extended his hitting streak to twenty-four games in a 5-2 loss at Cincinnati. The streak was the best in the bigs in 1963 and tied the Giants' modern record, shared by Freddie Lindstrom in 1930 and Don Mueller in 1955. Joe Nuxhall of the Reds snapped the string the next day.

August 22—Mays flashed his all-around excellence in an 8-6 victory over the Braves. In addition to a game-winning single, he scored on a passed ball only four or five feet behind catcher Del Crandall, walked and scored another run, robbed Lee Maye of extra bases with a diving catch in the third, and broke up a double play to keep the winning rally alive and set the stage for Felipe Alou's three-run homer.

August 27—Mays hit his four-hundredth career homer, a shot off the Cardinals' Curt Simmons, to power a 7-2 victory.

Sept. 3—Juan Marichal defeated the Cubs 16-3 for his first twenty-win season.

Sept. 7—Home runs by McCovey, Mays and Cepeda defeated Don Drysdale and the Dodgers, 5-3. The round-tripper was McCovey's tenth among his twenty-four lifetime hits off Drysdale.

Sept. 10—The Giants lost 4-2 at New York, but Jesus and Matty Alou were pinch hitters and Felipe started, marking the first time three brothers appeared in the same batting order in major league history.

Sept. 15—The Giants had an all-Alou outfield for one inning during a 13-5 romp at Pittsburgh. The eighteen-hit attack featured four apiece by Cepeda and Hiller. Mays scored three runs and knocked in four.

Sept. 22—McCovey rapped three home runs off the Mets in the first four innings during a 13-4 runaway. The blasts accounted for five RBI and included two-run pokes off Jay Hook and Galen Cisco. The outburst hiked his total to forty-three homers, tops in the league. He finished with 44.

Dec. 3—One of the biggest trades in Giants history sent Felipe Alou and Ed Bailey to Milwaukee in exchange for pitchers Bob Shaw and Bob Hendley and catcher Del Crandall.

1964

April 14—Opening Day at Candlestick Park produced a surprise when the Giants purchased Duke Snider and his 403 lifetime homers from the Mets. Mays hit two home runs off Warren Spahn and Haller and Orlando Cepeda and Jim Ray Hart homered in an 8-4 victory over the Braves.

April 15 — Mays' three-run homer in the tenth inning lifted the Giants to a 10-8 victory over the Braves, who had taken the lead in the top of the inning.

April 22—McCovey walloped three home runs in an 8-6 victory at Milwaukee. Stretch connected off Denny LeMaster in the second, Tony Cloninger in the third, and Phil Niekro in the fifth.

May 16—The Giants rallied with two outs in the fifteenth to edge the Mets, 6-4. Tom Haller started things with a single and Jim Davenport followed with a game-ending homer off Galen Cisco.

May 17—The Giants registered their second double shutout in their San Francisco history when Bob Hendley and Ron Herbel pitched a 6-0, 1-0 sweep of the Mets. Hendley fired a three-hitter in the opener and Herbel, making his first major league start, hurled a seven-hitter and struck out eight in the nightcap.

May 31—The Mets had won the first two games of the series, so 57,037 jammed Shea Stadium for a doubleheader with the Giants. S.F. won the opener 5-3, but blew a 6-1 lead in the second game, and the game was tied 6-6 in the seventh. The score remained tied until the Giants scored twice in the twenty-third for an 8-6 victory, ending the longest game (7 hours and 23 minutes) in history. The twin bill took thirty-two innings and lasted 9 hours and 52 minutes. The Giants won it on Davenport's triple, Cap Peterson's intentional walk, Del Crandall's ground-rule double, and Jesus Alou's run-scoring infield single. Haller and Alou each had four of the seventeen S.F. hits, and Gaylord Perry struck out nine in ten shutout innings of relief. Several years later, Perry admitted this was the game in which he began experimenting with a spitter.

June 17—McCovey's pinch-hit home run with one on in the ninth downed Joe Nuxhall and the Reds, 3-2.

June 20—Harvey Kuenn belted three singles, a double, and a home run to crush the Cardinals 14-3 at St. Louis.

June 21—Hal Lanier, playing in his fourth major league game, ripped two singles, a double, and a home run to help the Giants overcome the Cardinals 7-3 at St. Louis.

June 22—McCovey slugged a grand slam off John Tsitouris in the sixth inning at Cincinnati to lift the Giants from a 0-2 deficit to a 6-2 victory.

June 24—Ron Herbel struck out fourteen batters and outdueled Jim O'Toole for a 2-1 victory at Cincinnati.

June 27—Tom Haller belted two homers, including a three-run shot, to fuel a 9-1 romp at Los Angeles.

June 28—Herbel shaded Don Drysdale and the Dodgers 1-0 at L.A., with ninth-inning relief from Billy O'Dell.

July 10—Rookie Jesus Alou slashed five singles and a home run during a 10-3 romp over the Cubs at Wrigley Field. Alou connected off six different pitchers in the only six-hit performance in S.F. history. It was the first six-hit effort in the National League in four years.

July 26—Sandy Koufax had a 2-1 lead at Dodger Stadium until the Giants erupted for four runs in the ninth for a 5-4 victory, their first ever over the great lefty at L.A. Mays doubled for a 3-2 lead in the dramatic ninth, and Jim Ray Hart followed with a 400-foot homer off Koufax.

August 14—Former teammate Ed Bailey had the only hit as Bob Bolin fired a one-hit, 3-0 victory over the Braves in his finest major league performance.

August 24—A crowd of 36,034 at Los Angeles gave Willie Mays a standing ovation after his two spectacular catches paced a 4-2 Giants victory. Each catch was regarded better than his fabled 1954 World Series grab of Vic Wertz's long drive. Mays robbed Ron Fairly of extra bases when he made a catch on his knees in left center. Then he took at least a double away from Tommy Davis with a superb catch in right center.

Sept. 1—Masonari Murakami, the first Japanese to play in the majors, made his debut in a 4-1 loss at New York. Murakami went on to pitch eleven scoreless innings in his first five games.

Sept. 12—Orlando Cepeda hit a grand slam and a two-run homer for six RBI in a 9-1 trampling of the Phillies.

Oct. 3—Mays hit home runs off the Cubs' Bob Buhl and Lindy McDaniel, but the Giants were eliminated from pennant contention after a 10-7 loss to the Cubs.

1965

Feb. 1—The Giants reacquired catcher Ed Bailey by sending pitcher Billy O'Dell to the Braves.

April 12—Juan Marichal pitched nine scoreless innings on Opening Day at Pittsburgh but the Pirates and Bob Veale ruined the Giants' day with a 1-0 victory on Bob Bailey's tenth-inning homer off the Dominican Dandy.

May 2—Willie McCovey hit two home runs, including the game-winner in the tenth off Bob Miller, for a 4-2 victory at Dodger Stadium.

May 4—Dissatisfied with their roster, the Giants began a series of May swaps by sending pitcher Jim Duffalo to the Reds for reliever Bill Henry. On May 22, Jose Pagan went to Pittsburgh for Dick Schofield in a trade of infielders. Finally, on May 30, Bailey, Harvey Kuenn, and Bob Hendley were dealt to the Cubs for young slugger Len Gabrielson and catcher Dick Bertell.

June 20—Jim Ray Hart was the hitting hero in a 4-3, 7-3 sweep of the Pirates at Candlestick. In the opener, he hit an RBI double in the seventh inning for a 2-2 tie and cracked a 420-foot, game-winning homer off Alvin McBean leading off the fifteenth. Hart added a two-run triple in the second game.

June 28—Juan Marichal blanked the Dodgers 5-0 for his tenth straight victory over them at Candlestick.

July 10—Marichal was heading for his third career one-hitter with two down in the ninth, but settled for a two-hit, 7-0 victory over the Phillies. Juan posted his seventh shutout among fourteen wins and Jim Davenport stroked a home run.

July 19—The Giants signed left-hander Warren Spahn following his release by the Mets. Spahn, forty-four years old, came to the Giants with a 360-241 lifetime record.

July 27—Spahn pitched a four-hitter in his second start for S.F., picking Lou Brock off base twice, but was a 3-0 loser to the Cardinals' Bob Purkey.

August 8—Spahn hurled his 361st victory, and his first with the Giants, when he won at St. Louis, 6-4. Baseball's number six all-time winner received home run support from Mays, McCovey, and Jesus Alou.

August 15—Murakami made his first major league start and Hart hammered his first grand slam, the Giants overcoming a 4-1 Philadelphia lead to win, 15-9.

August 22—Bloody Sunday at Candlestick and 42,807 watched in amazement as Marichal struck the Dodgers' John Roseboro on the head with a bat. Marichal, who was suspended for nine days and fined $1,750, scuffled with the L.A. catcher in the third inning and there was a 14-minute delay while order was restored. Then, Mays's 450-foot, three-run homer beat Sandy Koufax 4-3 before the largest Giants crowd of the season.

August 26—The Giants were short of pitchers during an 8-0 loss to the Pirates, so outfielder Matty Alou went to the mound and fired two scoreless innings, striking out three.

August 27—The largest crowd of the season, 56,167 at New York, saw McCovey smash two home runs and Mays one in a 9-2 victory over the Mets. Mays' fortieth homer was his sixteenth of the month, equaling the National League record set by Ralph Kiner in 1949.

August 29—Mays hit his record seventeenth home run of the month, a three-run blow off Jack Fisher in the third, to power an 8-3 victory at New York. The homer was Mays' 494th, passing Lou Gehrig and making Willie fifth on the all-time list. Mays was the unanimous National League Player of the Month for his seventeen homers and twenty-nine RBI.

Sept. 7—Hart knocked in all three S.F. runs and Bob Shaw shackled the Dodgers 3-1 at L.A. to give the Giants the league lead.

Sept. 9—Marichal four-hit the Astros 4-0 for his tenth home win, Tom Haller accounting for two RBI with a home run and a sacrifice fly. The victory maintained the Giants' half-game lead over the Reds and the Dodgers, who downed the Cubs 1-0 on Koufax's perfect no-hitter over Bob Hendley's one hitter.

Sept. 10—The score was tied and the bases were loaded when McCovey strode to the plate as a pinch hitter against the Reds' Ted Abernathy. Stretch hit a grand slam and the Giants went on to a 5-3 victory.

Sept. 13—Mays hit his five-hundredth career homer and his forty-seventh of the season in the fourth inning at Houston against Don Nottebart, and Juan Marichal pitched his twenty-second victory, 5-1. The win was the Giants' eleventh straight and gave them a 2 1/2-game league lead.

Sept. 14—The Giants were behind 5-2 entering the ninth inning at Houston. They scored a run, and Jesus Alou was on base with two outs and Mays at the plate. Everyone knew Willie was going for the fences, and he was embroiled in a battle with reliever Claude Raymond. Mays fouled off four 3-2 pitches before sending one soaring for a 450-foot home run and a 5-5 tie. Davenport's pinch single in the tenth produced a 7-5 victory, the club's twelfth straight.

Sept. 16—Bob Bolin was a 5-1 winner at Houston, extending the winning streak to fourteen games.

Sept. 28—Mays hit his fifty-first home run in the first inning off Larry Jaster, tying Johnny Mize's all-time Giants record, in an 8-6 loss to the Cardinals at Candlestick. It also was Willie's two-thousandth career game.

Oct. 3—Mays's fifty-second home run, coming against the Reds' Billy McCool on the final day of the season, established a new Giants single-season record and powered a 6-3 victory.

Dec. 1—Reserve outfielder Matty Alou was traded to Pittsburgh for pitcher Joe Gibbon and catcher Ozzie Virgil. Mateo went on to win a batting championship for the Bucs.

1966

April 12—Juan Marichal pitched a perfect game for six innings and finished with a three-hit, 9-1 rout of the Cubs on Opening Day. Willie Mays contributed a two-run homer.

April 24—Mays hit his 511th home run, a 415-foot, two-run shot off Jim Owens at Houston, to tie Giant great Mel Ott's National League record. The Giants won, 4-2.

May 4—Mays, in a 3-for-23 slump after his 511th homer, belted Claude Osteen's first pitch in the fifth inning for number 512, becoming the all-time National League record-holder. Osteen had gone 96 2/3 innings without yielding a gopher ball prior to the historic blast. Joe Gibbon pitched a four-hit, 6-1 victory over the Dodgers at Candlestick.

May 7—The Giants erupted for thirteen runs in the third inning at St. Louis and crushed the Cardinals 15-2 behind Juan Marichal.

May 8—Apparently feeling they had more than enough offense following the outburst, and unable to convince Orlando Cepeda to shift from first base, the Giants swapped The Baby Bull to the Cardinals for left-hander Ray Sadecki. It was a controversial swap because of Cepeda's popularity. Sadecki felt the heat and went 3-7 the rest of the season, whereas Cepeda kept hitting and went on to become the league's MVP in 1967.

May 13—Jim Davenport's home run in the seventeenth inning beat the Mets 5-4 at New York. Bob Priddy pitched three scoreless innings for the victory, the Giants' twelfth in a row.

May 17—Mays recorded three throwing gems in a 2-1 loss at Los Angeles. Playing right field because of an injury, Mays nailed Willie Davis at third in the fourth; robbed Maury Wills and doubled Don Drysdale off first in the sixth; and threw to Willie McCovey, whose relay nipped Wills at the plate in the eleventh.

May 26—Marichal went the distance in a six-hit, fourteen-inning victory over the Phillies. Jim Bunning was taken out in the eleventh after hooking up with Juan in a scoreless duel, and the Giants scored the only run of the game in the fourteenth on Davenport's triple and Bob Barton's sacrifice fly.

May 31—Marichal defeated the Reds 5-3 at Cincinnati for a 10-0 record, best in the majors.

June 27—Mays' homer produced a 2-1 victory over Bob Gibson at St. Louis. It was his 522d homer, passing Ted Williams and into the number three spot on the all-time list. Ron Herbel was the winner.

July 9—The Giants staged two great comebacks to edge the Reds 8-7 in twelve innings. McCovey drove in the club's first six runs, belting two homers among four hits. Stretch hit a two-run shot in the first, but the Reds were ahead entering the bottom of the ninth. Mays singled and McCovey's 420-foot homer to center made it 6-6. After the Reds scored an unearned run in the twelfth,

Tito Fuentes doubled with two outs and Tom Haller hit a homer for the win.

July 8—Davenport hit a pinch-hit grand slam and infielder Bob Schroder hit a game-tying single in his major league debut. Marichal downed the Cardinals 7-2 for his fourteenth victory.

July 22—Gaylord Perry struck out fifteen Phillies, the most by a Giants pitcher since Christy Mathewson's sixteen in 1903, in a two-hit, 4-1 victory. Perry, who fanned Richie Allen four times, had a no-hitter until Clay Dalrymple singled with one out in the eighth.

August 12—Perry registered a three-hit, 1-0 victory over the Astros on Mays' 400-foot homer off Mike Cuellar in the ninth.

August 16—Mays hit a solo homer off the Cardinals' Al Jackson in the third inning of Perry's 3-1 victory. It was Willie's 534th, tying Jimmy Foxx for number two on the all-time chart.

August 17—Mays waited only one day to pass Foxx, hitting 535 off the Cardinals' Ray Washburn in the fourth inning, triggering a 4-3 victory. Plate umpire Chris Pelekoudas was so excited over the record smash, he was the first to shake Willie's hand, later apologizing to National League President Warren Giles for the instinctive gesture.

August 20—Gaylord Perry defeated the Braves 6-1 for a 20-2 record, becoming the majors' first twenty-game winner. He then proceeded to lose six straight.

August 31—Marichal mastered the Mets 2-1 at New York and the victory marked the first time the club had two twenty-game winners the same season since Sal Maglie and Larry Jansen in 1951.

Sept. 6—Sadecki pitched his finest game with the Giants, firing a three-hit, 6-0 victory at Dodger Stadium.

Sept. 7—Mays had a sore leg, so he was playing right field instead of center. He singled in the twelfth and took off on Frank Johnson's single to right center, scoring the winning run by knocking the ball out of catcher John Roseboro's glove for a 3-2 victory at L.A.

Sept. 16—Willie McCovey hit what is regarded as the longest home run in Candlestick Park history, a 500-foot bolt to right, in a 5-4 loss to the Mets.

Sept. 17—McCovey hit three home runs against the Mets, the first two off Dennis Ribant and a two-run shot in the tenth off Larry Miller for a 6-4 victory.

Oct. 1—The Giants swept a doubleheader at Pittsburgh, 5-4 and 2-0, to leapfrog over the Bucs into second place, two games behind the Dodgers. Outfielder Ollie Brown drove in three runs with a homer and a double in the opener, but the best was yet to come. Bob Bolin fired a one-hitter and belted a run-scoring double in the second game, Bill Mazeroski spoiling the no-hit bid in the second inning.

Oct. 2—There was an outside chance for a San Francisco pennant if the Giants won and the Dodgers lost a doubleheader at Philadelphia, a situation that would have forced a makeup of an S.F. rainout. The Giants did their part; McCovey's two-run pinch homer in a four-run eleventh downed the Bucs, 7-4. But L.A. split at Philly and won by 1 1/2 games.

Dec. 13—One of the Giants' greatest trades sent Bob Priddy and Cap Peterson to the Senators for left-hander Mike McCormick, who was the Cy Young Award winner in 1967.

1967

April 13—Mays and McCovey homered, and Gaylord Perry pitched a four-hitter in a 2-0 victory at Atlanta.

April 29—Juan Marichal struck out eleven and fired a five-hit shutout in a 5-0 victory at Los Angeles. It was the middle game of the Giants' first-ever, three-game sweep at Dodger Stadium.

May 3—Marichal hurled a four-hitter at New York, winning 8-0 and boosting his career record against the Mets to 18-0, including eight shutouts.

May 4—Mike McCormick posted his first victory for the Giants since 1962 and launched his Cy Young Award campaign with a 3-1 decision at New York.

May 14—Ollie Brown, two days after being struck on the jaw by a Claude Raymond pitch, gained revenge against the Houston reliever with a two-run, 400-foot homer off him for a 4-3 victory over the Astros. Brown also doubled and scored in the two-run eighth off Don Wilson before connecting in the ninth with two outs.

May 26—Marichal six-hit the Dodgers 4-1 for his eighth straight win following an 0-3 start. Juan extended his mastery over L.A. to 14-0 at Candlestick, raised his career record to 138-61 and upped his won-lost percentage to .693, surpassing Whitey Ford's major league record of .690.

June 1—Gaylord Perry two-hit the Pirates 7-1, and catcher Dick Dietz belted his first major league home run, a three-run shot off Pete Mikkelsen.

June 4—The Giants recorded the third double shutout in their San Francisco history, 7-0 and 5-0 against the Mets. Joe Gibbon pitched a four-hitter in the opener and McCormick fired an eight-hitter in the second game.

June 13—Mays' grand slam off Barry Latman in the tenth inning at Houston earned a 6-2 victory. Mays, who failed as a pinch hitter with the bases full in the sixth, connected for his first slam since 1962. The game-winning blow also was his career home run number 550. Shortstop Hal Lanier made his first error in seventy-two games.

June 29—An eleven-run first inning chased Bob Gibson and the Giants rolled to a 12-4 victory at St. Louis. The outburst came on the heels of a nineteen-hit attack in Ray Sadecki's 9-1 romp over the Cardinals on June 28.

July 4—The Mets posted an historic, 8-7 victory over the Giants at Shea Stadium. They defeated Marichal for the first time in twenty decisions, belting fourteen hits and scoring eight runs (five earned) off the flashy right-hander in 5 1/3 innings.

July 8—Marichal upped his record to 15-0 against the Dodgers at Candlestick, but Jim Ray Hart was the hero of the 8-4 victory. Hart belted two homers, including the one-hundredth of his career, and pulled the Giants from a 4-2 deficit to a 5-4 lead with a three-run wallop off Don Drysdale in the fifth.

July 9—Mike McCormick, who entered the starting rotation on June 19, went ten innings to beat Claude Osteen and the Dodgers 1-0 on a five-hitter.

July 15—McCormick defeated the Astros 9-1 for his eighth consecutive victory and a 12-3 record.

July 23—Jim Ray Hart went wild in a doubleheader at Chicago. His two homers off Ferguson Jenkins won the opener 5-2, and he added a home run and a double in a 6-3 loss to Joe Niekro in the nightcap.

July 31—Jack Hiatt's pinch-hit grand slam off Elroy Face cracked a 4-4 tie and downed the Pirates 8-4 at Candlestick.

August 6—Jesus Alou belted seven hits in eleven trips, lifting his average to .303, in a 9-7, 4-1 doubleheader sweep of the Mets.

August 27—McCormick fired a 2-0 victory over the Braves for his second straight five-hit shutout. He previously had downed the Cardinals 6-0 on August 23.

Sept. 1—In one of the greatest wasted efforts in S.F. history, Gaylord Perry pitched sixteen shutout innings at Cincinnati and didn't get a decision in the Giants' 1-0, twenty-one-inning victory. Perry, who scattered ten hits and struck out twelve, was 15-17 with nine one-run losses during the season. Frank Linzy fired five shutout innings for the win in the longest night game (5 hours and 41 minutes and twenty-one innings) in National League history.

Sept. 15—McCovey belted two home runs off Steve Blass, including a two-run game winner in the sixth, to power Perry's 6-3 triumph at Pittsburgh.

Sept. 22—Tom Haller's ninth-inning homer off Alvin McBean edged the Pirates 1-0 for Ray Sadecki, who pitched a four-hitter and struck out seven.

Sept. 23—The Giants were behind 4-3 in the eighth, but Willie McCovey's grand-slam homer off Juan Pizarro produced an 8-4 victory over the Pirates.

Sept. 26—Mays hit two home runs in an 8-3 rout of the Mets, increasing his National League record to fifty-six two-homer games.

Sept. 27—McCovey hit his third grand slam of the season, and his second in four days, handing Tug McGraw and the Mets a 7-2 defeat.

Sept. 30—McCovey's run-scoring single in the sixth inning gave the Giants a 3-2 victory over the Phillies in the opener of a doubleheader and clinched second place for the club.

Oct. 1—McCormick pitched a five-hit, 2-1 victory over the Phillies to finish his Cy Young Award season with a 22-10 record and a 2.84 ERA. His victory total tied Jim Lonborg of Boston and Earl Wilson of Detroit for the major league lead.

1968

Feb. 13—Catcher Tom Haller was traded to the Dodgers for infielders Ron Hunt and Nate Oliver, marking the first deal between the clubs since Jackie Robinson was acquired by the Giants in 1956 and did not report.

April 11—Mike McCormick pitched thirteen innings against the Pirates, yielding only six hits and one run, but was not involved in the decision in Pittsburgh's 3-1 victory.

April 14—Jim Ray Hart hammered three home runs in a 13-2, 3-1 doubleheader sweep of the Phillies. His two-run shot in the fourth inning broke a 1-1 tie in the second game.

April 23—Jim Davenport's third career grand slam downed Chris Short and Philadelphia 7-1 for Juan Marichal.

May 4—Willie McCovey set a Giants record with his eighth career grand slam in an 11-6 loss to the Cardinals' Larry Jaster. Stretch had been tied with Mel Ott, George Kelly, and Willie Mays.

May 31—Dick Dietz apparently walked with the bases loaded and no outs in the ninth inning at L.A., but plate umpire Harry Wendelstedt ruled he didn't make a sufficient effort to get out of the way of the pitch. Don Drysdale worked out of the jam, posted a 3-0 victory for a record-tying fifth straight shutout, and went on to a record for scoreless innings.

June 6—Hart belted three-run homers off Rick Wise and Turk Farrell in a 7-2 victory over the Phillies.

June 15—Marichal scattered sixteen hits in a 9-5 victory over the Mets for his sixth straight complete game and eighth win in a row. McCovey's single kayoed Tom Seaver in the first and Stretch homered on his next at bat.

June 23—McCovey clouted home runs in the first and third innings off Jim Bunning, powering Marichal's tenth straight victory, a 2-1 decision at Pittsburgh.

June 25—Bobby Bonds hit a grand slam off John Purdin in the sixth inning for a smashing major league debut in a 9-0 rout of the Dodgers. It was the first grand slam by a rookie in his first major league game since Willie Duggleby hit one for the Philadelphia Nationals in 1898! Bonds' blast stole the thunder from Ray Sadecki, who pitched a two-hitter and struck out ten.

June 26—Dave Marshall's two-out, eighth-inning pinch single broke up Don Drysdale's no-hit bid in a 2-1 loss to the Dodgers right-hander.

June 27—Willie McCovey hit two homers for four RBI off Bill Singer, but the Dodgers defeated Juan Marichal 6-5 for their first victory in sixteen decisions against him at Candlestick.

July 14—Hank Aaron's five hundredth home run, a three-run shot off Mike McCormick, paced the Braves to a 4-2 victory at Atlanta.

July 20—Sadecki fired another two-hitter and struck out eleven in a 1-0 victory over Houston. Mays scored from first on a single by Hart.

July 23—McCovey's tenth-inning homer off right-hander Jack Lamabe downed the Cubs 4-3 for Marichal's eighteenth victory.

July 28—Marichal's run-scoring single in the eleventh defeated the Astros 4-2 at Houston for his fifteenth straight complete game and a 19-4 record.

August 1—Marichal three-hit the Dodgers 2-0 for a 20-4 record. It was his sixteenth consecutive complete game and his seventh career shutout against Drysdale.

August 4—Bobby Bolin continued his mastery of the Pirates with a five-hit, ten-strikeout, 2-0 victory. In his previous start against them, at Pittsburgh on June 21, he hurled a four-hit shutout.

August 7—Willie McCovey hit two home runs against the Phillies, including a game-winning shot in the eighth off Dick Hall, for a 4-3 victory.

August 11—Sadecki fired a four-hitter, struck out thirteen, and walked none in a 2-1 victory over the Mets.

August 14—McCovey's tenth-inning single at Pittsburgh produced a 2-1 victory and snapped Ron Kline's streak of ten straight relief wins. Gaylord Perry pitched a three-hitter and the run off him was unearned.

August 19—Bobby Bolin pitched an eleven-inning, 1-0 victory at New York, striking out ten Mets.

August 24—Ty Cline hit his first home run in four years, a three-run blast in the fifth inning off Don Drysdale, to boost the Giants from a 3-2 deficit to a 9-7 victory over the Dodgers.

August 26—Gaylord Perry pitched a one-hit, 3-0 victory over the Cubs, losing a no-hitter on Glenn Beckert's seventh-inning single.

Sept. 14—Mays hit a pair of homers off the Reds' Gerry Arrigo, including a three-runner in the fifth, during Bolin's 9-1 victory. It was Willie's fifty-eighth two-homer performance.

Sept. 17—Perry fired a no-hitter in a 1-0 victory over the Cardinals before 9,546 under the lights at Candlestick. Perry struck out nine and walked two in the one-hour, 40-minute gem. Ron Hunt's one-out homer in the first provided all the scoring off Bob Gibson, who pitched a four-hitter and fanned ten Giants.

Sept. 18—Ray Washburn returned the favor the next afternoon, hurling the first St. Louis Cardinal no-hitter since Lon Warneke in 1941. Washburn was embroiled in a scoreless duel with Bolin until the Cardinals scored in the seventh and eighth for a 2-0 victory.

Sept. 20—Marichal defeated the Braves 9-1 on a five-hitter, lifting his record to 26-8. It was the most victories for a Giants pitcher since Carl Hubbell's twenty-six in 1936. Nobody had won more since Christy Mathewson notched twenty-seven in 1910.

Sept. 27—Mays' home run in the fifteenth inning off Ted Abernathy gave the Giants a 3-2 victory at Cincinnati.

Oct. 11—Clyde King, forty-three years old, was named manager of the Giants. Herman Franks stepped down after four consecutive second-place finishes.

Oct. 14—In the expansion draft to stock the new San Diego and Montreal franchises, Giants Jesus Alou, Ty Cline, and Don Hahn went to the Expos, and Ollie Brown, Mike Corkins, and Rafael Robles were taken by the Padres.

1969

April 12—Juan Marichal did it all in a 5-1 victory over the Padres, belting two doubles and a home run against the expansion club.

April 25—Jack Hiatt's greatest day as a Giant produced seven RBI in a 12-8 victory over Houston. The catcher started things with a two-run homer in the first and capped his performance with a game-winning grand slam in the thirteenth.

April 27—Willie McCovey's three-run homers in each game powered an 8-5, 4-3 doubleheader sweep of the Astros. His three-run shot off Dan Schneider cracked a 5-5 tie in the seventh inning of the opener, and it was 2-1 Houston when he connected in the second game off Jack Billingham. Mac's eight home runs tied the National League record for April.

April 29—Bobby Bonds belted a home run off George Culver in the thirteenth inning for a 4-3 victory over the Reds. Bonds finished with three RBI.

June 6—McCovey hit two home runs off Rick Wise to support Gaylord Perry's five-hit, 4-0 victory orver the Phillies. Willie, with nineteen homers, moved five games ahead of Roger Maris' record 1961 pace. The power show came in the midst of a sixteen-game batting streak in which Stretch socked eleven homers and batted .453.

June 24—Willie Mays and Giant Manager Clyde King had an angry exchange in the Houston dugout over Mays' exclusion from the starting lineup. Each played down the incident, which insiders say was the beginning of King's demise as the S.F. skipper.

June 28—McCovey blasted two homers, including a first-inning grand slam off Jack Fisher, and finished with five RBI to power a 12-5 rout at Cincinnati.

July 4—The Giants erupted with some holiday fireworks in a 7-6, 7-3 sweep at Atlanta. Bob Burda's two-run pinch homer tied the opener in the ninth inning, and he delivered a game-winning two-run double in the eleventh. Bonds hit three homers in the twin bill, two in the first game.

July 20—Gaylord Perry hit his first major league homer off the Dodgers' Claude Osteen, 25 minutes after Neil Armstrong and Buzz Aldrin walked on the moon. The Giants won, 7-3.

July 23—McCovey's home runs off Blue Moon Odom and Denny McLain led the National League to a 7-3 victory in the All-Star Game at Washington. Stretch was named the game's MVP.

August 5—Marichal, Ron Hunt, and Bonds hit home runs on successive at bats off John Boozer for a 6-2 victory in the opener of a doubleheader at Philadelphia. The Giants also won the second game 5-3 for a half-game lead in the National League West.

August 9—The Giants purchased reliever Don McMahon from Detroit. The veteran stabilized the bullpen and went on to become the club's pitching coach.

August 26—Willie McCovey drove in six runs, four with his tenth career grand slam, in a 13-4 romp over the Phillies.

Sept. 12—Marichal fired a one-hitter for a 1-0 victory over the Reds. "It was my best game ever," remarked Juan, who posted his eighteenth victory and lost a no-hitter on Tommy Helms's single in the third.

Sept. 13—The Reds shaded the Giants 6-4 but Bobby Bonds' thirtieth homer made him only the fourth player in history to join the thirty-homer, thirty-steals club. On August 13, Bonds stole his thirty-second base, erasing Mays' S.F. record of thirty-one, set in 1958.

Sept. 16—Juan Marichal pitched a five-hitter for a 2-0 victory over the Braves, his nineteenth. Coupled with the one-hitter over the hard-hitting Reds in his last start, Juan regarded the games his best back-to-back career victories.

Sept. 22—Mays' six-hundredth career homer, coming with one on and the game tied in the seventh inning at San Diego, gave the Giants a 4-2 victory. The blast came in a pinch-hit role (for George Foster) and was belted off Mike Corkins. In the same game, Bonds struck out for the 176th time, breaking Dave Nicholson's major league mark. Five days later, Foster collected his first major league hit in a 2-1 loss at L.A.

Sept. 28—McCovey homered off Pete Mikkelsen at L.A. for his forty-fifth, and final, home run of the season, a career high.

Dec. 9—McCovey was named National League MVP, edging Tom Seaver 263-243, in the baseball writers' voting. Each collected eleven first-place votes.

Dec. 12—The Giants swapped pitcher Ray Sadecki and outfielder Dave Marshall to the Mets for outfielder Jim Gosger and infielder Bob Heise. They also sent pitcher Bob Bolin to Seattle for outfielders Steve Whitaker and Dick Simpson.

1970

Jan. 17—Willie Mays was named Player of the Decade by *The Sporting News.*

April 17—Second baseman Ron Hunt and infielder Bob Heise were unlikely heroes in a 16-9 victory at Cincinnati. Hunt hit his first major league grand slam as a pinch hitter, tagging Ray Washburn, and finished with six RBI. Heise added five RBI as S.F. overcame an 8-3 deficit.

May 8—Willie Mays hit his 605th and 606th career homers, both off Gary Gentry, in a 7-1 victory at New York. Miguel Puente was the winner.

May 10—Willie McCovey walloped two homers, including his twelfth grand slam, to hammer the Mets, 11-7. Stretch slugged a two-run shot off Nolan Ryan in the third and the four-run job off Tug McGraw in the fourth to finish with six RBI. It was his second grand slam of the season, the first having come off Bill Stoneman of the Expos on April 26.

May 13—Tito Fuentes' three-run homer and two-run triple accounted for all the scoring in Rich Robertson's 5-1 triumph at San Diego.

May 19—Right-hander Frank Linzy was traded to St. Louis for Jerry Johnson in a swap of relievers.

May 23—The Giants pounded out twenty-three hits, but San Diego scored a team-record seventeen runs in a 17-16, 15-inning donnybrook at Candlestick. Following the wild one, Clyde King was replaced as manager by Charlie Fox, who guided the club to a 67-53 record. Willie Mays had four hits, four RBI, and two homers. McCovey added a double, a home run, and four RBI. Nate Colbert, who had five hits, smashed a two-run homer in the eleventh for a 6-4 Padres lead, but Ron Hunt's two-run single made it 6-6 in the bottom of the inning. The 5-hour, 29-minute contest and King's S.F. managerial career ended shortly after Steve Huntz hammered a leadoff homer in the fifteenth off Miguel Puente.

May 24—Charlie Fox's first day as Giant manager produced two McCovey home runs off ex-teammate Ron Herbel in a 6-1, 7-6 doubleheader sweep of the Padres.

June 26—Gaylord Perry pitched a three-hit, 4-1 victory over the Braves for his fifth straight win. It was his second three-hitter in ten days, following a 3-2 decision over the Cubs on June 16.

July 8—Jim Ray Hart, in his second game after returning from an injury, hit for the cycle within five innings in a 13-0 victory at Atlanta. He capped his performance with a three-run homer off Phil Niekro and a bases-loaded triple off Aubrey Gatewood in the Giants' eleven-run fifth. The six RBI in an inning were the most for a National Leaguer since Fred Merkle turned the trick in 1911.

July 18—Willie Mays collected his three-thousandth hit in the second inning of a 10-1 drubbing of the Expos at Candlestick. Ron Hunt was hit by a pitch for the 119th time in his career, breaking Frank Robinson's previous National League record of 118.

August 8—The Giants entered the bottom of the ninth trailing 5-1, but scored six times for a 6-5 victory over the Astros. Tito Fuentes' bases-loaded walk made it 5-4, and Mays followed with a two-run single. Pitcher Skip Pitlock homered for S.F.

August 22—Hal Lanier's one-out single in the eighth spoiled Chicago lefty Ken Holtzman's no-hit attempt during the Cubs' 15-0 rout.

August 28—Juan Marichal posted his two-hundredth major league victory by stopping the Pirates, 5-1. The Dominican Dandy, off to a slow start following a negative reaction to penicillin, won his sixth straight for a 9-9 record and became the only post-World War II pitcher to win two-hundred games within eleven years.

August 29—Bobby Bonds struck out three times as the Giants fell behind the Astros 9-2, but his three-run homer was the big blow in a seven-run eighth for 9-9. Bonds' run-scoring single won it in the tenth, 10-9.

August 30—Giants left-hander Ron Bryant hurled his first major league complete game, smothering the Pirates on two hits, both by Roberto Clemente, in a 2-1 victory.

Sept. 6—Gaylord Perry began a string of three consecutive four-hit shutouts by baffling the Braves 1-0 at Atlanta. Four days later, Houston succumbed to him 11-0, and on September 15, the Braves were thumped 8-0 at Candlestick, giving Gaylord a 21-13 record.

Sept. 9—Mays walloped two homers off Larry Dierker, notching five RBI in a 9-5 victory over the Astros. Willie's fifth two-homer game of the season raised his career total to 626.

Sept. 19—Perry fired a three-hit shutout at San Diego, 3-0, the fourth straight whitewash equaling Sal Maglie's club record set in 1950. Perry's scoreless-innings streak was snapped at thirty-nine in his next start.

Sept. 23—The host Dodgers bolted to an 8-0 lead after six innings, but Dick Dietz's grand slam off Jim Brewer was the telling blow in the Giants' nine-run seventh. L.A. tied the game, but S.F. won it 14-10 on Ken Henderson's three-run homer in the tenth.

Sept. 25—Willie McCovey hit two homers off Pat Dobson, including a 450-footer, and George Foster hit his first major league homer, but the Giants were beaten by the Padres, 7-4.

Oct. 1—Bobby Bonds tripled on his final at bat of a season-ending, 5-4 loss at Houston for his two-hundredth hit, the first S.F. player to reach that total since Mays bashed 208 in 1958. Bonds also scored his 134th run, a new S.F. mark. Russ Hodges retired after twenty-two years as the Giants announcer. Hodges, who made "Bye, Bye Baby" his trademark and had seen all of Mays' 628 homers to that point, died the following April.

Oct. 19—One of the greatest swaps in S.F. history seemed insignificant at that time. Former bonus baby pitcher Bob Garibaldi was traded to Kansas City for catcher Fran Healy. It was Healy who eventually was swapped back to the Royals for Greg Minton, who became the greatest right-handed reliever in modern Giants history.

Dec. 30—Ron Hunt, not one of manager Charlie Fox's favorites, was traded to the Expos for first baseman Dave McDonald. It was a giveaway because McDonald never played for the Giants.

1971

April 6—It was a good omen when the Giants opened their championship season at San Diego with a 4-0 victory. Juan Marichal pitched the shutout and Willie Mays hit the first pitch he saw for a first-inning homer off Tom Phoebus.

April 7—Giant shortstop Chris Speier made his major league debut a smash with a double, single, and two RBI in Gaylord Perry's 7-3 victory over the Padres. Mays homered again, added a grand slam in a 7-6 loss the next day, and made it four in four games during a 6-4 victory at St. Louis on April 10.

April 12—A crowd of 29,847 turned out for the home opener and Perry responded with a three-hitter and eleven strikeouts to stump the Padres, 5-0. Alan Gallagher hit a two-run homer in the five-run second off Clay Kirby. It was Perry's eighth straight win.

April 14—Tito Fuentes' two-out single in the eleventh edged the Astros 2-1, giving the Giants sole possession of first place, a lead they never relinquished.

April 16—Marichal had a no-hitter until Ken Rudolph of the Cubs led off the ninth with a single to left. Juan finished with a two-hit, 9-0 victory, retiring twenty-four of the first twenty-five batters despite a 32-minute rain delay. Dick Dietz, George Foster, and Healy homered, the latter going 4-for-4.

April 23—Right-hander Steve Stone registered his first major league complete game, pitching a five-hit, 2-0 victory at Pittsburgh. For an encore, left-hander Ron Bryant blanked the Bucs 2-0 on three hits the next day.

April 28—Rookie George Foster, playing because Mays was injured, went 4-for-4 with a double, homer, and three RBI in a 5-3 victory at Atlanta.

May 2—Willie McCovey hit two home runs, including the game-winner off Tony Cloninger in the thirteenth inning for a 4-3 victory at Cincinnati.

May 6—The Bay Area baseball writers threw a fortieth birthday party for Mays at a downtown hotel. Commissioner Bowie Kuhn was among the guests and manager Charlie Fox, an Irish tenor, sang "Willie Boy" to the music of "Danny Boy."

May 15—Marichal blanked the Dodgers on a six-hitter, 1-0. The Giants collected only two hits off Bill Singer, but they came in the seventh when Mays doubled and scored on Dietz's single. S.F. increased its division lead to nine games.

May 20—Fran Healy continued to exhibit his Midas touch, belting a three-run, eighth-inning double to trigger a comeback at Wrigley Field. McCovey's three-run homer in the ninth downed the Cubs, 8-7.

May 29—A day that will remain infamous for Giants fans. The club, bulging with young outfielders, traded George Foster to Cincinnati for shortstop Frank Duffy and pitcher Vern Geishert, who never played for San Francisco.

May 30—Mays' two-run, eighth-inning homer lifted the Giants to a 5-4 victory over the Expos. Mays's 1,950th run broke Stan Musial's National League record.

June 6—Mays' double triggered a two-run ninth for a 3-3 tie against the Phillies in the nightcap of a doubleheader. Mays' one-out homer off Joe Hoerner in the twelfth earned a 4-3 victory, snapping a five-game losing streak.

June 18—The Giants began a five-game sweep of San Diego by winning a doubleheader, but it wasn't easy. The Padres scored five runs in the ninth inning of the second game to lead 9-5, but S.F. erupted for five in the bottom of the inning for a 10-9 thriller. Dietz's two-run pinch double did the big damage, the winning run scoring on an error following the blow.

June 20—Another doubleheader sweep in the series. McCovey's three-run pinch homer capped a five-run eighth for a 6-2 victory over the Padres in the opener and Steve Stone fired a three-hit, 2-0 gem in the second game.

June 23—Juan Marichal and Milt Pappas were hooked up in a 2-2 battle until Ken Henderson homered to start the three-run eighth. After Dietz walked, Marichal belted a two-run homer for a 5-2 victory over the Cubs.

July 3—Left-hander John Cumberland, acquired by the Giants the previous year from the Yankees in a trade for Mike McCormick, pitched a four-hitter for his first major league complete game, a 10-1 conquest of the Cardinals.

July 9—The Giants erupted for six runs in the ninth inning to jolt the Dodgers 7-4 at L.A. Chris Speier and Tito Fuentes triggered the rally with singles, but the crushing blows were a two-run triple by outfielder Jimmy Rosario and a two-run single by Dick Dietz.

July 21—McCovey's ninth-inning grand slam off Pittsburgh right-hander Dave Giusti downed the Pirates 8-4 at Three Rivers Stadium.

July 31—Dave Kingman, playing his second major league game, put on a power display in a 15-11 thumping of the Pirates. Kingman replaced McCovey early in the game and belted a run-scoring double in the fourth, setting the stage for his grand slam off Giusti in the seven-run seventh. Willie Stargell homered twice for the Bucs.

August 1—The Giants power crushed the Pirates 11-7 and 8-3 in a homer-filled doubleheader. Mays' two-run double and McCovey's three-run homer in a five-run eighth won the opener. Then Kingman clouted a pair of two-run homers off Dock Ellis in the second game. Stargell hit two homers again.

August 4—Bob Gibson posted his two-hundredth victory and his tenth in a row over the Giants since Gaylord Perry's no-hitter in 1968. The Cardinals' right-hander won 7-2 at St. Louis and Ted Kubiak hit a three-run homer.

August 8—Perry's home run in the fifth created a 2-2 tie, and he went the distance in a 4-2, 11-inning victory at Chicago. Speier's two-run single won the game, snapping a six-game Giants losing streak.

Sept. 1—Left-hander John Cumberland pitched a four-hit, 4-0 victory over the Braves. Dave Kingman was hospitalized following an emergency appendectomy.

Sept. 3—The Giants exploded for a 16-6 destruction of the Astros behind Mays' four hits, including two of them in the seven-run eighth. Willie belted two doubles and a triple; his three-run double and Dick Dietz's three-run homer were the big hits in the eighth. Fuentes also had four hits among the Giants' season-high twenty.

Sept. 4—Right-hander Don Carrithers pitched a three-hitter and Bobby Bonds' first-inning homer off Ken Forsch held up for a 1-0 victory over the Astros. Carrithers struck out eight and did not allow a hit after the third inning.

Sept. 5—Houston right-handers Jack Billingham and J.R. Richard stifled the Giants in a 1-0, 5-3 doubleheader sweep by the Astros, beginning a seven-game slide by the Giants. The second game was significant because Richard struck out a record fifteen batters in his major league debut.

Sept. 13—Losing for the eighth time in nine games, the Giants had their lead slashed to two games in a wild, 5-4 loss to the Dodgers. Marichal was ejected by umpire Shag Crawford for giving the choke sign. Jerry Johnson, Maury Wills, and Bill Buckner also were booted during a beanball duel. On a positive note for S.F., Dave Kingman returned to the lineup with a single, a double, and a triple.

Sept. 14—The Giants trailed the Dodgers 3-1 entering the bottom of the seventh, but Chris Speier's homer and a three-run shot by Bobby Bonds gave S.F. the lead until Manny Mota's three-run double in the ninth earned a 6-5 L.A. victory, cutting the Giants' league lead to one game.

Sept. 30—Marichal won at San Diego on the final day, 5-1, giving the Giants the division crown by one game over the Dodgers. Kingman's two-run homer in the fourth off Dave Roberts was the key blow. S.F. won only eight of its final twenty-four games, but Marichal was responsible for four of those victories and the team finished 90-72.

Oct. 2—The Giants hosted the playoff opener against the Pirates and were confident following their season dominance of Pittsburgh. A crowd of 40,977 watched McCovey and Fuentes rip two-run homers in the four-run fifth as the Giants posted a 5-4 victory.

Oct. 3—Pirate first baseman Bob Robertson hit three home runs, a National League Championship Series record, to give the Bucs a 9-4 victory before 42,562 at Candlestick, and snapping a six-game losing streak on the Giants' field.

Oct. 5—Marichal pitched a four-hitter when the playoffs shifted to Three Rivers Stadium, but home runs by Robertson and Richie Hebner gave the Pirates a 2-1 victory behind Bob Johnson and Giusti.

Oct. 6—Pittsburgh earned a World Series trip by blasting the Giants 9-5 for a third consecutive playoff victory. Hebner belted a three-run homer off Perry in the second, and Al Oliver homered in a four-run sixth that snapped a 5-5 tie. McCovey had a three-run homer and four RBI in a losing cause.

Nov. 29—Compounding the felony following the earlier Foster trade, the Giants sent Duffy and Perry to the Indians for left-hander Sam McDowell, who went from "Sudden Sam" to "Seldom Sam" in a horrible 1972 effort.

1972

April 2—The Giants traded reserve catcher Fran Healy to Kansas City for minor league pitcher Greg Minton, who ten years later would blossom into the greatest reliever in San Francisco Giant history.

April 15—The baseball season began following a ten-day strike. Juan Marichal wasn't hindered by the layoff, firing a 5-0 shutout of the Astros on Opening Day.

May 11—The end of an era for the Giants. Willie Mays was traded to the Mets for pitcher Charlie Williams and $150,000. Mays was batting .184 in nineteen games and had not homered since September 26, 1971, when he belted his 646th against the Reds. This was the beginning of a housecleaning that helped Horace Stoneham financially, but stripped the club of its fading superstars.

May 22—The Giants were trailing 8-0 at Dodger Stadium, but Dave Kingman clouted a pair of home runs, including a grand slam, to pace a 9-8 comeback. His slam was hit in the third inning off Tommy John.

May 27—Rookie Ed Goodson belted four hits, including his second major league homer and a double in an 11-9 victory at Atlanta.

June 11—Ron Bryant pitched a five-hit, 3-1 victory over the Cubs in the second game of a doubleheader. The win snapped an eight-game losing streak, longest in S.F. history. Ex-Giant Bill Hands pitched a 4-0 victory for Chicago in the opener.

June 27—Bobby Bonds smashed a 3-2 curve for a home run off Atlanta's Cecil Upshaw in the tenth inning, giving the Giants a 3-2 triumph.

July 4—Rookie Jim Barr joined the Giants' rotation, and celebrated the occasion with a three-hit, 3-1 victory over the Phillies.

July 2—Willie McCovey's fourteenth career grand slam tied Hank Aaron and Gil Hodges for the National League record and guided the Giants to a 9-3 rout of the Dodgers. Reliever Randy Moffitt posted his first major league victory and received a congratulatory telegram from his tennis-star sister, Billie Jean King, who was playing at Wimbledon.

August 15—Garry Maddox slugged a two-run homer in the fifth inning and a grand slam in the sixth, each off Hands, in a 7-5 victory over the Cubs.

August 16—Ken Henderson belted four hits, scored four runs, and knocked in five to power a twenty-hit, 14-9 romp over the Cubs. Tito Fuentes added a pair of two-run singles.

August 22—Marichal was the victim of a one-hitter for the second time in the season. Pittsburgh's Nelson Briles retired twenty in a row before losing a perfect game on Henderson's searing liner off the top of first baseman Willie Stargell's glove with two outs in the seventh. Stargell's double in the first drove home the Pirates' unearned run.

August 23—Jim Barr fired a two-hit, 8-0 victory over the Pirates, retiring the last twenty-one batters after Bob Moose led off the third with a walk.

August 29—Barr retired the first twenty batters at St. Louis, setting a major league record of forty-one in a row over two games, in a 3-0 victory. (Harvey Haddix held the former mark of thirty-eight straight outs in 1959.) Bernie Carbo's two-out double in the seventh snapped the string, and Barr settled for a three-hitter. Kingman chased home all the runs with a three-run double in the ninth.

Sept. 9—Jim Willoughby edged Don Gullett 2-1 in a pitching gem that found each youngster firing a three-hitter. The Reds led 1-0 until Jim Ray Hart walked with one away in the ninth and Kingman followed with a home run on an 0-2 pitch.

Sept. 16—McCovey, who missed two months of the season with a broken arm, and rookie Gary Matthews each slammed a pair of homers in an 8-5 victory at Atlanta. Matty's homers were the first two of his major league career.

Nov. 29—Steve Stone, who would become a Cy Young Award winner in 1980, and Henderson were swapped to the White Sox for right-hander Tom Bradley.

1973

April 9—Chris Speier's one-out homer in the fifth off Mike Caldwell cracked a 1-1 tie and gave the Giants a 2-1 Opening Day victory at Candlestick. Ron Bryant didn't allow a hit over the final five innings and finished with a four-hitter over the Padres.

April 11—Jim Wynn's two homers had the Astros ahead by one entering the ninth, but Chris Speier led off with a walk and Willie McCovey belted a game-winning, two-run homer for a 5-4 victory.

April 12—McCovey became the eighth National Leaguer to wallop a pair of homers in one inning, connecting off Ken Forsch and Jim Crawford in the eight-run fourth during a 9-3 crunching of the Astros. The first two-homer inning in the National League since Sid Gordon did it for the 1949 Giants included a three-run blast and a solo shot. Gary Thomasson added a two-run homer in the fourth.

April 25—Juan Marichal required only eighty-nine pitches to shackle the Cubs 5-0 at Wrigley Field. Juan's fifty-first career shutout gave him a 4-1 record.

April 27—Jim Barr fired a two-hit, 5-0 victory at St. Louis, defeating Bob Gibson.

April 28—For an encore, Jim Willoughby pitched a four-hit, 1-0 victory at St. Louis, getting the run on Bobby Bonds' leadoff homer in the first.

May 1—One of the greatest comebacks in Giants history occurred after the Pirates held a 7-1 lead with two outs in the bottom of the ninth and Speier on first. The club scored seven times to win 8-7, with Chris Arnold providing a pinch-hit grand slam and Bonds a three-run double.

May 8—Bonds hit a leadoff homer in the first, a two-run shot in the fifth, and a two-run single in the eighth to pace a 9-7 victory over the Cardinals. McCovey and Dave Kingman stroked back-to-back homers in the fourth off Gibson, Mac's smash going some 500 feet.

May 26—Garry Maddox cracked a double and four singles, collecting five hits off four different Montreal pitchers in a 10-3 runaway. The splurge raised Maddox' average to .377.

June 3—The Giants rallied for four runs in the ninth to shade the Phillies, 5-4. Kingman started the comeback with a single and Dave Rader homered. Tito Fuentes singled with two outs and Maddox hit a 1-2 pitch for the game-winning homer.

June 15—McCovey's three-run homer in the top of the tenth outlasted Greg Luzinski's two-run shot in the bottom of the inning, hoisting the Giants to a 4-3 victory at Philadelphia, Bryant's eighth in a row.

June 20—The Giants were beaten by the Reds 7-5, but Bonds' leadoff homer in the first was his twenty-second as the first batter, erasing Lou Brock's National League record of twenty-one.

June 22—Jim Barr retired the last fifteen batters in a six-hit, 5-1 victory over Houston. Ed Goodson did the damage with a three-run homer in the first off Don Wilson and a two-run blast in the seventh off Jim Crawford.

July 15—McCovey became the fifteenth player to hit four-hundred home runs when he belted a pair of solos to back Marichal's four-hit pitching in a 12-0 drubbing of the Pirates in the opener of a doubleheader. Pittsburgh won the second game, 7-2. The shutout was Marichal's fifty-second and last.

July 24—Bobby Bonds, climaxing his finest season, was the All-Star Game MVP at Kansas City, belting a home run and a double and collecting two RBI in the Nationals' 7-1 victory.

July 26—Picking up where he left off in the dream game, Bonds slapped a three-run homer in the first game and a two-run shot in the nightcap to power a 10-2, 6-5 sweep at San Diego.

August 12—Bonds, who earlier tripled and homered, hit a run-scoring single in the thirteenth to down the Mets, 8-7. The victory gave the Giants a 10-0 record in extra innings.

August 17—McCovey hit his twenty-second and twenty-third homers off Bob Moose and Bryant hurled six perfect innings in a 5-3 victory at Pittsburgh.

August 25—Tom Bradley hurled a four-hitter and defeated Tom Seaver 1-0 at New York. The performance reversed the Mets' 1-0 decision August 24, when Jerry Koosman prevailed over Marichal in ten innings.

Sept. 3—The Dodgers were ahead 8-1 entering the seventh inning, but the Giants came out on top, 11-8, on Bonds's grand slam in the ninth inning. Kingman hit his seventh homer in ten games.

Sept. 30 — Ron Bryant beat the Reds 4-3 on the final day for his twenty-fourth victory, the last Giants pitcher in 13 years to win twenty. Elias Sosa registered his eighteenth save and appeared in his seventy-first game, equaling Hoyt Wilhelm's club record. Bonds hit his thirty-ninth homer, just missing becoming the first forty-home-run, forty-stolen-base man in history. Second baseman Fuentes made only six errors in 160 games.

Oct. 25—McCovey and outfielder Bernie Williams were traded to the San Diego Padres for left-hander Mike Caldwell, interrupting McCovey's career with the club after fifteen years.

Nov. 17—Bonds was named Player of the Year and Bryant was selected Pitcher of the Year by *The Sporting News,* the first time both awards went to players from the same team.

Dec. 7—Marichal, with 238 victories and a 2.78 ERA in his illustrious Giants career, was sold to the Red Sox. Within a span of nineteen months, the club had disposed of the three greatest players in San Francisco's major league history: Mays, McCovey, and Marichal.

1974

March 15—Ron Bryant was injured in a swimming pool accident at Yuma, requiring thirty stitches in his side. His record dipped from 24-12 to 3-15 and he never regained his winning form.

April 8—On the day Henry Aaron hit home run number 715 at Atlanta, Garry Maddox belted a run-scoring single in the first and a three-run homer in the fifth for a 4-3 victory over the Reds at Candlestick. John D'Acquisto, Elias Sosa, and Randy Moffitt collaborated on the shutout, giving the Giants first place with a 4-0 record.

May 1—Maddox belted two doubles and had three RBI in the fifth inning, the Giants chasing Steve Carlton with nine runs in a 13-8 rout of the Phillies. Gary Matthews led off and ripped four hits, including a homer, scored four times, and knocked in three runs.

June 28—Charlie Fox resigned as manager after the Giants lost fourteen of their last seventeen games for a 33-42 record and dropped 16 1/2 games out of first place. Wes Westrum was promoted from the coaching ranks and took over the club.

July 3—Matthews' home run off Vicente Romo in the tenth gave the Giants a 3-2 victory over the Padres.

July 13—Matthews and Dave Rader each belted four hits in an eighteen-hit, 13-3 romp over the Phillies. Steve Ontiveros added three hits and four RBI, and Dave Kingman walloped a two-run homer.

July 21—The fourth doubleheader shutout in the club's S.F. history found the Expos falling, 4-0, 2-0. Jim Barr pitched a six-hitter in the opener and D'Aquisto had a no-hitter for six innings of the second game, finishing with Sosa's help in the ninth and a combined two-hitter.

August 4—The Giants dropped the opener of a doubleheader 4-2 to the Braves, but Mike Caldwell fired a no-hitter in the second game until Aaron rapped a one-out double in the eighth. Caldwell finished with a four-hit, 5-2 victory, raising his record to 7-0 at Candlestick.

August 31—D'Aquisto downed the Cardinals 3-2 for his tenth victory, becoming the first Giants rookie to win that many since Ruben Gomez in 1953.

Sept. 3—John Montefusco made an auspicius major league debut, replacing Bryant while the Giants trailed 3-2 at Dodger Stadium. He worked out of a bases-loaded, first-inning jam, blasted a two-run homer, and went the rest of the way on a six-hitter to win, 9-5. Matthews hit a grand-slam homer.

Sept. 6—D'Aquisto pitched a four-hit, 2-0 victory at Atlanta. The hard-throwing right-hander struck out five for a total of 148, most by a Giants rookie since 1900.

Sept. 16—Jim Barr needed only one hour and 38 minutes to stop the Braves on seven hits, 4-2. Bobby Bonds and Gary Thomasson homered, but the big news was that only 748 attended, representing the smallest crowd in Candlestick history.

Sept. 22—Montefusco beat the Reds 6-0 on a seven hitter and hammered a home run in the eighth. Kingman and Chris Speier socked back-to-back homers off Don Gullett in the second.

Oct. 1—Fuentes doubled for his one thousandth career hit as the Giants pounded the Padres, 7-2. A little more than two months later, on December 6, the popular second baseman and minor league pitcher Butch Metzger were traded to San Diego for infielder Derrel Thomas.

Oct. 22—Bonds, only one year after he was regarded the best player in the National League, was traded to the Yankees for outfielder Bobby Murcer. It was the first swap ever involving ballplayers with six-figure salaries.

1975

Feb. 28— Dave Kingman was sold to the Mets.

April 13—John Montefusco pitched a four-hit, 5-0 victory over the Braves in the opener of a doublheader. Gary Matthews had a homer, a double, and a single to power a 3-1 second-game triumph for a sweep.

May 4—Continuing to trade away promising young talent, the Giants swapped Garry Maddox to the Phillies for Willie Montanez. Maddox blossomed into a Gold Glove center fielder, whereas Montanez was unhappy with his S.F. surroundings and didn't last long with the club.

May 9—Bryant was traded to St. Louis for outfielders Larry Herndon and Tony Gonzalez, a good move for the Giants because Bryant was finished as a winning pitcher.

May 18—Jim Barr fired a two-hitter to down his "cousin" Cardinals 2-0. Gentleman Jim had a no-hitter until Lou Brock led off the seventh with a single. Von Joshua's double and a sacrifice fly by Murcer accounted for the first S.F. run. Montanez tripled and scored on Chris Speier's single for the other.

May 24—Bobby Murcer's most productive day with the Giants included a three-run homer and a bases-loaded triple for six RBI in a 10-3 demolition of the Cubs behind Barr.

May 27—Montefusco fired a 1-0 shutout at Philadelphia, the Giants winning in the tenth on a run-scoring double by Glenn Adams.

June 4—Adams blasted a pair of homers at Chicago, including a three run shot off Rick Reuschel, to lead the Giants' 10-8 victory.

June 1—Murcer connected for a pair of two-run homers in the eighth and ninth innings at Montreal to lead a 13-5 victory.

August 1—Montanez and Chris Speier opened the ninth with back-to-back home runs off J.R. Richard in a 3-2 win over the Astros.

August 24—Right-hander Ed Halicki fired a no-hitter and struck out ten, smothering the Mets 6-0 before 24,132 in the second game of a Candlestick Park twin bill. Montanez' two-run single in the first gave Halicki all the support he needed. Kingman's grand slam off Barr powered New York to a 9-5 decision in the opener.

August 27—Montefusco struck out a career-high fourteen Expos in a 9-1 victory.

August 31—The Count followed with thirteen strikeouts in 8 1/3 innings while defeating Steve Carlton and the Phillies, 5-4. Montefusco surpassed D'Acquisto's club rookie strikeout record in the process.

Sept. 2—Johnnie LeMaster became the forty-third player to hit a home run on his first major league at bat, connecting for an inside-the-park blast off Don Sutton in a 7-3 victory over the Dodgers.

Sept. 21—Montefusco concluded the Giants' home schedule with a 4-1 victory over the Padres. It was his fourteenth victory, most by a Giants' rookie since Larry Jansen in 1947.

Nov. 7—Montefusco was named National League Rookie Pitcher of the Year by *The Sporting News*. The Count, whose 215 strikeouts approached Grover Cleveland Alexander's rookie record of 227, was accorded a similar honor by the baseball writers.

1976

Jan. 9 — Charles Ruppert, vice-president of the Giants and Horace Stoneham's son-in-law, announced the sale of the Giants to Toronto interests for $13.35 million, provoking outrage in the Bay Area.

Feb. 11—A preliminary injunction, instigated by new San Francisco Mayor George Moscone, prevented an immediate move to Toronto.

March 2—Bob Lurie and Bud Herseth, introduced by Moscone, came up with a last-ditch deal to purchase the Giants for $8 million and keep them in the Bay Area.

April 9 Bill Rigney returned to manage the Giants after an eighteen-year absence. Opening Day attracted 37,261, the largest home crowd in ten years, to Candlestick. Montefusco responded with a 4-2 victory over the Dodgers behind home runs by Bobby Murcer and Gary Matthews.

May 23—Montefusco pitched a no-hitter until the sixth and settled for a three-hit, 1-0 victory over Phil Niekro and the Braves in ten innings. Derrel Thomas triggered the winning rally with a one-out single and advanced on Glenn Adams' grounder. Pinch hitter Dave Rader was walked intentionally and Larry Herndon was hit by a pitch, loading the bases. Chris Speier then hit a game-ending, fielder's-choice grounder.

May 25—Murcer belted a grand slam in the fifth, but the Giants needed two runs in the eighth to edge the Astros, 7-6. Murcer's one-out single and Willie Montanez' two-out homer did the damage. Monty slashed four hits.

June 11—Montefusco fired a three-hitter against the Mets, winning 5-0 on a three-run homer by Murcer in the first and a two-run shot by Marc Hill in the second.

June 13—Montanez, batting .309 and wishing to be traded, had his wish granted when he was dealt to the Braves for Darrell Evans and Marty Perez.

June 23—Evans made an impressive Candlestick Park debut with the Giants, powering a 7-6, 8-7 sweep of San Diego. His two-run homer in the eighth off Butch Metzger won the opener and he added a grand slam in the third inning of the nightcap off Rich Folkers.

July 15—Ed Halicki defeated the Phillies, 1-0 in a tidy one-hour, 32-minute game.

August 15—Evans belted two homers, including a three-run blow in the ninth, during a 9-5 victory at Philadelphia.

Sept. 11—Jack Clark, promoted from Phoenix, hit his first major league homer off Jack Billingham in an 8-5 loss to the Reds.

Sept. 25—Matthews smashed three home runs in support of Jim Barr's 10-0 blanking of the Astros. Matty became the first Giant to hit three in one game since Willie McCovey in 1966, the outburst raising his season total to nineteen. Barr pitched a six-hitter and helped himself with a two-run triple.

Sept. 29—Montefusco pitched the first away no-hitter in the Giants' San Francisco history, tripping the Braves 9-0 at Atlanta. The brash right-hander threw only ninety-seven pitches, ninety-two of which were fastballs in a four-strikeout performance. Johnnie LeMaster was the offensive star with a triple, a double, and three RBI.

Oct. 7—In a surprise move, Joe Altobelli was named manager for 1977, succeeding Bill Rigney, who announced his retirement on Sept. 21.

Oct. 30—Larry Herndon was named National League Rookie of the Year by *The Sporting News.*

Dec. 10—Ken Reitz, eager to return to the Cardinals following a lackluster year with the Giants, was swapped to St. Louis for pitcher Lynn McGlothen. The trade was the second between the clubs in two months. Dave Rader, John D'Acquisto, and Mike Caldwell were shipped to St. Louis on October 4 in exchange for Willie Crawford, Vic Harris, and John Curtis.

1977

Feb. 11—Bobby Murcer and Steve Ontiveros were traded to the Cubs for two-time National League batting champion Bill Madlock.

April 19—Jack Clark became a regular at age twenty-one and slapped three hits in a 7-4 victory at Houston.

April 26—A contract hassle, similar to the one that cost the Giants Gary Matthews between seasons, prefaced the swapping of three-time All-Star Game shortstop Chris Speier to the Expos for shortstop Tim Foli.

May 8—Left-hander John Curtis pitched a two-hitter and belted a triple among his three hits in a 10-0 domination of the Mets.

June 18—Clark cracked a pinch homer off Goose Gossage in the eleventh inning for a 7-5 victory over the Pirates.

June 27—Willie McCovey, who returned to the Giants after a three-year exodus, became the only player in major league history to connect for a pair of home runs in the same inning twice in his career when he came through in a ten-run sixth at Cincinnati, powering a 14-9 thriller. Mac began with a one-out blast off Jack Billingham and capped the uprising with a grand slam off Joe Hoerner. The slam was his seventeenth, earning a tie with Henry Aaron for the National League record.

July 22—A pair of unexpected heroes combined talents to beat Steve Carlton and the Phillies, 6-2. Tim Foli ripped a solo homer in the sixth and a two-run shot in the seventh. Randy Elliott added a two-run homer in the sixth.

August 1—McCovey walloped two home runs including his eighteenth grand slam, off Wayne Twitchell in a 9-3 victory at Montreal. The slam gave Stretch the all-time National League record, leaving only Lou Gehrig ahead of him with twenty-three.

Sept. 3—Bill Madlock hit two solo homers, but it took Foli, snapping a 0-for-26 slump, to belt a pinch single in the fourteenth inning for a 6-5 victory over the Cardinals.

Sept. 7—McCovey doubled off Mario Soto for his two-thousandth hit and belted his 489th home run in a 6-3 victory over Cincinnati.

Sept. 18—It was Willie McCovey Day at Candlestick Park, honoring the great slugger's comeback season. He didn't disappoint, exhibiting his flair for the dramatic with a two-out, run-scoring single in the bottom of the ninth, beating the Reds, 3-2.

Oct. 2—Gary Alexander belted a pinch homer in a 3-1 loss to the Padres, setting a club record of 11 such home runs. The previous Giants high was ten, by the championship 1954 aggregation.

1978

Feb. 28—The Giants sent Derrel Thomas to the Padres for first baseman Mike Ivie, a good move until off-the-field problems compelled the Giants to trade Ivie in 1981.

March 15—The biggest swap in San Francisco history: the Giants obtained left-hander Vida Blue from the A's after Commissioner Bowie Kuhn disallowed his shift to the Reds over the winter. To get the Oakland ace, the Giants gave up seven players: Gary Alexander, Dave Heaverlo, Jerry Johnson, Gary Thomasson, Alan Wirth, Mario Guerrero, and Phil Huffman.

April 28—Willie McCovey's bases-loaded double in the eighth inning at Pittsburgh gave John Montefusco a 5-4 victory over John Candelaria.

May 14 — The Giants, who went into first place on May 12, padded their lead with a 5-4, 4-3 doubleheader sweep of the Cardinals, each victory attained in extra innings. Terry Whitfield's two-out homer in the twelfth won the opener, and he triggered the winning rally with a leadoff double in the tenth inning of the nightcap. After Mike Sadek sacrificed and Bill Madlock was walked intentionally, Marc Hill belted a two-out pinch single.

May 19—Rick Monday hit a pair of three-run homers off Montefusco before 53,846 at Dodger Stadium, but the Giants parlayed sixteen hits into a 10-7 victory. Darrell Evans hit a pair of solo homers and Madlock mashed a three-run blow.

May 23—The Giants erupted for three runs in the bottom of the ninth to edge the Astros, 3-2. Hill, pinch hitter Tom Heintzelman, and Madlock each hit run-scoring singles.

May 26—A crowd of 44,688, largest ever to see a night game at Candlestick, watched Knepper and McCovey baffle the Dodgers, 6-1. Knepper fired a six-hitter and McCovey took care of the offense with a two-run single in the first and a three-run, 497-foot homer in the fifth.

May 28—Mike Ivie's pinch-hit grand slam capped an electrifying, 6-5 victory over the Dodgers before 57,475. Los Angeles had a 3-0 lead erased in the five-run sixth, an inning featuring Ivie's smash off Don Sutton.

June 12—Ed Halicki pitched a one-hitter and Clark cracked a run-scoring double in the sixth for a 1-0 victory over the Expos. Ellis Valentine's leadoff single in the second was the only hit off Halicki. Steve Rogers lost on a three-hitter.

June 21—Halicki came through again, pitching a three-hit, 3-0 victory over the Reds. The Giants collected only five hits off Tom Seaver and scored all three of their runs in the fourth. Roger Metzger's two-run double did the big damage.

June 30—The Giants wasted a lot of slugging in a 10-9, 10-5 doubleheader loss at Atlanta. McCovey belted home run number five-hundred, off Jamie Easterly, and Ivie added a pinch-hit grand slam in the opener, becoming the only player ever to achieve the feat twice in the same season. Clark also got into the act, blasting three home runs in the twin bill.

July 11—Vida Blue became the first pitcher to start for both leagues in the All-Star Game when he went to the mound for the Nationals at San Diego. The lefty was roughed up for three runs, but his team rallied for a 7-3 victory.

July 17—The Giants registered a rarity in a 9-7 victory at St. Louis when Evans and Whitfield each belted five hits.

July 23—Jim Barr defeated the Pirates 3-1, but the big news was Clark's first-inning single. It extended his batting streak to twenty-five games, erasing the modern Giants mark of twenty-four by Freddie Lindstrom, Don Mueller and McCovey. Clark's closest call came on July 16, when he doubled as a pinch hitter against the Cardinals to make it seventeen in a row. The streak ended at twenty-six, a span of games in which Clark batted .300 with twenty nine RBI.

July 25—St. Louis scored twice in the ninth for a 2-1 lead over Blue, but the Giants roared back with a pair in the bottom of the ninth for a 3-2 victory. Larry Herndon hit a one-out single, and Ivie followed with his specialty, a pinch homer.

August 4—Blue pitched a two-hitter to edge the Dodgers 2-1 before 49,317. Vida retired twelve straight before Ron Cey hit a leadoff homer in the fifth. Madlock cracked a 1-1 tie with a leadoff homer off Doug Rau in the eighth, helping Blue to his tenth straight victory.

August 12—History repeated for Madlock, whose eighth-inning homer off Tommy John broke a tie and gave the Giants and Bob Knepper a 3-2 triumph at Dodger Stadium.

Sept. 1—Clark's eighth-inning home run downed Steve Carlton and the Phillies, 4-3.

Sept. 27—Bob Knepper edged the Padres 1-0 for his sixth shutout, most for the Giants in one season since 1969.

1979

March 9—The Giants signed outfielder Billy North as a free agent. He went on to set a San Francisco record with fifty-eight stolen bases, four shy of the club's all-time mark.

April 10—Vida Blue defeated the Padres 4-2 before 57,484, the largest Opening Day crowd in the Giants' history. It was 2-2 entering the last of the ninth. Willie McCovey hit a two-out pinch single off John D'Acquisto and John Tamargo followed with a game-winning pinch homer.

May 12—Del Unser stood between a second no-hitter for Ed Halicki, who pitched a two-hit, 4-1 victory over the Phillies. A pair of singles by Unser were the only hits off the rangy right-hander. Johnnie LeMaster had three hits and Darrell Evans had two RBI.

May 17—Halicki recorded his second straight two-hitter, stopping the Astros 3-0 at Houston. Halicki was at the peak of his game with the back-to-back gems, but a bacterial infection struck him shortly thereafter and he seldom pitched effectively again.

May 25—The Giants won a battle of homers over the Braves, 6-4. The clubs tied a major league record with five home runs in one inning. After Jeff Burroughs and Bob Horner connected in the top of the fourth to give Atlanta a 4-1 lead, the Giants blasted three homers in the bottom of the inning to lead, 5-4. McCovey, Mike Sadek, and Bob Knepper did the damage. Jack Clark added a homer in the eighth.

June 9—McCovey came off the bench at Pittsburgh and powered a three-run homer off Grant Jackson in a 6-2 victory for Blue. The blast was his 512th, lifting him over Mel Ott as the number one left-handed home run hitter in National League history. It also was Stretch's sixteenth pinch homer, second on the all-time list.

June 15—McCovey's three-run homer in the thirteenth off Darold Knowles beat the Cardinals, 9-6. It was his second of the game for a career total of 515. Big Mac would never hit two in a game again.

June 26—Darrell Evans, batting as a pinch hitter, led off the ninth with a home run for a 6-5 victory over the Braves. Billy North's homer triggered a five-run first for the Giants.

June 28—Satisfied that they would not be able to keep Bill Madlock in San Francisco, the Giants swapped him and pitcher Dave Roberts to Pittsburgh for pitchers Ed Whitson, Al Holland, and Fred Breining. It seemed like a poor move at the time, Mad Dog leading the Bucs to a pennant, but the Giants needed pitching help and they got it for years to come. They also indirectly landed Mike Krukow, Al Oliver, and Duane Kuiper by making Madlock expendable.

July 20—Bob Knepper beat Steve Carlton 4-1 on the strength of a four-run third inning. Clark hit a two-run homer and Mike Ivie followed with a homer to spark the rally.

August 6—Whitson dazzled the Dodgers 7-1 for his first major league complete game, snapping the Giants' eight-game losing string at Los Angeles.

August 24—McCovey hit his first home run in six weeks and Ivie added a bases-loaded triple in a 5-2 victory over the Cubs. The homer was McCovey's 520th, and his last at Candlestick Park.

Sept. 5—Coach Dave Bristol replaced Joe Altobelli, who was fired as manager after the club slipped to 61-79. The Giants finished the season 10-12 under Bristol.

Dec. 17—The Giants wholeheartedly entered the free agent market by announcing the signing of second baseman Rennie Stennett, catcher Milt May, and outfielder Jim Wohlford.

1980

May 3—Willie McCovey's 521st and final home run snapped an 0-for-15 slump and helped the Giants shade the Expos 3-2 at Montreal. Mac's homer, a 385-foot shot to right center off Scott Sanderson in the fourth, moved him into a tie on the all-time list with boyhood idol Ted Williams.

May 13—Vida Blue fired a four-hit, 5-0 victory over the Pirates, Jack Clark driving in a pair with a single and a home run.

May 17—Darrell Evans smashed his fifth career grand slam to lift Blue to a 4-2 victory over the Cardinals.

May 24—Clark enjoyed his second straight four-hit day, and the Giants edged the Pirates 10-9 in fourteen innings. Jim Wohlford entered the game in the sixth and finished with four hits.

June 9-10—The Longest Night in baseball history. Clark's two-run homer produced a 3-1 victory in a game that finished at 3:11 A.M. in Philadelphia. Steve Carlton had retired twelve straight Giants when the first in a series of rain delays came. The contest consumed 7 hours and 35 minutes from start to finish, but only 2 hours and 36 minutes was used to play baseball.

June 11—Rich Murray, playing his fifth game, belted his first major league homer and finished with three hits and four RBI in a 7-4 victory at Philadelphia.

June 18—The Giants dusted off the Mets 8-5, but the big story occurred in Dave Bristol's office long after the game had concluded. The manager and pitcher John Montefusco, who didn't appreciate his removal from the game, became involved in a pushing match and the Count received a black eye in the scuffle.

June 27—Left-hander Jerry Reuss pitched the Dodgers' first no-hitter in ten years, an 8-0 gem at Candlestick Park.

June 29—McCovey's run-scoring double in the bottom of the ninth earned a 4-3 victory over the Dodgers before 50,229 at Candlestick. Rennie Stennett started the rally with a single and Stretch came through off Buddy Castillo with two away.

July 10—McCovey was placed on the voluntary retired list, but not before one last hurrah. His final at bat produced an eighth-inning sacrifice fly off Rick Sutcliffe at Dodger Stadium, giving the Giants a 4-3 lead. They eventually won in the tenth, 7-4, on Milt May's run-scoring single and a two-run single by Stennett.

July 12—John Montefusco and Bill Bordley pitched a wild, 7-4, 10-7 sweep at Cincinnati. Jack Clark hit a three-run homer in the opener and joined Darrell Evans for back-to-back shots in the five-run sixth of the second game.

July 14—Clark's 400-foot homer and Al Hargesheimer's pitching gave the Giants their seventh straight victory, a 5-3 decision over the Reds. San Francisco thereby recorded the first four-game sweep ever by an opponent at Riverfront Stadium.

July 18—Milt May's grand slam was the telling blow in a four-run ninth at St. Louis, giving the Giants an 8-7 victory. Larry Herndon belted two triples and scored three runs.

July 23—The Giants turned on the power in a 14-6 romp over the Cubs. Mike Ivie and Rennie Stennett each clouted four hits among the club's twenty-one, and Clark contributed a three-run homer and four RBI.

Sept. 2—Vida Blue pitched a two-hitter for ten innings, but left the game tied 1-1 in a contest eventually won by the Phillies, 2-1.

Oct. 3—The only triple play in Candlestick Park history involved three rookie infielders for the Giants. San Diego's Dave Cash was the batter and his liner turned into a triple play handled by second baseman Guy Sularz, shortstop Joe Pettini and first baseman Rich Murray.

Dec. 8—The Giants began a busy week of wheeling and dealing at the winter meetings in Dallas. Bob Knepper and Chris Bourjos were sent to Houston for Enos Cabell and a player to be named; John Montefusco and Craig Landis went to Atlanta for Doyle Alexander, and Jerry Martin and Jose Figueroa were obtained from the Cubs for Joe Strain and Phil Nastu. Owner Bob Lurie also pulled a shocker by firing manager Dave Bristol during the meetings.

1981

Jan. 14—Frank Robinson was named manager of the Giants, becoming the first black skipper in the National League.

Feb. 9—Free agent second baseman Joe Morgan was signed by the Giants, Little Joe citing Robinson's presence as a key factor in his decision.

April 20—The Giants acquired outfielder Jeff Leonard and utility man Dave Bergman from Houston for first baseman Mike Ivie, the last great deal executed by General Manager Spec Richardson.

April 28—Right-hander Allen Ripley fired a three-hit, 6-1 victory at Dodger Stadium. Jack Clark cracked a three-run homer and Joe Morgan added a solo shot.

May 9—Billy North, hardly a power hitter, belted a grand-slam homer and a double off Steve Rogers, totaling six RBI in Vida Blue's 8-2 breeze at Montreal.

May 10—North didn't have much time to savor his slugging prowess. One day later, unheralded Expos right-hander Charlie Lea pitched a no-hitter, downing the Giants 4-0 in the second game of a doubleheader at Olympic Stadium.

May 22—Darrell Evans and Jerry Martin pooled their talents for a 6-3, fifteen-inning victory at Houston. Evans' triple and Martin's single gave the Giants a 3-2 lead in the fourteenth, but Houston tied the game in the bottom of the inning. Evans belted a two-run single and Martin added a run-scoring single in the fifteenth.

June 2—The Giants' last hurrah before the strike produced a nine-run fourth and a 15-7 romp over the Reds. Martin had a grand slam and a single in the fourth, and Morgan belted a two-run homer.

July 7—Tom Haller succeeded Spec Richardson as general manager, carrying the title of vice-president of baseball operations. The change occurred during the strike, a period in which the club also released Billy North and Randy Moffitt.

August 9—The All-Star Game at Cleveland marked the resumption of play and Blue was the winner of the Nationals' 5-4 victory. Vida thereby became the only man to win for each league in the All-Star Game.

August 15—Doyle Alexander posted a 5-2 victory at Cincinnati, becoming one of four active major leaguers to defeat all twenty-six existing major league teams.

August 27—Clark's one-out home run in the thirteenth inning defeated the Pirates, 5-4. Clark previously belted a three-run double.

Sept. 3—Doyle Alexander pitched a two-hit, 12-0 rout of the Cubs, retiring the last twenty batters. Evans, Leonard, and Larry Herndon each rapped three hits, and Clark hammered his one-hundredth career homer.

Sept. 4—Clark's two-out homer in the tenth nudged the Cubs, 3-2.

Sept. 6—Blue pitched six hitless innings before Bill Buckner spoiled the no-hit bid with a one-out single in the seventh. Vida settled for a three-hit, 3-0 victory over the Cubs, also slapping a run-scoring single.

Oct. 1—Doyle Alexander downed the Braves for his team-leading eleventh victory. Doyle finished with a 6-0 record and a 2.08 ERA at Candlestick, but announced he wouldn't be back if his contract was not renegotiated. He was traded to the Yankees the next spring.

Nov. 15—Right-hander Ed Whitson was traded to Cleveland for second baseman Duane Kuiper, triggering a rash of winter dealings by Haller. At the winter meetings in Florida, Herndon was swapped to Detroit for pitchers Dan Schatzeder and Mike Chris. One day later, Jerry Martin went to the Royals for pitchers Rich Gale and Bill Laskey.

1982

April 25—Jeff Leonard's grand slam capped a five-run eighth, and the Giants downed the Dodgers 6-3 before 47,808 at Candlestick.

April 28—Rookie Bill Laskey became an instant sensation by pitching a three-hit, 7-0 victory over the Expos shortly after his recall from Phoenix. Champ Summers, acquired in the spring from Detroit, had three singles and a walk.

April 30—The club's flair for late-inning triumphs surfaced in a 5-4 victory over the Mets, who entered the bottom of the ninth leading, 4-2. Jim Wohlford led off with a single, Jeff Ransom walked, and pinch hitter Reggie Smith smashed a three-run homer off Neil Allen.

May 28—Jack Clark snapped a prolonged slump with a three-run homer and a two-run homer off John Candelaria, powering a 10-5 victory at Pittsburgh.

May 29—Clark's grand slam and a two-run homer produced a 9-5 victory at Three Rivers Stadium. The S.F. slugger had eleven RBI and four home runs in two games.

June 1—Clark's pinch single in the eleventh earned a 4-3 victory at St. Louis.

June 5—Right-hander Rich Gale belted a two-run homer off Doug Bird at Chicago to beat the Cubs, 2-1.

June 19—Rookie Chili Davis' grand-slam homer was the big blow in a six-run ninth at Atlanta, downing the Braves, 9-4.

June 29—Rookie left-hander Atlee Hammaker, obtained from Kansas City in a swap for Vida Blue on March 30, pitched a four-hitter and cracked an RBI single in a 3-0 conquest of the Reds.

July 3—Chili Davis' leadoff homer in the fifteenth inning broke a tie and lifted the Giants to a 4-3 victory at San Diego.

July 5—Undaunted by a Veterans Stadium record crowd of 63,501, Laskey pitched the Giants to a 3-1 victory over the Phillies.

July 11—Milt May's tenth-inning homer edged the Expos 8-7 at Montreal. Smith, May, and Summers hit successive home runs in the second inning off Scott Sanderson, the first time the Giants hit three in a row since 1969.

August 1—Frank Robinson was inducted into the Hall of Fame at Cooperstown, N.Y., while coach Jim Davenport handled the club in a weekend series at the Astrodome.

August 3—The Giants, in fourth place and thirteen games behind the Braves, triggered their amazing comeback with a 6-3 victory at Atlanta. Rookie Tom O'Malley's two-run homer was the big blow in a four-run ninth, starting S.F. toward ten straight victories.

August 6—The most stirring victory during the streak found the Giants overcoming a 6-0 lead by Nolan Ryan in the sixth inning to win 7-6 with a three-run ninth. Clark and Smith hit back-to-back homers in the ninth for a tie. Pinch hitter Bob Brenly singled and eventually scored the winning run on a single by pinch hitter Darrell Evans. Clark and Smith each had two solo homers.

August 11—Morgan's walk and Smith's two-run homer in the twelfth edged the Braves 8-6 at Candlestick, giving the Giants ten straight wins and pulling them to within four games of first place.

August 20—The Cardinals were ahead 7-0 after six innings at St. Louis, but the Giants tied it with seven runs in the seventh, featuring a three-run homer by Leonard. Bruce Sutter took over in the eighth and was an 8-7 loser on Evans' triple and May's one-out, run-scoring grounder.

Sept. 4—The Giants did it again, falling behind the Cardinals 4-0 before winning 5-4 with three in the ninth at Candlestick. Leonard started things with a leadoff single, Morgan singled, and Clark clouted a game-winning, three-run homer.

Sept. 24—The Dodgers led 2-0 in the opener of a three-game series at Los Angeles, but Chili Davis' two-run double off Bob Welch in the fifth created a tie. The Giants won 3-2 when Davis singled and scored on Evans' two-out single in the eighth off Steve Howe before 50,606.

Sept. 25—Run-scoring singles by Davis and Morgan knocked home a pair of unearned runs in the eighth, and the Giants shaded the Dodgers 5-4 in front of 51,172 disbelievers.

Sept. 26—A three-run fifth off Burt Hooton carried the Giants to a 3-2 victory and a sweep of the three-game series, leaving S.F. one game out of first place entering the final week of home games. Morgan's walk started the winning rally, Clark followed with a run-scoring double, and Evans hammered a two-run homer. Fred Breining was the winner with help from Al Holland, who had his relief string snapped at 17 2/3 innings and fifty-eight batters without a hit.

Sept. 30—Another improbable victory kept the flag hopes flickering. The Astros were ahead 5-0 entering the seventh, but Ron Pruitt's two-run, two-out single in the bottom of the ninth produced a thrilling, 7-6 victory. It was Pruitt's first hit of the season.

Oct. 3—If the Giants couldn't win, they could do the next best thing—knock the hated Dodgers out of the race. Morgan's three-run homer off Terry Forster in the seventh downed the Dodgers 5-3 and gave the division crown to Atlanta by one game.

Dec. 14—The most controversial swap in General Manager Tom Haller's regime sent Joe Morgan and Al Holland to Philadelphia for pitchers Mike Krukow and Mark Davis, plus minor league outfielder Charles Penigar. The deal was made to assure added pitching depth for the future, but Morgan's leadership qualities contributed to the chemistry of the '82 club and were to be missed in '83.

1983

Feb. 8—The Giants acquired free agent outfielder Joel Youngblood, who was to prove a great addition—as an infielder—during the upcoming season. Youngblood, with no room to play in the outfield, filled in at second and third, and was a virtual regular in the second half, batting .317.

April 17—Left-hander Atlee Hammaker pitched a perfect game for seven innings in the opener of a doubleheader with Cincinnati at Candlestick Park. Johnny Bench's leadoff single snapped the string, but Hammaker finished with a two-hit, 3-0 victory, aided by Jeff Leonard's homer.

April 23—Hammaker fired his second consecutive shutout, a three-hit, 5-0 triumph at Chicago. The Cubs didn't have a hit until Larry Bowa led off the sixth with a single. Chili Davis' two-run homer and a sacrifice fly did most of the offensive damage.

May 14—Darrell Evans, in the midst of a blazing May that would earn him National League Player of the Month honors, belted two home runs for three RBI in an 8-7 victory at Cincinnati, helping the Giants sweep the four-game series.

May 18 — Jack Clark, who entered the game with only four hits in 36 trips with runners in scoring position, belted a run-scoring grounder in the first, a sacrifice fly in the fifth and a grand-slam homer in the seventh at Philadelphia to power a 8-1 romp. The six RBI gave Mike Krukow and Greg Minton plenty of support on a combined six-hitter.

May 26—Picking up where they left off the previous year, the Giants began 1983 play at Dodger Stadium with a 5-3 victory. Leonard connected for a pair of homers off Jerry Reuss to lead the attack. Bill Laskey, National League Pitcher of the Month for May at 6-0, earned the victory with help from Greg Minton.

June 11—Evans, ending a 6-for-41 slump, erupted with four straight hits, including a pair of home runs, to drive in five runs in a 7-6 victory at Atlanta.

June 15—Evans enjoyed the most prodigious slugging performance of his career by belting three home runs at Candlestick to drive in six runs during a 7-1 romp over the Astros. Evans hit a solo shot off Mike LaCoss in the first, a three-run homer off La Coss in the third, and a two-run poke off Vern Ruhle in the seventh for his 250th career homer. It was the club's first three-homer game since Gary Matthews did it on September 25, 1976.

June 18 — The Giants continued to give the Braves trouble by rallying from a 4-0 deficit after five innings to edge Atlanta, 5-4, at Candlestick. Clark's two-run homer in the sixth triggered the comeback and the Giants won it in the bottom of the eighth when Leonard's solo homer followed a two-run blast by Davis.

June 24—Krukow's first major league two-hitter stifled the

Padres, 5-0. He retired twenty-one of the last twenty-two batters after Luis Salazar singled in the third. Salazar also doubled in the first for the other hit. Rookie John Rabb powered the victory with a pair of doubles.

July 15 — Hammaker seemed destined for defeat when the Cardinals scored twice in the eighth for a 4-2 lead, but the Giants rallied for three runs in the bottom of the inning to down the champs, 5-4. Leonard, who had a two-run triple in the third, hit a sacrifice fly for the first run in the eighth and Davis followed with a two-run homer.

July 22—Clark tagged his "cousin" Pirates for five hits in five trips during a 5-3 victory at Pittsburgh. The five Clark singles resulted in the Giants' first five-hit performance since Evans and Terry Whitfield each turned the trick on July 17, 1978.

July 24 — Leonard's second career grand-slam came in the 10th inning at Pittsburgh and produced an 8-5 victory, salvaging a doubleheader split. Youngblood had a homer, double, single and three RBI.

July 30 — Left-hander Mark Davis made his Giants starting debut a memorable occasion by blanking the Dodgers on seven hits to prevail over Reuss   8-0 at Candlestick.

Aug. 5 — Johnnie LeMaster hit two home runs in a game for the first time as a professional and the Giants rolled to a 7-1 victory over Houston behind Laskey, Minton and Gary Lavelle.

August 10—Evans, returning to the park where he broke into the majors, smashed a three-run, 400-foot home run to center off Terry Forster in the top of the ninth, snapping a tie and propelling the Giants to a 7-4 victory at Atlanta's Fulton County Stadium.

Aug. 15 — Leonard, continuing a torrid August, knocked in four runs with a three-run homer and a triple and Evans blasted a two-run homer among four hits in a 7-3 crunching at Dodger Stadium.

Aug. 23 — Krukow didn't allow an earned run in eight strong innings and the Giants erupted for three runs off ex-teammate Al Holland in the bottom of the eighth for a 3-1 conquest of the Phillies. Steve Nicosia, recently acquired from Pittsburgh in exchange for Milt May, made it 1-1 with a pinch-single and Evans followed with a two-run homer.

August 24—Youngblood's two-run homer off Steve Carlton in the bottom of the ninth snapped a tie and gave the Giants a 5-3 victory and a sweep of the series with Philadelphia at Candlestick. Bob Brenly also belted a two-run homer as the winners posted their first home sweep of a three-game series from the Phillies since June 1-3, 1973.

Sept. 11—Hammaker, though winless since July 10, struck out a career-high fourteen Astros, but was not involved in the decision when the Giants rallied for three runs in the bottom of the ninth to defeat Nolan Ryan, who fanned eleven. No Giants pitcher had struck out more batters since Gaylord Perry's club-record fifteen in 1966. It also was a National League strikeout high for 1983. A two-run single by pinch hitter Dave Bergman tied the game, and Tom O'Malley's pinch single won it.

Sept. 16—Mark Davis extended his streak to eighteen scoreless innings against the Dodgers with a two-hit, 1-0 victory. Davis also singled and scored the only run in the sixth, on Leonard's single off Fernando Valenzuela, who was winless at Candlestick since April of 1981. It was Davis' second major league shutout, both against L.A.

Sept. 18—Youngblood knocked in four runs with a two-run homer and a single, and Breining pitched eight shutout innings in a 6-3 victory for a sweep of the three-game series. It was the first sweep of more than two games against L.A. at Candlestick since June 26-29, 1975, and gave the Giants ten victories in their last thirteen games with the Dodgers.

Oct. 1—Mark Davis continued his mastery over the Dodgers, limiting them to one hit for eight innings before giving way to Gary Lavelle in the ninth during the Giants' 4-1 victory at Los Angeles. Before the Dodgers erupted in the ninth, the left-handed Davis had shut them out in twenty-six consecutive innings. Rookie Chris Smith did the big damage offensively with a two-run double. The Giants also won the season finale on Oct. 2, giving them a 13-5 record against the division champions.

Dec. 20—Manny Trillo, winner of four Gold Gloves, was signed as a free agent to play second base.

1984

Feb. 26—First baseman Al Oliver, with a .305 lifetime average and eight consecutive .300-plus seasons, was acquired from the Montreal Expos for pitcher Fred Breining and a player to be named.

April 7—Rookie righthander Jeff Robinson, making the jump from Class A to the majors, fired six innings of shutout ball and allowed only four singles in his major league debut. He also had the game-winning RBI with a grounder to second on his first at bat in an 11-0 rout of the Cardinals.

May 6 — Jack Clark knocked in the first two runs with a homer and a sacrifice fly before singling and scoring the winning run on Dusty Baker's triple in a 3-2 victory at St. Louis. The win enabled the Giants to sweep the Cardinals on the road for the first time since May 6-8, 1966, the final series at old Busch Stadium.

June 13 — Chili Davis, Jeff Leonard, Jack Clark, Al Oliver, Joel Youngblood, Bob Brenly, Brad Wellman and pinch-hitter Duane Kuiper cracked a club-record eight straight hits in a seven-run, fifth-inning rally at Dodger Stadium. The eruption, which included seven singles and Wellman's double, buried the Dodgers, 10-5.

June 16 — Chili Davis slammed a two-run homer in the first inning and added a three-run homer in the fifth to power a 6-3 victory at San Diego.

June 17 — Run-scoring singles by Al Oliver and Jeff Leonard in the 15th inning cracked a tie and earned a 5-3 victory at San Diego after Oliver's single in the eighth created a 3-3 deadlock.

June 27 — Dusty Baker stole second, third and home in the third inning against the Reds, the first player to do so since Pete Rose in 1980. But it took Chili Davis' pinch-hit grand-slam to produce a 14-9 victory for the Giants. Baker, curiously, stole only one other base all season.

June 29 — The game was delayed 57 minutes because of a lighting failure at Candlestick. Then Jeff Robinson put out the Pirates' lights with a five-hit shutout that consumed a mere one hour and 57 minutes.

July 13 — The Giants and the Pirates played 18 innings and 5:11 in the nightcap of a doubleheader at Three Rivers Stadium. The Longest Night concluded on Jason Thompson's bases-loaded single in the 18th, earning a 4-3 Pittsburgh victory. Frank Williams pitched six innings of three-hit shutout relief for the Giants.

Aug. 5 — Danny Ozark's first game as interim manager resulted in a 7-4 victory at Atlanta when Jeff Leonard belted a ninth-inning grand-slam off Donnie Moore. Leonard dedicated the homer to Frank Robinson, who was fired in the late hours the previous night after guiding the club to a 42-64 record.

Aug. 7 — Jeff Leonard belted five hits in five trips and knocked in three runs during a 9-2 romp at The Astrodome.

Aug. 17 — New York Mets rookie Dwight Gooden struck out 12 Giants and Wally Backman's two-run homer in the top of the 10th sent Mike Krukow down to a disheartening 2-0 defeat at Candlestick. Gooden and Krukow were locked in a scoreless duel for nine innings and Krukow finished with a career-high 10 strikeouts.

186   GIANTS DIARY

Aug. 19 — Brad Wellman, a late-inning replacement, walloped a two-run homer off Mets relief ace Jesse Orosco in the bottom of the ninth at Candlestick, lifting the Giants to a dramatic, 7-6 victory in the opener of a doubleheader.

Aug. 24 — The Giants continued to play spoiler against the Mets, sweeping a doubleheader at Shea Stadium. Frank Williams became the first S.F. Giants pitcher to win each end of a doubleheader, working a total of one and two-thirds innings in the 7-6, 6-5 decisions. Greg Minton saved each game.

Aug. 29 — Bob Brenly hit an inside-the-park home run at Montreal in the 11th inning to edge the Expos. Brenly, riding a hot streak, was N.L. Player of the Week, Aug. 20-25, with a .440 average and four homers. His outburst powered a 9-3 road trip, second best in S.F. history.

Sept. 14 — Bob Brenly's two-run homer lifted the Giants to a 3-0 victory at Atlanta. It was his 20th, making him the first Giants catcher to reach that level since Dick Dietz in 1970.

Sept. 16 — Chili Davis smacked two home runs and had four RBI at Atlanta, extending his hitting streak to 18 games, longest on the club since Jack Clark's 26 straight in 1978. Davis was N.L. Player of the Week, Sept. 10-16, with 10 hits in 19 trips, including three homers.

1985

Feb. 1 — Jack Clark finally got his wish when the Giants traded him to St. Louis for lefthander Dave LaPoint, shortstop Jose Gonzalez, first-baseman David Green and utilityman Gary Rajsich. Clark went on to power the Cardinals into the World Series, whereas most of the players the Giants acquired were a disappointment. Gonzalez, perhaps not wishing to be identified with the controversial swap, changed his name to Uribe and became the regular shortstop. The deal came five days after the club sent veteran reliever Gary Lavelle to Toronto for righthander Jim Gott and two minor leaguers.

April 12 — Righthander Mike Krukow posted his first Giants victory at Dodger Stadium, going the distance for a 4-1 decision. The winners scored all of their runs in the third inning, a rally capped by Jeff Leonard's 400-foot, two-run homer to center.

April 19 — In an incident which set the tone for the worst season in Giants history, outfielders Jeff Leonard and Dan Gladden scuffled near the batting cage prior to a 4-2 loss at Cincinnati. Leonard, who provoked the altercation, resigned his team captaincy. Two days later, he called a team meeting to apologize and was reinstated as captain by manager Jim Davenport.

April 26 — The Reds took a 6-1 lead into the bottom of the ninth at Candlestick, but were jolted by a six-run rally in the Giants' greatest comeback of the year. Chili Davis led off with a double and scored on Jeff Leonard's single. Scot Thompson singled and Bob Brenly advanced the runners with a grounder to short. Brad Wellman belted a two-run single, pulling the Giants to within 6-4. With two out, pinch-hitter David Green walked and Dan Gladden smacked a game-winning, three-run homer off Ted Power.

May 5 — Dave LaPoint, a victim of non-support most of the season, figured out the best way to win when he hooked up against his former St. Louis teammates. The southpaw fired a six-hit, 5-0 shutout and made general manager Tom Haller happy by holding Jack Clark hitless in four trips. LaPoint and Jeff Leonard each cracked run-scoring doubles in a three-run fifth off Joaquin Andujar.

May 9 — Atlee Hammaker scattered three singles over eight innings and new relief ace Scott Garrelts struck out five batters the last two innings as the Giants edged the Cubs, 1-0, in 12 innings. The winning rally off Lee Smith started with two outs and none on base. Pinch-hitter Rob Deer singled, Dan Gladden was struck by a pitch and Manny Trillo lined a game-winning single to center.

May 12 — Jim Gott, who didn't bat with the Blue Jays, smashed a pair of solo homers in a 5-4 Giants victory over the Cardinals. Gott became the first Giants pitcher to accomplish the power feat since Dave Koslo in 1949. Reliever Scott Garrelts got the win on David Green's run-scoring single in the bottom of the 10th.

May 18 — The Giants erupted for six runs in the top of the 10th at Shea Stadium to bury the Mets, 8-2. Former teammate Gary Rajsich ended a zero-for-11 slump for the Giants, who had nine of the first 10 batters reach base in the 10th. The rally included a run-scoring double by Chili Davis followed by rookie Chris Brown's two-run homer.

June 11 — Bob Horner's two homers gave Atlanta a 4-0 lead after four innings, but some amazing relief by the Giants manufactured a 5-4 triumph in 18 innings, tying for the club's longest game since 1967. Greg Minton, Scott Garrelts, Mark Davis, Vida Blue and Frank Williams blanked the Braves on three singles over the final 14 innings. The winning rally began with two outs and nobody on base. David Green singled and stole second. After Jeff Leonard was walked intentionally, Bob Brenly lined a run-scoring single to left off Gene Garber, giving the Giants their first lead in 63 innings!

June 14 — Padres righthander Andy Hawkins was 11-0, but he couldn't beat the Giants. Gary Rajsich's force grounder tied it in the bottom of the ninth and David Green's homer off Luis DeLeon with one down in the 11th won it, 5-4.

June 16 — Chris Brown knocked in four runs with a homer, double, and a single as the Giants won the opener of a doubleheader with San Diego, 7-3, before 25,845 at Candlestick. In the nightcap, each team dramatically scored once in the 12th before the Giants won it 5-4 in the 13th on Jeff Leonard's two-out triple and Brown's single.

June 17 — Atlee Hammaker gave his finest post-surgeries performance with a complete-game, four-hit, 4-0 victory over the Reds. Jeff Leonard had a run-scoring single in the first and a solo homer in the sixth.

June 27 — Jeff Leonard became the first Giants slugger since Dave Kingman in 1972 to hit for the cycle during a 7-6 loss at Cincinnati that capped an 0-7 trip. Manager Jim Davenport lost more respect by not fining or reprimanding Leonard for the player's verbal attack on third base coach Rocky Bridges. "What happened in the dugout united 25 guys against Davvy," remarked a player.

June 30 — Vida Blue's 7-4, second-game victory over Houston in a Candlestick Park doubleheader earned him a spot in the rotation. More importantly, it snapped a 10-game losing streak, longest in the club's San Francisco history, and ended a string of 12 straight defeats to the Astros. Blue also registered his 2,000th strikeout during the game.

July 5 — The Giants quieted a crowd of 38,766 at Wrigley Field by posting season highs for hits and runs in a 17-hit, 12-6 romp. The winners erupted for seven runs in the seventh inning for a 10-2 lead. Chris Brown had four hits, including a two-run homer.

Aug. 31 — Dwight Gooden hadn't lost since May 25, winning 14 in a row, and Jim Gott hadn't won since July 2, so 22,887 assembled at Candlestick Park to watch the Mets marvel attempt to continue his mastery of the Giants. Instead, Gott didn't yield an earned run in seven innings and Gooden was handed a 3-2 defeat, making him 20-4. Run-scoring singles by Ron Roenicke and Jose Uribe made it 2-0 after two innings and Chili Davis' sacrifice fly added a run in the eighth.

Sept. 6 — Rookie Chris Brown belted a three-run homer, a two-run double and a run-scoring double among his four hits, crushing the Expos with six RBI in an 8-3 romp. Jose Uribe and Chili Davis hit solo homers for the other runs.

Sept. 18 — Owner Bob Lurie, at a morning press conference, introduced Al Rosen as the club's new president and general manager. Rosen then announced Roger Craig as the field boss. The pair replaced Tom Haller and Jim Davenport, who had guided the Giants to a 56-88 record. The new leaders were treated to a 9-6 victory over the Padres that night.

Oct. 4 — Righthander Roger Mason, acquired from the Tigers in an April swap for Alejandro Sanchez, posted his first National League victory, stopping the Braves on a 10-strikeout, four-hitter, 1-0. It was Mason's initial major league shutout and the first for the Giants since July 18. Doubles by Alex Trevino and pinch-hitter Chris Brown in the bottom of the ninth defeated Rick Mahler.

Oct. 6 — "Bye-bye Love" and "I Left My Heart in San Francisco" played over the sound system in what potentially was the Giants' final game at Candlestick Park. A crowd of 14,537 showed up for the season finale, and was treated to a seven-run, sixth-inning rally by the home club. But Atlanta posted an 8-7 victory that made the Giants the biggest loser in the history of the franchise at 62-100.

Oct. 7 — As promised, Al Rosen began his shakeup by trading Dave LaPoint, Matt Nokes, and Eric King to Detroit for catcher Bob Melvin and pitchers Juan Berenguer and Scott Medvin the day following the conclusion of the season. In the coming months, he also would deal David Green, Manny Trillo, and Alex Trevino, the latter to the Dodgers for Candy Maldonado, Dec. 11.

1986

Jan. 29 — Bay area baseball fans issued a sigh of relief when owner Bob Lurie finally announced the Giants would stay in San Francisco and play at Candlestick Park. The announcement was linked to efforts for a new downtown stadium for the club.

Feb. 12 — Willie Mays concluded a six-year absence from baseball by becoming a special assistant to Al Rosen. Mays would appear in uniform at spring training, along with Hall of Fame-bound Willie McCovey.

April 8 — The new-look Giants made a rousing debut in an 8-3, Opening Night romp at the Astrodome. Will Clark's first major league swing resulted in a home run off Nolan Ryan, Robby Thompson doubled and Candy Maldonado hit a game-winning, three-run triple as a pinch-hitter.

April 9 — Will Clark's double produced the game-winning RBI and Scott Garrelts, now a starter, fired a 4-1 victory. The second straight triumph at the Astrodome doubled the club's 1985 total under glass.

April 20 — Lefthander Vida Blue became the 85th major leaguer to notch 200 victories when a 4-0 collaboration with Jeff Robinson capped a four-game sweep of the Padres before 39,548 paying customers. The Giants mustered only three hits, one of them a two-run homer by Chili Davis.

April 21 — Righthander Roger Mason pitched a three-hitter and Chili Davis cracked a pair of homers in a 5-1 victory that gave the Giants undisputed first place for the first time since Aug. 13, 1978.

April 22 — A seven-run first inning whereby the first nine Giants reached base produced a 10-3 rout of the Dodgers and a six-game winning streak. Chili Davis' two-run double was the big blow in the first and winning pitcher Mike Krukow contributed a run-scoring single.

April 26 — Will (The Thrill) Clark provided just what his nickname implied when his two-out homer in the top of the 10th gave the Giants a 3-2 victory at San Diego.

April 29 — Retread righthander Mike LaCoss, signed as a free agent in spring training, posted his first Giants victory, 2-0, with 7 1/3 scoreless innings against the Cardinals. Chris Brown's two-out double and Jeffrey Leonard's triple gave LaCoss all the support he required. (Leonard had decided to be called Jeffrey instead of Jeff.)

May 13 — San Francisco had blown a 4-0 lead when the host Cubs rallied for five runs in the bottom of the eighth, but pinch-hitter Candy Maldonado's two-out, two-run homer in the ninth vaulted the Giants to a 6-5 victory.

May 25 — Mike LaCoss enjoyed a dream game for a pitcher during an 11-3 romp over the Expos. He fell behind on Tim Wallach's three-run homer in the first and yielded only one hit the next seven innings. He also belted three singles and a double for three RBI to pace a 16-hit attack.

June 3 — Vida Blue was a winner for the first time since April 20 when the Expos were edged at Montreal, 7-6. The price was high because first-baseman Will Clark and centerfielder Dan Gladden suffered injuries that sidelined each for more than one month.

June 8 — The Giants' aggressive brand of ball stole a second-game victory and salvaged a doubleheader split with the Reds. With the score 1-1 in the eighth, successive squeeze bunts by Mike Woodard and Robby Thompson triggered a 3-1 victory. The winning rally also included Jeffrey Leonard's second sacrifice bunt in four years.

June 12 — General manager Al Rosen made his most vital in-season acquisition when the Giants signed utilityman Harry Spilman, recently released by the Tigers. Spilman was 13 for 32 (.406) with nine RBI as a pinch-hitter for his new club.

June 13 — Mike Scott entered the ninth inning with a three-hitter and a 1-0 lead at the Astrodome. Chris Brown walked with one out, Jeffrey Leonard singled and Dave Smith replaced Scott. Chili Davis promptly belted a three-run homer for a 3-1 victory on a combination three-hitter by Mike LaCoss and Mark Davis.

June 15 — Lefthander Bob Knepper had won eight in a row against his former team and topped the N.L. with 10 victories, but the Giants turned on him for a 7-2 triumph. Jeffrey Leonard and Chili Davis powered a 14-hit barrage with three apiece. Davis concluded a six-RBI, .333 spree which earned him N.L. Player of the Week honors.

June 22 — "It seemed like a World Series," crowed manager Roger Craig after a 4-2, 3-2 sweep of the Astros before 47,030 at Candlestick Park wrested first place from Houston. Mike Krukow posted his ninth victory in the opener and reliever Juan Berenguer won the nightcap. Berenguer was N.L. Player of the Week after winning one game and saving three others in five appearances.

June 23 — All 14 Giants who played hit safely and 12 of them scored in a 21-hit, 18-1 demolition of the Padres. It was the most runs for the franchise since an 18-7 drubbing of Cincinnati, Aug. 5, 1965. A five-run first featuring Mike Aldrete's two-run single got things going. Candy Maldonado hit a two-run triple in the five-run seventh. Mike LaCoss coasted to victory on a three-hitter and contributed four RBI with a double and a three-run homer.

July 3 — Mike Krukow, elated upon learning former Phillies teammate Steve Carlton was joining the Giants, fired a three-hit, 1-0 victory over the Cardinals. Randy Kutcher's two-out homer in the sixth took care of the scoring.

July 4 — Steve Carlton ended his silence with a press conference, but new teammates Mike LaCoss and Randy Kutcher stole the show in a 6-1 rout of the Cardinals. Kutcher homered leading off the first and added a two-run single in a five-run fourth. LaCoss, improving to 3-0 against St. Louis, didn't allow a hit after Vince Coleman opened the third with a double, finishing with a five-hitter and his eighth victory.

July 13 — Randy Kutcher hit his sixth homer in 24 major league games and first-baseman Harry Spilman had four RBI with a double and a three-run homer to give the Giants an 11-4 victory and a division lead at the All-Star break for the first time since 1978. Mike LaCoss improved to 9-3.

July 17 — The Giants opened the second half with a 6-4 victory at Wrigley Field, Vida Blue aiding his cause with his first home run since

1979 and Randy Kutcher adding a homer. The win placed the Giants nine games above .500 (49-40) for the first time since 1982 and gave them a two-game lead, biggest of the season.

July 22 — On the short end of a 10-7 decision at Busch Stadium, the Giants lost far more than a game following a bench-clearing brawl with the Cardinals. Upset with Vince Coleman's stolen bases with a 10-2 lead, the Giants responded by hitting the St. Louis speedster with a pitch, triggering the fight. While tackling Coleman, Giants ace Mike Krukow suffered a ribcage injury that cost him three starts and braked the club's momentum.

July 26 — Incomparable Steve Carlton posted his only Giants victory, blanking the host Pirates for seven innings in a 9-0 runaway. Frank Williams and Juan Berenguer completed the shutout. Bob Brenly's two doubles produced four runs. Carlton soon "retired," only to re-surface with the White Sox.

Aug. 11 — Catcher Bob Melvin knocked in four runs with a homer and a bases-loaded triple and Bob Brenly added a three-run homer in a 13-4 outburst at Cincinnati made memorable by Pete Rose's last hurrah. Amid rumors that Rose's days as a starter were numbered, the Cincy skipper set a record with the 10th five-hit game of his career, blasting a double and four singles.

Aug. 15 — Mike Krukow posted his first victory since July 12 and lifted his record to 12-6 with a seven-hit, 5-1 decision over the Dodgers. Will Clark knocked in three runs with a pair of homers.

Aug. 20 — Mike Krukow and Don Carman of the Phillies fired a double shutout through nine innings, but the Giants ace was beaten, 1-0, on Juan Samuel's 10th-inning homer. Carman retired the first 24 batters, Bob Brenly ruining the perfect game with a leadoff double in the ninth, the club's only hit.

Aug. 26 — Lefthander Vida Blue pitched his finest game of the season with nothing to show for it, but the Giants emerged with a 1-0 victory over the Expos on pinch-hitter Harry Spilman's 12th-inning single. Blue worked the first nine innings, relinquishing one hit, and Scott Garrelts fired one-hit relief for three innings and was the winner.

Sept. 2 — Mike Krukow capped a brilliant season of pitching against the World Champion Mets when he posted a 4-3 victory at Shea Stadium. Bob Brenly's three-run homer helped Krukow finish 4-0 against New York, a feat no other hurler could claim. In the four victories, two of them over Dwight Gooden, Krukow received 31 runs of support while the Mets scored nine.

Sept. 7 — The fast-charging Krukow pitched a two-hitter, retiring 19 in a row in one stretch, to improve to 15-8 with a 1-0 victory over the Expos. Floyd Youmans, who lost a one-hitter, gave up the only run in the first when Robby Thompson was struck by a pitch and scored on Mike Aldrete's double.

Sept. 14 — Bob Brenly experienced one of the most bizarre games in the history of ANY major leaguer when the Giants hosted the Braves. Brenly's four errors at third base in the fourth inning tied a major league record and staked Atlanta to a 4-0 lead. Brenly then mounted a remarkable personal comeback by homering in the bottom of the fifth for the first Giants run. His two-out, two-run single in the seventh created a 6-6 tie, and Brenly ended the game with a two-out homer in the ninth for a 7-6 victory. "I've never seen anything like that," said manager Roger Craig. Not too many people had.

Sept. 26 — One day after Mike Scott embarrassed the Giants with a division-clinching no-hitter, Mike Krukow continued his march to 20 victories with a three-hit, 3-0 stifling of the Dodgers. Krukow, 19-8, was locked in a scoreless tie until the Giants scored thrice in the eighth with the help of Mike Aldrete's two-run triple.

Sept. 28 — Reliever Greg Minton, of all people, doubled with two outs in the 16th inning and stumbled home on Bob Brenly's single for an incredible, 6-5 victory over the Dodgers. A total of 52 players were used in the five-hour, 45-minute marathon, each team adding to the drama by scoring twice in the 14th. The Dodgers had a 3-0 lead entering the seventh, but homers by Chili Davis and Candy Maldonado helped carry the game into extra innings. Harry Spilman's two-run single in the 14th kept the club alive for Minton's heroics.

Oct. 5 — The Giants, finishing ahead of the Dodgers for the first time since 1971, capped an exciting season with an 11-2 romp in the season finale at Dodger Stadium. Mike Krukow became the club's first 20-game winner since Ron Bryant in 1973 and Candy Maldonado tormented his former team with two homers and six RBI. The final outburst fulfilled a prophecy for Maldonado, who told Krukow at midsummer that the ace would win his 20th on a grand-slam by Candy in Los Angeles.

CHRISTY MATHEWSON
NEW YORK, N.L.,1900-1916.
CINCINNATI, N.L., 1918.
BORN FACTORYVILLE, PA., AUGUST 12,1880
GREATEST OF ALL THE GREAT PITCHERS
IN THE 20TH CENTURY'S FIRST QUARTER
PITCHED 3 SHUTOUTS IN 1905 WORLD SERIES.
FIRST PITCHER OF THE CENTURY EVER TO
WIN 30 GAMES IN 3 SUCCESSIVE YEARS.
WON 37 GAMES IN 1908
"MATTY WAS MASTER OF THEM ALL"

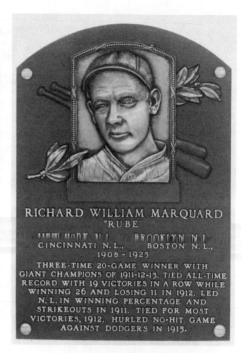

RICHARD WILLIAM MARQUARD
"RUBE"
NEW YORK N.L.,   BROOKLYN N.L.,
CINCINNATI N.L.,   BOSTON N.L.,
1908 - 1925
THREE-TIME 20-GAME WINNER WITH
GIANT CHAMPIONS OF 1911-12-13. TIED ALL-TIME
RECORD WITH 19 VICTORIES IN A ROW WHILE
WINNING 26 AND LOSING 11 IN 1912. LED
N.L. IN WINNING PERCENTAGE AND
STRIKEOUTS IN 1911. TIED FOR MOST
VICTORIES, 1912. HURLED NO-HIT GAME
AGAINST DODGERS IN 1915.

GEORGE LANGE KELLY
"HIGHPOCKETS"
NEW YORK N.L., PITTSBURGH N.L.
CINCINNATI N.L.,   CHICAGO N.L.
BROOKLYN, N.L.,1915-1930 AND 1932
ESTABLISHED MAJOR LEAGUE RECORD BY
HITTING SEVEN HOME RUNS IN SIX CONSECUTIVE
GAMES (1924). RAPPED HOMERS IN THREE
SUCCESSIVE INNINGS (1923). DROVE IN MORE THAN
100 RUNS FOUR CONSECUTIVE YEARS, 1921-24.
SET LEAGUE RECORDS FOR CHANCES ACCEPTED
(1,862) AND PUTOUTS (1,759) BY FIRST BASEMAN
IN 1920. ALSO LED IN CHANCES ACCEPTED
1921-22-23.

JOHN J. McGRAW
STAR THIRD-BASEMAN OF THE
GREAT BALTIMORE ORIOLES, NATIONAL
LEAGUE CHAMPIONS IN THE '90'S. FOR
30 YEARS MANAGER OF THE NEW YORK
GIANTS STARTING IN 1902.
UNDER HIS LEADERSHIP THE
GIANTS WON 10 PENNANTS AND 3
WORLD CHAMPIONSHIPS.

2

HISTORY OF THE GIANTS

The Giants came to New York in time for the 1883 season courtesy of the National League. The National League "invited" its Troy, New York, and Worcester, Massachusetts, members to withdraw their failing franchises. New York took over for Troy and Philadelphia replaced Worcester.

The Giants (known as the "Gothams" from 1883 to 1885) were purchased by New York City factory-owner John B. Day and James Mutrie, an energetic New York sports figure. Day and Mutrie operated the independent New York Metropolitans baseball club, which they had formed in 1881. In 1883 the dignified Day and the bustling Mutrie entered the "Mets" in the American Association and simultaneously began to build the National League Gothams.

Club President Day and business manager Mutrie stocked the Gothams with the cream of the Troy club's crop, players such as future Hall of Famers catcher Buck Ewing, first baseman Roger Connor, and pitcher Mickey Welch. Pitcher and jack-of-all-trades John Montgomery "Monte" Ward, another future Hall of Famer, was obtained from the Providence club. And several members of the Mets, including new Gotham manager John Clapp, were transferred in order to fill out the Gothams' thirteen-man roster.

The Gothams played their first game on May 1, 1883, decisioning the equally new Philadelphia Phils in a ragged 7-5 victory. The game was played at the first Polo Grounds, at 110th Street between Fifth and Sixth Avenues in Manhattan. The first Gotham lineup had catcher Buck Ewing leading off; the others, in order, were: first baseman Roger Connor, center fielder Monte Ward, left-fielder Pat Gillespie, right-fielder Mike Dorgan, pitcher Mickey Welch, second baseman Ed Caskins, shortstop Dasher Troy, and third baseman Frank Hankinson.

The Gothams finished their first season in sixth place but within a respectable four games of .500. Captain Ewing, Connor, and Welch led the team. Improvement occurred in 1884 as the same trio led the club to a fifth-place finish. Welch, the leading pitcher with a 39 and 21 record, was asked to explain his success. The carefree Welch, one of the great beer drinkers of the time, outdid himself with a cheerful little couplet:

Pure elixir of malt and hops,
Beats all the drugs and all the drops.

The National League had set attendance prices at 50 cents per admission compared with the American Association's 25 cents. Accordingly, in 1885 John Day concentrated on building up the Gothams, even at the expense of his fourth pennant winning Mets. He moved Mets manager Jim Mutrie over to manage the Gothams and transferred Mets star right-hander Tim Keefe to the Gothams. With these substantial additions — plus stellar work by Welch, Connor, Ewing, and outfielders "Orator Jim" O'Rourke and Mike Dorgan — the Polo Grounders vaulted into second place, just two games behind baseball immortal Cap Anson's Chicago White Stockings. Mutrie's jubilant, postgame victory shouts as his good-sized charges won, "My big fellows! My Giants! We are the people!" led to the club's adoption of the name "Giants" in 1886.

The Giants, led by Keefe and Welch who won a total of sixty-one of the club's eighty-four wins, won their first pennant in 1888 with relative ease over Cap Anson's club. Keefe won nineteen consecutive games, which remains a tie for the major league record. In 1889 the Polo Grounders were the beneficiary of the fifty-five wins accumulated by Welch and Keefe — they closed out the decade with another pennant.

Things worsened for the Giants in the 1890s. With little warning, city officials informed the Giants that the Polo Grounds site would be demolished in order to complete the area known now as Douglass Circle. Day hastily arranged to move the Giants to the Manhattan Field site further uptown at 155th Street and Eighth Avenue. The Giants played their first two 1890 home games at Oakland Park in Jersey City, then set up shop at Staten Island's St. George Grounds for their next twenty-five home games before moving into the second Polo Grounds on July 8, 1890.

The Giants sustained a more serious blow with the advent of the Players League in 1890. The new league was formed by the Brotherhood of Professional Baseball Players after a series of unresolved player-owner confrontations came to a head in 1889. The New York entrant in the Players League persuaded most of the Giants to join it; of the players who carried the Giants to successive

National League titles in 1888 and 1889, only Mickey Welch and outfielder "Silent Mike" Tiernan remained. As an added twist, the new Players League club took over a site just north of the Giants' new park, hardly a welcome neighbor to Day and Mutrie.

The Players League lasted only one year, but the Giants suffered big attendance losses and managed to survive only because President Arthur Soden of the National League's Boston club and a few others put up the money to keep the valuable New York franchise afloat. Day and Mutrie were ruined financially.

In March 1890, the Indianapolis club withdrew from the National League and owner John T. Brush sold his best players — most notably the fireballing Amos Rusie — to the Giants. Regardless, the decimated Giants finished in sixth place in 1890. With the demise of the Players League after the 1890 season, the Giants bought the larger Players League club's site, renamed it the "new Polo Grounds," and moved in for the next sixty-seven years. The Polo Grounders regained enough of their old players — Ewing, Connor, Keefe, O'Rourke, outfielder George Gore, and infielder Danny Richardson — to climb back up to third place in 1891.

In 1892 the National League and the American Association patched up their differences and together formed a twelve-club league with a split season. The Giants, with John B. Day still hanging on by his financial fingertips, joined the coalition. Day was pressured by new stockholders to release manager Jim Mutrie, and Pat Powers replaced Mutrie for the year. Powers finished an unspectacular eighth in 1892, his only managerial year.

Former Giant star Monte Ward, one of the key Players League figures, managed the Giants in 1893 and 1894. The second-place Giants played the pennant-winning Baltimore Orioles for the Temple Cup in 1894, and Ward's club beat the champions four straight. The Orioles had been odds-on favorites to beat the Giants for the Cup, but it was apparent that the Orioles had not given their best effort. It was learned later that several Baltimore players had agreed to split their shares with Giant players.

C. C. Van Cott was club president in 1893 and 1894, having replaced the financially crippled Day. Andrew Freedman, a New York insurance dealer and political operator, bought controlling interest in the National Exhibition Company (the Giants' corporate name) from Van Cott on January 24, 1895. Freedman conducted the club in a frenetic, uncoordinated manner during the eight years of his stewardship (1895-1902), continually quarreling with anyone with whom he came into contact. Umpires and managers resigned rather than deal with the insufferable Freedman, and his players publicly derided him. Newspapermen helped force Freedman out of the game with a devastating barrage of unfavorable caricatures and other ridicule. The Giants' performance suffered during the Freedman regime, including only one first-division finish in the eight-year period.

The abrasive Freedman made seventeen managerial changes in the eight years of his presidency. The George Steinbrenner of his day, he hired and fired Giant infielders George Davis and Bill Joyce twice each as manager. He hit his erratic peak in 1898 when he began the season with Joyce as manager, replaced Joyce in midseason with the famed Cap Anson (who could stand Freedman for only 22 games), then brought back Joyce to finish out the season. Freedman even hired destitute ex-Giant President John Day in 1899 to manage the Giants but Day lasted only seventy games, leaving with the Giants in ninth place. Freedman replaced Day with Fred Hoey, whose chief claim to sporting fame was his earlier prowess as a competing pigeon shooter. Not surprisingly, the Giants sank to a tenth-place finish.

The Giants' star players of the Freedman years were shortstop-third baseman (and sometimes manager) George Davis, infielder Kid Gleason, outfielders Mike Tiernan and George Van Haltren, and pitchers Amos Rusie, Cy Seymour, and Jouett Meekin. At age twenty-four in 1895, Davis took over the Giants, making him the youngest man to manage a major league team. He was also a fine hitter. He hit well over .300 in each of his nine years with the club, and he still holds the Giants' consecutive game hitting streak of thirty-three, achieved in 1893.

Seymour won a total of forty-five games during the 1897 and 1898 seasons. Meekin won thirty-six games in 1894 and had twenty-four and twenty wins in the 1896 and 1897 campaigns. Tiernan hit for a .311 career average and Van Haltren hit .316 in seventeen major league seasons.

Amos Rusie, elected to the Hall of Fame in 1977, won 230 games during his eight seasons with the Giants. The big Indiana right-hander, possessor of a great fastball, led the National League in strikeouts in five of the seasons. A proud man, he sat out the 1896 season when Freedman deducted a $200 fine (levied by Freedman in 1895) from his 1896 contract. Rusie brought suit to recover his 1896 salary because the club "had prevented him from following his profession." Rusie won his point and his money when all of the National League clubs chipped in to pay his 1896 salary, thereby avoiding a legal showdown on the reserve clause of player contracts. Rusie was a valuable Giant to the last — he was traded to Cincinnati in 1899 for the great Christy Mathewson.

Things improved for the Giants in the 1900-1910 period — the blundering Freedman left the Polo Grounds scene in 1902. Before he left he made his only certifiably wise decision — he hired Baltimore manager John McGraw as manager, a move that made the Giants the premier National League team for the next twenty-five years. McGraw assumed control of the Giants on July 19, 1902, bringing with him such talented Baltimore players as pitcher Joe "Iron Man" McGinnity, catcher Roger Bresnahan, and first baseman Dan McGann.

The 1902 Giants were a lost cause. Even the dynamic McGraw and his imported talent could not prevent a cellar finish. But in 1903, John T. Brush bought controlling interest in the Giants from the discredited Freedman, which helped McGraw drive the club to a second-place finish that year. The Giants' resurgence was led by McGinnity (31 and 20) and Mathewson, who won thirty games for the first of four times with the Giants. During the month of August, the remarkably rubber-armed McGinnity pitched and won an incredible three complete-game doubleheaders.

The Giants were overwhelming in 1904, winning the pennant by thirteen games over the second-place Cubs. Mathewson, McGinnity, and Luther "Dummy" Taylor won a total of ninety-five games. There had been a World Series in 1903, the American League's first year of operation, but Giant owner John Brush was still contemptuous of the new league and he did not permit the Giants to play the Boston Red Sox, who won the American League pennant. Because of Brush's attitude, baseball's National Commission immediately prepared rules for holding a World Series every year beginning in 1905.

The year 1905 repeated 1904 as the powerful Giants won the pennant by nine games over Pittsburgh. Mathewson, McGinnity, and Leon "Red" Ames accounted for seventy-four Giant wins, and McGraw's offensive stars were center fielder "Turkey Mike" Donlin, left fielder Sam Mertes, and catcher Roger Bresnahan. The Giants defeated Connie Mack's Philadelphia Athletics in the World Series, 4 games to 1, in a beautifully pitched five-game set. Christy Mathewson was brilliant, pitching three shutouts, and Joe McGinnity shut out the A's for the Giants' other win. The Athletics' only win came when Chief Bender beat McGinnity, 3-0.

The Giants did not win another pennant, but the 1900-1910 decade was marked by rapid improvement under McGraw nonetheless. McGraw also had a major impact on the game itself. His use of the platoon system — specialized deployment of his players — changed baseball strategy and was a prototype of Earl Weaver's masterful use of players' strengths.

McGraw intensified baseball's emotional aspect by motivating his players as no manager had yet done and by rousing fans, both for and against the Giants. As famed sportswriter Grantland Rice put it: "His very walk across the field in a hostile town is a challenge to the multitudes."

Frank Graham, in his classic *McGraw of the Giants,* described how

McGraw mounted a psychological campaign against a contending team, in this case the 1905 Pittsburgh Pirates:

> He [McGraw] fought with Fred Clarke, who managed the Pirates, and Barney Dreyfuss, the owner of the club. He raged at the umpires over every close decision against the Giants . . . . The result was that his players were set on fire at the very sight of Pittsburgh uniforms. Even the mild-mannered Mathewson, who seldom had a word to say to anyone on the field and almost never protested a decision, often found himself tangled with the umpires when the Giants and the Pirates were engaged . . . . The record of the games between the teams that year is one of almost unbroken strife that the umpires could only check now and then and never could quite put down.

McGraw's effect on the emotional level of fans led the stocky little Irishman and the Giants into a continuing series of controversial and often wildly exuberant scenes. For example, in August 1904, Giant catcher Frank Bowerman slugged a fan who had been riding him hard in a game in Cincinnati. The aggrieved fan, holding his badly cut jaw, claimed that McGraw had "ordered the assault." A week later, overenthusiastic Giant fans celebrated an exciting Giant doubleheader victory at the Polo Grounds by nearly trampling McGraw as he left the Giant dugout for the clubhouse. Several fans tried to carry McGraw off the field in triumph, but they dropped him and wild-eyed rooters walked all over the prostrate manager, nearly crushing him and severely injuring his ankle.

Mathewson's brilliance shone through the McGraw-generated turmoil. "Big Six" became the fans' idol early in the 1900s, not only because of his great pitching and famous "fadeaway" (screwball), but because of his style. Unlike the rough-tough, mercurial McGraw, Matty came across as a cool, gentlemanly craftsman who pitched as though he were playing chess. He preferred outguessing hitters to terrorizing them with brute force. He did not specialize in strikeouts but, with his superb control and stuff, induced hitters to hit the ball weakly to his fielders.

Mathewson had a reputation for letting up on opponents when he was well ahead in order not to humiliate the opposition unnecessarily (and not to tax his pitching arm unduly). His effect on the fans was heightened because he was so unlike the combative McGraw. Ironically, McGraw, Mathewson, and their wives were almost inseparable off the field.

Other Giants of early twentieth-century vintage also drew special attention from the writers and fans. Tough, aggressive outfielder Mike "Turkey Mike" Donlin spent six highly successful years with the

Giants, interspersed with years out of the game when he pursued a career in vaudeville. Donlin married stage star Mabel Hite and eventually worked in Hollywood in several films. Roger Bresnahan was a future Hall of Famer and innovative catcher who in 1906 became the first receiver to wear shinguards and the first hitter to wear a head protector. Second baseman "Laughing Larry" Doyle was a solid, upbeat player who coined the phrase, "It's great to be young and a Giant." Third baseman Art Devlin was the classic McGraw-type player whose steadiness and aggressiveness compensated for his just-average hitting. And alcoholic right-hander Arthur "Bugs" Raymond intrigued the fans with his heavy drinking antics, although his weakness led to his death at 30. (Raymond's favorite practice was to trade baseballs for drinks at bars near the ballpark.)

The 1911-1920 period began inauspiciously on April 14, 1911, when a fire of undetermined origin ravaged the Polo Grounds and demolished most of the structure. The Giants accepted an offer by the Yankees to use Hilltop Park, the American Leaguers' home park at 168th Street and Broadway in Manhattan. The Giants played there until they returned to the rebuilt and enlarged Polo Grounds on June 28, 1911.

The decade was marked by three straight pennant wins during the 1911-1913 period, a precipitous drop into last place in 1915, and a rebuilding program that carried the Giants to another pennant in 1917 and second-place finishes through the 1920 season.

Giant left-hander Richard "Rube" Marquard matured from a four-game winner in 1910 to a twenty-four game winner in 1911, and that improvement brought McGraw's club the pennant. The Giants repeated in 1912 and 1913 as Mathewson, Marquard, and right-hander Jeff Tesreau provided great pitching. The offensive load was carried by Fred Merkle (who had successfully shaken off the trauma of his 1908 "boner" with McGraw's strong support), Larry Doyle, right fielder Red Murray, center fielder Fred Snodgrass, and full-blooded-Indian catcher John "Chief" Meyers.

The Giants failed completely in the World Series of 1911-13. They lost to Connie Mack's Athletics in 1911 and 1913 so convincingly that Giant rooters could accept the defeats with equanimity. But the loss to the Boston Red Sox in 1912, on Snodgrass' "$30,000 muff" was difficult to take.

On November 26, 1912, President John T. Brush died. Harry N. Hempstead, his son-in-law, replaced him. Hempstead, who knew nothing about baseball, relied for advice on club Secretary John B. Foster rather than McGraw. The resulting front office friction continued until McGraw characteristically reestablished his complete control over the club a few years later.

After a second-place finish in 1914, the Giants fell apart in 1915, finishing last for the only time in McGraw's thirty-year tenure.The season was notable only because 1912 Olympic star Jim Thorpe joined the Giants (he proved allergic to curve balls and didn't stay) as did first baseman George "Highpockets" Kelly (who eventually made it). McGraw cleaned house and brought the Giants up to fourth place in 1916 with some assistance from outfielder Benny Kauff, the Ty Cobb of the short-lived Federal League. In midseason McGraw traded his friend Christy Mathewson to Cincinnati, where Matty took over as manager.

The 1916 Giants were models of inconsistency. The club lost eight straight games in late April, then ran off a string of seventeen victories in May, all of them on the road. Finally, the Giants escaped to fourth place from deep in the second division with a record 26-game winning streak in September.

The retooled Giants won the 1917 pennant by a ten-game margin. This was an unexpectedly easy flag considering that the Giants had only one twenty-game winner (Ferdie Schupp with a 21 and 7 record), only two .300 hitters (center fielder Benny Kauff and left fielder George Burns), and only one hitter with more than sixty-eight RBI (third baseman Heinie Zimmerman had 102). The Giants lost the World Series to the Chicago White Sox, 4 games to 2.

The Giants wound up the decade with second-place finishes in 1918 and 1919, but not without some taint of the game-throwing scandals that surfaced in the 1919 Black Sox affair. The Giants had obtained fancy-fielding first baseman Hal Chase from Cincinnati early in 1919 after the Reds had suspended the shady Chase for "indifferent play" in August 1918. The Reds also had charged Chase with attempting to influence players to throw games, but he was acquitted by the National League's Board of Directors.

During September 1919 both Chase and Zimmerman failed to play in a number of games and McGraw sent them home without public explanation. A year later, as part of the Black Sox investigation, McGraw testified that he had dismissed the players because they had thrown games and had attempted unsuccessfully to bribe Giant players to do the same. Both men eventually were banned from organized baseball.

Three of the great Giants and future Hall of Famers joined the club as the decade neared its end — outfielder Ross "Pep" Youngs, infielder Frank Frisch (straight off the Columbia University campus), and first baseman George Kelly (back from the minors). In addition, polished left-hander Art Nehf came over from the Braves and right-hander Jesse Haines arrived from the Cubs.

The Giants changed hands on January 14, 1919, when the club was purchased for more than one million dollars from the John T.

Brush estate by a syndicate headed by New York stockbroker Charles A. Stoneham, New York City Magistrate Francis X. McQuade, and John McGraw. Stoneham was elected president, McQuade treasurer, and McGraw vice-president while continuing as field manager.

The Giants sparkled in the first half of the 1920s, then frustrated McGraw and the fans by barely falling short in the second half. The 1920s also found the Giants in a losing struggle with the up-and-coming Yankees for supremacy in New York.

The Giants finished second in 1920, well behind old Oriole Wilbert Robinson's Brooklyn Robins. The season is remembered best for the Giants' acquisition from the Braves of shortstop Dave "Beauty" Bancroft, who sparked the team to pennant wins in 1921-1923. It also marked the first public indication of friction between the Giants and the Yankees. On May 14 the Giants informed the Yankees that the American Leaguers' lease to use the Polo Grounds would not be renewed after the 1920 season. No reason was given although it was obvious that the wide acclaim for the Yanks' recently-acquired Babe Ruth had been a great irritant. Yankee owner Jacob Ruppert responded angrily that the Giants had "gone back on their word," the understanding that had been in effect since the Yanks had begun using the Polo Grounds in 1912. The Giants' eviction order was rescinded a week later, but the Yanks began immediate efforts to obtain a site for their own ballpark.

The Giants won the first of four consecutive pennants in 1921 as Kelly, Bancroft, Frisch, Youngs, and veteran outfielder George Burns led the offense and Art Nehf anchored the pitching staff. The turning point of the season came in late August when the Giants, 7 1/2 games behind league-leading Pittsburgh, took five straight games from the overconfident Pirates at the Polo Grounds. McGraw's club went on to defeat the Yankees 5 games to 3 in the first "Subway Series."

The Polo Grounders repeated in 1922 with the same personnel, winning the pennant with relative ease and again defeating the Yankees in the World Series. The Giants' second straight World Series win over the hated Yankees was noteworthy because the Giants held Babe Ruth to a mere two hits and the second game was called surprisingly "on account of darkness" with the score tied at three-all and the sun high in the sky. There was such an uproar at the decision of umpire George Hildebrand to call the game that Commissioner Landis ordered the receipts of more than $120,000 sent to New York City charities and veterans' groups.

The Giants welcomed the 1923 season at the Polo Grounds, which had been expanded to its ultimate fifty-five thousand seating capacity. The original fifteen thousand bleacher seats were reduced to fifty-five hundred as many of the old bleacher seats in left center and right center were converted to covered, double-decked grandstands. This was the last significant addition to the Polo Grounds except for lights for night games, which were installed in 1940. It left the long, bathtub-shaped park with short foul lines (257 feet to right and 280 feet to left) and bleachers some 455 feet from the plate.

The Polo Grounders won their third straight pennant in 1923, led offensively by left fielder Emil "Irish" Meusel, Frisch, Kelly, and Youngs. Their rather pedestrian pitching staff (with a 3.90 ERA) was headed by American League castoff right-hander Jack Scott and right-hander Rosy Ryan with sixteen wins apiece. The Giants lost the World Series to the Yankees, now ensconced in brand-new Yankee Stadium. The key figures in the Series were Babe Ruth who hit .368 with three homers, and the Giants' Casey Stengel, who hit .417 and won two games with home runs.

The Giants nosed out Brooklyn for their fourth straight flag in 1924. This was substantially the same cast that had won pennants the past three years, with the addition of shortstop Travis Jackson (replacing Dave Bancroft), center fielder Hack Wilson, and part-timers first baseman Bill Terry and third baseman Fred Lindstrom. The Washington Senators beat the Giants in a seven-game World Series. Giant reliever Jack Bentley lost to the great Walter Johnson 4-3 in the bottom of the ninth of the deciding game when the Senators' Earl McNeely's easy bouncer hit a pebble and hopped over Giant third baseman Fred Lindstrom's head.

Hampered by inadequate pitching, the Giants did not win another pennant in the 1920s. The 1925, 1926, 1927, and 1929 clubs had on their rosters no less than seven future Hall of Famers, yet only the 1925 and 1928 clubs finished as high as second place. The Giants began to play an increasingly more obvious second fiddle to the mighty Yankees with each passing year, and McGraw's frustration increased correspondingly.

The Giant manager's increasing irritability caused the club to lose Frisch, who was then in his prime. Frisch, the Giant captain, jumped the club in St. Louis after receiving a vicious tongue-lashing from McGraw following a Giant loss. The Giants had been going poorly and, as was McGraw's custom, he took out his annoyance on the team captain. Frisch and McGraw met when the team returned to New York and Frisch rejoined the Giants shortly after. But it was clear that McGraw had not forgiven him and that Frisch would be gone as soon as McGraw could arrange it. The result was a midwinter trade of Frisch and pitcher Jimmy Ring to the Cardinals for the great Rogers Hornsby.

The Giants remained a star-studded club through the 1920s

despite McGraw's inability to bring another pennant to New York. Ross Youngs was a great outfielder and hustler who hit .322 over a ten-year career. His playing days ended abruptly with the onset of a serious kidney ailment that took his life in 1927 at age thirty.

Bill Terry was considered the finest-fielding first baseman of his day, and his .341 lifetime average is among the highest for modern era players. Memphis Bill was a powerful, straightaway hitter who specialized in blasting line drives into the power alleys. A blunt, outspoken man, Terry was described by a veteran Polo Grounds bleacherite as "basically a good businessman who happened to be a great first baseman and hitter only coincidentally."

Travis Jackson was the perfect "ballplayer's ballplayer," widely respected and liked by the players and the fans. He was a great shortstop with good range, a rifle arm, superb bunting and hit-and-run talents, and surprising power considering his slight figure.

Mel Ott's brilliant Giant career began in 1925 when he joined the club, just before the season ended, as a scared sixteen-year-old catcher referred to McGraw by a New Orleans friend. Ott played his first game at seventeen and became the regular right fielder in 1928. The most popular Giant of his time, Master Melvin carried the Giant offense for most of his twenty-two playing seasons with the club. Ott was the National League leader in career home runs with 511 before he retired as a player in 1947.

Carl Hubbell, a stylish, screwballing left-hander from Oklahoma, who joined the Giants in 1928, carried the Giant pitching load as effectively as his bosom buddy Ott spearheaded the offense. Noted for his ability to win crucial games, Hubbell retired in 1943 to become the Giants' farm club supervisor, a position he held for more than thirty years.

Freddy Fitzsimmons, a stout and stout-hearted knuckleballer from Indiana, became a Giant in 1925. Famed for his unusual "turntable" delivery, the right-hander won 170 games as a Giant until he was traded to Brooklyn in 1937 in a bad deal for the Giants.

Fred Lindstrom was a talented third baseman-outfielder who came to the Giants as an eighteen-year-old in 1924. Lindstrom had an impressive 231 hits in both the 1928 and 1930 seasons, winding up with a .311 lifetime average. The outspoken Chicago native was known for his quick wit and his willingness to challenge authority. On one occasion he silenced nagging acting manager Rogers Hornsby with the angry putdown, "Once you drop that bat, you're no bargain!"

McGraw permitted Lindstrom to stay with his parents overnight when the Giants played in Chicago, but after a tough loss to the Cubs in 1928, McGraw forgot about the arrangement. "Lindstrom," he roared, "You didn't check into your room last night and that'll cost you fifty dollars." Lindstrom protested, "But, Mr. McGraw, you always let me go home when we're in Chicago. It's not right to fine me."

"Enough of that," thundered McGraw. "The fine still goes."

"Okay, then, it goes," retorted Fred, "but I hope you break your leg to teach you a lesson."

The furious McGraw stomped out of the clubhouse, and while crossing a street outside Wrigley Field, walked into the path of an automobile — he didn't quite break his leg but he injured it badly and was laid low for a few weeks.

The decade ended with the Giant front office in turmoil. On December 24, 1929, officers of the Giant club filed a $200,000 damage suit against Francis X. McQuade, a major stockholder who had been deposed as club treasurer after serving in that post for nine years. The Giants' suit charged McQuade with seeking to "wreck and destroy" the club. McQuade filed a countersuit. After long and arduous litigation, the New York Supreme Court ordered the Giants to pay McQuade back salary as treasurer but refused to order his reinstatement to the post. The Giants successfully protested the payment order to a higher court, leaving McQuade out in the cold.

In the 1930s the Giants were dominated by three great players — Terry , Hubbell, and Ott. Terry hit .401 in 1930 (the last National Leaguer to hit .400), just missed winning the National League batting title in 1931 by the narrowest of margins, then replaced McGraw as manager in 1932. Memphis Bill, making excellent use of his skills as a defensive strategist, took the Giants to a surprise World Championship in 1933 and to pennants in 1936 and 1937. Hubbell was the Giant pitching leader and Ott was the club's offensive pillar throughout the decade.

The 1930s began with two more first-division finishes by the Giants but without McGraw's coveted eleventh National League pennant. As in the late 1920s, the Giants were able to finish in the first division but were not equal to winning the pennant. For New Yorkers, spoiled by McGraw's earlier successes, this simply was not good enough. McGraw's 1930 club managed to remain in the running through August, but wound up in third place. The story was the same in 1931 when the Giants finished well behind the pennant-winning Cardinals.

McGraw's health, poor for some time, worsened in 1932, and the jumpy, easily-irritated manager lost control of his players. The club floundered through April and May. Then, on June 3, an ill and aging McGraw stepped down and Bill Terry was named to succeed him. McGraw died less than two years later, on February 25, 1934.

Under Terry, the disorganized, last-place Giants regrouped and managed a sixth-place finish. Terry began maneuvering to improve the club as soon as the unhappy season ended. He swung a major deal with the Cardinals, obtaining second-string catcher Gus Mancuso. (Mancuso would be a key Giant in three pennant wins.)

Lindstrom, openly unhappy because he felt that he would be McGraw's successor, was traded to the Pirates. In other off-season transactions of note, pitchers Waite Hoyt and Clarence Mitchell were released and catcher Frank "Shanty" Hogan was sold back to the Braves.

Terry inherited several good ballplayers from McGraw, beginning with first baseman Terry himself. Shortstop Travis Jackson was still around, although hampered by knee ailments. Mel Ott, beginning his eighth year with the Giants at age twenty-four, was the only authentic Giant power hitter and one of the best right fielders in the game. Left fielder JoJo Moore, a gaunt, hollow-cheeked youngster with a great arm, had shown promise. Second baseman Hughie Critz was the other regular inherited from McGraw.

The Giants had a number of good pitchers. Hubbell was the staff leader and Freddy Fitzsimmons was an established starter. Terry was high on Hal Schumacher, a determined, sinker-ball-throwing right-hander who had pitched for the Giants in 1931 and 1932. Other pitchers included LeRoy "Tarzan" Parmelee, whose nickname derived from his wildness; Ray Starr, who had come from the Cardinals in the Mancuso deal; left-hander Al Smith; and Aldolfo Luque, a wily, forty-three-year-old Cuban relief pitcher whose National League career dated back to 1919 when he pitched for the Reds.

The Giants, picked to finish in sixth place by the annual Associated Press poll of sportswriters, surprised the experts by holding third place on Memorial Day. Well suited to the dead ball that had come into use in 1933, the Giants began to win a series of low-scoring games and moved into first place to stay in June. Hubbell, Fitzsimmons, Schumacher, and Parmelee rotated starting assignments and pitched effectively and Luque, Starr, and the all-purpose Hubbell excelled in relief. Mancuso proved a steadying influence behind the plate. Rookie shortstop Blondy Ryan was an adequate substitute for Travis Jackson. Ott led the hitters as expected.

One of the season's highlights came on July 2 when the Giants won a memorable doubleheader from the Cardinals at the Polo Grounds. Hubbell pitched an incredible eighteen scoreless innings to win the opening game 1-0 after Tex Carleton had thrown sixteen brilliant scoreless innings for the Cards and had been relieved by Jesse Haines. In the second game, which was played in semidarkness and a steady drizzle, Parmelee shut out the Cardinals for another 1-0 victory.

The Giants defeated Joe Cronin's Washington Senators in the World Series 4 games to 1 as Hubbell and Ott excelled. King Carl won the opening game at the Polo Grounds 4-2, supported by Master

Melvin's three-run homer and 4-for-4 hitting performance. Hubbell took the fourth game 2-1, and Ott won the last game with a tenth-inning home run to give the Giants a 4-3 decision.

As the year ended, an Associated Press poll voted the Giants' World Series triumph as the top team victory of 1933.

A triumphant Bill Terry attended the annual major league meetings in New York in January 1934 and talked with several of the writers about prospects for the coming season. On the edge of the group stood the *New York Times'* Roscoe McGowen, who normally covered the Dodgers. In the beginning he paid little attention to the conversation. But when Terry was questioned about the other clubs, McGowen became more attentive. He asked, "How about Brooklyn, Bill?" Terry turned to them and smiled. "Brooklyn, I haven't heard anything about them. Are they still in the league?" Everybody laughed and everybody printed the remark.

Terry, never known for his subtlety, had responded lightly, but it didn't come out that way in the writers' stories. Thousands of letters poured into the Giants' office, all of them from irate Dodger rooters. The Dodgers had left their fans cold since falling deep into the second division. But Terry's offhand comment had fired them up. Wait until the season started. Their team would show Terry whether Brooklyn was still in the league!

The Giants were favored to win the 1934 pennant and they played up to that form, leading the league by the time the All-Star game was played in early July. Terry piloted the National League squad in the second game of the series at the Polo Grounds on July 10. The National League's 9-7 loss was not the enduring story of the game; Hubbell's pitching was. The great left-hander struck out five Hall of Famers in a row — Babe Ruth, Lou Gehrig, Jimmy Foxx, Al Simmons, and Joe Cronin.

On Labor Day the Giants roosted in first place, six games ahead of St. Louis and Chicago. But by mid-September Terry's club was faltering badly while the "Gas House Gang" Cardinals, sparked by Dizzy Dean, were streaking, and the clubs were even with two games left to play. The relaxed Dodgers came into the Polo Grounds to complete the season.

Terry probably had given very little thought to the Brooklyn fans during the season when the Giants were riding high and the Dodgers were floundering in the second division. But now, at the rain-swept Polo Grounds that final Saturday of the season, the Dodger fans were out in force. They carried banners aimed at their arch-rival, Terry. There were banners that read "Bill Who?" or "I Wish *You* Were in Dixie," and the most prevalent, "Yeah, We're Still in the League." They screamed and taunted all the Giants, even the popular Ott, and Jackson who normally were cheered even at Ebbets Field. But they saved their choicest epithets for Terry, one of the most gentle being, "Is Brooklyn still in the league, Terry? You'll find out, you cocky bum. We'll show you."

And show Terry the Dodgers did. They took the Giants in the two games while the Cardinals won twice to win the pennant. Within the context of the Giant-Dodger rivalry, it was a bad year for the second-place Giants and a triumphant year for Casey Stengel's sixth place Dodgers.

The 1935 Giant team was essentially unchanged except for the addition of scrappy little shortstop Dick Bartell, who was obtained from the Phils. So were the results. A good start, with the Giants leading the league through much of the season, then the Terrymen falling before a tough western club — this time the Cubs, who stormed to the pennant with a devastating twenty-one game-winning streak.

Terry made one important trade after the 1935 season, picking up utility infielder Burgess Whitehead from the Cardinals. Some of the writers questioned whether the slight Whitehead had the stamina to play a full season, although even the doubters were intrigued because Whitehead had graduated Phi Beta Kappa from the University of North Carolina, hardly a requisite to being a member of the rough-and-ready Gas House Gang.

On January 6, 1936, Giant President Charles A. Stoneham died. He was the only survivor of the triumvirate that had purchased the Giants in 1919. A week later, thirty-two year-old Horace C. Stoneham replaced his father. A few weeks later, the popular Eddie Brannick, who had been associated with the Giants since he was a small boy running errands for John McGraw, became the team secretary.

After a good start, the 1936 Giants slipped badly, and were in fifth place at the All-Star Game break. After losing the first game of a doubleheader on July 15, the Terrymen were eleven games behind the league-leading Cubs. But they captured the second game when Terry, playing gamely with a badly-crippled knee against his doctor's advice, came off the bench and led the club with a single, a double, and a triple. This valiant effort revived the Giants, who won thirty-nine of their next forty-seven games to rocket into first place and remain there for the rest of the season. Bartell and Whitehead anchored the defense and Mancuso had his best year since 1933. But the blue-chip performers, as always, were Hubbell and Ott; at times, they carried the club on their backs. Hubbell, called the "Meal Ticket," racked up a league-leading twenty-six wins, finishing the season with sixteen straight wins and a 2.31 ERA. Ott had a league-leading thirty-three homers and 135 RBI.

The Giants lost the World Series to the overpowering Yankees, 4 games to 2. Hubbell won the first game, and Schumacher held on tenaciously to win the fifth game. But the Giants were overmatched by the Gehrig-DiMaggio-Dickey-Ruffing-et al. steamroller that had won the American League flag by a cool 19 1/2 games.

The Giants won the pennant in 1937 on the strength of twenty-game winning seasons by Hubbell, rookie left-hander Cliff Melton, powerful hitting by Ott, and some late-season hitting heroics by outfielder Jimmy Ripple. Hubbell won his first eight decisions of the campaign, running his two-year record to twenty-four straight wins before the Dodgers, his career-long nemesis team, broke the string on Memorial Day. Melton was an immediate sensation after Terry worked him into the starting rotation in May. Nevertheless, the Giants were seven games behind the league-leading Cubs in early August when Terry made a lineup change. He brought in the versatile Ott from right field to replace weak hitting third baseman Lou Chiozza and inserted Ripple into the outfield. The results were immediate and sensational. Powered by Ott and Ripple, the Giants vaulted into first place in early September and held on to win the pennant.

The 1937 World Series was a replay of the 1936 Series. The Giants again were badly overmatched and the Yanks won 4 games to 1, with the redoubtable Hubbell the only Giant winner.

The Giants were also-rans for the rest of the decade. The 1938 club started brilliantly, holding first place by the All-Star Game break. But the Polo Grounders faltered when play resumed and they wound up in third place, the downswing largely caused by serious elbow injuries to Hubbell and Schumacher.

After the season, Terry engineered a big trade with Chicago, sending Bartell, Lieber, and Mancuso to the Cubs for their opposite numbers — shortstop Billy Jurges, outfielder Frank Demaree, and catcher Ken O'Dea. First baseman Zeke Bonura, a powerful hitter but with no discernible mobility afield, was obtained from Washington. Regardless of the trades, the Giants sank into fifth place in 1939, by far their worst showing under Terry. To make matters worse, as the decade ended, the hated Dodgers moved past the Giants into third place.

The Giants' melancholia persisted through the 1940s. The remaining years of Terry's stewardship offered no relief. There was a brief improvement in Mel Ott's first year as manager in 1942, but Ott's remaining managerial years were unlucky and unhappy, Giant misfortune relieved only by the powerful, home-run-hitting 1947 club. And the Giants showed no immediate improvement under Leo Durocher, Ott's astonishing replacement, through the end of the decade.

The Giants finished sixth in 1940 and fifth in 1941, Terry's last two years as manager. Hal Schumacher led the pitching staff in wins both years with a meager thirteen in 1940 and twelve in 1941. First baseman Babe Young and catcher Harry Danning were the most effective hitters in 1940, and Ott, troubled with eyesight difficulties, had his first poor hitting season. Young and an improved Ott carried the attack in 1941. Meanwhile, the Giants continued to lose attendance and local prestige as the revived Dodgers came in second in 1940 and won the pennant in 1941.

Mel Ott was named to manage the Giants on December 2, 1941, just five days before Pearl Harbor and the U.S. active entry into World War II. Ott, easily the most popular Giant since joining the club in 1926, was a surprise choice, primarily because of his quiet, unassuming personality and his lack of managing experience. Terry, long desirous of moving into the front office, became the director of the Giants' shrinking farm system operation.

Ott's regime began on a high note. The New York fans, writers, and players rejoiced in the likable slugger's appointment, and his early trade for the Cardinals' Johnny Mize made a big hit. It also paved the way for an unexpectedly strong third-place finish in 1942 as Ott and Mize blasted the pitching-poor Giants to victory after victory. But Giant fortunes plummeted in 1943 as the Giants lost a disproportionately large number of regulars to the military draft. When the club gathered at its Lakewood, New Jersey, training camp (all clubs were required to train near their home cities because of the transportation and fuel shortages caused by the war), regulars Harry Danning, Johnny Mize, Babe Young, and Willard Marshall were in the service and several other Giants were expected to be called up at any time.

The undermanned Giants sank deep into the second division early in the season, the one bright spot coming on June 5 when Hubbell, approaching forty and in his final playing season, threw a brilliant one hitter against the Pirates for his 250th career win. The low esteem in which the lowly Giants were held and Ott's resulting frustration were illustrated in July when the *World Telegram*'s Tom Meany visited the Pirate clubhouse, scrounging for news. Meany noticed a blackboard in Pittsburgh manager Frankie Frisch's office, detailing how the Pirates planned to pitch each Giant. Frisch ordered Meany out, bellowing loudly, "Hey, Meany, get the hell out of here. I don't want you going back to those guys telling them what their weaknesses are. Some of those fellows don't even know themselves what they can't hit." The next day, after hearing Meany's story, Ott visited the Pirate clubhouse to chat with old comrade-in-arms Frisch and, most importantly, take a look at the blackboard. Frisch invited Mel in and they talked about old times at considerable length. Ott told Meany later, "Tom, we had a nice social visit but don't think for a moment I got a look at that blackboard. Frank had pulled a dark shade down over it and every once in a while he would look over at it, wink at me, and go right on talking about something else."

As the 1943 season drew to a merciful close, Ott was signed to a three-year, player-manager contract, and the freshly-retired Hubbell signed a long-term pact as farm system director, the post formerly held by Bill Terry. With the U.S. military effort approaching its peak of activity, the Giant farm system consisted only of the Jersey City team of the International League, the Class D Bristol club in the Appalachian League, and a small scouting staff.

Terry had remained inactive in 1943 after stepping down from his front office job earlier in the year. But in January 1944 he announced that he had abandoned the game to go into the cotton business. Memphis Bill said dourly, "It [baseball]'s too cheap a business and it's getting cheaper all the time." Then, completely underestimating the postwar profits and salaries to be made in the game, Terry continued, "With the low salaries they're paying, there's nothing in the game for me." The blunt, ex-Giant pilot said he was not worried about the game's future, concluding tartly, "No business in the world has ever made more money with poorer management. It can survive anything."

The 1944 Giants managed to finish in fifth place, reflecting the simple fact that other National League clubs had lost more talent to the military than the Polo Grounders since the 1943 season.

The Giants repeated their 1944 performance in 1945 — a fifth-place finish and no real chance for the pennant. The Giant highlight of the year came on August 1 when Ott blasted his five hundredth career home run. (At the time, the second-highest National League home run total was owned by Rogers Hornsby with 302.) An amusing sidelight — later that night there was a big party at Toots Shor's famous restaurant in Manhattan to celebrate Ott's milestone. Shor was a great Ott admirer and the story has it that the gregarious Toots was chatting that night with Sir Alexander Fleming, the discoverer of penicillin, when Ott arrived at the entrance to the restaurant. Spying Ott, Shor turned to a bemused Sir Alexander and said, in his impeccable New York accent, "Excuse me, I have to greet someone who's coming in who is *really* important."

The first post-World War II year, 1946, started promisingly. The Giants purchased catcher Walker Cooper from the Cardinals for $175,000, a lot of money in 1946. Before entering the service in 1944, Cooper had been considered the best young catcher in the game. In addition, the Giants acquired highly-ballyhooed pitcher-outfielder Clint "Hondo" Hartung from Minneapolis.

Then, with no warning before the season opened, several Giants jumped to the Mexican League, a newly-formed "outlaw" league operated by Mexican customs broker Jorge Pascual. Within a six-week period, the Giants lost Gardella; Reyes; pitchers Adrian Zabala, Sal Maglie, Harry Feldman, and Ace Adams; second baseman

George Hausmann; and reserve first baseman Roy Zimmerman. Adams had been the Giants' relief ace since 1942, and his loss was a particularly heavy blow to Ott's pitching-starved club. None of the other National League clubs suffered an equivalent loss to the Mexican League; the Giants' 1946 season was doomed.

The season began miserably. Ott injured his knee and played very little for the balance of the season. Cooper broke a finger, then rebroke it several weeks later. Hartung flopped as an outfielder and was tried as a pitcher. The pitching was woeful, and Adams was missed badly as game after game was lost because of relief pitching inadequacies. The club stumbled through June making little headway, then settled in last place to stay.

The only 1946 Giant achievement of note was their home attendance of 1,243,773, which far exceeded the club record set in 1945. After the season ended there were rumors that San Francisco's Frank "Lefty" O'Doul would replace Ott, but Stoneham retained Ott.

The sad state of Giant affairs was driven home at the annual dinner of the New York chapter of the Baseball Writers Association in February 1947. The writers lampooned the Giants with a satirical verse sung to Bing Crosby's then-popular "Swinging on a Star" as follows:

> A giant is a midget, gettin' by on his past,
> He can't hit a hook or nuthin' fast,
> His club makes money but it's gone to pot.
> The fans go there to dream of Hubbell and Ott.

The 1947 club, which finished in fourth place, was a reinforced version of the 1946 team but without the injuries. Rookie right-hander Larry Jansen shone through the cloud of pitching ineptitude with a remarkable 21 and 5 season, and second baseman Bill Rigney, along with young outfielders Bobby Thomson and Carroll "Whitey" Lockman, supplied the slow-moving Giants with some needed pep and speed. But the big story was the Giants' home-run-hitting power — they were affectionately referred to as "the windowbreakers" by the Polo Grounds faithful. By the All-Star Game break the Giants were in third place, but only because the overpowering offense bailed out the weak pitching staff. National League club records for home runs fell as the Giants homered in eighteen straight games and exceeded the Yankees' all-time major league record of 182. Ott's blasters wound up with 221 homers, a 154-game season record tied by the Cincinnati Reds in 1956 and exceeded only by the 1961 Yankees in a 162-game season.

Giant fans, despite their unshakable fondness for Ott, continually debated his merits as a manager. Some said he couldn't handle pitchers. Others faulted his tendency to play for one run late in the game despite his pitchers' inability to hold leads. Many felt vaguely that he was "too nice" to win. But, in retrospect, Ott's problems could best be summed up as: poor pitching.

The 1948 year began with Ott's future as Giant manager on the line as a preseason Associated Press poll projected a mere fourth-place finish for the club. After a fair start, the Giants faltered and Horace Stoneham decided to make a managerial change. He announced his move on July 16, 1948, with the Giants in fourth place, and what a change! Brooklyn Dodger manager Leo Durocher was named to replace Ott. A man Giant fans detested for his abrasive style as well as his Dodger affiliation was taking the place of their long-time hero who Durocher had dismissed contemptuously as a "nice guy."

Durocher was uncharacteristically restrained as the Giants finished an undistinguished fifth in 1948. But he took direct action when the Giants showed no improvement in 1949. (This, incidentally, was the first season in which black players, in this case Monte Irvin and Henry Thompson, played for the Giants). Leo was exasperated by the Giants' failure, and he was pressured further by a strong Dodger showing that brought another flag to Flatbush. He announced during the late summer that he was going to build "my kind of team," one built on speed and aggressiveness rather than power.

Durocher began to clean house long before the season ended. Cooper, having a poor season and never a Durocher admirer, was traded to Cincinnati. Mize, hitting .263 with a mere eighteen homers, was sold to the Yankees in time to star in the World Series against the Dodgers. During the winter the Giants made a whopper of a deal in which they sent Willard Marshall, Sid Gordon, and Buddy Kerr to the Braves for second baseman Eddie Stanky and shortstop Alvin Dark. Durocher was well on the way to having his kind of team as the decade ended.

The Giants moved up to third place in 1950, finishing only five games behind Philadelphia's famous Whiz Kids. Stanky and Dark played superbly and the pitching improved. After a so-so year in 1949, Larry Jansen rebounded to win nineteen games. And the Giants got a big break when Sal Maglie returned from Mexico as a tough, seasoned pitcher who had mastered the art of nicking the inside corner of the plate to the point that he was nicknamed, "The Barber."

Nineteen fifty-one was the incredible year of the Bobby Thomson home run, the year of the Miracle of Coogan's Bluff. The Giants' opening lineup included Monte Irvin at first base, Stanky at second, Dark at shortstop, and Henry Thompson at third. Don Mueller, called "Mandrake the Magician" because of his deft bat control, patrolled right field; Thomson was in center, and Lockman in left. Wes Westrum was the catcher. The regular starters were Jansen, Maglie, Dave Koslo, George Spencer, and Jim Hearn, who was acquired from the Cardinals in 1950.

The 1951 club started slowly and Durocher made some changes. He switched Lockman and Irvin and replaced Thomson in center with a young fellow just up from Minneapolis, the incomparable Willie Mays. After going hitless in his first twelve at bats, Mays stroked his first major league hit off Warren Spahn, a towering home run off the grandstand roof at the Polo Grounds. Shortly after, the effervescent Mays began to spark the club with his spirited play and morale-boosting good nature. Still, as late as August 11 the Giants were a distant 13 1/2 games behind Charlie Dressen's league-leading Dodgers. Durocher's club bounced back dramatically and cut the lead to five games with a sixteen-game winning streak, then pulled dead even as the regular season ended.

In the three-game playoff for the pennant, Hearn beat Ralph Branca 3-1 in the first game, but the Dodgers squared matters as Clem Labine won, 10-0. The deciding game came the next day at the Polo Grounds as the Giants won the "Miracle of Coogan's Bluff" game on Bobby Thomson's come-from-behind homer in the bottom of the ninth inning. The Giants' loss to the Yanks in a six-game World Series was an anticlimax.

The Giants finished in second place in 1952 as the Dodgers came back to win. Irvin missed most of the year with a broken ankle, and Mays was called up by the army early in the season. Hearn, Maglie, and reliever Hoyt Wilhelm carried the pitching load as Jansen faltered, but the Giants were outclassed. Durocher brought back memories of the McGraw days, drawing three separate suspensions for umpire-baiting in a three-week period.

With Mays in the service for the entire season, 1953 was a leaner year, and the Giants fell back to fifth place. Maglie, Jansen, and Hearn had poor years, Wilhelm was less effective, and the only bright spot was provided by rookie right-hander Ruben Gomez, who won thirteen games. The Giants were out of the race by mid-August and Dodger manager Charlie Dressen counted them out with the accurate, if ungrammatical, pronouncement, "The Giants is dead."

The 1953 season was marked by particularly bitter Giant-Dodger games. On September 4, Dodger pitcher Clem Labine and the Giants' Larry Jansen threw at several opposing hitters and Jansen narrowly escaped being spiked when Duke Snider and Jackie Robinson dropped bunts down the first base line in futile attempts to retaliate for close pitches. Then, two days later, Dodger right fielder Carl Furillo climaxed several seasons of hard feelings for Durocher when, after being hit on the wrist with a pitched ball, he raced to the Giant dugout to engage Durocher in a memorable brawl.

Nineteen fifty-four provided a pleasant surprise — the Giants came back to win the pennant. The offense was paced by the booming bat of the returned Willie Mays. Lockman, Dark, and Henry Thompson had good seasons, and a colorful Alabaman, Jim "Dusty" Rhodes, had a remarkable season as a pinch-hitter, coming through in the clutch time after time. Mays barely beat out Mueller to win the batting title. Left-hander Johnny Antonelli, a former bonus baby obtained from the Braves, led the pitching staff with a brilliant 21 and 7 record. Gomez, Maglie, Marv Grisson, and Wilhelm were the other pitching reliables as the Giants beat out the Dodgers by five games.

The Giants went on to defeat a strong Cleveland club in four straight in the World Series. The Series is remembered best for an unforgettable catch by Mays on Vic Wertz's long smash to deep center field at the Polo Grounds, which cut short a budding Indian rally.

In 1955 the club slipped back to third place 18 1/2 games behind another powerful Dodger club. The Giants had three new regulars' first baseman Gail Harris, second baseman Wayne Terwilliger, and catcher Ray Katt. None of them came through, the pitching was mediocre, and another great, 51-homer season for Mays was wasted. Durocher's contract ran out and was not renewed.

Bill Rigney, who had managed the Giants' farm club in Minneapolis in 1954 and 1955, succeeded Durocher. But the Giants finished sixth as Brooklyn's "Boys of Summer" won again. The peppery Rigney simply lacked the horses. Antonelli had another great year, but otherwise,the pitching staff's weakness reminded the fans of Ott's tribulations years before. Mays belted thirty-six home runs and rookie first baseman Bill White played well. Giant rooters were unhappy with the team's performance but even more concerned about rumors that the franchise might be moved.

The story was the same in 1957: A sixth-place finish, inept pitching except by Gomez, and a generally mediocre club with weaknesses relieved only by the brilliant play of Mays and the occasional power hitting of Hank Sauer, who had come over from the Cardinals.

In 1955 it had become public knowledge that Dodger President Walter O'Malley wanted to move his club out of Ebbets Field, which had limited capacity. At the same time, Stoneham was looking for another home for his team. With the Polo Grounds slated to be demolished and replaced by a housing development, it was rumored that Stoneham was considering renting Yankee Stadium — full cycle from the early 1920s when the Yanks were ousted from the Polo Grounds by John McGraw.

After long, unproductive negotiations between the Dodgers and Brooklyn borough officials, O'Malley openly expressed his interest in moving his team to Los Angeles and his disenchantment with the Brooklyn setup. At the same time, Stoneham told the writers that he had received an attractive offer to relocate the Giants to San

Francisco. Finally, on August 19, 1957, Stoneham announced that the Giants would move to the Bay Area in time for the 1958 season. Asked by a reporter how he felt about taking the Giants from kids in New York, Stoneham replied, "I feel bad about the kids, but I haven't seen many of their fathers at games lately." Stoneham's reference was to the attendance at the Polo Grounds, which had fallen from almost 1.2 million in 1954 to less than 630,000 in 1956.

The Giants played their last game at the Polo Grounds on September 29, 1957, and lost to the Pirates, 9-1. Just as Dusty Rhodes grounded out to the end of the game, most of the 11,606 fans raced out on the field as the players fled to the safety of the clubhouses. The crowd ripped out home plate, the pitching rubber, the bases, the bullpen fixtures — almost anything that wasn't steel, concrete, or otherwise fastened down. Fans gathered in forlorn groups in center field, many shouting unsuccessfully for the players to come out of the clubhouse. Others shouted insults at Stoneham's empty office over the clubhouse.

Mrs. John McGraw, a devoted Giant rooter even in the many years since his death, was the last "official" fan to leave the ball park. She lamented tearfully, "I still can't believe it. This would have broken John's heart. New York will never be the same." The other fans just stood there, then finally trudged sorrowfully out of the Polo Grounds. The Giants' historic seventy-five year stay in New York was over.

There was excitement and enthusiasm in the winter of 1957-58 because the Bay Area, a cradle for future major leaguers, finally was going to have a team of its own. But there also was a degree of apprehension. Proud Californians didn't want a hand-me-down. They didn't need a team with emotional ties to New York.

It was for that reason, more than anything, that Willie Mays wasn't embraced immediately as the leader of the Giants. It was important for the club to develop a local identity, and the timing couldn't have been better for Horace Stoneham, who spent some of his youth in California's gold country.

Stoneham made the transition smoothly, setting a fine example. "I don't even miss Broadway," chortled Horace, who regarded San Francisco, surrounded on three sides by water, as a mini-Manhattan — but with crisp, clean air and a lack of congestion.

Stoneham also had a fruitful farm system which was to prove a blessing in the franchise's fresh start. The 1958 squad featured no less than six rookies who played a prominent role in helping the Giants firmly plant Bay Area roots: Orlando Cepeda, Jim Davenport, Bob Schmidt, Willie Kirkland, Felipe Alou, and Leon Wagner.

Mays batted a career-high .347 with twenty-nine homers and ninety-six RBI, but he was treated like a Communist at an American Legion rally. So far as many Bay Area fans were concerned, there was only one great center fielder. Joe DiMaggio was born in crossbay Martinez and reared in San Francisco sandlots, so there was some resentment of Mays' intrusion.

Giants fans needed a new hero, and they got one in the powerful Cepeda, who earned the adoration with a team-leading .312 average, twenty-five home runs, ninety-six RBI, and Rookie of the Year distinction. The slick-fielding, clutch-hitting Davenport also became an instant hit. Schmidt was the regular catcher and Wagner batted .317 as a part-timer.

The rookies created a solid base for the club, which maintained its tradition of tape-measure home runs, late-inning rallies, and prodigious slugging feats. The Giants didn't skip a beat while switching from the Polo Grounds to Seals Stadium. The Bay Bombers, win or lose, made the game exciting.

They lived by the home run, and they died by it, a trend which was to continue under the Stoneham ownership. Beginning with the 8-0 victory over the Dodgers in the 1958 opener, the Giants featured a power-packed attack that laid the cornerstone for the club's Bay Area future.

The '58 Giants averaged almost five runs per game, led the league with 652 RBI, and boasted of nine hitters with ten or more home runs. The club also captured the fans' fancy with some amazing comebacks, like the May game with Pittsburgh in which the Giants entered the bottom of the ninth behind 11-1 before proudly emerging 11-10 losers.

That year the Giants began another tradition, the June Swoon. The club entered the jinx month in first place with a 27-17 record, only to go 10-16 in June and fall to third, where it ultimately finished with an 80-74 record.

The Giants also enhanced their popularity by winning sixteen of twenty-two games with the arch-rival Dodgers, something they hadn't been able to do as well since 1937. They also attracted 1,272,625 paying customers in a park with a capacity of 22,900, a successful season in every sense of the word.

"If we had any kind of pitching, we would have won the pennant by a dozen games," declared Stoneham, who had little to go with Johnny Antonelli (16-13) and league ERA leader Stu Miller (2.47). Horace, however, attacked the problem straight on by trading for Sam Jones and Jack Sanford prior to the 1959 season.

Jones pitched in fifty games, going 21-15 with a league-leading 2.83 ERA; Sanford won fifteen games, and Antonelli was 19-10, but the Giants had to stop printing World Series tickets in 1959 when the Dodgers and the Braves zoomed past the Bay Bombers in September, entering a playoff before Los Angeles won the pennant.

Mays, as usual, was outstanding with thirty-four homers, 104 RBI, and a .313 average, but he was once again upstaged by Cepeda, who belted twenty-seven homers, drove in 105 runs, and batted .317. Then something happened that challenged Cepeda's popularity and ultimately led to the Baby Bull's controversial departure, the arrival of another imposing slugger.

The 1959 Giants avoided a June Swoon and took the league lead until a late July slump. Something was needed to give the club a boost, and Pacific Coast League batting leader Willie McCovey proved an instant elixir, just as Mays had been when he jumped from Minneapolis to New York eight years earlier.

McCovey, a gangly first baseman batting .377 at Phoenix, made his debut against Robin Roberts and the Phillies on July 30 and proceeded to crush four hits, including a pair of triples. The Giants went on to win eight of the next nine games, with McCovey powering the surge. They built a four-game lead on August 23 and held a two-game lead with eight games remaining in the season.

But the Giants didn't yet learn to win the big games. They dropped a three-game series to the Dodgers and fell to third place with five games to go. They had to be content with an 83-71 record, another exciting race, a pitching turnaround, and a young stable of sluggers that was the envy of the National League. McCovey finished with a .354 average and was named Rookie of the Year.

"It was the best young lineup in baseball," Bill Rigney, who was the Giants manager in 1958-60, recalled. "You didn't play for one run because you knew you had to get a lot. I don't remember us bunting much. The Polo Grounds created the Giant's image. Horace lived by the home run. He seldom got involved in other areas.

"I really thought we had a dynasty going with that 1958 club. They were all such marvelous young hitters. Mays, of course, was outstanding, but Orlando was the best young right-handed hitter I ever managed. He had phenomenal power.

"One of our biggest problems in those early years was who to play," Rigney said. "I had guys like Alou, Kirkland, and Wagner on the bench. Then McCovey came up, and we had difficulty finding room for him. Those lineups were as feared as any in the league. There were headaches because you never could score enough runs, but it also was a lot of fun."

Well, most of the time. The 1960 Giants sagged to fifth place, a skid accelerated by an 11-16 June. Rigney was fired, with the team 33-25 and in third place June 18. Interim manager Tom (Clancy) Sheehan couldn't apply the brakes, going 46-50. The Giants' first bad trade of the San Francisco era made Don Blasingame the second baseman and leadoff hitter, but he batted .235 and was gone one year later.

On a positive note, the Giants moved into Candlestick Park and set a franchise attendance record of 1,795,356, one which still stands twenty-six years later. They also received solid seasons from Mays, Cepeda, and Jones, and introduced a third great rookie in three years when Juan Marichal was promoted from Triple-A a few days after Rigney's departure and proceeded to one-hit the Phillies in his debut.

The Candlestick wind immediately became a topic of conversation, but the conditions actually weren't much better at Seals Stadium. In fact, Antonelli's angry reaction to a pair of wind-aided homers at Seals Stadium quickly put him in disfavor with the natives and contributed to his departure from the Giants. The lefty was swapped, along with Willie Kirkland, to Cleveland for Harvey Kuenn in 1961.

Kuenn had adjustment problems in 1961, but rookie manager Alvin Dark had enough offense to keep the club in contention much of the year. The fans warmed to Mays, who belted four home runs in one game and finished with forty round trippers, 123 RBI, and a .308 average. But Cepeda was still the top dog with forty-six homers, a league-leading 146 RBI, and a .311 average.

Stu Miller, who was forced into a balk by a wind gust during the All-Star Game at Candlestick, was the Giants' biggest winner, going 14-5 in relief with seventeen saves and a 2.66 ERA. That someone out of the bullpen was the staff "ace" strongly suggests why the club didn't finish higher than third despite a solid 85-69 record.

But Dark was placing the pieces together and a winter swap gave the Giants the pitching that would make the difference in 1962. Giving up nothing of consequence, the club acquired Billy Pierce and Don Larsen from the White Sox, which added up to twenty-one victories and one dozen saves on the most successful Giants team in fifty years, the biggest winner at 103-62 since the 1913 club won 101.

Pierce, a crafty left-hander, was unbeaten at Candlestick Park; Sanford won twenty-four games, including sixteen in a row; Miller saved nineteen games; Billy O'Dell, unspectacular when acquired in 1961, was a nineteen-game winner; and Marichal had his first of several solid seasons at 18-11. The Giants, at last, had a pitching staff to match their offense.

Mays was the home-run king with forty-nine, knocking in 141 runs and batting .304; Cepeda batted .306 with 35 homers and 114 RBI; Kuenn batted .304 with nine game-winning RBI; Davenport enjoyed his finest season at .297; Felipe Alou batted .316 with twenty-five homers and ninety-eight RBI; McCovey blasted twenty homers in merely 229 at bats; and catchers Tom Haller and Ed Bailey pooled talents for thirty-five homers and one hundred RBI.

Despite the Giants' greatness, evidence supports the contention that it was more a case of the Dodgers losing the pennant than the Giants winning it. After all, Los Angeles lefty Sandy Koufax had piled up fourteen victories by mid-July and had to stop pitching the rest of the way because of a circulatory problem in his fingers.

When Koufax was knocked from the rotation, the Dodgers led the Giants by two games. The lead increased to 5 1/2 games when L.A. visited San Francisco for a three-game series. The Giants found a way to slow down Maury Wills on his record swath of 102 stolen bases. When the Dodgers arrived at Candlestick, they found the infield extensively watered down between first and second.

"An aircraft carrier wouldn't have run aground .... They found two abalone under second base," mused Jim Murray of the *Los Angeles Times.* Another Southland scribe suggested Giants groundskeeper Matty Schwab be named Most Valuable Player after the Giants slowed down the Dodgers with a sweep that pulled them to within 2 1/2 games of first place.

The Dodgers were eager to avenge that series loss to Swamp Fox Dark when the Giants visited Dodger Stadium for a four-game series the first week of September. The Giants entered trailing by 3 1/2 games, but won three out of four to climb to within 1 1/2 games.

Dark regarded the final game of the series as the most important game he ever managed. It was 5-5 in the top of the ninth when Kuenn batted for Haller with the bases loaded and smoked a three-run double off Ron Perranoski. The Giants' winning streak reached seven, so they were only one-half game out of first place on September 11.

The Dodgers, who had been in first place most of the way, lost five out of nine on the road, but the Giants couldn't capitalize. They dropped six in a row on the road, and with thirteen games remaining, they were four games out. "The Giants is dead," was written, but Dark was a picture of determination. "We aren't through," he insisted. "The race will go down to the last day."

They remained four out with seven games to go. While the Giants won two out of three at home from the Cardinals, the Dodgers lost two of three to Houston, so their lead was two games with three remaining. Rain washed out the Giants' game with Houston on the final Friday, but St. Louis edged the Dodgers 3-2, to slice their lead to 1 1/2.

In a doubleheader with Houston the following day, the Giants cut the lead to one by romping 11-5 in the first game behind Sanford's twenty-fourth victory with home runs by McCovey, Haller, and Cepeda. But the enthusiasm dimmed when Bob Bruce downed the Giants in the nightcap, 4-2. The Dodgers, however, obliged by losing to the Cardinals 2-0 and remaining only one game up with one to go.

The final day was dripping with drama and tension. Giants announcers Russ Hodges and Lon Simmons were listening to the Los Angeles broadcast and relaying the information to their audience. While O'Dell and Miller held Houston to one run, a home run by Bailey had the clubs tied until Mays smashed a home run in the eighth for a 2-1 victory. Many spectators remained at Candlestick, though, because the Cardinals and the Dodgers had only completed five innings of a scoreless tie. Then Gene Oliver homered in the ninth and the Cardinals held on to win 1-0, thereby creating a tie. Bedlam erupted throughout the Bay Area. The Giants would not quit. They would not die. They forced a playoff, as they did in 1951.

And, like '51, there were vivid reminders of a glorious past. Leo Durocher, now a Dodgers coach, reportedly brought the same T-shirt he had worn in the '51 playoff finale to the '62 opener. Dark, who was Leo's captain in 1951 an 1954, was asked if he brought any memento of Bobby Thomson's memorable game. "Yeah," Dark replied, "Willie Mays!"

The playoff opener at Candlestick was an 8-0 rout powered by Mays' two home runs and Pierce's thirteenth straight victory at home. The Dodgers, scoreless in three straight games, overcame a 5-0 deficit, won the second game at Los Angeles 8-7, and had the homefield advantage entering the final playoff game.

A two-run homer by Tommy Davis helped the Dodgers take a 4-2 lead into the fateful ninth. Pinch hitter Matty Alou led off with a single and one-out walks to McCovey, and Felipe Alou loaded the bases. Mays' single off pitcher Ed Roebuck's glove made it 4-3 and left the bases bulging.

Stan Williams replaced Roebuck and the slumping Cepeda lofted a sacrifice fly to right, creating a tie. A wild pitch advanced Mays and Bailey was walked intentionally, loading the bases with two outs. Davenport then walked on five pitches, forcing home the go-ahead run in a 6-4 triumph. Pierce then retired the Dodgers in the bottom half to place a lock on the Giants' first, and only, San Francisco pennant.

The Giants were bubbling over, but they were drained. Cepeda, when asked if he was ready for the World Series opener the next day, jokingly said, "Who we playing?" Cepeda wasn't far from the truth, because the clash with the Yankees was regarded as anti-climactic following such a gut-wrenching final few weeks.

Giants fans probably felt the same way. On the club's flight to the Bay Area following the stirring playoff clincher, approximately 75,000 people jammed into S.F. International Airport and spilled onto the field. There was a delay of close to one hour before the circling airplane could land and taxi to a maintenance area, away from the swarming public.

"In all my born years, I've never seen anything like this," said Giants general manager Chub Feeney. "It certainly wasn't this way when we won in 1951." But this was a Bay Area hungry for its first professional champion. The Giants provided that hope in dramatic fashion, and perhaps for the first time, finally had cut their emotional ties to New York.

The World Series was much closer than anyone could have expected, and rainouts added to the buildup, extending it to thirteen days before the Giants finally succumbed on their final at bats in the seventh game, October 16. The two clubs simply traded victories after the Yankees won the opener 6-2 at Candlestick Park.

Sanford's three-hitter and McCovey's home run produced a 2-0 victory in Game 2. The Yankees won two out of three at New York; San Francisco's only victory came in Game 4, when Chuck Hiller hit the first National League grand slam in Series history en route to a 7-3 victory in relief by ex-Yankee Larsen.

When action shifted back to Candlestick, Pierce maintained his mastery at Candlestick with a three-hit, 5-2 victory over Whitey Ford, setting the stage for the final duel between Ralph Terry and Sanford. The Yankees scored on a double-play grounder in the fifth and Terry took a two-hit, 1-0 shutout into the frenzied ninth.

Pinch hitter Matty Alou beat out a bunt single and went to third on Mays's two-out double to right. That brought up McCovey, who homered off Terry in Game 2. Teeing off on a 1-1 pitch, McCovey lined a rope that second baseman Bobby Richardson grabbed slighty to his left. It wasn't a difficult chance, but the ball was struck with such ferocity that a couple of inches either way may have meant a game-winning hit instead of a season-ending out.

There was temporary dejection, but the 1962 Giants had made a city proud. There was sadness, but many more tears of joy. According to Art Rosenbaum and Bob Stevens, who authored *The Giants of San Francisco* in 1963, a disconsolate McCovey was in a downtown nightclub many hours after the game.

Duke Ellington's orchestra spotted Stretch and saluted him with one of The Duke's classics, changing the title to "You Hit it Good, and That Ain't Bad," an appropriate tribute to a great day, win or lose.

The Giants figured 1962 was the beginning of a string of pennants. They seemingly had it all, particularly power. McCovey erupted to stardom in 1963 with forty-four homers and 102 RBI, as did Marichal at 25-8, a 2.41 ERA, and a no-hitter. Mays, Cepeda, and Felipe Alou also were solid, but others tailed off sharply, especially Davenport and Pierce, who lost his magic and went 3-11.

It added up to a third-place finish at 88-74, and an improved 90-72 in 1964 couldn't keep the Giants out of fourth in Dark's final year as manager. The '64 season featured Mays' forty-seven homers, Marichal's twenty-one victories, and a thirty-one-homer rookie season for Jim Ray Hart. But McCovey slumped badly and it seemed the club's chemistry wasn't right with Cepeda and Stretch each better suited to playing first base.

When Cepeda was injured most of the 1965 season, McCovey

returned to first base and clouted thirty-nine home runs. Mays was the MVP a second time, hitting a career-high fifty-two home runs. Hart avoided the sophomore jinx with a .299 average and ninety-six RBI, Marichal was 22-13, and rookie manager Herman Franks, once a catcher with the club in New York, guided the Giants to their first of five consecutive second-place finishes.

Franks came closest to going all the way in his first two seasons, the Giants finishing two games behind the Dodgers in 1965 and 1 1/2 in back of their primary nemesis the following year. A lack of pitching depth frequently was blamed for the near misses, and it could be argued the club failed to win the pennant despite a 95-67 finish in '65 because Marichal missed some turns following his altercation with John Roseboro at Candlestick on August 22.

Regardless, the Giants soared into the lead in mid-September on the strength of a fourteen-game winning streak, but the Dodgers later won thirteen in a row and the Giants were beaten despite a solid September. Convinced that pitching was the difference, Cepeda was swapped to St. Louis in May of 1966 for left-hander Ray Sadecki.

The controversial swap placed great pressure on Sadecki, who was a flop in his first season with the Giants. But the club stayed close with a 93-68 record in 1966 because Marichal and Gaylord Perry combined for forty-six victories, and Mays (thirty-seven homers), McCovey (thirty-six), Hart (thirty-three), and Haller (twenty-seven) supplied a lot of punch.

It actually was a two-team battle between the Dodgers and the Pirates most of the way, but the Giants finished fast, swept a three-game series at Pittsburgh, and hurdled the Bucs for second. Another great trade prior to the 1967 season bolstered the pitching when Mike McCormick was acquired from the Senators.

McCormick, who came west with the Giants in 1958, won the Cy Young Award with a 20-10 season. Unfortunately, Perry had a tough-luck, 15-17 campaign, and an injury limited Marichal to fourteen victories. But even with Mays showing advancing age (.263, twenty-two homers), the club went 21-7 down the stretch to finish with a strong record, though languishing 10 1/2 games behind St. Louis.

The club's personality began to change in 1968. The skills of Mays and Hart were diminishing, so only McCovey (thirty-six homers, 105 RBI) and rookie Bobby Bonds were ascending offensive forces. The 88-74 finish behind the Cardinals was attributed to a club-record (S.F.) 2.71 ERA. Marichal was 26-9 with a 2.43 figure and Bobby Bolin went 10-5 with a 1.99 ERA.

Franks announced in mid-season that he was retiring if the Giants didn't win, but the second-place rut continued under Clyde King in the first two-division alignment in 1969. King was 90-72 as a rookie skipper, keeping the team close until a ten-game Atlanta winning streak outlasted the Giants by three games.

McCovey developed into a bona fide superstar in '69, winning MVP honors with a .320 average, forty-five homers, and 126 RBI. In his first full season as a major leaguer, Bonds produced thirty-two homers and 90 RBI, but there was a big dropoff thereafter. Marichal and Perry combined for forty victories, and again there wasn't much support.

So the Giants completed the sixties by averaging 91.4 victories the last five years and having little to show for it but individual glory and consistent runner-up status. Those were great teams to watch, full of stars and excitement, but annual high expectations led to disappointment. There always seemed to be something missing, especially defensively.

"Those were good terms, or else we wouldn't have been winning so many games," Franks recalled, "but the main reason we didn't win a couple of pennants was our double-play combination. I can still remember several games we blew because we couldn't turn a double play. We could have used a left-handed reliever, too."

Hal Lanier, whose father, Max, pitched for the Giants in New York, was among those infielders in the late sixties. His version of why pennants were elusive: "We just weren't fundamentally sound. The Giants always waited for the home run. We could hit the long ball with anyone and we had some pretty good pitching, but we never seemed to do the little things we needed to do in the close games."

A lack of execution continued to be a Giants' malady in the seventies and eighties, but there was to be one more bright moment, in 1971, before the demise of the Stoneham Empire nearly cost Bay Area fans their beloved Giants.

Following a 19-23 start in 1970, King was fired and replaced by Charlie Fox who like Franks, was a New York Giants catcher. The club went 67-53 under Fox, McCovey once again was the league's most dangerous hitter (thirty-nine homers, 126 RBI), and Perry notched twenty-three victories. But the best was yet to come.

Fox did his best managing in 1971 guiding a mixture of youngsters and veterans to the Western Division title by one game over the hated Dodgers. For the first time since 1876, a team went all the way without a .300 hitter or a twenty-game winner; as a result, Fox was named Manager of the Year.

Bolting to an 18-5 start, the Giants took the lead on April 12 and never looked back. Bonds was the major offensive threat with thirty-three homers and 102 RBI, and Marichal topped the pitchers with eighteen wins, including a 5-1 decision over the Padres on the final day, clinching the division crown.

The Pirates were pounded to defeat nine times in twelve regular-season meetings, and Perry beat them 5-4 in the playoff opener. But the Bucs jolted the Giants in the next three games to advance to the

World Series. One year later, the club was to begin a slide from which it never really recovered, posting a losing record (69-86) in 1972 for the first time in the Giants' Bay Area history.

It also marked the first time the incomparable Mays didn't finish the season with the club. Willie was traded to the Mets, primarily to save Stoneham from paying his salary, but there were two other factors that had a far greater impact on the club: McCovey's broken arm and an atrocious trade engineered by Fox, sending Perry to the Indians for Sudden Sam McDowell. Granted, Perry didn't relate well to the younger players on the squad, but McDowell definitely wasn't the answer. Perry went on to win a Cy Young Award and three hundred games, but McDowell became not so sudden and was out of baseball.

Whereas 1971 was known as The Year of the Fox, 1973 definitely was The Year of the Bonds. The Giants' regrooping was delayed one year simply because Bonds did everything right in an 88-74 season, including All-Star Game MVP honors. He was regarded as the finest talent in the league after belting thirty-nine homers and swiping forty-three bases.

McCovey returned to form with twenty-nine homers, Gary Matthews batted .300 and was Rookie of the Year, and left-hander Ron Bryant enjoyed a dream season at 24-12. *The Sporting News* honored Bonds and Bryant as Player and Pitcher of the Year, respectively, the first time one club had two players so honored by the publication.

The Giants fell to 72-90 in 1974 and Wes Westrum, yet another ex-Giants catcher, replaced Fox at mid-season. The club was going with youth now that McCovey and Marichal were gone, but there were four managers in four years and little success except for flashes of brilliance like Ed Halicki's no-hitter and John Montefusco's Rookie of the Year distinction, each in 1975.

The bottom almost fell out on the club in 1975 despite a respectable 80-81, third-place finish under Westrum. The 1974-75 combined seasons' attendance was 1,042,916, as Stoneham was running out of money even though the high-salaried superstars were gone. In January of 1976, Stoneham sold his beloved Giants to Labatt's Breweries of Toronto, ending fifty-seven years of ownership by his family.

It seemed the National League would beat the American League to the Canadian city, but San Francisco Mayor George Moscone received a temporary restraining order against the move. The hunt began for new owners who would keep the club in the Bay Area. Bob Lurie, son of a wealthy San Francisco financier, pulled out his checkbook. But Lurie, a member of the Giants Board of Directors for most of the Stoneham years in San Francisco, couldn't do it alone, so a search was made for a partner as the league deadline approached. March 2 was the target date, but that morning Lurie was still without an angel. But with Mayor Moscone serving as an intermediary, Lurie was placed in contact with Arizona cattleman Bud Herseth, who ultimately saved the Giants' bacon.

Within minutes of the 5 P.M. deadline imposed by the league, Lurie and Herseth had pooled resources to save the Giants for San Francisco. Mayor Moscone, informing the Bay Area media of the good news, summed up the successful, last-ditch effort by declaring, "Bobby Thomson lives!"

Lurie and Herseth didn't have time to bask in the glory of their heroic deed. They had to field a winner and give the fans reason to return to Candlestick Park. Rigney was rehired as manager, but there were no young lions as he had enjoyed in 1958. Montefusco came closest to that status, pitching a no-hitter, but he was merely 16-14 and the Giants finished fourth at 74-88.

There was a one-game improvement in 1977, but things were looking up under rookie manager Joe Altobelli. Lurie, who was about to buy out Herseth and become sole owner, had the good judgment to sign McCovey, who went to spring training as a nonroster player after being released by the crossbay A's. Willie's presence rekindled a spark.

McCovey batted .280 and slammed twenty-eight home runs for Comeback of the Year honors. Bill Madlock, acquired in the off season, batted .302. Rookie Jack Clark gave a hint of what was to come and reliever Gary Lavelle had a 2.06 ERA and a club-record twenty saves.

The Giants finally climbed out of their rut in 1978, more than doubling attendance with 1,740,477 customers, leading the league much of the season, and finishing third at 89-73. Altobelli was named Manager of the Year and general manager Spec Richardson, who masterminded the preseason swap that brought Vida Blue from the A's, was selected the top executive.

Vida Blue was the catalyst for the club's resurgence, going 18-10 with a 2.79 ERA. Fellow lefty Bob Knepper was right behind at 17-11, 2.63. Madlock batted .309, and new addition Mike Ivie followed at .308. But Clark, only twenty-two years old, was the big gun with a .306 average, twenty-five home runs, ninety-eight RBI, and a club-record forty-six doubles. He also set a Giants' record with a twenty-six-game hitting streak, surpassing Freddie Lindstrom's, Don Mueller's and McCovey's twenty-four.

When the 1979 club didn't live up to its predecessor, Madlock was swapped in mid-season (and pushed the Pirates to a championship), and Altobelli was replaced by third base coach Dave Bristol in September. Ivie and Clark carried the offense and McCovey, who passed Mel Ott on the career-home-run list, swatted .393 as a pinch hitter.

Blue bounced back in 1980 and Clark and Darrell Evans did some damage offensively, but the club plunged to fifth at 75-86 and Bristol was relieved of his duties during the winter meetings. Frank Robinson was named as his replacement in January, becoming the first black manager in the National League, a distinction he received in the American League in 1975.

The 1981 season was ripped apart by the strike, which proved to be a boon for the Giants. They were 27-32 prior to the walkout and 29-23 following the resumption of play, finishing 56-55 overall. Newcomer Doyle Alexander was the pitching ace at 11-7, and the offensive load was carried by Clark and Evans, with Jeff Leonard coming up from the minors and enjoying a blazing second half with a .307 average. Milt May batted .310.

The upward trend continued in '82. By virtue of the strongest second half in the league, the Giants posted an 87-75 record and finished third, two games out of the division lead. This was done despite a complete revamping of the starting rotation by general manager Tom Haller, who replaced Richardson during the 1981 strike.

Haller replaced veterans like Alexander and Blue with rookies like Bill Laskey and Atlee Hammaker, who combined for twenty-five victories. Clark responded with his finest season, belting twenty-seven homers and knocking in 103 runs. Free agent Reggie Smith provided eighteen homers and a .284 average, while Joe Morgan contributed leadership and a team-leading .289 average. Greg Minton posted a club-record thirty saves.

In a controversial off-season swap, Morgan and reliever Al Holland were sent to Philadelphia for right-hander Mike Krukow and two minor league prospects, and Smith elected to play in Japan. Evans compensated for Smith's absence by switching to first base and enjoying this finest season with the Giants while ranked among the league leaders in many offensive categories.

Leonard developed into a solid slugger and an outstanding left fielder, and Johnnie LeMaster had his greatest all-around season at shortstop. Free agent Joel Youngblood made a big contribution in the infield and outfield, Lavelle returned to eminence as a reliever, and Laskey and Hammaker continued to flash brilliance.

But Clark and Chili Davis slumped miserably, Minton was a shadow of his former self, and the injury-riddled Giants were slightly out of sync most of the 1983 season. A poor second half dropped the club near the basement and had the front office talking about sweeping changes for the rebuilding process over the winter months.

That 1984 would become the losingest season in the Giants' San

Francisco history was disguised by an 18-9 spring training record, best in the Cactus League. With Darrell Evans signing with Detroit as a free agent, the Giants filled their first base void by acquiring veteran Al Oliver from Montreal during spring training.

But the early enthusiasm was dampened by a 7-16 April, and by the time a productive offense got into gear, the pitching was in disarray. The Giants fell 10 games behind on May 1, at the end of a nine-game losing streak, and they never recovered.

By the All-Star break, the club trailed by 16 games at 33-50, and five straight losses at the start of the second half suggested the early slump was no fluke. With the club 22 games in arrears, Aug. 4, Bob Lurie fired Frank Robinson with two years remaining on his contract and coach Danny Ozark took over on an interim basis.

The Giants improved slightly, going 24-32 under the former Phillies manager, yet couldn't escape a last-place finish because of a 4-12 nosedive down the stretch. The highlight of Ozark's tenure was a 9-3 swing through New York, Montreal and Phildelphia, Aug. 24-Sept. 2, the club's most successful East Coast trip ever.

Oliver batted .298, but failed to provide the required punch (zero homers, 34 RBI in 91 games), so he was swapped to Philadelphia. Jack Clark was off to his finest start, but a knee injury ended his season June 26, when he was batting .320 with 11 homers and 44 RBI in 57 games. But the injury proved to be a blessing in disguise and paved the way for the winter trade of the moody slugger.

With Clark shelved, outfielder Dan Gladden was promoted from Phoenix, where he was batting .397. The feisty Gladden batted .351 in 86 major league games, joining Chili Davis (.315) and Jeff Leonard (.302) to give the Giants a trio of young flyhawks who collectively batted .319 and augured well for the future.

Davis, Leonard and catcher Bob Brenly each had at least 20 home runs and 80 RBI for an offense that ranked second in batting (.265) and fourth in runs scored in the National League. But that pop couldn't compensate for the worst pitching (4.39 ERA) and the worst defense (173 errors) in the league.

Among the starters, only Mike Krukow had reasonable success at 11-12. Rookie Jeff Robinson made the jump from Class-A to the rotation and tailed off following a quick start. Atlee Hammaker did not pitch until June 26 following rotator cuff surgery, winning twice.

Reliever Gary Lavelle set an all-time Giants record with his 635th game, breaking Christy Mathewson's mark, and worked in 77 games in what was to be his final season with the club. Greg Minton had a team-leading 19 saves and rookie Frank Williams was 9-4, performing an oddity by winning each end of a doubleheader, Aug. 24, at New York.

Following the dismal 1984, it generally was felt the Giants couldn't be any worse in 1985, but they were. The only non-expansion franchise to avoid losing 100 games had its streak snapped in a 62-100 campaign rife with dissension and disappointment. It was a Murphy's Law season in which everything which could go wrong did.

Improvement was expected because personable Jim Davenport was an easygoing sort who was to be the antithesis of the demanding Robinson. Moreover, the club acquired two regulars (first-baseman David Green and shortstop Jose Uribe) and a starting pitcher (Dave LaPoint) for Clark, who was not missed during Gladden's rookie spree.

A 7-12 April which included a seven-game losing streak set the tone for the season. And while Clark and the Cardinals were heading toward a pennant, Green batted .080 during his first 21 games and became a scapegoat — much as was the case with Ray Sadecki in the Orlando Cepeda swap.

Green recovered to bat .318 after July 1, but it was too late. Public opinion and Oliver-like production (five homers, 20 RBI) cooked his goose and he virtually was given away at season's end. LaPoint, pitching in bad luck, lost 17 games and also was sent packing. Uribe survived, leading the club with 147 games played and fielding solidly.

Green wasn't alone. Leonard, Davis and Brenly also tailed off sharply from their 1984 success, and Gladden was a bust at the leadoff spot. Nothing seemed to click in a season which found the club plunging from second to last in batting (.233) and also finishing at the bottom in runs scored.

The lone bright spot in the offense was rookie third-baseman Chris Brown, who broke in with a team-leading .271 average and a career-high 16 home runs while making only 10 errors. But he had little help on a club which had nobody knock in more than 62 runs or any starting pitcher post more than eight victories.

From the morass of despair emerged two significant pitching performances. Scott Garrelts was switched from a starter to the bullpen and promptly became one of the best in the bigs with a 9-6 record, a 2.30 ERA and 13 saves. Vida Blue returned to the mound following a one-year exile and was 8-8 for a club which finished 38 games below .500.

There also was a silver lining around the dark cloud that hovered the entire season. The situation became so bleak, Lurie was compelled to make a sweeping change that would profoundly affect the future of the club. On Sept. 18, the owner gave the Giants much-needed new direction by replacing general manager Tom Haller and Davenport with Al Rosen and Roger Craig, respectively.

For the first time in several years, the Giants had a plan for success and the leadership to implement it. The club finished 6-12 under Craig, who "saw a lot of things I didn't like" and quickly worked with Rosen to rectify them. The plan would bear fruit one year later, but not before a winter of uncertainty regarding the club.

Lurie, intent on not playing at Candlestick Park in 1986, considered playing home games in Oakland or in Denver until a downtown stadium were built. It wasn't until Jan. 29, 1986, that Giants fans knew for sure that the club once again would call San Francisco home. What followed was one of the most exciting seasons in recent Giants history.

Craig boldly gave starting jobs to rookies Will Clark (first base) and Robby Thompson (second base) during spring training. The club bolted to a 10-4 start and enjoyed its first winning April (13-8) since 1973, acquiring Craig's confidence and Hum-Baby attitude.

Despite myriad roster moves (a total of 61!) and constant lineup juggling because of injuries, the Giants remained in contention most of the season. With a 48-40 record, they topped the division at the All-Star break for the first time since 1978. The club led or shared first place 47 days.

An injury which sidelined Leonard the final two months cost the club dearly, but it still showed a 21-game improvement from 1985, the greatest one-year turnaround in S.F. history and the most by the franchise since 1954. The Giants also became only one of 10 teams since 1900 to post a winning record (83-79) after losing 100 the previous year.

Character and confidence exemplified the club's turnaround. There were 40 come-from-behind victories, including 26 on the final at bats. The Giants avoided a June Swoon with a 16-12 record and were 16-11 in September without help from Leonard or Brown, who missed most of the final month with a shoulder injury.

Individually, Krukow's 20-win season stood out and typified the comeback character of the club. Injured in a St. Louis scuffle after the All-Star break, the veteran righthander missed a few turns. But he turned a 6-0 September (earning N.L. Pitcher of the Month honors) into the first 20-win season for the club since Bryant in 1973.

Righthander Mike LaCoss helped the club to its first-half lead by going 9-3 before fading. Garrelts began the season as a starter, but returned to the bullpen and again established himself as a premier reliever. His 13-9 record and 3.11 ERA ranked behind Krukow's 20-9 and 3.05 marks.

The offensive resurgence was powered by newcomer Candy Maldonado, whose 17 pinch hits set a club record. When Leonard was sidelined, Maldonado became a regular down the stretch and finished with a team-leading 18 home runs and 85 RBI in only 133 games and 405 at bats.

Clark and Thompson made a big impact and were instant favorites of the fans. Clark missed one month with an elbow injury and batted a solid .287. Thompson was named *The Sporting News* Rookie Player of the Year after batting a career-high .271 and exhibiting a hard-nosed style of play reminiscent of Eddie Stanky.

Brown was the team battting leader at .317, tailing off after entering his first All-Star Game with a .338 average. Davis made his second

All-Star appearance, knocking in 55 runs at the time, but added only 15 thereafter in a second-half slump (and disenchantment with Candlestick Park) that stamped him prime winter trade bait.

In addition to the attitude adjustment created by Rosen and Craig, the factors most responsible for the club's improvement were deft execution and production off the bench. The Giants, devoid of consistent power, emphasized the little things and registered 18 squeeze bunts among 101 sacrifices. They also set a San Francisco record with 148 stolen bases.

Giants pinch-hitters topped the majors with 10 homers and 59 RBI. Maldonado led the league with four homers and 20 RBI in a pinch. Joel Youngblood's 16 hits also surpassed the previous mark of 14 (Duane Kuiper, 1982) and Harry Spilman, acquired in mid-June, came through with 13 hits and a .400 average off the bench.

3

THE GREAT GIANTS

Hall of Famers Significantly Associated with the Giants	Year Elected to Hall of Fame
Christy Mathewson	1936
John McGraw	1937
Roger Bresnahan	1945
Jim O'Rourke	1945
Buck Ewing	1946
Joe McGinnity	1946
Frank Frisch	1947
Carl Hubbell	1947
Mel Ott	1951
Bill Terry	1954
Tim Keefe	1964
Monte Ward	1964
Dave Bancroft	1971
Rube Marquard	1971
Ross Youngs	1972
Monte Irvin	1973
George Kelly	1973
Mickey Welch	1973
Roger Connor	1976
Fred Lindstrom	1976
Amos Rusie	1977
Willie Mays	1979
Travis Jackson	1982
Juan Marichal	1983
Hoyt Wilhelm	1985
Willie McCovey	1986

Other Hall of Famers Who Played for the Giants	Year Elected to Hall of Fame
Willie Keeler	1939
Rogers Hornsby	1942
Dan Brouthers	1945
Mike"King" Kelly	1945
Jesse Burkett	1946
Ray Schalk	1955
Edd Roush	1962
Burleigh Grimes	1964
Joe Medwick	1968
Waite Hoyt	1969
Jake Beckley	1971
Warren Spahn	1973
Casey Stengel	1974
Hack Wilson	1979
Duke Snider	1980
Ernie Lombardi	1986

Sketches of the Greats

Christy Mathewson

Christy Mathewson was the greatest pitcher ever according to many baseball experts. Mathewson combined sheer physical ability with an unusual degree of pitching wizardry to win 373 career games, the third highest total in major league history. The great right-hander was the first modern-era pitcher to win thirty games in three successive seasons (thirty, thirty-three, and thirty-one in 1903-1905, respectively). Matty also won a career-high thirty-seven games in 1908. "Big Six" was the winner of twenty or more games for twelve consecutive years, and he pitched a remarkable three shutout wins in the 1905 World Series against the Philadelphia Athletics. Noted for his "fadeaway" (known today as a screwball), the Factoryville, Pennsylvania, native was the consummate control pitcher, walking only 846 hitters in 4,783 innings.

Despite his aloof, austere personality, Matty's "all-American boy" image made him perhaps the most widely-loved sports figure of the 1900-1915 era, an age when baseball dwarfed all other U.S. professional sports in crowd appeal and commercial importance. Mathewson joined the Giants in 1900, shortly after his graduation from Bucknell College. John McGraw, his close friend, traded him to Cincinnati in midseason of 1916 to permit him to take over the managership of the Reds. Mathewson served in World War I, when he was gassed, and then returned to the Giants as a coach in 1921-1922.

While serving as president of the Boston Braves in 1925, Matty contracted tuberculosis. He died of the ailment on October 7, 1925, at forty-five, mourned by the Nation's fans to whom he represented the best in American sports, both on and off the field.

John McGraw

Most experts consider John McGraw the greatest manager ever. His record and his overall contributions to the game support this view. He ranks second only to Connie Mack in major league games managed (4,879) and in games won (2,840). He won ten pennants in thirty years with the Giants, and most incredibly, had only two second-division finishes in the twenty-nine full seasons that he managed the New Yorkers. McGraw's managerial genius also is reflected by other achievements — his strategic and tactical innovations, the superb players whom he attracted and developed, and his continuing impact on the game through the leadership exerted by men who learned the game under his direction.

McGraw is remembered best for the high excitement and emotions that he engendered during his thirty-year domination of the National League. Most fans either liked or disliked him intensely, but either way the ballpark turnstiles clicked furiously as fans came in increasing numbers to cheer for or root against his Giants. Thus, McGraw's influence stimulated the growth of baseball from the early 1900s until the 1920s, when the lively ball era moved the game into a still higher level of popularity and commercial importance.

McGraw gained early prominence in the 1890s as an infielder and leading member of the famed Baltimore Orioles. McGraw and Wee Willie Keeler were credited with developing one of the Orioles' major innovations, the hit-and-run play. The scrappy McGraw hit over .300 in seven straight Oriole seasons, then managed the Baltimore club from 1899 until July 16, 1902, when he took over as Giants manager. He moved the ineffectual Giants into second place in 1903, won the pennant in 1904, and the Giants became the most consistently successful National League team for the next thirty years under the Little Napoleon's leadership.

McGraw's career was a continuous string of arguments, fistfights, and controversies with a succession of National League presidents, owners, umpires, opposing managers and players, and off-the-field acquaintances. Yet he also was known as a bon vivant, a raconteur, a man of many nonbaseball interests, and a benefactor of down-and-out ballplayers.

McGraw demanded unquestioning obedience from his players and strict compliance with curfew rules. His iron-fisted approach was highly successful until the mid-twenties, when several of his players rebelled openly at his long clubhouse diatribes, vicious tongue-lashings, and fines. Not surprisingly, McGraw failed to win another pennant after 1925 through June 3, 1932, when he turned the managership of the Giants over to first baseman Bill Terry.

McGraw was born in Truxton, New York, on April 7, 1873, and he died on February 25, 1934.

Roger Bresnahan

Roger Bresnahan, one of the best catchers of his day, gained fame as Christy Mathewson's batterymate during the 1902-1908 period. A nimble, all-purpose player who played all positions capably and with brisk assurance, the right-hand-hitting Bresnahan hit .280 in a seventeen-year career with the Giants, Cardinals, and Cubs. Possessing unusual speed for a catcher, the "Duke of Tralee" often batted in the leadoff position.

Bresnahan also gained fame as an innovator. In 1907 he became the first major league catcher to wear shinguards, an equipment adaptation he made after watching a cricket match. Later in 1907 Bresnahan became the first big league hitter to wear a head protector when he returned to the lineup after a head injury resulting from a beaning.

McGraw traded Bresnahan to St. Louis in December 1908 to permit him to take over the managership of the Cardinals. After an unsuccessful managerial career in St. Louis, Bresnahan moved to the Cubs in 1913, where he finished out his playing career in 1915. He was born in Toledo, Ohio, on June 11, 1879, and died on December 4, 1944.

Jim O'Rourke

"Orator Jim" O'Rourke was an outfielder-utility player who hit .310 in a nineteen year major league career that spanned thirty years. The right-hand-hitting O'Rourke's career began in 1876 with Boston, where he had the distinction of obtaining the very first National League hit on April 22, 1876, in a game against Philadelphia. He came to the Giants in 1885 after several seasons with Providence and Buffalo as well as Boston. O'Rourke played with the Giants for seven full seasons, hitting over .300 in five of them. His playing career actually ended in 1893 when he played with Washington. However, the Giants called the popular fifty-two-year-old "Orator Jim" out of thirteen years of retirement to catch their first pennant-clinching game on September 22, 1904.

O'Rourke, born in Bridgeport, Connecticut, on August 24, 1852, died on January 8, 1919.

Buck Ewing

William "Buck" Ewing was rated as the finest catcher of the 1880s by most experts. He had a .303 lifetime batting average in eighteen seasons and was an all-around player with a great arm and fine speed, stealing more than twenty-five bases in eight seasons. A spirited field leader, Ewing captained the Giants in 1888 and 1889 as the club won its first two pennants.

Ewing was the playing-manager of the New York Players League club in 1890, managed Cincinnati from 1895 to 1899, and managed the Giants for part of the 1900 season. Ewing was born in Hoaglands, Ohio, on October 17, 1859, and died on October 20, 1906.

Joe McGinnity

The legendary Joe "Iron Man" McGinnity is remembered best for having pitched two complete games in one day no less than five times. In the month of August 1903, McGinnity pitched and won two complete games on three occasions. McGinnity had a ten-year career record in the majors of 247 and 145, winning twenty games in eight seasons. The sturdy right-hander reached his peak in 1903 and 1904, winning thirty-one games and pitching 434 innings in 1903 and racking up a magnificent 31 and 8 season in 408 innings in 1904.

McGinnity joined the Giants in 1902, coming over from Baltimore when John McGraw became the Giants' manager. After leaving the Giants in 1908, McGinnity pitched for and managed seven minor league teams before leaving the active ranks at the age of fifty-four. McGinnity was born in Rock Island, Illinois, on March 19, 1871, and died on November 14, 1929.

Frank Frisch

Second baseman Frank Frisch joined the Giants in 1919 just after graduating from Fordham University. Almost immediately Frisch exhibited the spectacular infielding, timely hitting, and brilliant baserunning that marked his career. The switch-hitting "Fordham Flash," who hit .316 over nineteen seasons, starred for the Giants through 1926. John McGraw traded him to the St. Louis Cardinals for Rogers Hornsby after Frisch jumped the Giants following violent verbal abuse by McGraw.

Frisch moved to even greater heights with the Cardinals, playing in four World Series, including the 1934 classic when Frisch was the Cards' player-manager. Frisch held many World Series records for a number of years and he still ranks first in career two-base hits, with ten, and third in total hits with fifty-eight.

The Fordham Flash managed the famed "Gas House Gang" Cardinals for six seasons, the Pirates for seven and the Cubs for three. In addition, he did the Giants' play-by-play radio coverage and served as a Giants coach. The aggressive Frisch was born in New York City on September 9, 1898, and died on March 12, 1973, after an auto acident.

Carl Hubbell

Carl Hubbell might well be described as a left-handed, latter-day Christy Mathewson. The lanky Oklahoman, affectionately referred to as "King Carl" or "The Meal Ticket," was a master in throwing Mathewson's reverse curve screwball. Hubbell also had marvelous control, a good fastball and curve, and complete mastery of pitching. The Giants' Meal Ticket won 253 games for them in a sixteen-year career that began in 1928. In his prime, King Carl won twenty-four straight decisions over two seasons, his last sixteen decisions in 1936 and his first eight games in 1937.

Hubbell pitched a remarkable 46 1/3 consecutive scoreless innings in 1933, a year in which he pitched ten shutouts. His most famous feat came in the 1934 All-Star Game when he fanned five future Hall of Famers in succession — Babe Ruth, Lou Gehrig, Jimmy Foxx, Al Simmons, and Joe Cronin. Hubbell's major single-game achievement, in addition to a no-hitter in 1929, was an eighteen-inning shutout win over the Cardinals on July 2, 1933, during which King Carl allowed only six hits and no walks. But Hubbell's contribution to the Giants' effort in the 1930s, when they won three hard-fought pennants, cannot adequately be described by his pitching record. He was the ultimate stopper, consistently winning important games as a starter and saving games for the other Giants pitchers as a reliever. As testimonial to his value to the club, Hubbell was named the National League's Most Valuable Player in 1933 and 1936.

The quiet, unassuming left-hander retired as a player after the 1943 season and managed the Giants' farm system for more than thirty years. Born in Carthage, Missouri, on June 22, 1903, Hubbell has been a part-time scout for the Giants in the Arizona area since his retirement.

Mel Ott

Mel Ott's storybook Giant playing career began when he joined the club in September 1925 as a scared sixteen-year-old, fresh from a Louisiana high school, and extended through the 1947 season. The left-hand-hitting Ott's durability, and his ability to pull the ball sharply toward the friendly Polo Grounds right-field stands, gave him ownership of a number of National League career offensive records to go with his .304 batting average for twenty-two seasons. The career records, all of which have since been overtaken, include 511 home runs, 1,860 RBI, 1,859 runs scored, and 1,708 walks.

In the field, Master Mel's great throwing arm, flychasing skill, and mastery of the caroms off the Polo Grounds right-field wall gained him recognition as the National League's premier right fielder for much of his career. An extremely versatile player, Ott filled in at third base acceptably in several seasons to give the Giants their needed flexibility.

Similar to his close friend Hubbell, also a Hall of Famer, Ott's records do not reflect completely his value to the club. For most of the 1930s, Ott was the only major offensive threat — the club relied primarily upon solid pitching, tight defense, and Ott to carry the run-making responsibilities. Opposing pitchers were able to pitch around Ott and it is testimony to his greatness that he was able to hit so well under the circumstances. (For example, in the seventeen-year period from 1929 through 1945, Ott led the Giants in home runs each year and led the club in RBI nine times).

The pleasant, gentlemanly little slugger was by far the most popular Giant during his long tenure with the club. He succeeded Bill Terry as manager in December 1941 and retained his "nice guy" image despite a lackluster, unlucky 7 1/2 year managerial regime during which the Giants had only two first division finishes. Born in Gretna, Louisiana, on March 2, 1909, Ott died on November 21, 1958, as the result of an automobile accident.

Bill Terry

Bill Terry was the nonpareil National League first baseman for most of his fourteen-year major league playing career, during which the big left-handed swinger compiled a .341 batting average. He also was ranked with Hal Chase and George Sisler among the all-time fielding first basemen. Terry's playing years were highlighted by his .401 batting average in 1930, the last year in which a National Leaguer reached the .400 mark. Memphis Bill had more than two hundred hits in six seasons, reaching his peak with a phenomenal total of 254 hits in 1930 (still a tie for the National League record). Terry preferred to hit straightaway to all parts of the field rather than pull hit. As a result, he hit for a high average but had relatively low home-run totals.

The blunt, businesslike Terry succeeded John McGraw as Giant manager on June 3, 1932, and by a combination of shrewd trading and clever defensive strategy, he led the Giants to a surprise pennant and World Series win over Washington in 1933. The quietly efficient Giants won again in 1936 and 1937, succumbing both times to the overpowering Yankees in the World Series. Terry relinquished the Giants' managership to Mel Ott after the 1941 season, then directed the Giants' farm system for a year before going into private business. He returned to the game as president of the South Atlantic League in

1955, but left the game again for a lucrative business career.

Terry was born in Atlanta, Georgia, on October 30, 1898.

Tim Keefe

Tim Keefe won 346 major league games in fourteen seasons, 174 of them with the Giants in only 5 1/2 seasons. Sir Timothy led the National League with forty-two wins in his second season with the Giants in 1886, and won thirty-five games in both the 1887 and 1888 campaigns. He won nineteen straight games in 1888, still the major league record although it was tied by Giants left-hander Rube Marquard in 1912. Keefe ranks eighth on the all-time list in career wins with 344, third in complete games with 558, and seventh with 5,072 innings.

This wiliily built right hander was noted for his artful use of the change-of-pace delivery. He pitched for Troy and the New York Metropolitans before John B. Day, who owned both the Giants and the Metropolitans, transferred him to the Giants in 1885. He was born in Cambridge, Massachusetts, on January 1, 1856, and died on April 23, 1933.

Monte Ward

John Montgomery "Monte" Ward was one of the most versatile and important baseball figures of his time. He began as an eighteen-year-old right-handed pitcher for Providence of the National League in 1878, winning forty-four games in 1879 and forty games, including a perfect no-hitter, in 1880. Ward joined the Giants when they entered the National League in 1883, and was shifted to shortstop in 1884 because of an arm injury.

Ward was one of the Giants' stalwarts through 1889. He then managed the Brooklyn entry in the one-season Players League in 1890. He was one of the driving forces in the development of the Brotherhood of Professional Baseball Players, which organized the Players League. Ward managed the Brooklyn National League club in 1891-1892, then managed the Giants in 1893-1894.

A graduate of the Columbia Law School, Ward retired after the 1894 season to practice law. He served as president of the Boston Braves in 1911-1913 and later was the attorney for the National League. Born on March 3, 1860, in Bellefonte, Pennsylvania, Ward died on March 4, 1925, of pneumonia, which he contracted during a hunting trip.

Dave Bancroft

Shortstop Dave "Beauty" Bancroft was the key player in the three fine Giant infields that carried the club to pennants in 1921-1923. The smooth-fielding Bancroft handled 984 total chances in 1922, still the major league record for shortstops, and led National League shortstops in putouts in 1918, 1920, 1921, and 1922. Bancroft had a .279 batting average over sixteen seasons, hitting his offensive peak in 1922 with 209 hits and a .321 average.

Bancroft's major league career began with the Philadelphia Phillies in 1915. He was traded to the Giants on June 8, 1920, for shortstop Art Fletcher, pitcher Wilbur Hubbell, and $100,000. Four years later, John McGraw traded Bancroft to the Boston Braves as a favor to Braves President Christy Mathewson, who wanted Bancroft to manage the Braves. Bancroft was unsuccessful in four years as player-manager at Boston, failing to pull the club into the first division. He played for the Dodgers in 1928 and 1929, and rejoined the Giants as a player-coach in 1931 and 1932 until McGraw was replaced by Bill Terry in June 1932.

Bancroft was born in Sioux City, Iowa, on April 20, 1891, and died on October 9, 1972.

Rube Marquard

Left-hander Richard William "Rube" Marquard is remembered best for winning nineteen consecutive games in 1912, still a major league record held jointly with old-time Giant right-hander Tim Keefe. Actually, under the then-existing scoring rules, Marquard was not credited with a win that would have been credited under present rules. (See July 3, 1912, "Day by Day" section.)

The Giants purchased Marquard from Indianapolis in 1908 for $11,000, the highest price paid for a minor league player up to that time. Rube had mediocre seasons in 1909 and 1910, so mediocre that he was referred to as the "$11,000 lemon." But he came through with twenty-game seasons in 1911-1913 as the Giants won three straight pennants. Marquard pitched a no-hit game against Brooklyn on April 15, 1915, but slumped and was released in August 1915. He was picked up by Brooklyn in September 1915 and pitched for Brooklyn through 1920. Marquard played subsequently for the Cincinnati Reds and the Boston Braves before closing out his major league career in 1925.

Marquard was nicknamed "Rube" because he was left-handed and reminded fans of the Philadelphia Athletics' eccentric lefty, Rube Waddell. Actually, Marquard was a sophisticated man who married a Broadway actress and performed on stage during off seasons. A native of Cleveland, Marquard was born on October 9, 1889, and died on June 1, 1980.

Ross Youngs

Ross Middlebrook "Pep" Youngs joined the Giants in 1917 as a twenty-year-old lad from a military academy in Texas. He was one of the team pillars who sparked the Giants to four straight pennant wins in 1921-1924. The stocky, aggressive young hustler hit over .300 in nine of his ten major league seasons, compiling a .322 lifetime average. He also gained recognition as a great right fielder with a rifle arm. Youngs led the National League in assists twice and tied once for the lead.

Youngs, along with Christy Mathewson and Mel Ott, was a top McGraw favorite and McGraw often referred to him as "my greatest outfielder." In 1926, Youngs was stricken with a serious kidney ailment that terminated his playing career before the 1927 season and resulted in his death. He was born in Shiner, Texas, on April 10, 1897, and died on October 22, 1927.

Monte Irvin

Monte Irvin was elected to the Hall of Fame largely on his achievements as a Negro League player from 1937-1940 as the pre-Jackie Robinson racial barrier prevented him from playing in the major leagues until he was thirty years old. A fine outfielder, Irvin led the Negro National League with a .422 average in 1941. Irvin and infielder Henry Thompson were the Giants' first black players, both men appearing in their first Giant game on July 8, 1949.

Monte had his best major league season in 1951, hitting .312 with a league-leading 121 RBI, as the Giants won the "miracle at the Polo Grounds" pennant on Bobby Thomson's famous last-minute home run. Irvin had a great 1951 World Series in a losing cause, hitting .458 with eleven hits and stealing home in the first game of the Series.

The right-hand-hitting Irvin played with the Giants until 1955, then finished his major league career with the Chicago Cubs. The Columbia, Alabama, native, born on February 25, 1919, was a scout for the New York Mets before joining the Baseball Commissioner's staff.

Mickey Welch

"Smiling Mickey" Welch joined the Giants when they entered the National League in 1883 after spending the 1880-1882 campaigns with Troy, New York. The compact, little right-hander won seventeen straight games in 1885 on the way to a 44 and 11 season. Welch had a total of 311 wins in thirteen major league seasons, winning more than thirty games in three Giant seasons and in 1880 with Troy.

Welch was the only one of two Giant regulars who remained with the Giants in the 1890 season rather than play in the Players League. The jolly, beer-drinking Welch stayed with the Giants in the 1892 season, then left the major leagues for good. Born in Brooklyn on July 4, 1859, Welch died on July 30, 1941.

Roger Connor

Roger Connor was one of the members of the Troy club who moved to the Giants when the National League transferred the Troy franchise to New York in time for the 1883 season. Connor compiled a .318 career batting average over eighteen major league years, hitting over .300 in twelve of the seasons. He was one of the most dangerous power hitters of the dead-ball era, accumulating the most home runs (136) of any of the players of the 1800s. Connor led the National League in hitting with a .371 average in 1885, and hit three homers in a game against Indianapolis on May 9, 1888.

An excellent first baseman, Connor left the Giants in 1890 to play with the New York Players League club, but he returned to the Giants in 1893, moved to St. Louis in 1894, and managed St. Louis for a portion of the 1896 season.

Connor was born in Waterbury, Connecticut, on July 1, 1857, and died on January 4, 1931.

Fred Lindstrom

Third baseman Fred Lindstrom preceded Mel Ott as the Giants' boy wonder, playing in the 1924 World Series against Washington at age eighteen, hitting .333 with ten hits, and touching up the great Walter Johnson for four hits in the fifth game of the Series. Regardless, Lindstrom's participation is best remembered for a ground ball that took a lucky hop over his head to bring in the Senators' Series-winning run. Actually, Lindstrom was a superb outfielder as well as third baseman. But he was better known for his hitting, compiling a .311 average in thirteen seasons. He collected a remarkable total of 231 hits twice, in 1928 when he hit .358 and in 1930 when he averaged .379.

Lindy also was known for his sharp wit and his willingness to take on his bosses if he felt the situation called for it. He suffered a major disappointment when Bill Terry replaced John McGraw as manager. Lindstrom felt that he had been promised the job, and because of his continuing bitterness, he was traded to Pittsburgh after the 1932 season. His career with the Giants covered the 1924-1932 period, and after playing with the Pirates in 1933 and 1934, he played for the Cubs and the Dodgers before calling it a career after the 1936 season.

After his retirement, Lindstrom coached college baseball and then became U.S. postmaster in Evanston, Illinois. He was born on November 21, 1905, in Chicago and died on October 4, 1981.

Amos Rusie

Amos Wilson Rusie was considered the hardest-throwing pitcher of the 1800s and accordingly nicknamed "The Hoosier Thunderbolt."

The big right-hander racked up remarkable statistics in his eight years with the Giants. He won 230 games for the Giants overall, winning more than thirty games in three seasons and winning twenty-nine games in three other campaigns. Rusie led the league in both shutouts and strikeouts in five seasons.

The big fellow also was a man of principle. He sat out the entire 1896 season because Giant owner Andrew Freedman deducted a protested $200 fine levied in 1895 from Rusie's 1896 contract. Rusie brought suit successfully and subsequently was paid in full for 1896 when all the National League clubs chipped in to pay him and thereby avoid a legal showdown on the reserve clause in the standard player contract.

The Hoosier Thunderbolt played for Indianapolis in 1889, was with the Giants through 1898, and was traded to Cincinnati in 1900 for twenty-year-old Christy Mathewson. Rusie was born in Mooresville, Indiana, on May 30, 1871, and died on December 6, 1942.

Willie Mays

Willie Mays unquestionably was the greatest all-around player in Giants history, displaying his extraordinary skills for six seasons in New York and for fifteen more in San Francisco. He was hailed for his consummate excellence in all facets of the game, but is best remembered for his home runs, all but fourteen of his 660 coming as a member of the Giants.

The Say Hey Kid, as he was known in his New York days, tied John Mize's club record with fifty-one home runs in 1955 and set a new standard by blasting fifty-two for San Francisco ten years later. He became the National League's first 30-30 man by belting thirty-six homers and stealing forty bases in 1956. One year later, he became the first man to do it twice.

Mays, who wore No. 24, was purchased from the Birmingham Black Barons for $14,000 in 1950 at age nineteen. One year later he was in the bigs, helping the Giants win a miracle pennant. Following two years in the military service, he returned to New York in 1954 and parlayed an MVP season into victory in the World Series, one best remembered for his catch of Vic Wertz's long fly to center. Mays won the batting title that year at .345.

Although Willie was a hero in New York, he was greeted with skepticism when the Giants moved west in 1958. Despite a career-high .347 average that maiden season, the Bay Area fans didn't fully accept Mays until his slugging feats rewarded San Francisco with its only pennant winner in 1962. He hit forty-nine homers and knocked in a career-high 141 runs that year.

Mays's one last gasp of glory for the Giants came at age forty, when his hot first half gave the 1971 club the division lead en route to the title. One year later, Mays was traded to the Mets and his beloved New York, where he went out in style by appearing in the 1973 World Series. It's been many years since he last wore a Giants uniform, but the incomparable Mays still tops the San Francisco Giants in all offensive categories except batting average, games played, and home runs.

Travis Jackson

Travis Calvin "Stonewall" Jackson was one of the premier shortstops of the 1920s and early 1930s, with one of the most powerful throwing arms and greatest ranges at the position. He led National League shortstops in assists four times, in total chances accepted for three seasons, and in fielding average and double plays twice. Jackson suffered recurrent knee ailments, which slowed him enough to require his shift to third base in 1935 and 1936, his last two years playing with the Giants.

Jackson had a lifetime batting average of .291 in fifteen seasons, all of them with the Giants. He hit with surprising power considering his slight stature, batting in more than seventy-five runs in seven seasons. For many years he was considered one of the most accomplished bunters in the game.

The popular Jackson, the Giants' captain for several seasons, coached for the Giants and managed in the minor leagues for many years after his retirement as a player. Jackson was born in Waldo, Arkansas, on November 2, 1903.

Juan Marichal

Nobody did it better than the Dominican Dandy. Juan Marichal simply was the finest pitcher to wear a San Francisco uniform, winning 104 more games than anyone else in the Giants' West Coast history. Marichal was 238-140 with the Giants, including fifty-two shutouts and a 2.84 earned run average over fourteen seasons.

Marichal required only 2½ years of minor league seasoning before he joined the Giants to stay with a one-hit debut against the Phillies in 1960. He had his first great season in 1963 with a 25-8 record and a 2.41 ERA plus a no-hitter against Houston (the Giants' first since 1929!), and a sixteen-inning, 1-0 victory over Warren Spahn of the Braves.

That season began a string of six twenty-win campaigns in seven years, the exception being 1967, when injury deprived him of approximately one dozen starts and restricted him to a 14-10 record. Contemporaries Bob Gibson, Sandy Koufax, and Don Drysdale received more attention in the sixties, but none could match Juan's 191 victories for the decade.

Marichal was the complete pitcher, a right-handed Spahn with his high-kicking delivery. Others were faster and had sharper-breaking pitches, but none could master their repertoire like Juan could. His ability to nick the corners with all of his vast assortment of pitches baffled hitters. Durability was another Marichal asset — he completed sixteen games in a row en route to a 26-9 season in 1968.

Orlando Cepeda

The Baby Bull enjoyed only seven full seasons in the Giants' livery, yet he made the greatest impact on the San Francisco franchise in the shortest amount of time. Nobody, not even the great Mays, took the Bay Area by storm as Orlando Cepeda did in his and the Giants' rookie year in San Francisco. Anxious fans desperately wanted a new hero and Cepeda won their hearts with a .312 average, twenty-five home runs and Rookie of the Year honors.

The Puerto Rican powerhouse won batting titles in his first two minor league seasons for Kokomo (.393) and St. Cloud (.355) before using Triple-A Minneapolis as a stepping stone to the majors. Cepeda smacked a home run in his first big league game, the historic Giants-Dodgers West Coast inaugural, and was dear to the hearts of Bay Area fans ever since that sensational debut.

He already was an All-Star Game performer by 1959, and in 1961 he enjoyed one of the finest seasons in the club's history. Cepeda set a San Francisco record in 1961 with 142 runs batted in and led the National League with forty-six home runs, a career high. Despite a late-season slump, he helped the Giants to the 1962 pennant with thirty-five homers and 114 RBI.

Cepeda never hit below .297 in his seven full seasons with the club, and his .308 career average with the Giants is the highest in the history of the franchise on the West Coast. Mays, at .301, is the only other player to post a lifetime mark above .300. But Cepeda was deemed expendable in 1966 when it finally was determined that neither he nor Willie McCovey could play anywhere but first base.

Willie McCovey

The presence of Willie McCovey made the trading of Cepeda to St. Louis tolerable, because Stretch proved beyond a doubt that if one of the popular youngsters had to go, the Giants made the correct decision. As soon as Cepeda departed, McCovey settled at first base, brought consistency to his game, and blossomed into one of the greatest sluggers in history.

McCovey became the most popular player in the club's West Coast history, enjoying a career that spanned four decades and produced 521 home runs. He hit 469 of those with the Giants, ten more than Mays accumulated in a San Francisco uniform. McCovey retired in 1980 with eighteen grand-slam home runs, more than anyone in National League history.

But it was a rocky path to stardom for No. 44. He made a big splash as a rookie in 1959, batting .354 with thirteen home runs in fifty-two games in 1959 and earning Rookie of the Year distinction. One year later, he struggled and was returned to the minors. When he rejoined the Giants, his playing time was reduced by Cepeda's presence, yet he helped the Giants to the 1962 flag with a .293 average and twenty home runs in only 229 at bats in 1962.

Stretch was used as a left fielder in 1963, responding with a club-record forty-four home runs at that position and tying Hank Aaron for the league lead. There was a woeful slump in 1964, but by 1965 an upward trend began that earned the big fellow MVP honors in 1969 with forty-five homers, 126 RBI, and a .320 average.

McCovey was the most feared slugger in the league during his peak years. In 1969-70, for instance, he totaled eighty-four homers and 252 RBI despite a staggering 258 walks. He was swapped to San Diego in 1974, but his heart remained in San Francisco. In 1977, Willie Mac was signed by the Giants as a free agent and said "thank you" with twenty-eight home runs as the Comeback Player of the Year. To some, he'd never left.

Gaylord Perry

Some might argue that Gaylord Perry doesn't belong among the Giants greats, but the 300-game winner spent more complete seasons (eight) with San Francisco than with any other club. Only Marichal has better numbers in most of the S.F. pitching lists, which show Gaylord with 134 victories and a 2.96 ERA.

Perry, a $90,000 bonus baby, made it to the big leagues to stay in 1964; a performance at New York, May 31, 1964, started him on the road to stardom. It was the second game of the longest doubleheader in history and Perry worked ten innings, striking out nine, to gain the victory in the Giants' 8-6, twenty-three-inning decision. That was the first time, by Gay's admission, that he used his so-called "spitter."

Perry always pitched in Marichal's shadow and was a tough-luck hurler for the Giants. In 1967-68, for instance, his ERAs were 2.61 and 2.44, yet his combined record was 31-32. His first great season with the Giants was 1966, when Gaylord went 21-8 and set a San Francisco strikeout record with fifteen against the Phillies on July 22. That was the most strikeouts by a Giants pitcher since Christy Mathewson's sixteen in 1904.

He fired the second no-hitter in S.F. history by shackling the Cardinals in 1968, won nineteen games with a 2.49 ERA in '69, and enjoyed his finest Giants season in 1970, topping the National League with a 23-13 record. He aided the club's 1971 pennant drive with sixteen victories, added one more in the playoffs, and was traded to Cleveland for Sam McDowell in one of the more controversial and ill-fated swaps in Giants history. Perry won more games (twenty-four) for the Indians in '72 than McDowell did in his S.F. career.

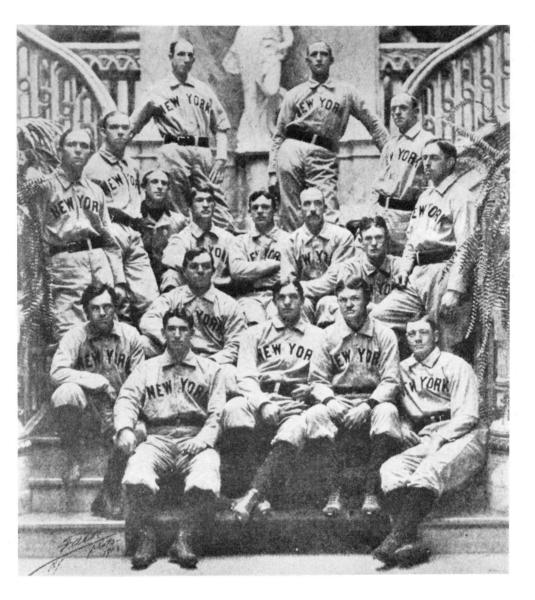

1903 Giants

Dunn.   Warner.
Gilbert.   McGann.   Miller
Mertes.   Babb.   Bowermann.   McGraw.   Van Haltren.   Brown.
Lauder.   Bresnahan.   McGinnity.   Mathewson.   Taylor.   Cronin.

Polo Grounds, New York City,
Home of the New York Giants.

Vintage Polo Grounds postcards with inset photos of John McGraw

National League Baseball
Park, New York

John McGraw (left) greeted Christy Mathewson after 1916 trade of star pitcher to Cincinnati

Christy Mathewson at peak of 372-win New York career

Stars of 1912 champs, l. to r., Fred Merkle, Larry Doyle, Christy Mathewson, John McGraw and Fred Snodgrass

JOHN McGRAW . . . greatest manager

FREDDY LINDSTROM . . . lifetime .311 hitter

TRAVIS JACKSON . . . slick-fielding shortstop

LEFTY O'DOUL . . . Mr. Baseball of San Francisco

1922 champions, l. to r., (top row) Travis Jackson, Mike Cvengros, Mahlon Higbee, Ralph Shinners, Claude Jonnard, George Kelly, Jesse Burkett, Jack Scott; (second row) Irish Meusel, Fred Johnson, Freddie Maguire, Rosy Ryan, Carmen Hill, Jesse Barnes, Virgil Barnes, Dave Robertson, Frank Snyder; (third row) Ross Youngs, Art Nehf, Casey Stengel, Hughie Jennings, John McGraw, Cozy Dolan, Alex Gaston, Earl Smith, Frankie Frisch; (bottom row) Hugh McQuillan, Waddy MacPhee, Davey Bancroft, Clint Blume, Bill Cunningham, Heinie Groh, Lee King, Johnny Rawlings

1933 champions, l. to r., (top row) Bill Clark, Homer Peel, Jack Salveson, Bill Shores, Dolph Luque, Lefty O'Doul, Herman Bell, Harry Danning, Joe Moore; (second row) Gus Mancuso, Johnny Vergez, Freddy Fitzsimmons, George Davis, Carl Hubbell, Blondy Ryan, Hal Schumacher, Joe Malay, Mel Ott, LeRoy Parmelee; (third row) Hughie Critz, Travis Jackson, Frank Snyder, Bill Terry, Tom Clarke, Chuck Dressen, Byrnie James; (bottom row) Willie Schaeffer, Phil Weintraub, Al Smith, Tom Troy, Glenn Spencer, Paul Richards

Christy Mathewson at leisure outside Saranac Lake, N.Y., home

Pallbearers at Christy Mathewson's funeral in 1925 included John McGraw and Davey Bancroft

Bill Terry (left) met new Braves' slugger Babe Ruth in 1935 (Associated Press photo)

Manager Bill Terry (foreground) addressed his Giants in early 1930s (Associated Press photo)

MEL OTT...great slugger early in his career

CARL HUBBELL...a 253-game winner in 1928–43

Polo Grounds, longtime home (1912–57) of the Giants, as viewed from above

Bill Terry managed the Giants 10 years, 1932–41, and batted .341 for his career, including a .401 average in 1930, making him the last National Leaguer to reach .400

After becoming Giants' manager in 1942, Mel Ott admired photographs of predecessors John McGraw (left) and Bill Terry (Associated Press photo)

Hall of Fame slugger Johnny Mize belted a career-high 51 homers as N.L. power champion in 1947, also leading league with 137 runs and 138 RBI that year

Jubilant Giants whooped it up in clubhouse following pennant-winning playoff homer in 1951. From left, coach Fred Fitzsimmons, Larry Jansen, Bobby Thomson, owner Horace Stoneham and Don Mueller (foreground) celebrated Thomson's historic shot heard 'round the world (Associated Press photo)

1951 champions, l. to r., (top row) Wes Westrum, George Spencer, Ray Noble, Sal Yvars, Dave Koslo, Lucky Lohrke, Davey Williams, Don Mueller, Al Corwin, Sheldon Jones; (middle row) Jim Hearn, Sal Maglie, Monte Irvin, Whitey Lockman, Larry Jansen, Clint Hartung, Monte Kennedy, Bobby Thomson, Alex Konikowski; (front row) Hank Thompson, Alvin Dark, Willie Mays, Herman Franks, Leo Durocher, Fred Fitzsimmons, Hank Schenz, Bill Rigney, Eddie Stanky, Doc Bowman

MONTE IRVIN . . . league-leading 121 RBI in 1951

RUSS HODGES . . . longtime radio voice of the Giants

HOYT WILHELM . . . began great bullpen career in 1952

SAL MAGLIE . . . The Barber shaved them close

Manager Leo Durocher (left) posed with rookie Willie Mays in 1951. Mays, Leo's protege, contributed 20 homers to pennant push (Associated Press photo)

The most famous catch in World Series history found Giants' centerfielder Willie Mays chasing down Vic Wertz' long blast in Game 1 of the 1954 sweep of the Cleveland Indians (Associated Press photo)

NEW YORK
GIANTS'
YEAR BOOK
1954
GIANTS
1951
THE LITTLE MIRACLE of COOGAN'S BLUFF
50 CENTS
PASTE
1954 EDITION

A beaming Willie Mays displayed the bat and ball used for his major league-leading 51st home run in 1955. Mays became the seventh player in history to surpass 50 home runs (Associated Press photo)

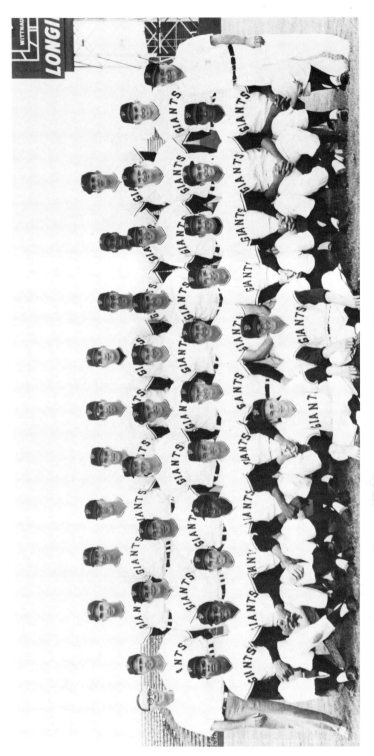

San Francisco's first Giants, 1958, l. to r. (top row) Ramon Monzant, Hank Sauer, Bob Schmidt, Bob Speake, Eddie Bressoud, John Antonelli, Ray Jablonski, Valmy Thomas, Mike McCormick; (middle row) Eddie Logan, Don Johnson, Paul Giel, Nick Testa, Al Worthington, Jackie Brandt, Stu Miller, Danny O'Connell, Gordon Jones, Whitey Lockman, Daryl Spencer, Doc Bowman; (bottom row) Felipe Alou, Willie Mays, Jim Davenport, Willie Kirkland, Wes Westrum, Bill Rigney, Herman Franks, Salty Parker, Ruben Gomez, Orlando Cepeda, Bill White; (batboys) Roy McKercher and Frank Iverlich

WILLIE MAYS . . . after move to S.F. in 1958

ORLANDO CEPEDA . . . rookie listened to records

SEALS STADIUM . . . first home of the San Francisco Giants, 1958–59

Willie Mays (right) posed with Stan Musial at Seals Stadium

Rookie Willie McCovey's powerful swing at Seals Stadium, 1959

CANDLESTICK PARK...a capacity crowd at new home of the Giants

ALVIN DARK...managed N.L. champs in 1962

FELIPE ALOU...a .316 average in 1962

STU MILLER...won 14 in relief in 1961

SAD SAM JONES...a 21-game winner in 1959

Giants' Murderers Row of early Sixties, (from left) Willie McCovey, Willie Mays and Orlando Cepeda terrorized N.L. pitchers

BILLY PIERCE . . . contributed 16 wins in 1962   JACK SANFORD . . . Giants' 1962 ace at 24–7

FELIPE ALOU . . . slid into Dodgers' catcher John Roseboro

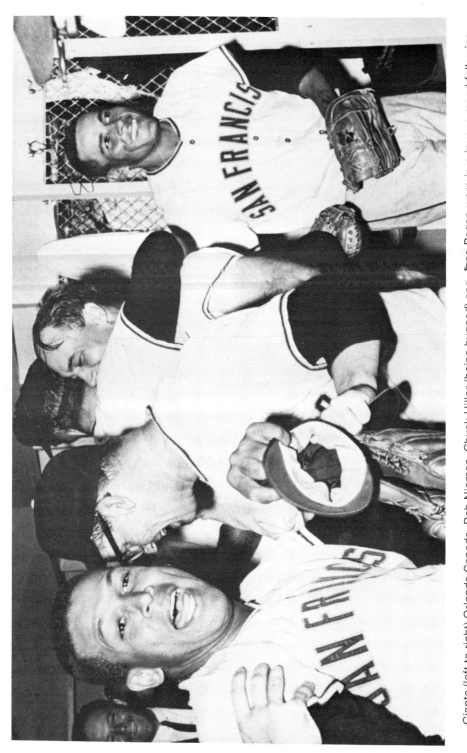

Giants (left to right) Orlando Cepeda, Bob Nieman, Chuck Hiller (being hugged) and Jose Pagan were in a joyous mood following pennant-clinching 6–4 playoff victory at Los Angeles in 1962 (Associated Press photo)

Chuck Hiller watched the flight of the ball after becoming the first N.L. player ever to hit a grand-slam in a World Series game. The blow occurred at Yankee Stadium in 1962 (Associated Press photo)

1962 champions, l. to r. (top row) Jim Davenport, Willie Mays, Bob Bolin, Harrey Kuenn, Manny Mota, Bob Nieman; (second row) Don Larsen, Ed Bailey, Tom Haller, Juan Marichal, Felipe Alou, Willie McCovey, Mike McCormick; (third row) Eddie Logan, Jim Duffalo, Whitey Lockman, Larry Jansen, Alvin Dark, Wes Westrum, Jack Sanford, Orlando Cepeda, Doc Bowman; (bottom row) Stu Miller, Billy Pierce, Ernie Bowman, Chuck Hiller, Ernie Reddick, Matty Alou, Jose Pagan, Billy O'Dell, Joe Pignatano

Willie McCovey belted a three-run homer to down the Cubs, 6–4, at wide-open Candlestick Park in 1965. That's Jesus Alou heading for third and Willie Mays approaching second

Willie Mays, as he looked in the mid-Sixties, when his consistent excellence carried the club to perennial second-place finishes

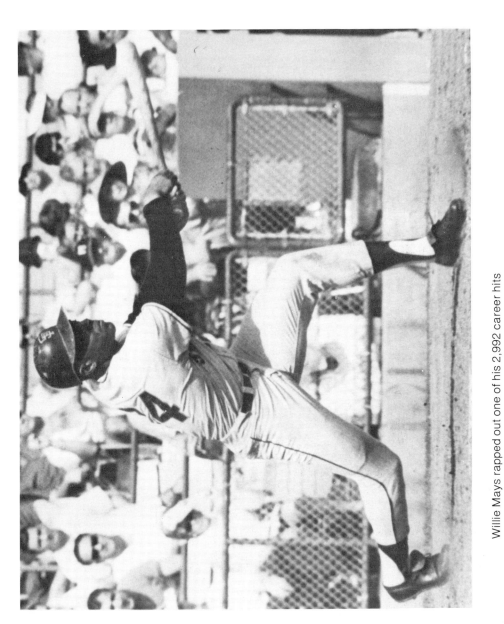

Willie Mays rapped out one of his 2,992 career hits

Stylish righthander Juan Marichal was the winningest N.L. pitcher in the Sixties, posting 20-victory seasons six of seven years, 1963–69. He's the biggest winner in S.F. history with 238

GAYLORD PERRY ... began 300-win career with Giants

JIM RAY HART ... blasted 139 homers in first five years

Hal Lanier (left), who managed Houston to a division title in 1986, beat the throw to Mets' catcher Jerry Grote in 1966

A grim moment in Candlestick Park history found Juan Marichal (27) attacking Dodgers' catcher John Roseboro with a bat as coach Charlie Fox and Sandy Koufax looked on

Lefthander Mike McCormick rejoined the Giants in 1967 and promptly was the N.L.
Cy Young Award winner with a 22–10 record and a 2.85 earned run average

HERMAN FRANKS . . . four straight runners-up, 1965–68

CLYDE KING . . . managed 90–72 Giants of 1969

CHARLIE FOX . . . Year of the Fox brought title in 1971

WES WESTRUM . . . guided Stoneham Era's last hurrah in 1975

Gaylord Perry displayed the 1970 form which produced a 23–13 record, including four straight September shutouts

Bobby Bonds, who bounced around the majors after leaving S.F., enjoyed his finest season with the 1973 Giants, belting 39 homers, stealing 43 bases and knocking in 96 runners. He also was the All-Star Game MVP

1971 division champions, l. to r. (top row) Eddie Logan, Mike Murphy, Willie Mays, Jerry Johnson, Bobby Bonds, Jim Barr, Tito Fuentes, Steve Hamilton, Jim Ray Hart, Jim Willoughby, Willie McCovey, Fran Healy, Hal Lanier, Al Wylder, Chris Arnold, Dave Rader, Doc Hughes, Rich Robertson; (middle row) Frank Bergonzi, Dick Dietz, Russ Gibson, Ozzie Virgil, John McNamara, Wes Westrum, Charlie Fox, Larry Jansen, Alan Gallagher, Don McMahon, Gaylord Perry; (bottom row) Chris Speier, Juan Marichal, Frank Duffy, Steve Sockolov, Jim Saunders, Ron Bryant, Don Carrithers, Steve Stone, John Cumberland, Jimmy Rosario

JIM DAVENPORT . . . greatest third baseman in S.F. history

CHRIS SPEIER . . . rookie whiz sparked 1971 title

JUAN MARICHAL . . . at dusk of a Hall of Fame career

DAVE KINGMAN...29 homers in 1972

GEORGE FOSTER...a bad trade for Giants

GARY MATTHEWS...Rookie of the Year
in 1973

GARRY MADDOX...a .319 hitter in 1973

These four starters (clockwise from top left), Bob Knepper, Jim Barr, John Montefusco and Vida Blue, posed by the Golden Gate Bridge for a Sporting News cover after getting the 1978 Giants off to a fast start. Newcomer Blue won 18 games and Knepper added 17

BILL MADLOCK...batted .309 in 1978

FRANK ROBINSON...first black manager in N.L.

JACK CLARK...blowing bubbles during spring training exercises

JACK CLARK...Giants' most feared slugger, 1978–84, in batting cage

WILLIE McCOVEY...finished with 521 homers, 1980

ROGER CRAIG...a Hum Baby success in 1986

BILL MADLOCK...batted .309 in 1978

FRANK ROBINSON...first black manager in N.L.

JACK CLARK...blowing bubbles during spring training exercises

JACK CLARK ... Giants' most feared slugger, 1978–84, in batting cage

WILLIE McCOVEY ... finished with 521 homers, 1980

ROGER CRAIG ... a Hum Baby success in 1986

JEFFREY LEONARD . . . club's leader of the mid-Eighties

MIKE KRUKOW . . . a 20-game winner in 1986

BOB BRENLY . . . team homer leader in 1985

CHILI DAVIS . . . a switch-hitter with power

CHRIS BROWN . . . batted .317 in 1986

SCOTT GARRELTS . . . club's new relief ace

WILL CLARK . . . jumped from Class-A to majors

ROBBY THOMPSON . . . rookie sensation of 1986

4

WORLD SERIES GAMES

The Giants have played in fifteen World Series, fourteen of them before the club left New York for San Francisco. They have won only five of the Series, in the process winning forty-two of the eighty-seven World Series games played. The Giants have played the Yankees most frequently, winning two and losing five of these Series. They have played the Philadelphia Athletics next most frequently, winning one Series and losing two. In the other five Series, the Giants split two Series with the Washington Senators, lost once to the Boston Red Sox and the Chicago White Sox, and defeated the Cleveland Indians.

Despite their great record during the McGraw years (only two second-division finishes in the twenty-nine years that McGraw managed for the entire season), the Giants won only three of the nine World Series in which they were managed by McGraw. They lost two of their three Series under Bill Terry's leadership, and won both Series played during Leo Durocher's managerial years. Alvin Dark managed the Giants in 1962 when they lost a seven-game Series to the Yankees.

The following table lists the records of the fifteen championship Giants teams, including season records, managers, and Series records.

CHAMPIONSHIP GIANT CLUBS, 1902–1982
15 NATIONAL LEAGUE PENNANTS — 5 WORLD CHAMPIONSHIPS

Year	Games Won	Games Lost	Winning Percentage	Games Won Pennant By	Giant Manager	World Series Opponent	World Series Record Won	Lost
1904	106	47	.693	13	McGraw	Elected not to play		
*1905	105	48	.686	9	McGraw	Philadelphia	4	1
1911	99	54	.647	7.5	McGraw	Philadelphia	2	4
1912	103	48	.682	10	McGraw	Boston	3	4
1913	101	51	.664	12.5	McGraw	Philadelphia	1	4
1917	98	56	.636	10	McGraw	Chicago	2	4
*1921	94	59	.614	4	McGraw	New York	5	3
*1922	93	61	.604	7	McGraw	New York	4	0
1923	95	58	.621	4.5	McGraw	New York	2	4
1924	93	60	.608	1.5	McGraw	Washington	3	4
*1933	91	61	.599	5	Terry	Washington	4	1
1936	92	62	.597	5	Terry	New York	2	4
1937	95	57	.625	3	Terry	New York	1	4
1951	98	59	.624	1	Durocher	New York	2	4
*1954	97	57	.630	5	Durocher	Cleveland	4	0
1962	103	62	.624	1	Dark	New York	3	4
						Total	42	45

*World Champions

A summary of each Giant World Series follows. The line scores list the pitchers, with the winning team's pitcher(s) listed first and the winner and the loser indicated by bold type. If a pitcher gained a save, this is indicated by "SV."

1905

This was the Giants' first World Series, although the Giants won the 1904 pennant. Giant owner John T. Brush, still contemptuous of the new American League, had refused to permit his club to play the 1904 Boston Red Sox, the American League pennant winner. Accordingly, shortly after Brush's decision, baseball's National Commission issued a rule requiring the National League and American League winners to meet in a World Series beginning in 1905.

John McGraw's Giants, decked out in spanking-new black uniforms with white trim, defeated Connie Mack's Athletics 4 games to 1 in a superbly-pitched set of games. Giant right-hander Christy Mathewson dominated the Series with three shutout wins, and right-hander Joe "Iron Man" McGinnity captured the other Giant win, also with a shutout. Athletics' right-hander Chief Bender won the only Philadelphia victory, a whitewash of the Giants.

Game 1: October 9 at Shibe Park

Mathewson held the A's to four scattered hits and defeated Eddie Plank, 3-0. Giant second baseman Billy Gilbert led the Giants with three hits.

```
GIANTS        000  020 001    3  10  1
ATHLETICS     000  000 000    0   4  0
Pitchers: Mathewson vs. Plank     Att: 17,955
```

Game 2: October 10 at Polo Grounds

Athletics' right-hander Charles "Chief" Bender duplicated Mathewson's opening-game win by shutting out the Giants, 3-0. Philadelphia center fielder Bristol Lord drove in two of the A's runs as Joe McGinnity took the loss.

```
ATHLETICS  001  000 020    3  6  2
GIANTS     000  000 000    0  4  2
Pitchers: Bender vs. McGinnity, Ames (9)    Att: 24,992
```

Game 3: October 12 at Shibe Park

With an intervening rainy-day postponment, Mathewson came back to shut out the A's for an easy 9-0 win, again on a four-hitter. Giant first baseman Dan McGann drove in four runs with three hits.

Giants	200 050 002	9	8	1
Athletics	000 000 000	0	4	4

Pitchers: **Mathewson** vs. **Coakley**   Att: 10,991

Game 4: October 13 at Polo Grounds

Joe McGinnity pitched a four-hit, 1-0 shutout to defeat Eddie Plank. Billy Gilbert singled in Giant left fielder Sam Mertes in the fourth inning with the only run of the game.

Athletics	000 000 000	0	5	1
Giants	000 100 000	1	4	0

Pitchers: **McGinnity** vs. **Plank**   Att: 13,598

Game 5: October 14 at Polo Grounds

Mathewson shut out the Athletics for the third straight time as the Giants won the World Series. His brilliant five-hit, 2-0 win topped off the greatest World Series performance by a pitcher and a staff (four shutouts). Billy Gilbert drove in the first Giant run in the fifth inning with a sacrifice fly, and Mathewson scored the second run on a grounder by Giant right fielder George Browne.

Athletics	000 000 000	0	6	0
Giants	000 010 01#	2	5	2

Pitchers: **Mathewson** vs. **Bender**   Att: 24,187

Total Attendance: 91,723
Winning Player's Share: $1,142
Losing Player's Share: $832

1911

The Giants lost the World Series to the Philadelphia Athletics 4 games to 2 in a Series remembered for the hard hitting of A's third baseman Frank Baker. Baker had led the American League in 1911 in home runs with eleven, but he did not gain the nickname "Home Run" until he homered in the second and third games to turn the Series around in the A's favor. Christy Mathewson pitched three solid games for the Giants, but won only one of them as the outgunned Polo Grounders went down in a Series that lasted twelve days because of six straight rainouts after the third game.

Game 1: October 14 at Polo Grounds

Giant left fielder Josh Devore doubled in the go-ahead Giant run in the seventh inning to break a 1-1 tie and give Mathewson a decision over Chief Bender.

Athletics	010	000	000	1	6	2
Giants	000	100	10#	2	5	0

Pitchers: **Mathewson** vs. **Bender**   Att: 38,281

Game 2: October 16 at Shibe Park

A's third baseman Frank Baker was the hero of this game. With Rube Marquard facing Eddie Plank, the score was 1-1 after five innings. In the bottom of the sixth, Eddie Collins cracked a two-out double and Baker followed with a sharply pulled drive over the right-field fence for a 3-1 victory.

Giants	010	000	000	1	5	3
Athletics	100	002	00#	3	4	0

Pitchers: **Plank** vs. **Marquard,** Crandall (8)
Home Run: Baker   Att: 26,286

Game 3: October 17 at Polo Grounds

Mathewson held a 1-0 lead as the A's came to bat in the top of the ninth. Frank Baker earned his new "Home Run" tag with a game-tying home run. The one-all tie carried into the eleventh when the A's scored two runs on three hits and errors by Buck Herzog (his third of the game) and Art Fletcher. The Giants could manage only one run in the bottom of the inning and went down to a 3-2 loss.

Athletics	000	000	001	02	3	9	2
Giants	001	000	000	01	2	3	5

Pitchers: **Coombs** vs. **Mathewson**
Home Run: Baker   Att: 37,216

Game 4: October 24 at Shibe Park

After six straight rainouts, the Series resumed with Mathewson facing Bender. The A's overcame a two-run Giant lead with three runs in their fourth. Baker, right fielder Danny Murphy and shortstop Jack Barry each had two doubles for Philadelphia as the Athletics won, 4-2.

Giants	200	000	000	2	7	3
Athletics	000	310	00#	4	11	1

Pitchers: **Bender** vs. **Mathewson,** Wiltse (8)   Att: 24,355

Game 5: October 25 at Polo Grounds

The A's took a three-run lead on center fielder Rube Oldring's home run in the third inning and held a 3-1 lead in the ninth inning. The Giants tied the game in the last of the ninth on doubles by Art Fletcher, pitcher Doc Crandall, and a single by Josh Devore. In the bottom of the tenth, Larry Doyle doubled off relief pitcher Eddie Plank, was sacrificed to third, and scored the winning run on Fred Merkle's sacrifice fly. After the game, plate umpire Bill Klem told writers that Doyle had missed home plate when he slid in but that the A's had not noticed the omission.

```
Athletics        003  000  000  0    3   7   1
Giants           000  000  102  1    4   9   2
```
Pitchers: Marquard, Ames (4), **Crandall** (8) vs. Coombs, **Plank** (10)
Home Run: Oldring   Att: 33,228

Game 6: October 26 at Shibe Park

The Athletics won the game 13-2 to win the Series. Chief Bender was the winner as the A's iced the game with a seven-run outburst in the bottom of the seventh. The A's Danny Murphy was the hitting star with four hits.

```
Giants           100  000  001    2    4   3
Athletics        001  401  70#   13   13   5
```
Pitchers: **Bender** vs. **Ames,** Wiltse (5), Marquard (7)   Att: 20,485

Total Attendance: 179,851
Winning Player's Share: $3,655
Losing Player's Share: $2,436

1912

The Giants lost a seven-game World Series to the Boston Red Sox on outfielder Fred Snodgrass' famous "$30,000 muff" in the last inning of the deciding game. Down 3 games to 1 (plus a tie game), the Giants fought back to win the sixth game behind Rube Marquard, and the seventh with Jeff Tesreau the winner. But the Giants lost the dramatic final game, after appearing to have the game in hand, as the Sox capitalized on Snodgrass' mechanical error and a mental lapse by first baseman Fred Merkle.

Game 1: October 8 at Polo Grounds

The Red Sox defeated surprise Giant rookie starter Jeff Tesreau 4-3 at the Polo Grounds as second baseman Steve Yerkes singled in two Boston runs in the seventh inning. Boston's thirty-four-game winner Smokey Joe Wood snuffed out a Giant rally in the bottom of the ninth with his tenth and eleventh strikeouts to leave the tying and winning Giant runs stranded.

Red Sox	000	001	300	4	6	1
Giants	002	000	001	3	8	1

Pitchers: **Wood** vs. **Tesreau,** Crandall (8)   Att: 35,730

Game 2: October 9 at Fenway Park

The clubs played to a 6-6 tie at Fenway Park before the game was called after eleven innings because of darkness. With the game tied at five-all after nine innings, the Giants scored a run on Merkle's triple and a single by Moose McCormick. But the Red Sox tied the game again in the bottom of the tenth when Tris Speaker tripled to deep center, and scored when Giant catcher Dutch Wilson dropped the throw to the plate. Christy Mathewson pitched the entire game, but the Sox scored four unearned runs on three errors by shortstop Art Fletcher and Wilson's miscue.

Giants	010	100	030	10	6	11	5
Red Sox	300	010	010	10	6	10	1

Pitchers: **Mathewson** vs. **Collins**, Hall (8), Bedient (11)   Att: 30,148

Game 3: October 10 at Fenway Park

Rube Marquard outpitched Boston right hander Buck O'Brien and won 2-1. Giant right fielder Josh Devore saved the game with a running catch of catcher Josh Cady's liner with two out and two on in the bottom of the ninth.

Giants	010	010	000	2	7	1
Red Sox	000	000	001	1	7	0

Pitchers: **Marquard** vs. **O'Brien,** Bedient (9)
Att: 34,624

Game 4: October 11 at Polo Grounds

Jeff Tesreau lost to Joe Wood, 3-1. Wood scattered nine hits, struck out eight hitters, and drove in the last Boston run.

Red Sox	010	100	001	3	8	1
Giants	000	000	100	1	9	1

Pitchers: **Wood** vs. **Tesreau,** Ames (8)   Att: 36,502

Game 5: October 12 at Fenway Park

Boston right-hander Hugh Bedient defeated Mathewson 2-1, yielding the Giants only three hits. Matty gave up the Boston runs in the third inning on triples by Harry Hooper and Steve Yerkes plus an error by Giant second baseman Larry Doyle, then set down Boston in order from the fourth inning on in a losing effort.

```
Giants         000  000 100    1   3   1
Red Sox        002  000 00#    2   5   1
Pitchers: Bedient vs. Mathewson      Att: 34,683
```

Game 6: October 14 at Polo Grounds

Rube Marquard held off Boston 5-2 as the Giants drew back to a 3-2 deficit in games. The New Yorkers scored all of their runs in the bottom of the first inning on hits by Doyle, Murray, Merkle, Herzog, and Fletcher, and on a double steal.

```
Red Sox        020  000 000    2   7   2
Giants         500  000 00#    5  11   1
Pitchers: Marquard vs. O'Brien, Collins (2)    Att: 30,622
```

Game 7: October 15 at Fenway Park

Jeff Tesreau tied the Series with an 11-4 victory. He defeated Joe Wood, who was removed from the game after the first inning during which he yielded six Giant runs on seven hits. It was a clever move by Boston manager Jake Stahl, because it enabled him to pitch Wood in the following day's climactic game.

```
Giants         610  002 101   11  16   4
Red Sox        010  000 210    4   9   3
Pitchers: Tesreau vs. Wood, Hall (2)
Home Runs: Doyle, Gardner     Att:32,694
```

Game 8: October 16 at Fenway Park

The Giants broke a one-all tie after nine innings when Merkle drove in Red Murray with the go-ahead run in the top of the tenth. The World Championship appeared to be well in hand, with Mathewson pitching a strong game, particularly when Boston pinch hitter Clyde Engle led off with an easy fly ball to center. The Giants' Fred Snodgrass camped under the ball, tapped his glove, then muffed the ball as Engle moved into second with the tying run. Snodgrass recouped some of the loss with a fine running catch of Harry Hooper's drive to deep center. Mathewson walked weak-hitting Steve Yerkes, then appeared to have the second out when Tris Speaker popped up softly near the first-base coaching box. Inexplicably, first baseman Fred

Merkle stood transfixed and the ball dropped foul when catcher Chief Meyers missed a last-second dive for it. The reprieved Speaker responded with a single that drove in Engle, and Yerkes scored the winning run on third baseman Larry Gardner's sacrifice fly. The loss would thereafter be attributed to Snodgrass' "$30,000 muff." A mortified McGraw absolved Snodgrass' mechanical error, but blamed Merkle for not making the play on Speaker's foul ball and Mathewson for not shouting directions to his infielders on the play.

Giants   001 000 000   1   2   9   2
Red Sox   000 000 100   2   3   8   5
Pitchers: Bedient, **Wood** (8) vs. **Mathewson**
Att: 17,034

Total Attendance: 252,037
Winning Player's Share: $4,025
Losing Player's Share: $2,566

1913

The Giants lost their third World Series in the past three years, losing to the Philadelphia Athletics, 4 games to 1. The A's were never in serious difficulty, winning the first game, losing the second, then taking the final three games with ease. The Giants were handicapped by pre-Series injuries to center fielder Fred Snodgrass and first baseman Fred Merkle, and a broken finger sustained by catcher Chief Meyers before the first game. Regardless, it was considered unlikely that their full availability would have changed the Series results.

Game 1: October 7 at Polo Grounds

Philadelphia right-hander Chief Bender defeated Rube Marquard as the A's won, 6-4. The Athletics moved to a 5-1 lead on a two-run homer by Home Run Baker in the top of the fifth inning, and Bender struggled through to win despite eleven Giant hits.

Athletics   000 320 010   6 11   1
Giants   001 030 000   4 11   0
Pitchers: **Bender** vs. **Marquard,** Crandall (6), Tesreau (8)
Home Run: Baker   Att: 36,291

Game 2: October 8 at Shibe Park

Christy Mathewson shut out the Athletics and won 3-0 in ten innings. The Giants scored their runs on hits by catcher Larry McLean, Mathewson, and Art Fletcher. Giant left-hander George "Hooks" Wiltse played a surprise role as he replaced the crippled Fred

Snodgrass at first base in the third inning and threw two men out at the plate to prevent the A's from breaking the scoreless tie in the ninth inning.

Giants	000	000	000	3	3	7	2
Athletics	000	000	000	0	0	8	2

Pitchers: **Mathewson** vs. **Plank**   Att: 20,563

Game 3: October 9 at Polo Grounds

Jeff Tesreau lost to Athletics right-hander Bullet Joe Bush. Philadelphia took a 5-0 lead in the second inning and moved to an easy 8-2 win. Second baseman Eddie Collins led the A's with three hits and three RBI.

Athletics	320	000	210	8	12	1
Giants	000	010	100	2	5	1

Pitchers: **Bush** vs. **Tesreau,** Crandall (7)
Home Run: Schang   Att: 36,896

Game 4: October 10 at Shibe Park

The Giants fell behind 6-0 after five innings and lost 6-5 despite rallying for five runs in the seventh and eighth innings. Chief Bender defeated Giants right-hander Al Demaree, who gave way to Rube Marquard after four innings. Philadelphia catcher Wally Schang led the A's with three RBI, matching a three-run homer by Fred Merkle in the Giant seventh.

Giants	000	000	320	5	8	2
Athletics	010	320	00#	6	9	0

Pitchers: **Bender** vs. **Demaree,** Marquard (5)
Home Run: Merkle   Att: 20,568

Game 5: October 11 at Polo Grounds

Eddie Plank outpitched Christy Mathewson for a 3-1 Philadelphia win and the Series. Matty pitched a solid six hitter, allowing only two earned runs. But Plank was superb, yielding singles only to McLean and Mathewson and facing only twenty-nine batters.

Athletics	102	000	000	3	6	1
Giants	000	010	000	1	2	2

Pitchers: **Plank** vs. **Mathewson**   Att: 36,632

Total Attendance: 150,992
Winning Player's Share: $3,246
Losing Player's Share: $2,164

1917

The Giants lost their fourth straight World Series, this time to the Chicago White Sox, 4 games to 2. The Sox won the first two games, but the Giants came back to even the Series at two-all. The Sox took the pivotal fifth game, then won the sixth game to take the Series. This classic is remembered for a play in the last game: Chicago broke a scoreless tie on a mistake by Giant catcher Bill Rariden which was erroneously blamed on Giant third baseman Heinie Zimmerman.

Game 1: October 6 at Comiskey Park

Chicago's twenty-eight game winning right-hander Eddie Cicotte outpitched Slim Sallee for a 2-1 White Sox win. Center fielder Happy Felsch's solo homer in the fourth inning provided the winning margin as Cicotte scattered seven Giant hits.

Giants	000	010	000	1	7	1
White Sox	001	100	00#	2	7	1

Pitchers: **Cicotte** vs. **Sallee**
Home Run: Felsch   Att: 32,000

Game 2: October 7 at Comiskey Park

The White Sox knocked Giant left-hander Ferdie Schupp out of the box in a two-run second inning and went on to a 7-2 win as Chicago spitballer Red Faber pitched a steady eight-hit game. The Sox put the game away in the fourth inning with a five-run assault on Giant relievers Fred Anderson and Pol Perritt. Left fielder "Shoeless Joe" Jackson and shortstop Buck Weaver led the White Sox attack with three hits apiece.

Giants	020	000	000	2	8	1
White Sox	020	500	00	7	14	1

Pitchers: **Faber** vs. Schupp, **Anderson** (2), Perritt (4), Tesreau (8)   Att: 32,000

Game 3: October 10 at Polo Grounds

The Giants fought back to win their first Series game as Rube Benton shut out Chicago, 2-0. The Giants scored their runs off Cicotte in the fourth inning on right fielder Dave Robertson's triple, first baseman Walter Holke's double, and left fielder George Burns' single.

White Sox	000	000	000	0	5	3
Giants	000	200	00#	2	8	2

Pitchers: **Benton** vs. **Cicotte**   Att: 33,616

Game 4: October 11 at Polo Grounds

The Giants tied the Series with a 5-0 win at the Polo Grounds. Schupp came back to hold the White Sox to seven scattered hits, and center fielder Benny Kauff brought in the first Giant run with an inside-the-park home run off Red Faber in the fourth inning. Kauff hit his second homer of the day in the eighth.

```
White Sox      000  000 000    0   7   0
Giants         000  110 12#    5  10   1
Pitchers: Schupp vs. Faber, Danforth (8)
Home Runs: Kauff (2)     Att: 27,746
```

Game 5: October 13 at Comiskey Park

The White Sox won 8-5 to take a 3-2 advantage in games. The Giants moved out to a 5-2 lead after 6 1/2 innings, but the Sox came back with three-run bursts in the seventh and eighth innings off Giant starter Slim Sallee to win the game. Second baseman Eddie Collins singled in Chicago's go-ahead run in the eighth inning.

```
Giants         200  200 100    5  12   3
White Sox      001  001 33#    8  14   6
Pitchers: Russell, Cicotte (1), Williams (7), Faber (8) vs.
Sallee, Perritt (8)     Att: 27,323
```

Game 6: October 15 at Polo Grounds

Chicago clinched the Series with a 4-2 victory at the Polo Grounds as Sox right-hander Red Faber outpitched Rube Benton. The game is best remembered for a play in the Chicago fourth that led to three unearned White Sox runs and which was mistakenly considered a "boner" by third baseman Heinie Zimmerman. With none out and Chicago's Joe Jackson at first and Eddie Collins at third, pitcher Benton fielded a bouncer and threw to Zimmerman at third. The trapped Collins, seeing catcher Bill Rariden well up the line near third base with no one behind him protecting the plate, sprinted past Rariden to score. Zimmerman could do nothing but chase Collins hopelessly to the plate. Criticized after the game for his futile chase, Zimmerman answered his critics with an unanswerable question: "Who the hell was I going to throw the ball to? [plate umpire] Bill Klem?"

White Sox	000	300	001	4	7	1
Giants	000	020	000	2	6	3

Pitchers: **Faber** vs. **Benton,** Perritt (6) Att: 33,969

Total Attendance: 186,654
Winning Player's Share: $3,669
Losing Player's Share: $2,442

1921

After four straight World Series losses, John McGraw won the Series he *had* to win— the Giants' first Series with their New York City rivals, the Yankees. The Yanks had won their first pennant ever, led by Babe Ruth with fifty-four home runs in his first season in New York. This was a best five-out-of-nine game set with all games played at the Polo Grounds, which both clubs shared. To McGraw's special satisfaction, the Giants came back to win after falling behind 2 games to 0 and 3 games to 2.

Game 1: October 5 at Polo Grounds

Yankee submariner Carl Mays shut out the Giants with five hits and defeated the Giants' Phil Douglas, 3-0. Frank Frisch obtained four of the Giants hits as the Giant attack all but folded up shop for the day.

Yankees	100	011	000	3	7	0
Giants	000	000	000	0	5	0

Pitchers: **Mays** vs. **Douglas,** Barnes (9)   Att: 30,203

Game 2: October 6 at Polo Grounds

The Giants lost again, 3-0, with Yankee right-hander Waite Hoyt limiting them to two singles, one by Frisch and the other by second baseman Johnny Rawlings. Giant left-hander Art Nehf held the Yanks to three hits but gave up seven walks, three of them to Babe Ruth. The first, and winning, Yankee run scored on Hoyt's ground ball in the fourth inning.

```
Giants        000 000 000    0  2  3
Yankees       000 100 02#    3  3  0
Pitchers: Hoyt vs. Nehf    Att: 34,939
```

Game 3: October 7 at Polo Grounds

The Giants won their first game of the Series, 13-5, smashing out twenty hits. McGraw's club put the game away with eight runs on eight hits in the bottom of the seventh. The Giant attack was led by left fielder George Burns and catcher Frank "Pancho" Snyder with four hits apiece, and right fielder Ross Youngs, who doubled and tripled in the big seventh inning and drove in four runs on the day. Right-hander Jesse Barnes was the beneficiary of the powerful Giant hitting.

```
Yankees       004 000 010    5  8  0
Giants        004 000 81#   13 20  0
Pitchers: Toney, Barnes (3) vs. Shawkey, Quinn (3),
Collins (7), Rogers (7)    Att: 36,509
```

Game 4: October 9 at Polo Grounds

The Giants tied the Series at two-all as the opening game pitchers reversed their earlier performances and Phil Douglas defeated Carl Mays, 4-2. George Burns' double in the eighth drove in the final two Giant runs and overcame an earlier 1-0 Yankee lead. Babe Ruth homered in the ninth inning, his first of fifteen lifetime World Series home runs.

```
Giants        000 000 031    4  9  1
Yankees       000 010 001    2  7  1
Pitchers: Douglas vs. Mays
Home Run: Ruth    Att: 36,372
```

Game 5: October 10 at Polo Grounds

The Yankees took a 3-2 lead in games as Waite Hoyt outpitched Art Nehf for a 3-1 win. The Giants scored on first baseman George Kelly's first inning hit, but the Yanks tied the game in the third inning and scored their last two runs in the fourth with a rally that began with Babe Ruth's surprise bunt.

```
Yankees      001  200  000     3   6   1
Giants       100  000  000     1  10   1
Pitchers: Hoyt vs. Nehf     Att: 35,758
```

Game 6: October 11 at Polo Grounds

The Giants tied the Series with an 8-5 triumph. Jesse Barnes relieved Giant starter Fred Toney, who was knocked out of the box in the first inning as the Yanks scored three times, and struck out ten Yankees. Both of the Yankee runs scored on Barnes came on Chick Fewster's home run. George Kelly led the Giants with three hits, and left fielder Irish Meusel and catcher Pancho Snyder homered for the National Leaguers. The Giants got a break when Babe Ruth was unable to play because of an infected arm and a damaged knee.

```
Giants       030  401  000     8  13   0
Yankees      320  000  000     5   7   2
Pitchers: Toney, Barnes (1) vs. Harper, Shawkey (2),
Piercy (9)
Home Runs: Fewster, Irish Meusel, Snyder     Att: 34,283
```

Game 7: October 12 at Polo Grounds

The Giants pulled to within one game of the Series clincher with a 2-1 win as Phil Douglas again outpitched Carl Mays. Pancho Snyder drove in Johnny Rawlings with a tie-breaking double in the Giant seventh.

```
Yankees      010  000  000     1   8   1
Giants       000  100  10#     2   6   0
Pitchers: Douglas vs. Mays     Att: 36,503
```

Game 8: October 13 at Polo Grounds

The Giants won the Series as Art Nehf beat Waite Hoyt 1-0 in a superbly-pitched game. Giant shortstop Dave Bancroft scored the only run in the first inning when Yankee shortstop Roger Peckinpaugh permitted George Kelly's grounder to go through his legs. The Yankees appeared to have a rally going in the bottom of the ninth when second baseman Aaron Ward walked with one out. Home

Run Baker pulled a hard smash between first and second on which
Rawlings made a diving stop to his left and threw to first to nail the
hitter. Inexplicably, Ward rounded second base and was easily
gunned down at third on a bullet throw from George Kelly to Frank
Frisch to end the game and the Series.

```
Giants      100  000 000    1   6   0
Yankees     000  000 000    0   4   1
Pitchers: Nehf vs. Hoyt      Att: 25,410
```
Total Attendance: 269,976
Winning Player's Share: $5,265
Losing Player's Share: $3,510

1922

The Giants beat the Yankees in the World Series for the second
straight year, this time taking four consecutive wins with a
controversial tie game interspersed. It was a triumphant victory for
John McGraw, not only because the Yanks were whitewashed, but
because Giant pitchers held Babe Ruth to a meager two hits, a .118
batting average, and only one RBI. The Series is best remembered for
the second game, a ten-inning one-to-one tie that was called
unexpectedly with almost an hour of sunlight remaining. Baseball
Commissioner Kenesaw M. Landis, who was mistakenly blamed for
calling the game, ordered all of the $120,000 game receipts to be
donated to war veteran benefits.

Game 1: October 4 at Polo Grounds

The Yankees' Bullet Joe Bush failed to hold a 2-0 lead and lost the
game to Giant right-hander Rosy Ryan, 3-2. Ryan relieved Art Nehf in
the eighth inning and was the beneficiary of three Giant runs, two
scoring on Irish Meusel's single and the other run coming in on Ross
Youngs' sacrifice fly.

```
Yankees     000  001 100    2   7   0
Giants      000  000 03#    3  11   3
Pitchers: Nehf, Ryan (8) vs. Bush, Hoyt (8)    Att: 36,514
```

Game 2: October 5 at Polo Grounds

The clubs played to a ten-inning, three-all tie. The Giant runs came
on Meusel's first-inning home run. Yankee second baseman Aaron
Ward homered for one run, and first baseman Wally Pipp and left-
fielder Bob Meusel drove in the other two Yankee runs. To the
amazement and vociferous reaction of the fans, Umpires Bill Klem

and George Hildebrand called the game overcautiously after only 2 hours and 40 minutes of play with the sun still high in the sky.

```
Giants        300 000 000  0   3  8  1 (a)
Yankees       100 100 010  0   3  8  0
```
(a) Game called after ten innings because of darkness
Pitchers: J. Barnes vs. Shawkey
Home Runs: Irish Meusel, Ward   Att: 37,020

Game 3: October 6 at Polo Grounds

Rehabilitated Giant right-hander Jack Scott threw a 3-0 shutout win to defeat Yankee pitcher Waite Hoyt. The Giants scored their first two runs in the bottom of the third inning on a sacrifice by Frisch and a single by Irish Meusel.

```
Yankees       000 000 000  0   4  1
Giants        002 000 10#  3  12  1
```
Pitchers: **Scott** vs. **Hoyt,** Jones (8)   Att: 37,630

Game 4: October 7 at Polo Grounds

The Giants moved into a commanding three-game lead with a 4-3 win. The Yankees jumped off to a 2-0 lead off Giant starter Hugh McQuillan in the first inning on hits by Wally Pipp and Bob Meusel. But the Giants came back with four runs in the fifth on a bad-hop single by Dave Bancroft, a run-scoring grounder by Irish Meusel, and a single by Ross Youngs. McQuillan yielded a solo home run to Aaron Ward but held on to win over Yankee right-hander Carl Mays.

```
Giants        000 040 000  4   9  1
Yankees       200 000 100  3   8  0
```
Pitchers: **McQuillan** vs. **Mays**, Jones (9)
Home Run: Ward   Att: 37,242

Game 5: October 8 at Polo Grounds

The Giants won their second straight Series from the Yanks with a 5-3 win as Art Nehf won the clinching game for the second consecutive year. George Kelly drove in the tying and winning runs in the eighth inning with a bases-loaded single.

```
Yankees       100 010 100  3   5  0
Giants        020 000 03#  5  10  0
```
Pitchers: **Nehf** vs. **Bush**   Att: 38,551

Total Attendance: 185,947
Winning Player's Share: $4,470
Losing Player's Share: $3,225

1923

The Yankees came back after two straight World Series losses to the Giants, and defeated the National Leaguers, 4 games to 2. This was the first season for the Yanks in their brand-new Yankee Stadium, making this the first New York "Subway Series." This classic is remembered best for the play of the Yankees' Babe Ruth and the Giants' Casey Stengel. Stengel's home runs won the first and third games for the Giants and Ruth's two home runs won the second game.

Game 1: October 10 at Yankee Stadium

The Giants won 5 4 on Stengel's inside-the-park home run in Yankee Stadium off Bullet Joe Bush. The Yanks moved out to a 3-0 lead after two innings off surprise Giant starter John "Mule" Watson, but the Giants countered with a four-run third inning, driving out Waite Hoyt. The Yanks tied the game in the seventh on third baseman Joe Dugan's triple, and Stengel won it in the ninth. Casey lost a shoe running out his game-ending homer and he hobbled around the bases, barely beating the throw to the plate with a desperate slide.

```
Giants        004  000 001    5   8   0
Yankees       120  000 100    4  12   1
```
Pitchers: Watson, **Ryan**(3) vs. Hoyt, **Bush**(3)
Home Run: Stengel   Att: 55,307

Game 2: October 11 at Polo Grounds

The Yankees tied the Series as Herb Pennock held the Giants in check for a 4-2 win. Aaron Ward and Irish Meusel traded second-inning home runs for a one-all tie, but the Yanks moved ahead with two runs in the fourth, one run scoring on Ruth's drive over the right-field roof. The Babe hit his second homer in the next inning, but his hardest drive of the game was pulled down in deep center by Stengel in the ninth inning.

```
Yankees       010  210 000    4  10   0
Giants        010  001 000    2   9   1
```
Pitchers: **Pennock** vs. **McQuillan**, Bentley(4)
Home Runs: I. Meusel, Ruth 2, Ward   Att: 40,402

Game 3: October 12 at Yankee Stadium

Art Nehf shut out the Yanks 1-0 with a workman-like six hitter. Stengel accounted for the only run with a long drive into the right-field bleachers. Right-hander "Sad Sam" Jones pitched a superb four hitter in the losing Yankee cause. The game was played before 62,430, the largest crowd to see a World Series game up to that time.

```
Giants        000  000 100    1   4   0
Yankees       000  000 000    0   6   1
```
Pitchers: **Nehf** vs. **Jones**, Bush(9)
Home Run: Stengel   Att: 62,430

Game 4: October 13 at Polo Grounds

The Yankees tied the Series with an 8-4 win. Starting pitcher Bob Shawkey was hit hard, but the Giant pitching was completely ineffective as Giant starter Jack Scott, knocked out of the box in the second inning, took the loss. Ross Youngs provided the only Giant high spot with four hits, including an inside-the-park home run in the ninth.

```
Yankees       061  100 000    8  13   1
Giants        000  000 031    4  13   1
```
Pitchers: **Shawkey**, Pennock(8)SV vs. **Scott**, Ryan(2), McQuillan(2), Jonnard(8), Barnes(9)
Home Run: Youngs   Att: 46,302

Game 5: October 14 at Yankee Stadium

The Yanks moved ahead in the Series with an easy 8-1 win. They put the game away early by scoring seven of their runs in the first two innings. Irish Meusel, with a single, a double, and a triple, had all of the Giant hits.

```
Giants        010  000 000    1   3   2
Yankees       340  100 00#    8  14   0
```
Pitchers: **Bush** vs. **Bentley**, Scott(2), Barnes(4), Jonnard(8)
Home Run: Dugan   Att: 62,817

Game 6: October 15 at Polo Grounds

The Yankees won the classic with a 6-4 win at the Polo Grounds. Babe Ruth homered in the first inning, but Ross Youngs tied the game with a run-scoring single in the bottom of the inning. The Giants moved out to a 4-1 lead, but the Yanks came back with a five-run eighth on bases-loaded walks to Fred Hofmann and Joe Bush, a two-

run single by Bob Meusel, and a throwing error by Giant center fielder
Bill Cunningham.

```
Yankees        100  000  050     6   5   0
Giants         100  111  000     4  10   1
```
Pitchers: **Pennock**, Jones(8)SV vs. **Nehf**, Ryan(8)
Home Runs: Ruth, Snyder   Att: 34,172

Total Attendance: 301,430
Winning Player's Share: $6,143
Losing Player's Share: $4,113

1924

After three straight World Series with the Yankees, the Giants took on
Clark Griffith's Washington Senators. John McGraw's club lost a
tough, seven-game Series when the Giants lost the deciding game
on a bad-hop single by Washington center fielder Earl McNeely. The
Series is remembered for McNeely's lucky hit and because the great
Walter Johnson appeared in his first World Series after eighteen
years with the Senators.

Game 1: October 4 at Griffith Stadium

The Giants took the first game 4-3 with two runs in the top of the
twelfth, the first scoring on Ross Youngs' base-loaded hit and the
winning run on George Kelly's sacrifice fly. Both Art Nehf and Walter
Johnson pitched the entire game and Johnson, although touched for
fourteen hits, struck out twelve batters in a losing cause.

```
Giants      010  100  000  002   4  14   1
Senators    000  001  001  001   3  10   1
```
Pitchers: **Nehf** vs. **Johnson**
Home Runs: Kelly, Terry   Att: 35,760

Game 2: October 5 at Griffith Stadium

The Senators won a thriller, 4-3 as Tom Zachary, with relief help from
Firpo Marberry, defeated Jack Bentley. Washington took a 2-0 lead
on Goose Goslin's homer in the first inning and added another run in
the fifth inning on player-manager Bucky Harris' homer. The Giants
fought back to tie the game with a run in the seventh and two runs in

the top of the ninth on hits by George Kelly and Hack Wilson. Senators' shortstop Roger Peckinpaugh won the game in the bottom of the ninth with a double past third base.

```
Giants          000 000 102    3  6  0
Senators        200 010 001    4  6  1
```
Pitchers: **Zachary**, Marberry(9)SV vs. **Bentley**
Home Runs: Goslin, Harris   Att: 35,922

Game 3: October 6 at Polo Grounds

The Giants went ahead in the Series with a 6-4 victory at the Polo Grounds. They scored twice in the second after Bucky Harris botched a double play, and staggered through to the win despite mediocre pitching from starter Hugh McQuillan and Rosy Ryan. Ryan homered in the fourth inning.

```
Senators        000 200 011    4  9  2
Giants          021 101 01#    6 12  0
```
Pitchers: **McQuillan**, Ryan(4), Jonnard(9), Watson(9)SV vs. **Marberry**, Russell(4), Martina(7), Speece(8)
Home Run: Ryan   Att: 47,608

Game 4: October 7 at Polo Grounds

The Senators defeated the Giants for an easy 7-4 victory to tie the Series. Left-hander George Mogridge pitched adequately, until relieved by Marberry, to decision Giant right-hander Virgil Barnes. Goslin was the big Senator hitter with four hits, including a three-run homer and four RBI.

```
Senators        003 020 020    7 13  3
Giants          100 001 011    4  6  1
```
Pitchers: **Mogridge**, Marberry(8)SV vs. **Barnes**, Baldwin(6), Dean(8)
Home Run: Goslin   Att: 49,243

Game 5: October 8 at Polo Grounds

The Giants defeated Walter Johnson again, this time by a 6-2 score, with Jack Bentley getting the win. Bentley contributed a two-run homer and Goslin hit his third home run of the Series. Eighteen-year-old Fred Lindstrom was the Giants' hitting star with four singles and two RBI.

```
Senators        000 100 010    2  9  1
Giants          001 020 03#    6 13  0
```
Pitchers; **Bentley**, McQuillan(8) vs. **Johnson**
Home Runs: Bentley, Goslin   Att: 49,271

Game 6: October 9 at Griffith Stadium

The Senators tied the Series at three-all as Tom Zachary pitched a fine 2-1 win over Art Nehf. Kelly singled in the Giant run in the first inning and Harris drove in the Senators' runs in the fifth inning.

```
Giants        100  000 000    1  7  1
Senators      000  020 000    2  4  0
```
Pitchers: **Zachary** vs. **Nehf**, Ryan(8)   Att: 34,254

Game 7: October 10 at Griffith Stadium

The Senators won 4-3 in twelve innings as Walter Johnson, who pitched the last four scoreless Giant innings, defeated Jack Bentley. Bucky Harris broke a scoreless tie with a solo home run in the fourth inning. The Giants took the lead with a three-run sixth inning, but the Senators tied the game with two runs in the eighth when Harris' routine grounder hopped over Fred Lindstrom's head to bring in two runners.

In the bottom of the twelfth with one out, Giant catcher Hank Gowdy tripped over his mask, thereby failing to catch a pop foul hit by Washington catcher Muddy Ruel. Ruel then doubled and Johnson was safe on Travis Jackson's error. Earl McNeely followed with another routine grounder to third, which also bounced over the snake-bit Lindstrom's head, and Ruel came across with the winning Senator run.

```
Giants      000  003 000 000   3  8  3
Senators    000  100 020 001   4 10  4
```
Pitchers: Ogden, Mogridge(1), Marberry(6), **Johnson**(9) vs. Barnes, Nehf(8), McQuillan(9), **Bentley**(11)
Home Run: Harris   Att: 31,667
Total Attendance: 283,665
Winning Player's Share: $5,970
Losing Player's Share: $3,820

1933

The Giants, a surprise pennant winner in Bill Terry's first full year as manager, beat Joe Cronin's Washington Senators 4 games to 1 as the Giants gained belated revenge for their loss to the Senators in 1924. Mel Ott and Carl Hubbell, who carried much of the club's offensive and pitching load through the regular season, starred for the Giants. Ott's hitting accounted for two of the victories and Hubbell won two games without a loss or yielding an earned run in twenty innings.

Game 1: October 3 at Polo Grounds

Carl Hubbell defeated Senator left-hander Walter Stewart 4-2 in the first game. The masterful Hubbell struck out ten hitters and neither of the Washington runs were earned. Mel Ott represented most of the Giants' attack, going 4-for-4 and driving in three runs, two of them on a first-inning homer.

```
Senators        000  100  001     2   5   3
Giants          202  000  00#     4  10   2
```
Pitchers: **Hubbell** vs. **Stewart**, Russell(3), Thomas(8)
Home Run: Ott   Att: 46,672

Game 2: October 4 at Polo Grounds

Hal Schumacher pitched a solid five-hitter to win the second game 6-1 over right-hander Alvin Crowder. The only Washington run came in the third inning on Goose Goslin's home run. The Giants struck back with six runs in the sixth inning to put the game away. The big Giant hits were Lefty O'Doul's bases-loaded single (years later O'Doul admitted he had stepped across the plate while swinging at the pitch and should have been called out), another single by Travis Jackson, a surprise bunt by the slow-footed Gus Mancuso, and singles by Schumacher and Joe Moore.

```
Senators        001  000  000     1   5   0
Giants          000  006  00#     6  10   0
```
Pitchers: **Schumacher** vs. **Crowder**, Thomas(6), McColl(7)
Home Run: Goslin   Att: 35,461

Game 3: October 5 at Griffith Stadium

Senator left-hander Earl Whitehill shut out the Giants and defeated Freddy Fitzsimmons, 4-0. The Senators took a 3-0 lead after two innings and won with relative ease as Whitehill scattered six Giant hits.

```
Giants          000  000  000     0   6   0
Senators        210  000  10#     4   9   1
```
Pitchers: **Whitehill** vs. **Fitzsimmons**, Bell(8)   Att: 25,727

Game 4: October 6 at Griffith Stadium

The Giants took a 3-1 lead in games with a 2-1, eleven-inning win. Hubbell yielded eight hits in defeating Monte Weaver, topping off a great performance by getting reserve catcher Cliff Bolton to hit into a game-ending double play with the bases loaded.

```
Giants      000 100 000   01  2 11  1
Senators    000 000 100   00  1  8  0
```
Pitchers: **Hubbell** vs. **Weaver**, Russell(11)
Home Run: Terry   Att: 26,762

Game 5: October 7 at Griffith Stadium

The Giants won the Series as they defeated the Senators 4-3 in ten innings on Mel Ott's home run into the temporary bleachers in deep center. The Giants took a 2-0 lead in the second inning on Schumacher's two-run single. Mancuso doubled in the third run in the top of the sixth, but veteran right-hander Dolph Luque relieved Schumacher and held the Senators scoreless the rest of the way to earn the win.

```
Giants      020 001 000   1  4 11  1
Senators    000 003 000   0  3 10  0
```
Pitchers: Schumacher, **Luque**(6) vs. Crowder, **Russell**(6)
Home Runs: Ott, Schulte   Att: 28,454

Total Attendance: 164,076
Winning Player's Share: $4,257
Losing Player's Share: $3,010

1936

The Giants had won a hard-fought pennant race by five games. The Yankees had torn the American League apart, winning by an overwhelming 19 1/2-game margin. Accordingly, it was hardly a surprise when the Yanks defeated the Giants in the World Series, 4 games to 2.

Manager Joe McCarthy's Bronx Bombers were led offensively by Lou Gehrig, Bill Dickey, rookie Joe DiMaggio, George Selkirk, and Tony Lazzeri, all of whom had more than 100 RBI. Yet, two other Yanks, third baseman Red Rolfe and outfielder Jake Powell, led the club with ten hits apiece in the classic. Red Ruffing, Lefty Gomez, Monte Pearson, and reliever Johnny Murphy were the pitching leaders.

Game 1: September 30 at Polo Grounds

Carl Hubbell ended a string of twelve winning Yankee World Series games, holding the Bombers to seven hits as the Giants won, 6-1. Hubbell's pitching was so masterful that none of the Giant outfielders had a fielding chance, and the only Yankee run came on George Selkirk's third-inning homer. The Giants came back with a run in the fifth inning on Dick Bartell's homer, another run in the sixth, and four game-breaking runs in the eighth.

Yankees	001 000 000	1	7	2
Giants	000 011 04#	6	9	1

Pitchers: **Hubbell** vs. **Ruffing**
Home Runs: Bartell, Selkirk   Att: 39,419

Game 2: October 2 at Polo Grounds

The Yanks overpowered the Giants in an 18-4 slaughter at the Polo Grounds. Every Yankee regular, including weak-hitting Lefty Gomez, had at least one hit and one run scored as the American Leaguers whacked out seventeen hits. The fireworks included a grand-slam homer by Tony Lazzeri (only the second in Series history) and a three-run blast by Bill Dickey as both men had five RBI. Gomez coasted to an easy win as none of the five Giant pitchers were effective.

Yankees	207 001 206	18	17	0
Giants	010 300 000	4	6	1

Pitchers: **Gomez** vs. **Schumacher**, Smith(3), Coffman(3), Gabler(5), Gumbert(9)
Home Runs: Dickey, Lazzeri   Att: 43,543

Game 3: October 3 at Yankee Stadium

Freddy Fitzsimmons lost a 2-1 heartbreaker despite holding the Yankees to four hits. The Yanks scored first on Gehrig's second-inning home run. Giant outfielder Jimmy Ripple tied it with a solo homer in the fifth. The Yanks broke the deadlock in the bottom of the eighth when Frank Crosetti singled off Fitzsimmon's glove to drive in the winning run.

Giants	000 010 000	1	11	0
Yankees	010 000 01#	2	4	0

Pitchers: **Hadley**, Malone(9)SV vs. **Fitzsimmons**
Home Runs: Gehrig, Ripple   Att: 64,842

Game 4: October 4 at Yankee Stadium

The Yankees took a commanding 3 games to 1 lead in the Series with a workman-like 5-2 win. Yankee right-hander Monte Pearson outpitched Hubbell, who lost his first game after seventeen straight wins (his last sixteen decisions in the regular season and his victory in the first game of the Series). After taking a 1-0 lead in the second inning, the Yanks scored three runs in the third on an RBI single by Red Rolfe and a two-run homer by Gehrig.

```
Giants       000  100  010    2   7  1
Yankees      013  000  01#    5  10  1
```
Pitchers: **Pearson** vs. **Hubbell**, Gabler(8)
Home Run: Gehrig   Att: 66,669

Game 5: October 5 at Yankee Stadium

The Giants won 5-4 in ten exciting innings as Hal Schumacher pitched a courageous game to defeat Pat Malone, who was in relief of starter Red Ruffing. The Giants took a 3-0 lead in the first inning as Dick Bartell, Jimmy Ripple, and Burgess Whitehead drove in runs. The Yankees retaliated with a run in the second on Selkirk's homer and another run in the third. Schumacher pitched heroically in the third as, with the bases loaded and none out, he struck out DiMaggio and Gehrig and got Dickey on a fly ball. The Giants broke a four-all tie in the top of the tenth with the winning run when Terry's sacrifice fly drove in Joe Moore.

```
Giants       300  001  000  1    5   8  3
Yankees      011  002  000  0    4  10  1
```
Pitchers: **Schumacher** vs. Ruffing, **Malone**(7)
Home Run: Selkirk   Att: 50,024

Game 6: October 6 at Polo Grounds

The Yankees overwhelmed the Giants with seventeen hits for a 13-5 win and the Series. Mel Ott drove in three of the Giant runs with a home run and a double; Joe Moore also homered. But the powerful Yanks, leading 6-5 after eight innings, put the game away in the ninth with a seven-run inning as Giant pitching collapsed.

```
Yankees      021  200  017    13  17  2
Giants       200  010  110     5   9  1
```
Pitchers: **Gomez**, Murphy(7)SV vs. **Fitzsimmons**,
Castleman(4), Coffman(9), Gumbert(9)
Home Runs: Moore, Ott, Powell   Att: 38,427

Total Attendance: 302,924
Winning Player's Share: $6,431   Losing Player's Share: $4,656

1937

The Yankees easily defeated the Giants again in a virtual rerun of the 1936 World Series. There was no pivotal game or play in the Series as the Yanks methodically won the first three games, paused to absorb a loss to Carl Hubbell, then polished off the Giants in the fifth game.

Game 1: October 6 at Yankee Stadium

Lefty Gomez pitched a solid six-hit, one-run effort to defeat Hubbell 8-1 at Yankee Stadium. The Giants scored their only run in the fifth inning, but the Yankees knocked out Hubbell in a seven-run sixth inning featured by two-run, bases-loaded singles by DiMaggio and Selkirk and two walks to Gomez. There was an amusing interlude during the unhappy Giant inning. Manager Bill Terry intended to replace Hubbell with Dick Coffman. But Captain Gus Mancuso informed the umpires that Harry Gumbert would be the relief pitcher and the announcement was made. As a result Gumbert came off the bench cold, pitched to one batter, then turned the game over to Coffman.

```
Giants        000  010 000    1   6   2
Yankees       000  007 01#    8   7   0
```
Pitchers: **Gomez** vs. **Hubbell**, Gumbert(6), Coffman(6), Smith(8)
Home Run: Lazzeri   Att: 60,573

Game 2: October 7 at Yankee Stadium

Red Ruffing easily defeated rookie Giant left-hander Cliff Melton and the Giants 8-1 to take a two-game lead in the Series. Ott drove in Bartell in the first inning for a 1-0 Giant lead, but the Yankees moved ahead to a commanding 6-1 lead after six innings. Selkirk and Ruffing drove in three runs apiece.

```
Giants        100  000 000    1   7   0
Yankees       000  024 20#    8  12   0
```
Pitchers: **Ruffing** vs. **Melton** , Gumbert(5), Coffman(6)
Att: 57,675

Game 3: October 8 at Polo Grounds

Monte Pearson, with relief help from Johnny Murphy, defeated Hal Schumacher in a 5-1 Yankee victory. The Yanks pecked away at Schumacher for a 5-0 lead after five innings; the only Giant run was driven in by first baseman Johnny McCarthy.

```
Yankees      012 110 000    5  9  0
Giants       000 000 100    1  5  4
```
Pitchers: **Pearson**, Murphy(9)SV vs. **Schumacher**, Melton(7), Brennan(9)
Att: 37,385

Game 4: October 9 at Polo Grounds

Hubbell stopped the Yanks, for the time being at least, with a 7-3 win over right-hander Bump Hadley. The Giants scored six runs in the second inning on six hits, two of them by outfielder Hank Leiber. Lou Gehrig homered in the ninth, but Hubbell had the game well in hand.

```
Yankees      101 000 001    3  6  0
Giants       060 000 10#    7 12  3
```
Pitchers: **Hubbell** vs. **Hadley,** Andrews (2), Wicker (8)
Home Run: Gehrig   Att: 44,293

Game 5: October 10 at Polo Grounds

The Yanks won the Series with a 4-2 win at the Polo Grounds. Lefty Gomez gave up ten hits but held the Giants to two runs, both scoring on Ott's third-inning home run. The Yankees scored in the second and third innings on solo home runs by left fielder Myril Hoag and Joe DiMaggio. With the score tied in the fifth, the Yanks scored the winning runs on Lazzeri's triple, a scratch hit by Gomez, and a double by Gehrig.

```
Yankees      011 020 000    4  8  0
Giants       002 000 000    2 10  0
```
Pitchers: **Gomez** vs. **Melton,** Smith (6), Brennan (8)
Home Runs: DiMaggio, Hoag, Ott   Att: 38, 216
Total Attendance: 238, 142
Winning Player's Share: $6,471
Losing Player's Share: $4,490

1951

The day after their miracle pennant win, climaxed by Bobby Thomson's "Shot Heart 'Round the World" home run, the Giants took on the Yanks in the World Series. The Giants won the first game of the

Series, seemingly through sheer momentum, but the exhausted Polo Grounders succumbed to reality, losing to the Yanks 4 games to 2. Shortstop Alvin Dark (.417) and outfielder Monte Irvin (.458) accounted for twenty-one of the forty-six Giant hits in the Series as Leo Durocher's club slumped at the plate. Giant pitchers were unable to stop the Yankee hitters. The Series is remembered best as the last appearance of aging Joe DiMaggio in a Yankee uniform (DiMag retired during the winter).

Game 1: October 4 at Yankee Stadium

Surprise Giant starter Dave Koslo pitched a strong game as the Polo Grounders won 5-1. The Giants went ahead 2-0 in the first inning as Whitey Lockman doubled in the first run and Monte Irvin, who had four hits, stole home for the second run. Alvin Dark supplied the other three Giant runs with a home run.

```
Giants      200  003 000    5 10  1
Yankees     010  000 000    1  7  1
Pitchers: Koslo vs. Reynolds, Hogue (7), Morgan (8)
Home Run: Dark      Att: 65,673
```

Game 2: October 5 at Yankee Stadium

The Yanks tied the Series as lefty Eddie Lopat outpitched Larry Jansen for a 3-1 decision. The Bombers scored a run in the first inning when third baseman Gil McDougald singled in Mickey Mantle, and first baseman Joe Collins hit a solo homer in the second inning. The only Giant run came in the seventh when Irvin, who had three more hits, scored on Bill Rigney's sacrifice fly.

```
Giants      000  000 100    1  5  1
Yankees     110  000 01#    3  6  0
Pitchers: Lopat vs. Jansen, Spencer (7)
Home Run: Collins      Att: 66,018
```

Game 3: October 6 at Polo Grounds

The Giants took the lead in the Series as right-hander Jim Hearn outpitched Vic Raschi to win, 6-2. The pivotal play came in the Giant fifth inning. With the Giants leading 1-0 and one out, Eddie Stanky walked. Stanky was apparently out on a steal attempt, but he was safe when he kicked the ball out of shortstop Phil Rizzuto's glove. Dark and Hank Thompson singled for a run and Dark scored when Yogi Berra dropped a throw to the plate. Lockman topped off the five-run outburst with a line-drive homer to bring in three runs and ice the game.

| Yankees | 000 000 011 | 2 5 2 |
| Giants | 100 050 00# | 6 7 2 |

Pitchers: **Hearn,** Jones (8) SV vs. **Raschi,** Hogue (5), Ostrowski (7)
Home Runs: Lockman, Woodling   Att: 52,035

Game 4: October 8 at Polo Grounds

Right-hander Allie Reynolds pitched a steady game to give the Yankees a 6-2 win over Sal Maglie. The Yanks held a 1-1 lead after five innings and Joe DiMaggio, hitless in the first three games, gave them a a decisive 6-1 margin with a two-run homer in the seventh.

| Yankees | 010 120 200 | 6 12 0 |
| Giants | 100 000 001 | 2 8 2 |

Pitchers: **Reynolds** vs. **Maglie,** Jones (6), Kennedy (9)
Home Run: DiMaggio   Att: 49,010

Game 5: October 9 at Polo Grounds

The Yankees took a 3 games-to-2 lead by routing the Giants, 13-1. Durocher's club led 1-0 after two innings, but the Bombers had a five-run third inning against Larry Jansen as Gil McDougald clouted a grand-slam homer. The Yankees bombed away for eight more runs against four other Giant pitchers; Eddie Lopat scattered five Giants hits.

| Yankees | 005 202 400 | 13 12 1 |
| Giants | 100 000 000 | 1 5 3 |

Pitchers: **Lopat** vs. **Jansen,** Kennedy (4), Spencer (6), Corwin (7), Konikowski (9)
Home Runs: McDougald, Rizzuto   Att: 47,530

Game 6: October 10 at Yankee Stadium

Yankee right fielder Hank Bauer broke up a one-all tie with a bases-loaded triple off Dave Koslo in the bottom of the sixth inning. Losing 4-1 in their last at bat, the Giants loaded the bases with none out. Monte Irvin and Bobby Thomson drove in runs with sacrifice flies, but the game ended sensationally when Bauer raced in to grab Giant catcher Sal Yvars' low liner to short right just before it hit the ground.

Giants	000 010 002	3 11 1
Yankees	100 003 00#	4 7 0

Pitchers: **Raschi**, Sain (7), Kuzava (9)SV vs. **Koslo**, Hearn (7), Jansen (8)   Att: 61,711

Total Attendance: 341,977
Winning Player's Share: $6,446
Losing Player's Share: $4,951

1954

The Giants surprised the baseball world by defeating the Cleveland Indians in four straight games. Al Lopez' Indians had played at a remarkable .721 pace (111 won and 43 losses) in taking the pennant by eight games. Lopez had a superb pitching staff: Early Wynn and Bob Lemon led with twenty-three wins apiece, Mike Garcia scored nineteen victories, and Art Houtteman and venerable Bob Feller had fifteen and thirteen wins, respectively. Outfielder Larry Doby, third baseman Al Rosen, and league-leading hitter Bobby Avila were the leading Cleveland hitters. Yet the powerful Indians club was outplayed in the Series by an all-around Giant club, some wonderful fielding by Willie Mays, and the magic bat of Giant outfielder Dusty Rhodes.

Game 1: September 29 at Polo Grounds

Cleveland took a 2-0 lead in the first inning when outfielder Vic Wertz tripled in both runs. The Giants tied the game in the third inning on hits by Whitey Lockman and Alvin Dark, Don Mueller's force-out, and another hit by Hank Thompson. The Indians threatened to break the game open in the eighth inning, but Mays made a memorable catch on Wertz's fly ball to deepest center field to cut off the rally. Dusty Rhodes won the game 5-2 in the bottom of the Giant tenth with a three-run homer that barely made the right-field seats, about 260 feet from the plate. Giant relief right-hander Marv Grissom won the game and Bob Lemon, who took the loss, went the route for the Indians.

Indians	200 000 000 0	2 8 0
Giants	002 000 000 3	5 9 3

Pitchers: Maglie, Liddle (8), **Grissom** (8), vs. **Lemon**
Home Run: Rhodes   Att: 52,751

Game 2: September 30 at Polo Grounds

Johnny Antonelli defeated Early Wynn in a well-pitched game. Cleveland left fielder Al Smith took one swing and hit Antonelli's first pitch of the game for a home run to begin and end the Indians' offense for the day. The Giants scored twice in the fifth inning on deluxe pinch hitter Rhodes' RBI single and Antonelli's force-out. Rhodes remained in the game and gave the Giants an insurance run with a solo home run in the seventh inning.

```
Indians        100  000 000    1  8  0
Giants         000  020 10#    3  4  0
```
Pitchers: **Antonelli** vs. **Wynn,** Mossi (8)
Home Runs: Rhodes, Smith   Att: 49,099

Game 3: October 1 at Municipal Stadium

Ruben Gomez, with relief help from Hoyt Wilhelm, defeated Mike Garcia 6-2 as the Giants won their third straight game. Mays singled in a first-inning run, but the key Giant hit came in the third when pinch hitter Rhodes singled in two more runs to set up a three-run inning. The Polo Grounders took a 6-0 lead after six innings and held on to win easily.

```
Giants         103  011 000    6 10  1
Indians        000  000 110    2  4  2
```
Pitchers: **Gomez**, Wilhelm (8) SV vs. **Garcia**, Houtteman (4), Narleski (6), Mossi (9)
Home Run: Wertz   Att: 71,555

Game 4: October 2 at Municipal Stadium

The Giants won the Series in four straight as lefty Don Liddle beat Bob Lemon. Leading by 3-0 after four innings, the Giants put the game out of Cleveland's reach with a four-run fifth inning, scoring their runs on a bases-loaded walk to Hank Thompson, a two-run single by Monte Irvin, and a sacrifice by Wes Westrum.

```
Giants         021  040 000    7 10  1
Indians        000  030 100    4  6  2
```
Pitchers: **Liddle**, Wilhelm(7), Antonelli (8) SV vs. **Lemon**, Newhouser (5), Narleski (5), Mossi (6), Garcia (8)
Home Run: Majeski   Att: 78,102
Total Attendance: 251,507
Winning Player's Share: $11,118
Losing Player's Share: $6,713

1962

The Giants lost a seesaw seven-game Series to the Yankees, their old New York rivals. Similar to the 1951 season, the Giants had caught up with the Dodgers late in the campaign and then beaten them in a playoff. Only two members of the 1951 cast remained with the club, center fielder Willie Mays and former shortstop Alvin Dark, now the manager of the Giants. This was an even Series, which neither team was able to dominate.

Game 1: October 4 at Candlestick Park

Yankee great lefty Whitey Ford scattered ten Giant hits en route to a 6-2 victory over Billy O'Dell. Outfielder Roger Maris doubled in two runs for a first-inning 2-0 Yankee lead, but the Giants tied the game with single runs in the second and third innings. Third baseman Clete Boyer put the Yanks ahead with a solo homer in the seventh and the Bronx Bombers iced the game with two more runs in the eighth.

Yankees	200	000	121	6	11	0
Giants	011	000	000	2	10	0

Pitchers: **Ford** vs. **O'Dell**, Larsen (8), Miller (9)
Home Run: Boyer   Att: 43,852

Game 2: October 5 at Candlestick Park

Giant right-hander Jack Sanford shut out the Yanks 2-0 to defeat Ralph Terry. The Giants scored in the first inning on second baseman Chuck Hiller's double and Matty Alou's groundout. Willie McCovey's long home run provided the other Giant run in the seventh inning.

Yankees	000	000	000	0	3	1
Giants	100	000	10#	2	6	0

Pitchers: **Sanford** vs. **Terry**, Daley (8)
Home Run: McCovey   Att: 43,910

Game 3: October 7 at Yankee Stadium

Starters Billy Pierce and Bill Stafford pitched shutout ball for six innings. Then the New Yorkers broke the deadlock with three runs in the bottom of the seventh on Maris' two-run single and Boyer's run-scoring ground ball. The Giants rallied with two runs on Mays' double and catcher Ed Bailey's home run, but Stafford retired Jim Davenport to end the game.

Giants	000	000	002	2	4	3
Yankees	000	000	30#	3	5	1

Pitchers: **Stafford** vs. **Pierce**, Larsen (7), Bolin (8)
Home Run: Bailey   Att: 71,434

Game 4: October 8 at Yankee Stadium

Juan Marichal outpitched Whitey Ford for four innings, but the Dominican Dandy had to leave the game after the fourth inning because he injured his hand while batting. At the time the Giants led 2-0 on Tom Haller's two-run homer. The Yanks tied the game in the sixth on run-scoring hits by Bill Skowron and Clete Boyer. But the Giants put the game away in the top of the seventh when Chuck Hiller hit a grand-slam home run off Yankee right-hander Tom Coates. Billy O'Dell held on in relief for a 7-3 win, tying the Series at two games apiece.

```
Giants        020 000 401    7  9  1
Yankees       000 002 001    3  9  1
```
Pitchers: Marichal, Bolin (5), **Larsen** (6), O'Dell (7) SV vs. Ford, **Coates** (7), Bridges (7)
Home Runs: Haller, Hiller   Att: 66,607

Game 5: October 10 at Yankee Stadium

Ralph Terry and Jack Sanford dueled to a 2-2 tie after seven innings. Yankee left fielder Mike Tresh hit a three-run homer in the bottom of the eighth to power the Yankees to a 5-3 win.

```
Giants        001 010 001    3  8  2
Yankees       000 101 03#    5  6  0
```
Pitchers: **Terry** vs. **Sanford**, Miller (8)
Home Runs: Pagan, Tresh   Att: 63,165

Game 6: October 15 at Candlestick Park

The Giants tied the Series at three-all with a 5-2 win in San Francisco. Bill Pierce bested Whitey Ford by pitching a steady game, allowing only three hits, including a home run by Roger Maris. Orlando Cepeda led the Giant attack with three hits and two RBI.

```
Yankees       000 010 010    2  3  2
Giants        000 320 00#    5 10  1
```
Pitchers: **Pierce** vs. **Ford**, Coates (5), Bridges (8)
Home Run: Maris   Att: 43,948

Game 7: October 16 at Candlestick Park

Ralph Terry outpitched Jack Sanford as the Yanks won 1-0 to win the Series. The only run of the game was scored in the fifth inning on Tony Kubek's double-play grounder. The Giants threatened to score in the bottom of the ninth, but with men on second and third and two out, Yankee second baseman Bobby Richardson reached up and pulled down Willie McCovey's liner to right.

Yankees	000 010 000	1 7 0
Giants	000 000 000	0 4 1

Pitchers: **Terry** vs. **Sanford**, O'Dell (8)   Att: 43,948

Total Attendance: 376,864
Winning Player's Share: $9,883
Losing Player's Share: $7,291

TRAVIS CALVIN JACKSON
NEW YORK N.L., 1922-1936

PREMIER DEFENSIVE SHORTSTOP WHO SWUNG
PRODUCTIVE BAT. KNOWN FOR OUTSTANDING
ARM AND EXCEPTIONAL RANGE AFIELD. LED
N.L. SHORTSTOPS IN ASSISTS FOUR TIMES,
TOTAL CHANCES THREE YEARS AND FIELDING
PCT. AND DOUBLE PLAYS TWICE. ADEPT AS
BUNTER, HE BATTED OVER .300 SIX YEARS
WHILE COMPILING .291 LIFETIME AVERAGE.
DROVE IN MORE THAN 90 RUNS SIX TIMES,
REACHING 101 ON .268 AVERAGE IN 1934.

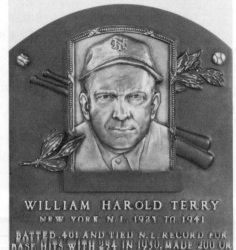

WILLIAM HAROLD TERRY
NEW YORK N.L. 1933 TO 1941

BATTED .401 AND TIED N.L. RECORD FOR
BASE HITS WITH 254 IN 1930. MADE 200 OR
MORE HITS IN SIX SEASONS. RETIRED WITH
LIFETIME BATTING AVERAGE OF .341, A
MODERN N.L. RECORD FOR LEFT-HANDED
BATTERS. MOST VALUABLE PLAYER IN 1930.
SUCCEEDED JOHN McGRAW AS MANAGER IN
1932 AND WON PENNANTS IN 1933-36-37.

CARL HUBBELL
NEW YORK N.L. 1928-1943

HAILED FOR IMPRESSIVE PERFORMANCE IN
1934 ALL-STAR GAME WHEN HE STRUCK OUT
RUTH, GEHRIG, FOXX, SIMMONS AND CRONIN
IN SUCCESSION. NICKNAMED GIANTS'
MEAL-TICKET. WON 253 GAMES IN MAJORS,
SCORING 16 STRAIGHT IN 1936. COMPILED
STREAK OF 46 1/3 SCORELESS INNINGS IN
1933. HOLDER OF MANY RECORDS.

MELVIN T.(MEL)OTT
NEW YORK (N.L.) 1926-48

ONE OF FEW PLAYERS TO JUMP FROM A HIGH
SCHOOL TEAM INTO MAJORS. PLAYED OUTFIELD
AND THIRD BASE AND MANAGED CLUB FROM
DEC.1941 THROUGH JULY 1948. HIT 511 HOME
RUNS, N.L. RECORD WHEN HE RETIRED. ALSO
LED IN MOST RUNS SCORED, MOST RUNS BATTED
IN, TOTAL BASES, BASES ON BALLS AND EXTRA
BASES ON LONG HITS. HAD A .304 LIFETIME
BATTING AVERAGE. PLAYED IN ELEVEN ALL STAR
GAMES AND IN THREE WORLD SERIES.

5

ALL-STAR GAMES

Perhaps no team has meant more to the National League's success in the All-Star Game than the Giants, who have used the midsummer classic as a showcase for the talent. Their feats abound in the first fifty years of the spectacle.

King Carl Hubbell's magnificent strikeout achievement in 1934 is regarded as the finest pitching performance in the game's history, and Larry Jansen, Juan Marichal, Stu Miller, and Vida Blue have had their moments. Willie Mays has no peers as an All-Star Game hitter, holding many of the game's records. But Bill Terry was dynamite in the early classics and Willie McCovey and Bobby Bonds were MVPs of modern All-Star Games.

Hubbell's accomplishment, before 48,363 at the Polo Grounds, deserves special mention. The American League won the game 9-7, but that didn't diminish what Hub achieved against five Hall of Fame hitters.

"I never had any more control and stuff in my life than for that All-Star Game," recalled Hubbell, who made history by striking out Babe Ruth, Lou Gehrig, Jimmy Foxx, Al Simmons, and Joe Cronin in succession. "It was as big a surprise for me to strike out those fellows as it probably was to them. When I went over the hitters with Gabby Hartnett, my catcher, he told me to waste everything but the screwball."

It didn't start out like a superior performance by Hubbell. Leadoff batter Charley Gehringer singled, and Heinie Manush walked on a 3-2 pitch in the very first inning. The infielders converged around the mound to settle down the Giants ace. "I could imagine how they felt with two on, nobody out, and Ruth at bat," Hubbell said. "To strike him out was the last thing on my mind. The thing was to make him hit on the ground. He wasn't too fast and he'd be a cinch to double up. Babe never took the bat off his shoulder. You could have pushed me over with your little finger. I fed him three straight screwballs, all over the plate, after wasting a fastball,   and he just stood there. Hartnett was laughing when he threw the ball back.

"Up came Gehrig," Hub continued. "Striking out Ruth and Gehrig in succession was too big an order. By golly, he fanned on four pitches. He swung at the last screwball, and you should have heard that crowd. I felt a lot easier then, even though Gehringer and Manush pulled a double steal.

"We were really trying to strike Foxx out, so Gabby didn't bother to waste any pitches. I threw three more screwballs and he went down swinging. We had set down the side on twelve pitches.

"The second inning was easier because Simmons and Cronin both struck out with nobody on base" said Hubbell, who then yielded a single to Bill Dickey before fanning Lefty Gomez.

Hubbell retired the side in the third inning and finished with six strikeouts in three frames, throwing twenty seven strikes among forty-eight pitches to thirteen American League batters. He allowed two hits and then left the game winning 4-0.

When it comes to all-around All-Star play, nobody did it better than the incomparable Mays, who hit safely in twelve of his first fourteen games, belting twenty hits in forty-eight at bats (.417), and scoring fifteen runs through 1963.

The games that stick out in Mays' memory were played in Cleveland in 1954 and 1963. The first was his All-Star Game debut and the second had him batting cleanup following several stints as the lead-off hitter.

"You can't imagine how nervous I was in the 1954 game," said Mays, whose All-Star Game records include twenty-four appearances, twenty-three hits, and twenty runs. "I was in the service in '52 and '53, so it was like being a rookie again. I was more nervous in that game than in any other I've been in. I was so young, and here I was in the same clubhouse with guys like Duke Snider, Roy Campanella, and Stan Musial, and around the batting cage with guys like Ted Williams and Larry Doby. These were players I had idolized, and there I was, playing with them.

"I had my best game in Cleveland, too," Mays added. "That was in 1963, when I hit fourth for one of the few times. I drove in two runs, stole two bases, scored a couple of times, and made a catch to save a run."

Mays was the MVP of the 1973 affair, repeating in 1968 when he replaced injured Pete Rose in the starting lineup at Houston and came through in typical Mays fashion. Wondrous Willie led off the first with a single off Luis Tiant, advanced to second on Tiant's wild pickoff throw, reached third on a wild pitch, and scored the game's only run on McCovey's double-play grounder.

Like Mays, Marichal was in a class of his own as an All-Star game performer. Whereas Hubbell registered the game's greatest pitching moment, no hurler in either league was as consistently superb as the Dominican Dandy. Marichal pitched in eight games from 1962 to 1971, yielding but seven hits and one earned run in eighteen stingy innings. He struck out twelve, walked two, and posted an incredible 0.50 ERA. He was the winner in '62 and '64, and was named the game's MVP in '65.

A capsule summary of significant Giants' contributions in the All-Star Game follows.

1933—Hubbell set the stage for his 1934 heroics by working two scoreless innings in the first All-Star Game at Comiskey Park. Terry belted two hits in four trips, and the last National League player to hit .400 appropriately went on to collect four hits in ten All-Star trips.

1934—Terry had one of eight National League hits, but Hubbell stole the show by striking out the aforementioned five Hall of Famers in succession.

1935—Hal Schumacher struck out five in four innings and Terry had another hit, but the Americans won their third straight, posting a 4-1 victory at Cleveland.

1936 — The Nationals finally won a game, 4-3, at Braves Field, and Hubbell helped with three scoreless innings. Mel Ott singled as a pinch hitter for his first All-Star Game safety.

1938 — Ott tripled and scored a run in the Nationals' 4-1 triumph at Cincinnati.

1940—Harry (The Horse) Danning contributed a run-scoring single, Ott scored, and Hubbell worked a scoreless ninth to help the Nationals to a 4-0 victory at St. Louis.

1947 — Johnny Mize's fourth-inning homer off Spec Shea accounted for the only National League run in a 2-1 defeat at Wrigley Field.

1950—Jansen was the outstanding pitcher in a game won on Red Schoendienst's fourteenth-inning homer, 4-3 at Comiskey. With the Nationals trailing 3-2, Larry entered the game in the seventh inning and pitched a one-hitter for five innings, striking out six.

1951 — Sal Maglie, though not pitching particularly well, was the winner of the Nationals' 8-3 romp at Detroit. Alvin Dark singled.

1954—Mays singled and scored in his All-Star Game debut, Marv Grissom hurled scoreless relief, and Don Mueller ripped a run-scoring, pinch double, but the Americans won 11-9 at Cleveland.

1955—Mays had two singles, scored twice, and started the National League back from a 5-0 deficit to a 6-5 victory earned on Musial's twelfth-inning homer at Milwaukee.

1956—Mays belted a two-run, pinch homer off Whitey Ford, and Johnny Antonelli worked four scoreless innings during the Nationals' 7-3 romp at Washington.

1959—Mays' run-scoring triple in the bottom of the eighth capped a two-run rally and made the Nationals a 5-4 winner in the first All-Star Game that year. Antonelli pitched one-third of an inning and got the decision at Pittsburgh.

1960—The National League posted a 5-3, 6-0 sweep at Kansas City and Yankee Stadium. Mays was at his magnificent best. Willie, in the two games, was a combined six for eight with a double, a triple, and a homer. Mays led off with a triple and scored the first run in the opener, then made a triumphant return to New York in the second game, rapping a homer off Ford.

1961—Mays doubled and scored the winning run on Roberto Clemente's single as the National League scored twice in the tenth for a windy, 5-4 decision at Candlestick Park in the first game that year. Stu Miller worked a total of 4 2/3 innings in the two games, yielding one hit and no earned runs while striking out nine. He was the winner of the Candlestick clash, though victimized by the wind while throwing a costly balk in the Americans' game-tying, two-run ninth.

1962—Marichal made his All-Star Game debut and was the winner with two scoreless innings as the National League posted a 3-1 victory at Washington. Jim Davenport contributed a single and Felipe Alou a sacrifice fly in the eighth for an insurance run.

1963—The All-Star Game returned to a single-game format. Mays was the hero of a 5-3 victory at Cleveland that pulled the Nationals to within one game of the American League, which once had a 12-4 advantage in the series. Willie walked in the second, stole second, and scored on Dick Groat's single. Mays and Giants teammate Ed Bailey added run-scoring singles in the third, and Willie knocked in the winning run with a grounder in the fifth.

1964—Marichal was the winner when the National League erupted with four runs in the bottom of the ninth for a 7-4 victory at Shea Stadium. Mays walked and Orlando Cepeda singled in the winning rally.

1965—Marichal and Mays were the heroes as the National League posted a 6-5 victory at Minnesota to take a lead in the All-Star Game series for the first time. Juan was the MVP, facing a minimum of nine batters in a one-hit starting stint. Mays led off the game with a 415-foot homer off Milt Pappas and scored the winning run in the seventh. He walked, raced to third on Hank

Aaron's single, and scored on Ron Santo's grounder to short.

1966—Marichal and Gaylord Perry blanked the American League over the last five innings in a 2-1 victory at St. Louis. Juan worked three frames and Gaylord was the winner. Mays scored the first National League run in the fourth on Santo's infield hit.

1968—Mays scored the only run on McCovey's double-play grounder in the first, and Marichal pitched two hitless innings during a 1-0 National League decision at Houston.

1969—McCovey became the fourth All-Star Game performer to wallop two home runs in one game, connecting off Blue Moon Odom and Denny McLain to power a 9-3 runaway at Washington. MVP McCovey finished with three RBI.

1970—Dick Dietz and McCovey had big hits in the Nationals' 5-4, twelfth-inning victory at Cincinnati. The American League entered the bottom of the ninth leading 4-1, but Dietz triggered a three-run rally with a homer off Catfish Hunter. McCovey added a run-scoring single in the rally.

1971 — Marichal pitched two hitless innings, but two future Giants combined to give the American League its last victory in the series through 1982. Frank Robinson belted a two-run homer and was the MVP, while Blue was the winner in a 6-4 decision at Detroit.

1973—Bonds didn't enter the game at Kansas City until he replaced Billy Williams in the fourth. Bobby belted a homer off Bill Singer in the fifth and stretched a single into a double in the seventh to earn MVP honors in the Nationals' 7-1 rout.

1976—John Montefusco pitched two hitless innings to help the Nationals crush the Americans 7-1 at Philadelphia.

1981—Blue worked one hitless inning and was the winner of the Nationals' 5-4 decision at Cleveland following the strike layoff. That made Vida the only pitcher to win games for each league in the All-Star Game Series.

1986 — Chris Brown doubled in his All-Star game batting debut, then grounded into a double paly to kill a ninth-inning rally as the N.L. lost at Houston. Mike Krukow pitched a perfect ninth inning.

JAMES HOYT WILHELM

NEW YORK N.L. 1952-1956 ST. LOUIS N.L. 1957
CLEVELAND A.L., 1957-1958 BALTIMORE A.L., 1958-1962
CHICAGO A.L., 1963-1968 CALIFORNIA A.L., 1969
ATLANTA N.L., 1969-1970, 1971 CHICAGO N.L., 1970
LOS ANGELES N.L., 1971-1972
BASEBALL'S PREMIER RELIEF PITCHER. USED KNUCKLE
BALL TO WIN 143 GAMES (A RECORD 124 IN RELIEF)
AND AMASSED 227 SAVES OVER 21-YEAR CAREER.
NO-HIT YANKEES ON SEPT. 20, 1958 IN INFREQUENT
START FOR ORIOLES. PITCHED IN RECORD 1070
GAMES WITH LIFETIME ERA OF 2.52.

WILLIE HOWARD MAYS, Jr.
"THE SAY HEY KID"

NEW YORK N.L... SAN FRANCISCO N.L...
NEW YORK N.L., 1951 - 1973
ONE OF BASEBALL'S MOST COLORFUL AND
EXCITING STARS. EXCELLED IN ALL PHASES OF
THE GAME. THIRD IN HOMERS (660), RUNS (2,062)
AND TOTAL BASES (6,066); SEVENTH IN HITS
(3,283) AND RBI'S (1,903). FIRST IN PUTOUTS
BY OUTFIELDER (7,095). FIRST TO TOP BOTH
300 HOMERS AND 300 STEALS. LED LEAGUE IN
BATTING ONCE, SLUGGING FIVE TIMES, HOME
RUNS AND STEALS FOUR SEASONS. VOTED N.L.
MVP IN 1954 AND 1965. PLAYED IN 24
ALL-STAR GAMES - A RECORD.

JUAN ANTONIO (SANCHEZ) MARICHAL

SAN FRANCISCO N.L., 1960-1973 BOSTON A.L. 1974
LOS ANGELES N.L., 1975
HIGH-KICKING RIGHT-HANDER FROM DOMINICAN
REPUBLIC WON 243 GAMES AND LOST ONLY 142
OVER 16 SEASONS. WON 20 GAMES SIX TIMES AND
NO-HIT HOUSTON IN 1963. LED N.L. IN COMPLETE
GAMES AND SHUTOUTS TWICE AND IN ERA WITH
2.10 IN 1969. COMPLETED 244 GAMES DURING
CAREER, STRIKING OUT 2,303 AND FINISHING
WITH 2.89 ERA.

WILLIE LEE MC COVEY
"STRETCH"

SAN FRANCISCO, N.L., 1959 - 1973, 1977 - 1980
SAN DIEGO, N.L., 1974 - 1976
OAKLAND, A.L., 1976
TOP LEFT-HANDED HOME RUN HITTER IN N.L.
HISTORY WITH 521. SECOND ONLY TO LOU GEHRIG
WITH 18 CAREER GRAND SLAMS. LED N.L. IN HOMERS
THREE TIMES AND RBI'S TWICE. N.L. ROOKIE OF
YEAR IN 1959, MVP IN 1969 AND COMEBACK PLAYER
OF THE YEAR IN '77 TEAMED WITH WILLIE MAYS
FOR AWESOME 1-2 PUNCH IN GIANTS' LINEUP.

6

FAMOUS POLO GROUNDS GAMES

The Merkle Boner

September 23, 1908
In a dogfight for the pennant, the Giants and the Chicago Cubs were tied one-all in the bottom of the ninth inning at the Polo Grounds. With two out, Moose McCormick on third base, and Fred Merkle on first, Giant shortstop Al Bridwell smashed an apparent game-winning hit to center. McCormick raced home and the crowd swarmed on the field as the players ran for the clubhouse. But suddenly there was a commotion at second base, where Chicago second baseman Johnny Evers was calling for the ball. Merkle, it seemed, had not touched the bag, but seeing McCormick cross the plate and believing the game to be over, had stopped a few feet short of the bag and then joined in the rush for the clubhouse.

The mixup that followed was never cleared up. Evers claimed that the ball was thrown back to him and that he had stepped on second, forcing Merkle and nullifying the winning run. But umpires Bob Emslie and Hank O'Day paid no attention to him and trotted off the field. However, O'Day (who had showed no sign before leaving the field that he agreed with Evers) announced at 10 o'clock that night that Evers was right—and that Merkle was out.

McGraw was furious. "If Merkle was out," he roared, "then the ball game was a tie and O'Day should have ordered the field cleared and the game resumed. But he wasn't out and we won the game and they can't take it away from us!" But they could. President Pulliam ruled the game a tie that would have to be replayed if the pennant race was tied at the end of the regular season. The Giants and Cubs finished dead even and the Cubs won the playoff game. Although McGraw claimed that Merkle simply had followed common practice by not touching second base, history was not as charitable to the unfortunate Merkle. The event has always been known as "Merkle's Boner."

Bobby Thomson's
Home-Run Shot Heard
'Round the World

Oct. 3, 1951

The Giants were playing the Brooklyn Dodgers in the third, and deciding, game of a playoff for the pennant. Losing 4-1 in the bottom of the ninth, the Giants' chances were dim as they faced Dodger starter Don Newcombe.

Alvin Dark opened with a bloop single to right. For some unexplained reason, Dodger manager Charley Dressen had first baseman Gil Hodges playing a step or two behind the baserunner even though Dark was unlikely to steal because his run would be meaningless. Mueller, a master with the bat, grounded a single to right into the larger gap provided by Hodges' positioning near first base. Irvin popped to Hodges, but Lockman came through with a sliced double past third base, scoring Dark and moving Mueller to third. Mueller injured his ankle sliding into the bag and Hartung ran for him. Meanwhile, Dressen removed the tiring Newcombe and brought in right-hander Ralph Branca.

With one out, men on second and third, and the Giants losing 4-2, Bobby Thomson stepped in to hit as Willie Mays moved to the on-deck circle. Durocher, coaching at third base, called time and moved in to impart some wisdom to Thomson. (Durocher told the Flying Scot, "Bobby, if you ever hit one, this is the time!") The first pitch to Thomson was a called strike as Branca threw a waist-high fastball. And here is the way Giant announcer Russ Hodges described what transpired:

Bobby batting at .292. He's had a single and a double and he drove in the Giants' first run with a long fly to center ... Hartung down the line at third not taking any chances ... Branca throws ... there's a long drive ... it's gonna be, I believe ... THE GIANTS WIN THE PENNANT! THE GIANTS WIN THE PENNANT! THE GIANTS WIN THE PENNANT! ... Bobby Thomson hits into the lower deck of the left field stands. THE GIANTS WIN THE PENNANT! THE GIANTS WIN THE PENNANT AND THEY'RE GOING CRAZY! THE GIANTS WIN THE PENNANT! THE GIANTS WIN THE PENNANT!

After hitting the ball, Thomson left the plate with his usual greyhound speed, then slowed down as the ball hooked into the lower stands about 20 feet over the outstretched glove of left fielder Andy Pafko and some 315 feet from the plate. Almost all of the Giants mobbed Thomson as he leaped high and planted both feet on the plate. Two of the Giants not at the plate were Eddie Stanky and Leo Durocher. Stanky had raced down to the third-base coaching box, climbed Durocher's back, and the two men were rolling in the grass near the box in happy delirium. The thunderstruck Dodgers began to move off the field like zombies, except for the indomitable Jackie Robinson, who stood near second base, hands on hips, making sure that Thomson touched each base.

The Polo Grounds was a madhouse as the Giant fans shrieked joyfully, pounded each other in unabashed ecstasy, and raced onto the field to intercept the Giant players before they could escape to the center-field clubhouse. Long after the game, Giant fans could be seen in the stands and on the field shouting, dancing, and hugging complete strangers. The highest point came when Bobby Thomson emerged from the Giant clubhouse, stood at the top of the stairs, and waved to the crowd.

The jubilation at the Polo Grounds was matched all over the city as Russ Hodges' voice carried throughout the area. When the "Miracle at Coogan's Bluff" happened it was 3:58 P.M. Within a few seconds, Giant fans reacted. Motorists blew their horns in jubilation and the racket continued in city streets and on school campuses for the next couple of hours.

There were rumors that the staid old Polo Grounds had been the scene of a celebrating couple making love in the lower stands behind first base, which, in the unlikely event that it was true, would have been an even more unbelievable "Miracle at Coogan's Bluff."

Willie Mays's Miraculous Catch Against Cleveland

September 29, 1954

In the first game of the World Series between the Giants and the Cleveland Indians, Willie Mays caught Vic Wertz's tremendous clout to deepest center field at the Polo Grounds. The score was tied 2-2 in the top of the eighth inning, there were no outs, Larry Doby was at second base, and Al Rosen was on first. Giant left-hander Don Liddle replaced Sal Maglie to pitch to the left-hand-hitting Wertz. Liddle threw a high curve ball (a pitching sin to Wertz) and Vic smoked a long drive to center field which appeared headed for the bleachers slightly to the right-field side of dead center. The following scene is as familiar to today's fans watching a film of the game on TV as to those who saw the play in person.

Mays turned completely around at the crack of the bat and raced frantically toward the runway that separated the two bleacher sections. Running head down, Willie looked over his left shoulder, slowed a bit to avoid running into the bleacher wall and screen, then cupped his hands over his head and pulled the ball in like a football receiver. Mays whirled in front of the screen (characteristically losing his cap), and almost 450 feet from the plate, threw a strike to Davey

Williams at second base, spinning to his knees in the process. Doby had time to touch up at second base and move over to third base, but the astonished Rosen, having gone too far toward second, had to retreat to first base. Cleveland's Dave Pope struck out and catcher Jim Hegan flied out to end the inning. Mays's great catch and equally remarkable throw had prevented the Indians from scoring.

With none out in the top of the tenth, Wertz got his fourth hit, a drive to left center, which Mays held to a double with a sparkling barehand stop and a rifle throw to third base. The Indians did not score and Dusty Rhodes' homer won the game for the Giants 3-2 in the bottom of the inning.

The Last Giant Game at the Polo Grounds

September 29, 1957

The Giants lost to the Pittsburgh Pirates 9-1 before 11,606 in their last game at the Polo Grounds, their home park since 1891. Giant left-hander Johnny Antonelli pitched and lost the New York Giants' last game to Pirate right-hander Bob Friend. Pittsburgh rookie outfielder Johnny Powers scored the last run when he homered in the top of the ninth. Dusty Rhodes drove in the only Giant run with a sacrifice fly in the sixth inning. Giant manager Bill Rigney started as many of the Giants from the 1951 and 1954 pennant winners as he could—Willie Mays, Don Mueller, Dusty Rhodes, Bobby Thomson, Whitey Lockman, Wes Westrum, and Antonelli.

The sentimental crowd watched somberly as the Giants batted in the last of the ninth. Don Mueller opened with a soft flyball to right. With the franchise, season and game fading before their eyes, resident idol Willie Mays stepped up to hit. The crowd gave him a long cheer and kept up the clamor as Mays took the first pitch for a strike and the next two pitches for balls. Suddenly, with the cheers of the emotional crowd continuing to rise, Mays stepped out of the box and tipped his cap in appreciation. Satisfied emotionally for the time being, the throng settled down and Mays, obviously shooting for a home run to please the fans, bounced out to Pirate shortstop Dick Groat. The crowd applauded his every step back to the dugout. Dusty Rhodes worked the count to 3 and 2, then bounced to Groat for the final out as the hands of the clock over the center field clubhouses stood at 4:35 P.M.

After the last out, the crowd took over the Polo Grounds. It poured onto the field and tore up the bases, home plate, and the infield sod. Several hundred fans ripped away at the fences, the dugouts, and the bullpen benches and the awnings that shaded them. It was reminiscent of the remarkable scene after Bobby Thomson's last minute miracle home run won the 1951 pennant, but this was a different era and a different occasion. The Giants' sixty-seven-year stay at the Polo Grounds was over.

A number of Giant players of earlier years were at the Polo Grounds and many stayed long after the game was over. The night before, they had attended a dinner party hosted by Giant president Horace Stoneham and they were introduced before the game. Eighty-seven-year-old Jack Doyle, the Giants' manager seven years before John McGraw appeared on the scene, was there — and Red Murray, George Burns, Hooks Wiltse, Moose Marquard, Carl Hubbell, Billy Jurges, Monte Irvin, George "Kiddo" Davis, Willard Marshall, Sid Gordon, Buddy Kerr, Babe Young. They sat with Mrs. John McGraw, who said after the game, "It would have broken John's heart. I prefer to regard this as just the end of another season."

Garry Schumacher, the long-time New York sportswriter and Giant publicity director, brought things into focus with the comment, "If all the people who twenty years from now claim to have been at this last game at the Polo Grounds were really there, we would have drawn such a big attendance this year that there would have been no point in ever leaving New York."

ROGER BRESNAHAN

BATTERY MATE OF CHRISTY MATHEWSON
WITH THE NEW YORK GIANTS, HE WAS
ONE OF THE GAMES MOST NATURAL
PLAYERS AND MIGHT HAVE STARRED
AT ANY POSITION. THE "DUKE OF TRALEE"
WAS ONE OF THE FEW MAJOR LEAGUE
CATCHERS FAST ENOUGH TO BE USED
AS A LEADOFF MAN.

WM. B. "BUCK" EWING

GREATEST 19TH CENTURY CATCHER. GIANT
IN STATURE AND GIANT CAPTAIN OF
NEW YORK'S FIRST NATIONAL LEAGUE
CHAMPIONS 1888 AND 1889. WAS GENIUS
AS FIELD LEADER, UNSURPASSED IN
THROWING TO BASES, GREAT LONG-RANGE
HITTER. NATIONAL LEAGUE CAREER
1881 TO 1899 TROY, N.Y. GIANTS AND
CLEVELAND; CINCINNATI MANAGER.

ROSS MIDDLEBROOK YOUNGS
"PEP"
NEW YORK N.L. 1917-1926

STAR RIGHT FIELDER OF CHAMPION GIANTS
OF 1921·22·23·24 WHEN HE BATTED .327, .331,
.336, AND .356 COMPILED LIFETIME AVERAGE
OF .322, TOPPING .300 IN NINE OF TEN YEARS.
TWICE MADE 200 OR MORE HITS IN A SEASON.
LED LEAGUE IN DOUBLES IN 1919 AND RUNS
SCORED IN 1923. LED N.L. OUTFIELDERS
IN ASSISTS TWICE AND TIED ONCE.

FREDERICK CHARLES LINDSTROM
NEW YORK N.L., PITTSBURGH N.L.,
CHICAGO N.L., BROOKLYN N.L.,
1924 - 1936

COMPILED LIFETIME .311 BATTING MARK,
INCLUDING SEVEN SEASONS OF .300 OR
BETTER. ONE OF ONLY THREE PLAYERS TO
AMASS 230 OR MORE HITS A YEAR TWICE.
AS YOUNGEST PLAYER (AGE 18) IN WORLD
SERIES HISTORY, HE TIED RECORD WITH
FOUR HITS IN GAME IN 1924. EQUALLED
MAJOR LEAGUE RECORD BY COLLECTING
NINE HITS IN 1928 DOUBLEHEADER.

7

HOME BALL PARKS

Ball Park	Years Used	First Game	Last Game
First Polo Grounds (110th St. and Sixth Ave.)	1883-1888	N.Y. 7, Boston 5 May 1, 1883	Indianapolis 6, N.Y. 4 Oct. 13, 1888
Oakland Park (Jersey City)	1889 (2 games)	Boston 8, N.Y. 7 April 24, 1889	N.Y. 11, Bost. 10 April 25, 1889
St. George Grounds (Staten Island)	1889 (25 games)	N.Y. 4, Washington 2 April 29, 1889	N.Y. 14, Philadelphia 4 June 14, 1889
Second Polo Grounds (155th St. and 8th Ave.)	1889-1890	N.Y. 7, Pittsburgh 5 July 8, 1889	Boston 8, N.Y. 5 Sept. 10, 1890
Third Polo Grounds (157th St. and 8th Ave.)	1891-1957	Boston 4, N.Y. 3 April 22, 1891	Pittsburgh 9, N.Y. 1 Sept. 29, 1957
Seals Stadium (San Francisco)	1958-1959	S.F. 8, L.A. 0 April 15, 1958	L.A. 8, S.F. 2 Sept. 20, 1959
Candlestick Park (San Francisco)	1960-present	S.F. 3, St. Louis 1 April 12, 1960	

The original Polo Grounds, the Giants' home park from 1883 through 1888, was located at 110th Street and Sixth Avenue in Manhattan. The Giants shared the park with Giant owner John B. Day's other club, the New York Metropolitans, from 1883 until 1885. The champion Giants of 1889 were forced abruptly to vacate their first home park in February 1889 when New York City took over the site for inclusion in the Douglass Circle development.

Day hastily arranged for the Giants to move to Manhattan Field, which was situated at 155th Street and Eighth Avenue in Manhattan. Work began immediately on the construction of a wooden grandstand structure. But the new stadium was not sufficiently completed for the Giants' use on Opening Day. As a result, the Giants opened the 1889 season at Oakland Park in Jersey City. They played their second game at the same park, then moved to St. George Grounds in Staten Island for their next twenty-five home games. They played their first home game at the new Polo Grounds on July 8, 1889.

Day's club played in the second Polo Grounds for two seasons, 1889 and 1890. When the Players League folded after the 1890 season, the Giants purchased the larger Brotherhood Park (the home of the Players League New York entrant), which adjoined the second Polo Grounds to the north. Renamed the "New Polo Grounds," this would be the Giants' home park in New York for the next sixty-seven years.

The (third) Polo Grounds was destroyed by fire on April 14, 1911. The Giants used the Yankees' Hilltop Park at 168th Street and Broadway as a temporary home park until they returned to the partially rebuilt Polo Grounds on June 28, 1911. Their completely rebuilt home, which was dedicated on April 19, 1912, had double-decked, reinforced concrete and steel-supported stands that increased the park's seating capacity greatly, raising the pre-fire capacity of 17,300 to 34,000.

The Giants shared the Polo Grounds with the Yankees during the 1913-1922 period. The two clubs co-existed without noticeable hostility until the Yanks purchased Babe Ruth from the Red Sox before the 1920 season. The Yanks' resulting improvement on the field and at the box office led to increased friction between the two clubs, which culminated in an eviction notice issued to the Yankees by the Giants on May 14, 1920. Although the eviction action was rescinded shortly thereafter, Yankee owner Jacob Ruppert began to look for a location for his own park, finally selecting the Yankee Stadium site at River Avenue and 161st Street in the Bronx, just across the Harlem River from the Polo Grounds.

In 1924 the Polo Grounds playing field was completely enclosed by stands with the construction of double-decked, covered grandstands extending into the outfield, leaving only 4,600 uncovered bleacher seats (long, wooden planks rather than individual seats). This brought the capacity of the Polo Grounds to its eventual fifty-six thousand.

The only other significant modification to the Polo Grounds came in 1940, when the stadium was equipped for night baseball.

The San Francisco-bound Giants played their last game at the Polo Grounds on September 29, 1957, losing to Pittsburgh, 9-1.

The Polo Grounds, built in the 1890s and torn down in 1963 to make way for a housing development, was something special. Like many of the older parks, it had a unique charm and atmosphere that the newer stadiums are not likely to match.

The rectangular park was situated in a hollow overlooked by a mini-cliff known as Coogan's Bluff. It was bound on its home-plate side by Coogan's Bluff and the "Speedway" (now the Harlem River Drive), a road running along the Harlem River from 155th Street to 200th Street in upper Manhattan. Outside its first-base and right-field stands was an enormous lot used extensively by local cricket teams. The third-base and left-field stands were bound by subway yards, and the street bordering the park's center-field area was sun-sheltered by an IRT elevated station.

The green, double-decked, horseshoe-shaped stands seated 56,000. The unusual layout included high fences 257 feet down the right-field line and 279 feet down the left-field line, and a center field that terminated 483 feet from the plate at the base of the clubhouse wall. Right- and left-field bleachers, fronted by large, green "batters' background" screens 460 feet from the plate, were separated by 25 feet of open space extending from the screens back to the clubhouse. Each inner bleacher side had a flight of stairs leading to the separated clubhouses (the Giants' on the right-field side and their opponents' on the left-field side). The bullpens were in the outfield corners of the playing field. Owner Charles A. Stoneham's office, later used by his son Horace, was located above the clubhouses along with two ancient, iron loudspeakers and a large clock.

The Polo Grounds was ideal for hitters capable of pulling the ball directly down the line. However, the distances from the plate to the fences increased sharply from the foul lines out, and many long drives that were not hit close to the foul lines were converted into easy outs. The narrowness of the park also permitted outfielders to play relatively close to each other, thereby reducing the chances of hitting extra-base drives between the outfielders.

The outfield walls were probably the most difficult to play of any major league park, and not only because of their sharp angles. The right-field wall presented a solid stretch of concrete where most drives struck. Accordingly, a hard drive off the wall was likely to rebound back toward the infield. Balls hit not quite so hard usually caromed off toward center field, and softer drives, particularly those that just reached the wall, usually bounced off toward right center field or continued bouncing along the base of the wall.

The left-field wall was even more difficult to play. Compounding the problems of playing the carom, the left-field wall had a corrugated iron door on its gate that caused particularly unpredictable rebounds. Judgment of fly balls was complicated further because this was the sun field. In addition, the upper-deck facing extended well beyond the lower deck. This meant that, in cases where fly balls just missed the upper deck, there was a split second during which the fielder lost sight of the ball.

The outfield walls, as in all the older parks, were covered by advertisements (GEM razor blades, Stahl-Meyer frankfurters, Botany clothes, etc.) until 1948. After that the walls were painted a restful green to conform with the rest of the park, which may not have pleased the outfielders, who had used the letters in the advertisements as reference points for judging rebounds.

There was only one point outside the park from which any field action could be seen. High above Coogan's Bluff was an area from which the second-base area and a small part of the outfield was visible. An experienced viewer could have a good idea of what was taking place on the field simply by watching this sector and listening to the changing crowd noises. This was before the day of the portable radio and, for that matter, before the Giant games were on radio.

When the Giants shifted to San Francisco they played in the smallest major league park (23,741 capacity), but Seals Stadium was recognized among the most beautiful ballparks in the minors and certainly was major league in terms of beauty, location, and playing dimensions.

Seals was a cozy stadium, but home runs were not easy to come by because it was 365 feet down the left-field line, 355 to right, 410 to dead center, and 375 in the alleys. There were painted stars on the outfield walls, honoring some of the longest pokes. Names like Al Lyons, Joe Brovia, and Jerry Casale are recalled, the latter a pitcher in the Red Sox system who cleared the center-field wall with a mammoth blow in the mid-fifties.

Seals Stadium was built at a cost of $600,000 by three men who owned the Pacific Coast League's San Francisco Seals: Charles Graham, George Putnam, and Charles (Doc) Strub. The property at 16th and Bryant Streets once was the site of a mine, which by coincidence was listed as Home Plate Mine on the original deed.

The stadium was opened in April of 1931, and 14,235 attended an exhibition between the Seals and the Detroit Tigers. Former Yankees star Frankie Crosetti, a native San Franciscan, belted three hits, and the Seals stomped the Tigers, 5-2. That was the first in a series of eleven exhibitions in the new park, games that attracted close to one-hundred-thousand.

It wasn't until the fifth game, a spring skirmish between the Cubs and the Pirates, that a player was able to clear the wall with a homer; Gabby Hartnett connected for a 370-foot drive to left field that had to be at least 20 feet high to soar out of the park. One day later, Cubs manager Rogers Hornsby became the second man to turn the trick.

Jerry Donovan, a future Seals president and a Giants executive, hit the first home run that counted at Seals Stadium, blasting one for the Seals in the 1931 opener off Portland's Curt Fullerton. At the time, it took a clout of 385-plus feet for a home run to right. None of the big leaguers could do it in the exhibitions, but veteran outfielder Red Wingo of the Seals gained the distinction in the second Pacific Coast League series of the season against the crosstown arch-rival Mission Reds.

The Seals and the Missions shared Seals Stadium until 1938, when the Missions became the Hollywood Stars. Seals Stadium ranked as the largest uncovered park in organized baseball until the Dodgers moved into the Los Angeles Coliseum in 1958. Also, a minor league attendance record was established at Seals Stadium in 1946, when future Giants star Larry Jansen's thirty victories paced Lefty O'Doul's club to a pennant.

As much as Northern California fans craved major league baseball, they always had a soft spot for the Seals, who gave their followers a Pacific Coast League flag in 1957, a fitting going-away present. The Red Sox supplied the talent in those days, and Joe Gordon was the manager. There weren't many dry eyes at the final Pacific Coast League game in Seals Stadium because the club's fans knew the famed S.F. Seals were dead.

But enthusiasm abounded for the start of the city's first major league season (on April 15, 1958), and 23,449 were on hand for the Giants' 8-0 whipping of the Dodgers. After years of annual major league exhibitions, including visits by the Giants (who provided talent for the Oakland Oaks), the fans were eager for the real thing.

They watched Daryl Spencer of the Giants belt the first official major league homer at Seals Stadium. One day later, Duke Snider of the Dodgers cleared the right-field wall with one of the longest home runs in the park's history. More tears flowed when the Dodgers downed the Giants 8-2 on September 20, 1959, because the faithful fans realized it was the last game to be played at Seals Stadium, which was demolished by a wrecking crew a few months later.

Seals Stadium was the perfect location for a major league facility. It was five minutes from downtown, and there was talk of adding a deck to the park to bring it up to major league attendance standards. Unfortunately the plan was doomed because of inadequate parking. Too bad, because it wasn't nearly as windy at 16th and Bryant as it is at Candlestick Cove.

Moreover, expansion of Seals Stadium would have raised the capacity to only thirty-three-thousand, and the Giants insisted on a facility with a minimum of forty-thousand seats and plenty of parking when they elected to move from the Polo Grounds. The prospects for a new stadium were outstanding long before Horace Stoneham took Horace Greeley's advice.

In 1954, S.F. voters approved a $5 million bond issue to finance a stadium, but there was a catch. The funds would not be released unless a major league franchise was obtained within five years. The search was on and Supervisor Francis McCarty, author of the bond measure, discussed with Bill Veeck the possibility of moving the Browns to San Francisco. There also were talks with Calvin Griffith about shifting the Senators.

When George Christopher became mayor in 1956, his top priority was landing a major league baseball team. The Giants were considering a move to Minneapolis, so Christopher realized that a new ballpark was imperative to lure an established franchise. A site selection committee was appointed and Candlestick Point became the most feasible because downtown merchants opposed a stadium in their area.

Candlestick Park was a convenient alternative. A minimum of 75 acres were needed for a forty-thousand-capacity stadium with twelve-thousand parking spaces, and construction magnate Charles Harney happened to own 67 acres at Candlestick Point. Financially, it seemed like a sound move. Harney sold the city his property for $2.7 million, and Christopher later pointed out that it would have cost $33 million to purchase land downtown.

Construction on the new stadium began in September of 1958. Stoneham was anxious to have it completed by the 1959 World Series because the Giants were threatening to go all the way that year. As it was, the Giants folded down the stretch, and Candlestick Park, after a multitude of snags, wasn't opened until April 12, 1960.

Parts of Bay View Hill had to be cut to provide fill for the new park and its surroundings, so wind was a problem from the start. There were other problems, too, because it was the first stadium erected since the Depression, thus there were no standards by which to compare. The final announced cost was $14,855,990, less than $6 million of which went into the stadium itself.

For all its faults, Candlestick Park was attractive. It had 42,500 seats for the historic opener, and the playing dimensions were symmetrical: 335 feet down each foul line, 420 to dead center, and 390 in the alleys. An $850,000 lighting system was regarded as the finest in the nation at the time, and the curved seats were comfortable. A radiant heating system was designed to combat the cold for night games, but it didn't perform as promised.

A paid attendance of 42,269 for the opener shattered the S.F. record of 23,192 paid for the 1958 inaugural at Seals Stadium. The Giants downed the Cardinals 3-1, with Leon Wagner of St. Louis belting the initial home run in the new stadium, which had a deck but no stands beyond the fence in right and center. The open areas made hitting homers much easier for left-handed batters and worked against those who swung from the right side.

As a possible remedy, the Giants drastically moved in the fences for the 1961 season, dissatisfied that only eighty home runs were walloped in seventy-seven games at Candlestick in its maiden season. The distance in left-center was reduced to 365 feet and the new distances in center and right center were 410 and 375. A 45-foot backdrop was installed behind the center-field fence to reduce glare for batters.

After Stu Miller was blown off the mound in the 1961 All-Star Game, the park's capricious winds gained national attention. The City hired a firm to do a wind study in March of 1962. At a cost of $55,000, the Palo Alto firm released its findings in September of 1963, recommending a cut through the south end of Bay View Hill and a partial dome over the stadium. Those efforts to reduce wind would have cost an estimated $3 million, the firm pointed out.

Heels dragged and nothing was done at City Hall until Joseph Alioto became mayor and urged the demolition of Candlestick Park. "Why should we perpetuate mediocrity?" asked Alioto, whose joint committee recommended the construction of a fifty-five-thousand-seat stadium in downtown San Francisco. The report noted that it would cost $874,000 annually to improve Candlestick and $1.5 million annually to build a downtown stadium, but the committee stated it would be more advantageous to follow the latter plan because of the revenue that would be generated downtown.

Alioto's dream didn't gain much support, so steps were taken to improve Candlestick for the Giants and for its new tenants, the NFL's 49ers. Artificial turf was installed, as recommended by the Recreation and Parks Department in 1967, and the park was enclosed in an effort to reduce the wind and increase the capacity (to sixty-two-thousand) for football through use of movable stands. The work was completed in January of 1972.

The 49ers pushed for the synthetic surface, but numerous knee injuries made them change their mind and natural grass was planted in time for the 1979 baseball season. But that didn't calm the winds, which often make the game a nightmare for players and a nuisance for well-bundled fans. As a result, another study was launched and there was continuing talk of a dome for Candlestick or a downtown stadium as the Giants headed into the mid-eighties.

The much-maligned ballpark again was the focus of controversy following the 1984 season. Owner Bob Lurie's patience was running thin after attendance barely exceeded one million, so he vowed not to play at Candlestick Park beyond 1985.

Flames were fueled when the city of San Francisco announced major renovations at the stadium, most of them geared to appease the NFL's 49ers. Lurie and Giants brass deemed Candlestick unacceptable for baseball and their efforts to move to a new stadium increased after attendance dipped below one million in 1985.

When the 100-loss season concluded, it generally was felt the Giants had played at Candlestick for the last time. But plans to play temporarily at Oakland and Denver never got off the ground, parallelling the lack of success in obtaining a firm commitment for a new stadium in downtown San Francisco or elsewhere in the Bay Area.

There was moderate interest by San Jose officials but they backed off when S.F. Mayor Dianne Feinstein warned of tampering. Downtown stadium sites were mentioned, but those plans fell through. On Jan. 29, 1986, Lurie announced the club was to remain at Candlestick in 1986.

During the season, the club financed a feasibility study which discouraged downtown stadium plans because of the money involved in such a project. Lurie would not commit to Candlestick Park beyond 1987, hopeful that a stadium would be built somewhere in the Bay Area, perhaps as far away as Sacramento.

There was one notable change last year. Because of the club's success during the summer months, there was a reduction in grumbling about the ballpark by fans and players alike. The final attendance of 1,528,748 was the club's second highest in 20 years, representing an 87 percent increase over 1985.

Lurie, however, wasn't gushing. The businessman boss of the Giants noted that 1.8 million was the break-even figure for the club. He renewed his intentions of keeping the club in the Bay Area, but as of the end of the year there were no concrete plans for a new stadium west of Sacramento.

8

ALL-TIME TEAMS

Former National League President Chub Feeney's all-time Giants among the players he's seen perform:

New York
Bill Terry (1B), Eddie Stanky (2B), Travis Jackson (3B), Alvin Dark (SS), Monte Irvin (LF), Willie Mays (CF), Mel Ott (RF), Gus Mancuso and Wes Westrum (tie-C), Carl Hubbell (left-hander), Sal Maglie (right-hander), Hoyt Wilhelm (reliever), Sid Gordon (utility), Bill Terry (mgr).

San Francisco
Willie MCovey (1B), Tito Fuentes (2B), Jim Davenport (3B), Jose Pagan (SS), Bobby Bonds (LF), Willie Mays (CF), Felipe Alou (RF), Tom Haller (C), Mike McCormick (left-hander), Juan Marichal (right-hander), Frank Linzy (reliever), Orlando Cepeda (utility), Bill Rigney (mgr).

Long-time Giants front office man Eddie Brannick's all-time Giants (from 1905 through the 1960s):
Bill Terry (1B), Frankie Frisch (2B), Dave Bancroft (SS), Fred Lindstrom (3B), Joe Moore (LF), Willie Mays (CF), Ross Youngs (RF), Pancho Snyder and Chief Meyers (tie-C), Christy Mathewson (right-hander), Carl Hubbell (left-hander), Mel Ott and Heinie Groh (utility), and John McGraw (mgr).

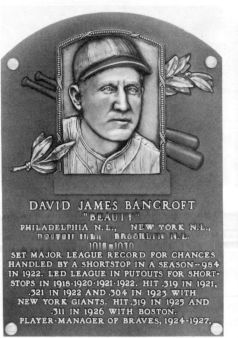

DAVID JAMES BANCROFT
"BEAUTY"

PHILADELPHIA N.L., NEW YORK N.L.,
BOSTON N.L., BROOKLYN N.L.
1915-1930

SET MAJOR LEAGUE RECORD FOR CHANCES
HANDLED BY A SHORTSTOP IN A SEASON--984
IN 1922. LED LEAGUE IN PUTOUTS FOR SHORT-
STOPS IN 1918·1920·1921·1922. HIT .319 IN 1921,
.321 IN 1922 AND .304 IN 1923 WITH
NEW YORK GIANTS. HIT .319 IN 1925 AND
.311 IN 1926 WITH BOSTON.
PLAYER·MANAGER OF BRAVES, 1924-1927.

FRANK FRISCH
NEW YORK N.L. 1919-1926
ST. LOUIS N.L. 1927-1938
PITTSBURGH N.L. 1940-1946
MEMBER BASEBALL HALL OF FAME
THE "FORDHAM FLASH" WAS AN OUTSTANDING
INFIELDER, BASE-RUNNER AND BATTER.
HAD A LIFETIME BATTING MARK OF .316.
HOLDS MANY RECORDS. PLAYED IN 50
WORLD SERIES GAMES. MANAGED ST. LOUIS
FROM 1933 THROUGH 1938 AND WON WORLD
SERIES IN 1934. MANAGED PITTSBURGH
FROM 1940 THROUGH 1946.

MONFORD (MONTE) IRVIN
NEGRO LEAGUES 1937-1948
NEW YORK N.L., CHICAGO N.L.,
1949-1956

REGARDED AS ONE OF NEGRO LEAGUES' BEST
HITTERS. STAR SLUGGER OF NEWARK EAGLES.
WON 1946 NEGRO LEAGUE BATTING TITLE.
LED N.L. IN RUNS BATTED IN AND PACED
"MIRACLE" GIANTS IN HITTING IN 1951
DRIVE TO PENNANT. BATTED .458 AND
STOLE HOME IN 1951 WORLD SERIES.

JOSEPH JEROME McGINNITY
"IRONMAN"

DISTINGUISHED AS THE PITCHER WHO HURLED
TWO GAMES ON ONE DAY THE MOST TIMES. DID
THIS ON FIVE OCCASIONS. WON BOTH GAMES
THREE TIMES. PLAYED WITH BALTIMORE,
BROOKLYN AND NEW YORK TEAMS IN N.L.
AND BALTIMORE IN A.L. GAINED MORE THAN
200 VICTORIES DURING CAREER. RECORDED
20 OR MORE VICTORIES SEVEN TIMES. IN TWO
SUCCESSIVE SEASONS WON AT LEAST 30 GAMES.

9

AWARDS AND HONORS

Retired Giant Uniform Numbers

Player	Uniform Number
Bill Terry	3
Mel Ott	4
Carl Hubbell	11
Willie Mays	24
Juan Marichal	27
Willie McCovey	44

Giant MVP Award Winners

Player	Year
Chalmers Award:	
Larry Doyle	1912
Baseball Writers Association of America:	
Carl Hubbell	1933
Carl Hubbell	1936
Willie Mays	1954
Willie Mays	1965
Willie McCovey	1969

Rookie of the Year Awards

	Year
Baseball Writers Association of America:	
Willie Mays	1951
Orlando Cepeda	1958
Willie McCovey	1959
Gary Matthews	1973
John Montefusco	1975
The Sporting News:	
Orlando Cepeda	1958
Willie McCovey	1959
Frank Linzy	1965
Dave Rader	1972
Gary Matthews	1973
John D'Acquisto	1974
John Montefusco	1975
Larry Herndon	1976
Robby Thompson	1986

Cy Young Award

Pitcher	Year
Mike McCormick	1967

10

TEAM STATISTICS

WHERE THE GIANTS FINISHED

1883–1986

Year	Pos	W	L	Pct	Manager
1883	6	46	50	.479	Clapp
1884	5	62	50	.554	Price
					Ward
1885	2	85	27	.759	Mutrie
1886	3	75	44	.630	Mutrie
1887	4	68	55	.553	Mutrie
1888	1	84	47	.641	Mutrie
1889	1	83	43	.659	Mutrie
1890	6	63	68	.481	Mutrie
1891	3	71	61	.538	Mutrie
1892	8	71	80	.470	Powers
1893	5	68	64	.515	Ward
1894	2	88	44	.667	Ward
1895	9	66	65	.504	Davis
					Doyle
					Watkins
1896	7	64	67	.489	Irwin
					Joyce
1897	3	83	48	.634	Joyce
1898	7	77	73	.513	Joyce
					Anson
					Joyce
1899	5	60	90	.400	Day
					Hoey
1900	8	60	78	.435	Ewing
					Davis
1901	7	52	85	.380	Davis
1902	8	48	88	.353	Fogel
					Smith
					McGraw

Year	Pos	W	L	Pct	Manager
1903	2	84	55	.604	McGraw
1904	1	106	47	.693	McGraw
1905	1*	105	48	.686	McGraw
1906	2	96	56	.632	McGraw
1907	4	82	71	.536	McGraw
1908	2	98	56	.636	McGraw
1909	3	92	61	.601	McGraw
1910	2	91	63	.591	McGraw
1911	1	99	54	.647	McGraw
1912	1	103	48	.682	McGraw
1913	1	101	51	.664	McGraw
1914	2	84	70	.545	McGraw
1915	8	69	83	.454	McGraw
1916	4	86	66	.566	McGraw
1917	1	98	56	.636	McGraw
1918	2	71	53	.573	McGraw
1919	2	87	53	.621	McGraw
1920	2	86	68	.558	McGraw
1921	1*	94	59	.614	McGraw
1922	1*	93	61	.604	McGraw
1923	1	95	58	.621	McGraw
1924	1	93	60	.608	McGraw
1925	2	86	66	.566	McGraw
1926	5	74	77	.490	McGraw
1927	3	92	62	.597	McGraw
1928	2	93	61	.604	McGraw
1929	3	84	67	.556	McGraw
1930	3	87	67	.565	McGraw
1931	2	87	65	.572	McGraw
1932	6	72	82	.468	McGraw
					Terry
1933	1*	91	61	.599	Terry
1934	2	93	60	.608	Terry
1935	3	91	62	.595	Terry
1936	1	92	62	.597	Terry
1937	1	95	57	.625	Terry
1938	3	83	67	.553	Terry
1939	5	77	74	.510	Terry
1940	6	72	80	.474	Terry
1941	5	74	79	.484	Terry
1942	3	85	67	.559	Ott
1943	8	55	98	.359	Ott
1944	5	67	87	.435	Ott
1945	5	78	74	.513	Ott
1946	8	61	93	.396	Ott
1947	4	81	73	.526	Ott
1948	5	78	76	.506	Ott
					Durocher
1949	5	73	81	.474	Durocher
1950	3	86	68	.558	Durocher
1951	1	98	59	.624	Durocher
1952	2	92	62	.597	Durocher
1953	5	70	84	.455	Durocher

Year	Pos	W	L	Pct	Manager
1954	1*	97	57	.630	Durocher
1955	3	80	74	.519	Durocher
1956	6	67	87	.435	Rigney
1957	6	69	85	.448	Rigney
1958	3	80	74	.519	Rigney
1959	3	83	71	.539	Rigney
1960	5	79	75	.513	Rigney
					Sheehan
1961	3	85	69	.552	Dark
1962	1	103	62	.624	Dark
1963	3	88	74	.543	Dark
1964	4	90	72	.556	Dark
1965	2	95	67	.586	Franks
1966	2	93	68	.578	Franks
1967	2	91	71	.562	Franks
1968	2	88	74	.543	Franks
1969	2	90	72	.556	King
1970	3	86	76	.531	King
					Fox
1971	1	90	72	.556	Fox
1972	5	69	86	.445	Fox
1973	3	88	74	.543	Fox
1974	5	72	90	.444	Fox
					Westrum
1975	3	80	81	.497	Westrum
1976	4	74	88	.457	Rigney
1977	4	75	87	.463	Altobelli
1978	3	89	73	.549	Altobelli
1979	4	71	91	.438	Altobelli
					Bristol
1980	5	75	86	.466	Bristol
1981	4	56	55	.505	Robinson
1982	3	87	75	.537	Robinson
1983	5	79	83	.488	Robinson
1984	6	66	96	.407	Robinson
					Ozark
1985	6	62	100	.383	Davenport
					Craig
1986	3	83	79	.512	Craig

*World Champions

GIANTS MANAGERS' RECORDS

1883–1986

Manager	Years	W	L	Pct
John Clapp	1883	46	50	.479
James Price	1884	56	42	.571
Monte Ward	1884	162	116	.583
	93-94			
James Mutrie	1885-91	529	345	.605
Pat Powers	1892	71	80	.470
George Davis	1895	108	139	.437
	1900-01			
Jack Doyle	1895	31	31	.500
Harvey Watkins	1895	18	17	.514
Arthur Irwin	1896	39	50	.418
Bill Joyce	1896-98	177	122	.592
Cap Anson	1898	9	13	.409
John B. Day	1899	30	40	.429
Fred Hoey	1899	30	50	.375
Buck Ewing	1900	21	41	.339
Horace Fogel	1902	18	23	.439
George Smith	1902	5	27	.156
John McGraw	1902-32	2,658	1,823	.593
Bill Terry	1932-41	823	661	.555
Mel Ott	1942-48	464	530	.467
Leo Durocher	1948-55	637	523	.549
Bill Rigney	1956-60	406	430	.486
	1976			
Tom Sheehan	1960	46	50	.479
Alvin Dark	1961-64	366	277	.569
Herman Franks	1965-68	367	280	.567
Clyde King	1969-70	109	97	.529
Charlie Fox	1970-74	348	325	.517
Wes Westrum	1974-75	118	129	.478
Joe Altobelli	1977-79	225	239	.485
Dave Bristol	1979-1980	85	98	.464
Frank Robinson	1981-84	264	277	.488
Danny Ozark	1984	24	32	.429
Jim Davenport	1985	56	88	.389
Roger Craig	1985-86	89	91	.494

GIANTS CLUB PRESIDENTS

President	Years
(New York)	
John B. Day	1883-92
C. C. Van Cott	1893-94
Andrew Freedman	1895-02
John T. Brush	1903-12
Harry N. Hempstead	1912-18
Charles A. Stoneham	1919-35
Horace C. Stoneham	1936-57
(San Francisco)	
Horace C. Stoneham	1958-75
Robert A. Lurie	1976-present

MISCELLANEOUS TEAM RECORDS
1883-1986

Overall Wins and Losses

Years	Games	Won	Lost	Pct
1883-1957	11,141	6,243	4,898	.560
1958-1986	4,618	2,367	2,251	.513
Total	15,759	8,610	7,149	.546

Most Giants Wins in
a season

Year	W	L	Pct	Pos
1904	106	47	.693	First
1905	105	48	.686	First
1912	103	48	.682	First
1962	103	62	.624	First
1913	101	51	.664	First

Most Consecutive Giants Wins

Year	Won	Home	Away
1916	26	26	0
1904	18	13	5
1907	17	14	3
1916	17	0	17
1912	16	11	5
1951	16	13	3
1936	15	7	8
1913	14	6	8
1965	14	6	8
1905	13	8	5

Most Consecutive Giants Losses

Year	Lost	Home	Away
1902	13	5	8
1944	13	0	13

Most Lopsided Decisions

	Date	Opponent	Score
Giant Win	April 30, 1944	Brooklyn	26-8
Giant Loss	June 7, 1906	Chicago	19-0

BATTING RECORDS

GIANTS WHO LED THE NATIONAL LEAGUE IN VARIOUS CATEGORIES

1883-1986

Walks

Year	Player	Total
1888	Roger Connor	73
1889	Mike Tiernan	96
1908	Roger Bresnahan	83
1917	George Burns	75
1919	George Burns	82
1920	George Burns	76
1921	George Burns	80
1927	Rogers Hornsby	86
1929	Mel Ott	113
1931	Mel Ott	80
1932	Mel Ott	100
1933	Mel Ott	75
1937	Mel Ott	102
1942	Mel Ott	109
1950	Eddie Stanky	144
1970	Willie McCovey	137
1971	Willie Mays	112

Runs

Year	Player	Total
1889	Mike Tiernan	147
1904	George Browne	99
1905	Mike Donlin	124
1907	Spike Shannon	104
1908	Fred Tenney	101
1914	George Burns	100
1916	George Burns	105
1917	George Burns	103
1919	George Burns	86
1920	George Burns	115
1923	Ross Youngs	121
1927	Rogers Hornsby	133
1938	Mel Ott	116
1942	Mel Ott	118
1961	Willie Mays	129
1969	Bobby Bonds	120
1973	Bobby Bonds	131

Slugging Percentage

Year	Player	Pct
1889	Roger Connor	.528
1890	Mike Tiernan	.495
1891	Mike Tiernan	.500
1938	Mel Ott	.588
1954	Willie Mays	.667
1955	Willie Mays	.659
1957	Willie Mays	.626
1964	Willie Mays	.607
1965	Willie Mays	.645
1968	Willie McCovey	.545
1969	Willie McCovey	.656
1970	Willie McCovey	.612

Stolen Bases

Year	Player	Total
1887	Monte Ward	111
1905	Art Devlin	59
1914	George Burns	62
1921	Frankie Frisch	49
1956	Willie Mays	40
1957	Willie Mays	38
1958	Willie Mays	31
1959	Willie Mays	27

Hits

Year	Player	Total
1885	Roger Connor	169
1890	Jack Glasscock	172
1909	Larry Doyle	172
1915	Larry Doyle	189
1923	Frankie Frisch	223
1928	Freddie Lindstrom	231
1930	Bill Terry	254
1954	Don Mueller	212
1957	Red Schoendienst	200
1960	Willie Mays	190

Triples

Year	Player	Total
1884	Bill Ewing	20
1885	Jim O'Rourke	16
1886	Roger Connor	20
1896	George Van Haltren	21
1911	Larry Doyle	25
1931	Bill Terry	20
1952	Bobby Thomson	14
1954	Willie Mays	13
1955	Willie Mays	13
1957	Willie Mays	20

Doubles

Year	Player	Total
1903	Sam Mertes	32
1915	Larry Doyle	40
1919	Ross Youngs	31
1951	Alvin Dark	41

LEADING GIANT HITTERS*

1883–1986

Year	Player	BA	Year	Player	BA
1883	R. Connor	.357	1929	B. Terry	.372
1884	R. Connor	.317	1930	B. Terry	.401*
1885	R. Connor	.371*	1931	B. Terry	.349
1886	R. Connor	.355	1932	B. Terry	.350
1887	M. Ward	.338	1933	B. Terry	.322
1888	B. Ewing	.306	1934	B. Terry	.354
1889	M. Tiernan	.335	1935	B. Terry	.341
1890	J. Glasscock	.336*	1936	M. Ott	.328
1891	M. Tiernan	.306	1937	J. Ripple	.317
1892	B. Ewing	.310	1938	M. Ott	.311
1893	G. Davis	.362	1939	Z. Bonura	.321
1894	J. Doyle	.369	1940	F. Demaree	.302
1895	M. Tiernan	.347	1941	D. Bartell	.303
1896	M. Tiernan	.369	1942	J. Mize	.305
1897	G. Davis	.358	1943	M. Witek	.314
1898	G. Van Haltren	.312	1944	J. Medwick	.337
1889	G. Davis	.346	1945	M. Ott	.308
1900	K. Selbach	.337	1946	J. Mize	.337
1901	G. Van Haltren	.335	1947	W. Cooper	.305
1902	D. McGann	.300	1948	S. Gordon	.299
1903	R. Bresnahan	.350	1949	B. Thomson	.309
1904	D. McGann	.286	1950	E. Stanky	.300
1905	M. Donlin	.356	1951	M. Irvin	.312
1906	C. Seymour	.320	1952	A. Dark	.301
1907	D. McGann	.298	1953	D. Mueller	.333
1908	M. Donlin	.334	1954	W. Mays	.345*
1909	L. Doyle	.302	1955	W. Mays	.319
1910	F. Snodgrass	.321	1956	J. Brandt	.299
1911	C. Meyers	.332	1957	W. Mays	.333
1912	C. Meyers	.358	1958	W. Mays	.347
1913	C. Meyers	.312	1959	O. Cepeda	.317
1914	G. Burns	.303	1960	W. Mays	.319
1915	L. Doyle	.320*	1961	O. Cepeda	.311
1916	D. Robertson	.307	1962	F. Alou	.316
1917	B. Kauff	.308	1962	O. Cepeda	.316
1918	R. Youngs	.302	1964	O. Cepeda	.304
1919	R. Youngs	.311	1965	W. Mays	.317
1920	R. Youngs	.351	1966	W. Mays	.317
1921	F. Frisch	.341	1966	W. Mays	.288
1922	F. Snyder	.343	1967	J. Alou	.292
1923	F. Frisch	.348	1968	W. McCovey	.293
1924	R. Youngs	.356	1969	W. McCovey	.320
1925	F. Frisch	.331	1970	B. Bonds	.302
1926	T. Jackson	.327	1971	B. Bonds	.288
1927	R. Hornsby	.361	1972	C. Speier	.269
1928	F. Lindstrom	.358	1973	G. Maddox	.319

*Led National League

Year	Player	BA	Year	Player	BA
1974	D. Rader	.291	1981	M. May	.310
1975	V. Joshua	.318	1982	J. Morgan	.289
1976	L. Herndon	.288	1983	J. Youngblood	.292
1977	B. Madlock	.302	1984	D. Gladden	.351
1978	B. Madlock	.309	1985	C. Brown	.271
1979	M. Ivie	.286	1986	C. Brown	.317
1980	T. Whitfield	.296			

GIANT HOME-RUN LEADERS

1883-1986

Year	Player	Home Runs	Year	Player	Home Runs
1883	B. Ewing	10*	1904	D. McGann	6
1884	A. McKinnon	4	1905	B. Dahlen	7
	R. Connor		1906	C. Seymour	4
1885	B. Ewing	6		S. Strang	4
1886	R. Connor	7	1907	G. Browne	5
1887	R. Connor	17	1908	M. Donlin	6
1888	R. Connor	14	1909	R. Murray	7*
1889	R. Connor	13	1910	L. Doyle	8
1890	M. Tiernan	13	1911	L. Doyle	13
1891	M. Tiernan	17*	1912	F. Merkle	11
1892	D. Lyons	8	1913	L. Doyle	5
1893	M. Tiernan	15		T. Shafer	5
1894	G. Davis	9	1914	F. Merkle	7
1895	G. Van Haltren	8	1915	F. Merkle	4
1896	M. Tiernan	7		L. Doyle	
1897	G. Davis	9	1916	D. Robertson	12*
1898	B. Joyce	10	1917	D. Robertson	12*
1899	T. O'Brien	6	1918	G. Burns	4
1900	P. Hickman	9	1919	B. Kauff	10
1901	G. Davis	7	1920	G. Kelly	11
1902	S. Brodie	3	1921	G. Kelly	23
1903	S. Mertes	7	1922	G. Kelly	17

GIANT HOME-RUN LEADERS

1883–1986

Year	Player	Home Runs	Year	Player	Home Runs
1923	E. Meusel	19	1956	W. Mays	36
1924	G. Kelly	21	1957	W. Mays	35
1925	E. Meusel	21	1958	W. Mays	29
1926	G. Kelly	13	1959	W. Mays	34
1927	R. Hornsby	26	1960	W. Mays	29
1928	M. Ott	18	1961	O. Cepeda	46
1929	M. Ott	42	1962	W. Mays	49*
1930	M. Ott	25	1963	W. McCovey	44**
1931	M. Ott	29	1964	W. Mays	47*
1932	M. Ott	38**	1965	W. Mays	52*
1933	M. Ott	23	1966	W. Mays	37
1934	M. Ott	35*	1967	W. McCovey	31
1935	M. Ott	31**	1968	W. McCovey	36*
1936	M. Ott	33*	1969	W. McCovey	45*
1937	M. Ott	31**	1970	W. McCovey	39
1938	M. Ott	36*	1971	B. Bonds	33
1939	M. Ott	27	1972	D. Kingman	29
1940	M. Ott	19	1973	B. Bonds	39
1941	M. Ott	27	1974	B. Bonds	21
1942	M. Ott	30*	1975	G. Matthews	12
1943	M. Ott	18	1976	B. Murcer	23
1944	M. Ott	26	1977	W. McCovey	28
1945	M. Ott	21	1978	J. Clark	25
1946	J. Mize	22	1979	M. Ivie	27
1947	J. Mize	51**	1980	J. Clark	22
1948	J. Mize	40**	1981	J. Clark	17
1949	B. Thomson	27	1982	J. Clark	27
1950	B. Thomson	25	1983	D. Evans	30
1951	B. Thomson	32	1984	J. Leonard	21
1952	B. Thomson	24		C. Davis	
1953	B. Thomson	26	1985	B. Brenly	19
1954	W. Mays	41	1986	C. Maldonado	18
1955	W. Mays	51*			

*Led National League
**Tied for National League Lead

GIANTS WITH 100 OR MORE RBI IN A SEASON

1883–1986

Year	Player	RBI	Year	Player	RBI
1889	R. Connor	130*	1933	M. Ott	103
	D. Richardson	100	1934	M. Ott	135*
1893	G. Davis	119		T. Jackson	101
	R. Connor	105	1935	M. Ott	114
	M. Tiernan	102		H. Leiber	107
1984	G. Van Haltren	104	1936	M. Ott	135
	J. Doyle	100	1938	M. Ott	116
1895	G. Van Haltren	103	1940	B. Young	101
	G. Davis	101	1941	B. Young	104
1897	G. Davis	134	1942	J. Mize	110*
	K. Gleason	106	1947	J. Mize	138*
1903	S. Mertes	104*		W. Cooper	122
1905	S. Mertes	108		W. Marshall	107
1908	M. Donlin	106	1948	J. Mize	125
1917	H. Zimmerman	102*		S. Gordon	107
1921	G. Kelly	122	1949	B. Thomson	109
	R. Youngs	102	1951	M. Irvin	121*
	F. Frisch	100	1952	B. Thomson	108
1922	E. Meusel	132	1953	B. Thomson	106
	G. Kelly	107	1954	W. Mays	110
1923	E. Meusel	125*	1955	W. Mays	127
	F. Frisch	111	1959	O. Cepeda	105
	G. Kelly	103		W. Mays	104
1924	G. Kelly	136*	1960	W. Mays	103
	E. Meusel	102	1961	O. Cepeda	142*
1925	E. Meusel	111		W. Mays	123
1927	R. Hornsby	125	1962	W. Mays	141
	B. Terry	121		O. Cepeda	114
1928	F. Lindstrom	107	1963	W. Mays	103
	B. Terry	101		W. McCovey	102
1929	M. Ott	151	1964	W. Mays	111
	B. Terry	117	1965	W. Mays	112
1930	B. Terry	129	1966	W. Mays	103
	M. Ott	119	1968	W. McCovey	105*
	F. Lindstrom	106	1969	W. McCovey	126*
1931	M. Ott	115	1970	W. McCovey	126
	B. Terry	112		D. Dietz	107
1932	M. Ott	123	1971	B. Bonds	102
	B. Terry	117	1982	J. Clark	103

*Led National League

GIANTS WITH THREE- AND FOUR-HOME-RUN GAMES

Player	HR/Game	Date	Opponent	Consecutive	Home/Away
Willie Mays	4	4/30/61	Milwaukee	no	away
Roger Connor	3	5/9/88	Indianapolis	no	away
George Kelly	3	9/17/23	Chicago	yes	away
George Kelly	3	6/14/24	Cincinnati	no	home
Mel Ott	3	8/31/30	Boston	yes	home
Bill Terry	3	8/13/32	Brooklyn	no	home
Johnny Mize	3	4/24/47	Boston	yes	away
Wes Westrum	3	6/24/50	Cincinnati	no	home
Don Mueller	3	9/1/51	Brooklyn	no	home
Dusty Rhodes	3	8/26/53	St. Louis	yes	home
Dusty Rhodes	3	7/20/54	St. Louis	yes	home
Willie Mays	3	6/29/61	Milwaukee	no	away
Willie Mays	3	6/2/63	Philadelphia	no	away
Willie McCovey	3	9/22/63	New York	yes	home
Willie McCovey	3	4/22/64	Milwaukee	yes	away
Willie McCovey	3	9/17/66	New York	no	home
Gary Matthews	3	9/25/76	Houston	no	home
Darrell Evans	3	6/15/83	Houston	no	home

PLAYERS WITH MOST GRAND-SLAM HOME RUNS DURING GIANT CAREERS

1883–1986

Player	Number of Grand Slams
Willie McCovey	18*
Willie Mays	8
Mel Ott	7
George Kelly	5
Babe Young	5
Wes Westrum	5
Travis Jackson	4
Bill Terry	4
Bobby Thomson	4
Bobby Bonds	4
Hank Thompson	4
Jack Clark	4
Dave Robertson	3
Ernie Lombardi	3
Walker Cooper	3
Sid Gordon	3
Monte Irvin	3
Alvin Dark	3
Orlando Cepeda	3
Jim Davenport	3
Jim Hart	3
Dick Dietz	3
Dave Kingman	3

*All-time National League leader

CAREER RECORDS OF TOP 20 NEW YORK GIANTS HITTERS, 1883–1957*

Hitter	Games	BA	Hits	Doubles	Triples	HR	RBI	Runs	Walks	SO	SB
B. Terry	1,721	.341	2,193	373	112	154	1,078	1,120	537	449	56
R. Youngs	1,211	.322	1,491	236	93	42	592	812	550	390	153
R. Connor	1,998	.318	2,480	442	233	136	1,078	1,621	1,002	449	227
F. Frisch	2,311	.316	2,880	466	138	105	1,244	1,532	728	272	419
G. Van Haltren	1,984	.316	2,582	289	161	69	1,014	1,639	868	305	583
J. Mize	1,884	.312	2,011	367	83	359	1,337	1,118	856	524	28
M. Tiernan	1,476	.311	1,834	255	162	108	851	1,313	747	318	428
F. Lindstrom	1,438	.311	1,747	301	81	103	779	895	334	276	84
E. Meusel	1,294	.310	1,521	250	93	106	818	701	269	199	113
M. Ott	2,732	.304	2,876	488	72	511	1,860	1,859	1,708	896	89
B. Ewing	1,315	.303	1,625	250	178	70	733	1,129	392	294	336
W. Mays	2,992	.302	3,283	523	140	660	1,903	2,062	1,463	1,526	338
J. Moore	1,335	.298	1,615	258	53	79	513	809	348	247	246
G. Davis	2,377	.297	2,688	452	167	73	1,435	1,544	870	180	616
G. Kelly	1,622	.297	1,778	337	76	148	1,020	819	386	694	65
T. Jackson	1,656	.291	1,768	291	86	135	929	833	412	565	71
L. Doyle	1,765	.290	1,887	299	123	74	793	960	625	274	297
G. Burns	1,853	.287	2,077	362	108	41	611	1,188	872	565	383
W. Lockman	1,666	.279	1,658	222	49	114	563	836	552	383	43
B. Thomson	1,779	.270	1,705	267	74	264	1,026	903	559	804	38

*Includes overall major league career totals

All players listed played at least 500 games as Giants

TOP 10 NEW YORK GIANTS
IN VARIOUS HITTING CATEGORIES

1883-1957

Extra Base Hits		Batting Average		Slugging Percentage	
Player	**Total**	**Player**	**Avg**	**Player**	**Pct**
M. Ott	1,071	B. Terry	.341	W. Mays	.593
B. Terry	640	G. S. Davis	.335	J. Mize	.549
M. Tiernan	516	R. Connor	.334	M. Ott	.533
T. Jackson	512	G. Van Haltren	.323	B. Terry	.506
L. Doyle	459	R. Youngs	.322	R. Connor	.500
R. Connor	445	F. Frisch	.321	B. Thomson	.484
B. Thomson	437	F. Lindstrom	.318	B. Ewing	.472
G. Kelly	393	M. Tiernan	.317	E. Meusel	.471
J. Moore	390	B. Ewing	.315	M. Tiernan	.468
G. J. Burns	383	E. Meusel	.314	G. S. Davis	.466

TOP 10 NEW YORK GIANTS
IN VARIOUS HITTING CATEGORIES

1883-1957

Games		At Bats		Runs	
Player	**Total**	**Player**	**Total**	**Player**	**Total**
M. Ott	2,732	M. Ott	9,456	M. Ott	1,859
L. Doyle	1,765	B. Terry	6,428	M. Tiernan	1,313
B. Terry	1,721	T. Jackson	6,086	B. Terry	1,120
T. Jackson	1,656	L. Doyle	5,995	G. Van Haltren	982
M. Tiernan	1,476	M. Tiernan	5,910	R. Connor	939
W. Lockman	1,393	W. Lockman	5,462	L. Doyle	906
G. J. Burns	1,363	J. Moore	5,427	G. J. Burns	875
J. Moore	1,335	G. J. Burns	5,312	G. S. Davis	844
A. Fletcher	1,306	G. Van Haltren	4,930	T. Jackson	833
G. Van Haltren	1,217	R. Youngs	4,627	M. Ward	826

Hits		Singles		Doubles	
M. Ott	2,876	M. Ott	1,805	M. Ott	488
B. Terry	2,193	B. Terry	1,553	B. Terry	373
M. Tiernan	1,875	M. Tiernan	1,359	T. Jackson	291
T. Jackson	1,768	L. Doyle	1,292	L. Doyle	275
L. Doyle	1,751	G. Van Haltren	1,279	G. J. Burns	267
J. Moore	1,615	T. Jackson	1,256	J. Moore	258
G. Van Haltren	1,592	J. Moore	1,225	M. Tiernan	249
W. Lockman	1,542	W. Lockman	1,175	R. Connor	240
G. J. Burns	1,541	G. J. Burns	1,158	R. Youngs	236
R. Youngs	1,491	R. Youngs	1,120	G. S. Davis	226

Triples		Home Runs		Total Bases	
M. Tiernan	159	M. Ott	511	M. Ott	5,041
R. Connor	129	B. Thomson	189	B. Terry	3,253
L. Doyle	117	W. Mays	187	M. Tiernan	2,766
B. Terry	112	J. Mize	157	T. Jackson	2,636
B. Ewing	108	B. Terry	154	L. Doyle	2,461
G. S. Davis	97	T. Jackson	135	J. Moore	2,216
R. Youngs	93	H. Thompson	129	R. Connor	2,186
G. Van Haltren	90	G. Kelly	123	W. Lockman	2,176
T. Jackson	86	W. Lockman	111	G. J. Burns	2,074
G. J. Burns	82	M. Tiernan	108	G. Van Haltren	2,051

CAREER RECORDS OF TOP
SAN FRANCISCO GIANTS HITTERS, 1958–1986*

Hitter	Games	BA	Hits	Doubles	Triples	HR	RBI	Runs	Walks	SO	SB
W. Mays	2,992	.302	3,283	523	140	660	1,903	2,062	1,463	1,526	338
O. Cepeda	2,124	.297	2,351	417	27	379	1,365	1,131	588	1,169	142
F. Alou	2,082	.286	2,101	359	49	206	852	985	423	706	107
G. Matthews	1,944	.282	1,972	315	52	231	983	1,070	921	1,092	180
T. Whitfield	732	.281	537	93	12	33	179	233	138	288	18
J. Alou	1,380	.280	1,216	170	26	32	377	448	138	267	31
J. Hart	1,125	.278	1,052	148	29	170	578	518	380	573	17
J. Clark	1,235	.275	1,213	235	35	194	705	702	535	717	62
J. Leonard	862	.273	808	127	31	81	428	379	228	628	120
W. McCovey	2,588	.270	2,211	353	46	521	1,555	1,229	1,345	1,550	26
C. Davis	725	.270	715	122	19	77	342	352	289	469	79
B. Bonds	1,849	.268	1,886	302	66	332	1,024	1,258	914	1,757	461

*Includes overall major league totals
All players listed played at least 500 games as Giants

TOP 5 SAN FRANCISCO GIANTS IN VARIOUS CATEGORIES*

1958–1986

Games		At Bats		Runs	
Player	**Total**	**Player**	**Total**	**Player**	**Total**
W. McCovey	2,248	W. Mays	7,578	W. Mays	1,480
W. Mays	2,095	W. McCovey	7,214	W. McCovey	1,113
J. Davenport	1,501	J. Davenport	4,427	B. Bonds	765
O. Cepeda	1,114	O. Cepeda	4,178	O. Cepeda	652
H. Lanier	1,101	B. Bondo	4,047	J. Clark	597

Hits		Singles		Doubles	
Player	**Total**	**Player**	**Total**	**Player**	**Total**
W. Mays	2,284	W. Mays	1,373	W. Mays	376
W. McCovey	1,974	W. McCovey	1,152	W. McCovey	308
O. Cepeda	1,286	J. Davenport	851	O. Cepeda	226
J. Davenport	1,142	O. Cepeda	812	J. Clark	197
B. Bonds	1,116	T. Fuentes	781	B. Bonds	188

Triples		Home Runs		Total Bases	
Player	**Total**	**Player**	**Total**	**Player**	**Total**
W. Mays	76	W. McCovey	468	W. Mays	4,199
B. Bonds	42	W. Mays	459	W. McCovey	3,729
L. Herndon	39	O. Cepeda	226	O. Cepeda	2,234
J. Davenport	37	B. Bonds	186	B. Bonds	1,946
T. Fuentes	33	J. Clark	163	J. Clark	1,780

Extra-Base Hits		Batting Average		Slugging Percentage	
Player	**Total**	**Player**	**Avg**	**Player**	**Pct**
W. Mays	911	O. Cepeda	.308	W. Mays	.554
W. McCovey	822	W. Mays	.301	O. Cepeda	.535
O. Cepeda	474	B. Madlock	.296	W. McCovey	.517
B. Bonds	416	G. Maddox	.292	B. Bonds	.481
J. Clark	390	T. Whitfield	.289	J. Clark	.477

*Based on at least 1,000 at bats
 for the Giants

PITCHING RECORDS

GIANT PITCHERS WHO LED THE NATIONAL LEAGUE IN VARIOUS CATEGORIES

1883–1986

Strikeouts

Year	Pitcher	Total
1888	Tim Keefe	333
1890	Amos Rusie	345
1891	Amos Rusie	337
1893	Amos Rusie	208
1894	Amos Rusie	195
1895	Amos Rusie	201
1903	Christy Mathewson	267
1904	Christy Mathewson	212
1905	Christy Mathewson	206
1907	Christy Mathewson	178
1908	Christy Mathewson	259
1910	Christy Mathewson	190
1911	Rube Marquard	237
1937	Carl Hubbell	159
1944	Bill Voiselle	161

Innings Pitched

Year	Pitcher	Total
1885	Tim Keefe	540
1893	Amos Rusie	482
1903	Christy Mathewson	434
1904	Joe McGinnity	408
1908	Christy Mathewson	391
1912	Christy Mathewson	310
1933	Carl Hubbell	309
1944	Bill Voiselle	313
1963	Juan Marichal	321
1968	Juan Marichal	326
1969	Gaylord Perry	325
1970	Gaylord Perry	329

ERA

Year	Pitcher	Total
1885	Tim Keefe	1.58
1888	Tim Keefe	1.74
1891	John Ewing	2.27
1894	Amos Rusie	2.78
1897	Amos Rusie	2.54
1904	Joe McGinnity	1.61
1905	Christy Mathewson	1.27
1908	Christy Mathewson	1.43
1909	Christy Mathewson	1.14
1911	Christy Mathewson	1.99
1912	Jeff Tesreau	1.96
1913	C. Mathewson	2.06
1922	Rosy Ryan	3.01
1929	Bill Walker	3.09
1931	Bill Walker	2.26
1933	Carl Hubbell	1.66
1934	Carl Hubbell	2.30
1936	Carl Hubbell	2.31
1949	Dave Koslo	2.50
1950	Jim Hearn	2.49
1952	Hoyt Wilhelm	2.43
1954	Johnny Antonelli	2.30
1958	Stu Miller	2.47
1959	Sam Jones	2.83
1960	Mike McCormick	2.70
1969	Juan Marichal	2.10
1983	Atlee Hammaker	2.25

Saves

Year	Pitcher	Total
1889	Mickey Welch	2
1904	Joe McGinnity	5
1905	Claude Elliott	6
1906	George Ferguson	6
1907	Joe McGinnity	4
1908	Christy Mathewson	5
1917	Slim Sallee	4
1918	Fred Anderson	3
1922	Claude Jonnard	5
1923	Claude Jonnard	5
1926	Chick Davies	6
1934	Carl Hubbell	8
1937	Cliff Melton	7
1938	Dick Coffman	12
1940	Jumbo Brown	7
1941	Jumbo Brown	8
1944	Ace Adams	13
1945	Ace Adams	15
1961	Stu Miller	17

GIANTS 20-GAME WINNERS

1883-1986

Year	Pitcher	W	L	Year	Pitcher	W	L
1883	Mickey Welch	27	21	1917	Ferdie Schupp	21	7
1887	Mickey Welch	23	15	1919	Jesse Barnes	25*	9
1888	Mickey Welch	26	19	1920	Jesse Barnes	20	15
1889	Mickey Welch	27	12		Art Nehf	21	12
	Tim Keefe	28	13		Fred Toney	21	11
1890	Amos Rusie	29	30	1921	Art Nehf	20	10
1891	John Ewing	21	8	1928	Larry Benton	25*	9
1892	Silver King	22	24		Freddy Fitzsimmons	20	9
1893	Amos Rusie	29	18	1933	Carl Hubbell	23*	12
1895	Amos Rusie	22	21	1934	Hal Schumacher	23	10
1896	Jouett Meekin	26	14		Carl Hubbell	21	12
1897	Amos Rusie	29	8	1935	Carl Hubbell	23	12
	Jouett Meekin	20	11	1936	Carl Hubbell	26*	6
1898	Cy Seymour	25	17	1937	Carl Hubbell	22*	8
	Amos Rusie	20	11		Cliff Melton	20	9
1901	Christy Mathewson	20	17	1944	Bill Voiselle	21	16
1904	Dummy Taylor	21	15	1947	Larry Jansen	21	5
1905	Joe McGinnity	21	15	1951	Larry Jansen	23*	11
	Red Ames	22	8		Sal Maglie	23*	6
1906	Joe McGinnity	27*	12	1954	Johnny Antonelli	21	7
	Christy Mathewson	22	12	1956	Johnny Antonelli	20	13
1907	Christy Mathewson	24*	13	1959	Sam Jones	21*	15
1908	Hooks Wiltse	23	14	1962	Jack Sanford	24	7
1909	Christy Mathewson	25	6	1963	Juan Marichal	25*	8
	Hooks Wiltse	20	11	1964	Juan Marichal	21	8
1910	Christy Mathewson	27*	9	1965	Juan Marichal	22	13
1911	Christy Mathewson	26	13	1966	Juan Marichal	25	6
	Rube Marquard	24	7	1967	Mike McCormick	22*	10
1912	Rube Marquard	26*	11	1968	Juan Marichal	26*	9
	Christy Mathewson	23	12	1969	Juan Marichal	21	11
1913	Rube Marquard	23	10	1970	Gaylord Perry	23*	13
	Christy Mathewson	25	11	1973	Ron Bryant	24*	12
1914	Jeff Tesreau	26	10	1986	Mike Krukow	20	9
	Christy Mathewson	24	13				

*League leader

GIANTS 30- AND 40-GAME WINNERS

1883–1986

Year	Pitchers	W	L
1884	Mickey Welch	39	21
1885	Mickey Welch	44	11
	Tim Keefe	32	13
1886	Tim Keefe	42*	20
	Mickey Welch	33	22
1887	Tim Keefe	35	19
1888	Tim Keefe	35*	12
1891	Amos Rusie	33	20
1892	Amos Rusie	32	28
1894	Amos Rusie	36*	13
	Jouett Meekin	36*	10
1903	Joe McGinnity	31*	20
	Christy Mathewson	30	13
1904	Joe McGinnity	35*	8
	Christy Mathewson	33	12
1905	Christy Mathewson	31*	8
1908	Christy Mathewson	37*	11

*League leader

GIANT PITCHERS' NO-HITTERS

1883–1986

Date	Pitcher	Score	Walks	Strikeouts	Opponent
July 31, 1891	Amos Rusie	6-0	8	4	Brooklyn
July 15, 1901	Christy Mathewson	5-0	4	4	St. Louis
June 13, 1905	Christy Mathewson	1-0	0	2	Chicago
July 4, 1908	Hooks Wiltse	1-0	0	6	Philadelphia
April 15, 1909	Red Ames	0-3 (lost)	2	9	Brooklyn
Sept. 6, 1912	Jeff Tesreau	3-0	2	2	Philadelphia
April 15, 1915	Rube Marquard	2-0	2	2	Brooklyn
May 7, 1922	Jesse Barnes	6-0	1	5	Philadelphia
May 8, 1929	Carl Hubbell	11-0	1	4	Pittsburgh
June 15, 1963	Juan Marichal	1-0	2	5	Houston
Sept. 17, 1968	Gaylord Perry	1-0	2	9	St. Louis
August 24, 1975	Ed Halicki	6-0	2	10	New York
Sept. 29, 1976	John Montefusco	9-0	1	4	Atlanta

LEADING GIANT SHUTOUT PITCHERS

1883–1986

Pitcher	Giant Shutouts	Career Shutouts
Christy Mathewson	83	83
Juan Marichal	52	52
Carl Hubbell	36	36
Hal Schumacher	29	29
Mickey Welch	28	40
Hooks Wiltse	27	27
Joe McGinnity	26	32
Tim Keefe	22	40
John Antonelli	22	26
Gaylord Perry	21	52
Rube Marquard	21	30
Freddy Fitzsimmons	20	29
Jim Barr	20	20
Mike McCormick	19	23
Red Ames	15	27
Art Nehf	14	30
Ed Halicki	13	13
Ray Sadecki	12	19
Bob Knepper	11	18
John Montefusco	11	11
Bob Bolin	10	10

MOST CONSECUTIVE
PITCHING WINS

1883–1986

Pitcher	Year	Consecutive Wins
Tim Keefe	1888	19
Rube Marquard	1912	19*
Mickey Welch	1885	17
Carl Hubbell	1936**	16
Jack Sanford	1962	16
Joe McGinnity	1904	14
Christy Mathewson	1909	13
Burleigh Grimes	1927	13
Hooks Wiltse	1904	12
Christy Mathewson	1909	11
Hal Schumacher	1935	11
Sal Maglie	1950	11
Johnny Antonelli	1954	11
Slim Sallee	1917	10
Jesse Barnes	1919	10
Clarence Mitchell	1930	10
Juan Marichal	1978	10
Juan Marichal	1966	10
Vida Blue	1978	10

*Under present scoring rules, Marquard would have been credited with twenty consecutive wins (see Day-by-Day entry for July 3, 1912).

**Hubbell won his last sixteen decisions in 1936 and his first eight decisions in 1937 for a two-season consecutive-game winning streak of twenty-four.

CAREER RECORDS OF GIANTS OVER-80-GAME WINNERS *

1883–1986

Pitcher	Wins for Giants	Games	W	L	Pct	Innings	Hits	Strikeouts	Walks	ERA
C. Mathewson	372	635	373	188	.665	4,783	4,216	2,511	846	2.13
C. Hubbell	253	535	253	154	.622	3,589	3,463	1,678	724	2.97
M. Welch	243	564	311	207	.600	4,802	4,587	1,850	1,297	2.71
J. Marichal	238	471	243	142	.628	3,506	3,081	2,303	709	2.89
A. Rusie	230	462	243	160	.603	3,770	3,384	1,957	1,716	3.07
T. Keefe	174	601	344	225	.605	5,072	4,452	2,533	1,231	2.62
F. Fitzsimmons	170	513	217	146	.598	3,224	3,335	870	846	3.51
H. Schumacher	158	391	158	120	.568	2,481	2,424	906	902	3.36
J. McGinnity	151	466	247	145	.630	3,458	3,276	1,068	812	2.64
H. Wiltse	138	357	141	90	.610	2,112	1,892	965	498	2.47
G. Perry	134	777	314	265	.542	5,352	4,938	3,534	1,379	3.09
L. Jansen	120	291	122	89	.578	1,765	1,751	842	410	3.58
J. Meekin	119	324	156	134	.538	2,603	2,831	900	1,058	4.07
J. Tesreau	118	247	118	72	.621	1,679	1,350	880	572	2.43
R. Marquard	113	536	201	177	.532	3,307	3,233	1,593	858	3.08
D. Taylor	111	274	112	106	.514	1,916	1,877	767	551	2.75
R. Ames	108	533	183	167	.523	3,192	2,893	1,702	1,034	2.63
A. Nehf	107	451	184	120	.605	2,708	2,715	844	640	3.20
M. McCormick	104	484	134	128	.511	2,381	2,281	1,321	795	3.73
S. Maglie	95	303	119	62	.657	1,723	1,591	862	562	3.15
D. Koslo	91	348	92	107	.462	1,591	1,597	606	538	3.68
J. Barr	90	446	100	112	.472	2,061	2,170	739	469	3.70
J. Sanford	89	388	137	101	.576	2,049	1,907	1,182	737	3.69
C. Melton	86	272	86	80	.518	1,454	1,446	660	431	3.42
J. Barnes	82	422	153	149	.507	2,570	2,686	653	515	3.22

GIANT CAREER RECORDS OF TOP SAN FRANCISCO GIANT WINNERS

1958-1986

Pitcher	Games	W	L	Pct	Innings	Hits	Strikeouts	ERA	Shutouts	Saves
J. Marichal	458	238	140	.630	3,443	3,081	2,281	2.84	52	2
G. Perry	367	134	109	.551	2,295	2,061	1,606	2.96	21	10
M. McCormick	357	104	94	.525	1,741	1,651	976	3.68	19	9
J. Barr	394	90	96	.484	1,800	1,863	650	3.41	20	11
J. Sanford	233	89	67	.571	1,404	1,289	781	3.62	9	4
B. Bolin	345	73	56	.566	1,282	1,088	977	3.26	10	21
G. Lavelle	647	73	60	.521	981	910	696	2.82	0	127
V. Blue	179	72	58	.554	1,132	1,030	704	3.51	7	0
J. Montefusco	185	59	62	.488	1,182	1,143	869	3.47	11	0
R. Bryant	195	57	55	.509	909	870	502	3.90	6	1
B. O'Dell	204	56	49	.533	921	912	620	3.55	7	7
E. Halicki	182	52	65	.444	1,028	968	691	3.58	13	1
M. Krukow	128	50	43	.538	823	803	605	3.70	5	1
F. Linzy	308	48	39	.552	532	510	268	2.71	0	79
S. Jones	126	47	37	.560	633	566	504	3.30	7	5
B. Knepper	136	47	50	.485	873	878	484	3.63	11	0
B. Laskey	131	41	48	.461	687	697	290	3.84	1	1
J. Antonelli	122	41	30	.577	636	569	365	3.28	5	15
G. Minton	537	44	52	.458	847	827	343	3.22	0	124
S. Miller	269	40	35	.533	681	626	446	3.07	1	46
R. Moffitt	459	35	46	.432	683	678	393	3.68	0	83
R. Herbel	240	33	29	.532	719	756	364	3.59	3	4
R. Sadecki	128	32	39	.451	685	652	517	3.52	12	0

*Pitchers with 32 or more Giants wins

11

PLAYER NICKNAMES

Abner
Chuck Hiller

Ace
Willis Hudlin

Admiral
George Schlei

Arch
Harvey Kuenn
Bob Lennon

Arlo
Chris Arnold

Available
Sheldon Jones

B.B.
Bob Brenly

Babe
Herbert Barna
Mario Picone
Norman Young

Baby Bull
Orlando Cepeda

Bad Bill
Bill Dahlen

Bad News
Odell Hale

Baldy
Dick Rudolph

Badges
Juan Berenguer

Bambi
George Bamberger

Bananas
Zeke Bonura

Bash
Pete Compton

Bear
Ron Bryant

Beauty
Dave Bancroft

Bedford Bill
Bill Rariden

Bee-Bee
Bob Bolin
Bobby Bonds

Big Bill
Willard Brown

Big Cat
Johnny Mize

Big Coop
Walker Cooper

Big Dan
Dan Brouthers

Big Dee
Daryl Spencer

Big Ed
Edward Hendricks

Big Jawn
Johnny Mize

Big Mike
Mike Sullivan

Big Money
Bobby Moore

Big Righthander
Roger Craig

Big Six
Christy Mathewson

Big Tom
Tom Gorman

Blackie
Otis Carter
Bill Clarkson
Alvin Dark
Bill Lohrman
Gus Mancuso
Leo Mangum

Blondy
John Ryan

Blood
Joel Bloodgood

Bobo
Louis Newsom

Boileryard
William Clarke

Bonehead
Fred Merkle

Bones
Johnnie LeMaster

Boot
Marc Hill

Boots
George Grantham

Boy Bomber
Mel Ott

Bosco
Colonel Snover

Brat
Eddie Stanky

Brickyard
William Kennedy

Broadway Aleck
Alexander Smith

Buck
James Becannon
William Ewing
Charles Herzog
Baxter Jordan
Willie Mays

Bud
William Byerly
William Heine

Buddy
Jack Brewer
Arthur Crump
John Kerr

Buffy
Mike LaCoss

Bugs
Arthur Raymond

Bull
Louis Durham
George Uhle

Bullet Joe
Joe Bush

Bump
Irving Hadley

Bumpus
Charles Jones

Bunker
Carmen Hill

Bunny
Bunn Hearn

Bunt
Charlie Frisbee

Buster
Frank Burrell
Jim Maynard

Butch
Walter Henline
Clarence Metzger

Cactus
Fred Johnson

California
Willard Brown

Candyman
Candy Maldonado

Cannonball
Ed Crane
Ledell Titcomb

Cap
Charles Peterson

Capone
Al Holland

Carney
Cornelius Flynn

Casey
Charles Stengel

Cash
Bill Taylor

Cat Man
Tom O'Malley

Cha-Cha
Orlando Cepeda

Champ
John Summers

Chauncey
Jean Dubec
Bill Stuart

Cheeks
Ron Herbel

Chick
Tony Cuccinello
Lloyd Davies
Charles Fullis
Walter Hartley

Chico
Jose Morales

Chief
Virgil Cheeves
John Meyers
Euel Moore

Chili
Charles Davis
Harvey Kuenn

Choo-Choo
Jesus Alou

Chuck
Charles Diering

Coaster Joe
Joe Connolly

Coca
Cesar Gutierrez

Colonel
Roy Beecher
Bill Terry

Columbia George
George Smith

Coochy
Tony Cuccinello

Country
Frank Linzy

Cowboy
Ray Harrell

Cozy
Patrick Dolan

Crab
Jesse Burkett

Crabapple Comet
Johnny Rucker

Cracker
Jim Hamby
Ray Schalk

Crane
Fred Reberger

Crazy
Frederick Schmidt

Cricket
Bill Rigney

Crip
Lou Polli

Crispy
Don Carrithers

Crow
Jim Ray Hart

Cy
Sutherland Bowen
James Seymour

Dad
William Clarke
Arthur Clarkson

Daddy Wags
Leon Wagner

Daffy
Paul Dean

Dandelion
Fred Pfeffer

Dasher
John Troy

Dauntless Dan
Danny Gardelia

Deacon
Bill McKechnie

Deerfoot
Tom Needham

Desperate
Des Beatty

Digger
Billy O'Dell

Dinty
Dennis Gearin

Dirty Al
Alan Gallagher

Dirty Jack
Jack Doyle

Dixie Thrush
Sammy Strang

Doc
James Crandall
Edward Farrell
Edward Marshall
William Marshall
Theodore Sechrist

Dominican Dandy
Juan Marichal

Doody
Darrell Evans

Doughnut Bill
Bill Carrick

Downtown
Chris Brown
Ollie Brown

Ducky
James Holmes
Joe Medwick
Dick Schofield

Dude
Thomas Esterbrook

Duke
Charles Farrell
Albert Kelleher
Edwin Snider

Duke of Tralee
Roger Bresnahan

Dummy
John Deegan
George Leitner
Luther Taylor

Dusty
Jim Rhodes

Dutch
Hal Bamberger
Fred Hartman
Frank Henry
Frank Hiller
Art Wilson

Eagle Eye
Jake Bentley

Fat Freddy
Freddy Fitzsimmons

Fatso
Bruce Sloan

Fiddler Bill
Bill McGee

Firpo
Fred Marberry

Fish Hook
Allyn Stout

Flaco
Jose Morales

Flaky
Jackie Brandt

Flip
Steve Filipowicz
Al Rosen

Floppy
Clint Hartung

Flying Scot
Bobby Thomson

Foghorn
George Myatt

Footie
Walter Ockey

Fordham Flash
Frank Frisch

Frenchie
Jim Lefebvre

Fresh
Arlie Latham

Fuzz
Albert White

Gabby
Frank Gabler
Leo Hartnett
Glen Stewart

Gause Ghost
Joe Moore

Glass Arm
Eddie Brown

Gob
Garland Buckeye

Goldie
Joseph Rapp

Groucho
Scott Garrelts

Gumbo
Harry Gumbert

Gummy
Joe Wall

Gracie
Grayson Pearce

Gyp
Manuel Salvo

Hack
Jeff Leonard
Lewis Wilson

Hal
Hugh Luby

Ham
Abraham Wade

Hammer
Atlee Hammaker

Handsome Hugh
Hugh McQuillan

Hank
Henry Leiber
William Ritter
Henry Thompson

Hans
Johnny Wittig

Harry the Horse
Harry Danning

Harvard Eddie
Eddie Grant

Hatch
Tom Haller

Heinie
Henry Groh
Clarence Mueller
George Smith
Henry Stafford
Charles Wagner
Henry Zimmerman

Hi
Herman Bell

Hickory
Walt Dickson
Elmer Johnson

Highpockets
George Kelly

Hodge
Joe Berry

Hoghead
Jack Sanford

Ho-Ho
Ed Halicki

Hondo
Clint Hartung

Honest Jack
Jack Boyle

Honker
Hank Sauer

Honus
Hans Lobert

Hooks
Clarence Iott
George Wiltse

Hoot
Walter Evers

Hopalong
Bill Howerton

Horse
John Orsino

Hum Babe
Brad Gulden

Hum Baby
Roger Craig

Hy
Harold Vanderberg

Irish
Charlie Fox
Emil Meusel

Iron Hands
Chuck Hiller

Iron Man
Joe McGinnity
Ray Mueller
Ray Starr

Jabbo
Ray Jablonski

Jackrabbit
Jack Gilbert

Jake
Merwin Jacobson

Jasper
Harry Davis

Jeff
Charles Tesreau

Jigger
Arnold Statz

Jocko
John Menefee
John Milligan

JoJo
Joe Moore

Judge
Tom Grubbs

Jumbo
Walter Brown

Junior
Lonny Frey
Gene Thompson

Kid
Wilfred Carsey
William Gleason

Kiddo
George Davis

King
Loren Bader
Michael Kelly
Fred Lear

King Carl
Carl Hubbell

King Kong
Dave Kingman

Kip
Albert Selbach

Knobby
Garland Lawing

Knucksie
Charlie Williams

Kruk
Mike Krukow

Kutch
Randy Kutchner

Laughing Larry
Larry Doyle

Lefty
Steve Carlton
Ken Chase
Jim Faulkner
Montia Kennedy
Thornton Lee
Howard Merritt
Frank O'Doul
Ewald Pyle
Al Stanek
Tom Sunkel

Lindy
Fred Lindstrom

Little Napoleon
John McGraw

Lollypop
Wade Killefer

Louie
Luis Quinones

Lucky
Jack Lohrke

Luke
Bobby Etheridge
Ray Lucas

Lumber
Joe Price

M.D.
Mark Davis

Mad Dog
Bill Madlock

Magoo
Gaylord Perry

Mandrake the Magician
Don Mueller

Manito
Juan Marichal

Mario
Mike Aldrete

Mashi
Masonari Murakami

Master Melvin
Mel Ott

Maxie
Hal Lanier

Max Headroom
Jeff Robinson

Meal Ticket
Carl Hubbell

Memphis Bill
Bill Terry

Mercury
George Myatt

Mickey
William Devine
Tullis McGowan
Manny Mota
Phil Weintraub
Michael Welch
Nicholas Witek

Moe
Morrie Arnovich
Moses Solomon

Mole Man
Randy Moffitt

Monte
John Montgomery Ward

Moon
George Gibson

Moonie
Greg Minton

Moonlight
Archibald Graham

"Peanut" Jim Davenport

Moon Man
Dave Kingman
Greg Minton

Moose
Harry McCormick

Moses
Joe Shipley

Mountain Music
Cliff Melton

Mudcat
Mark Grant

Muff
Dilly Muffett

Muggsy
John McGraw
Eddie Stanky

Mul
Howard Holland

Mule
Dick Dietz
John Watson

Muscles
Joe Medwick

Nasty
Phil Nastu

Nick
Steve Nicosia

Ninety-Six
Bill Voiselle

Offa
Theophilus Neal

Oil
Earl Smith

Old Stubblebeard
Burleigh Grimes

Old True Blue
Hardy Richardson

Orator Jim
Jim O'Rourke

Oyster
Thomas Burns

Pancho
Frank Snyder

Pappy
Bill Henry

Pat
Thomas Deasley
William Paterson

Peaceful Valley
Roger Denzer

Peach
Chauncey Fisher

Peanut
Jim Davenport

Pebbly John
Jack Glasscock

Pecks
George Daly

Peekskill Pete
Pete Cregan

Pee Wee
Nate Oliver

Pep
Paul Florence
Ross Youngs

Pepper
Royal Clark

Piano Legs
George Gore
Charles Hickman

Pink
Emerson Hawley

Pip
Horace Koehler

Poison
Mike Ivie

Pol
William Perritt

Pooch
Bill Fahey

Pop
Clarence Foster
Roy Joiner
William Schriver

Poosh 'Em Up
Tony Lazzeri

Preacher
Lindy McDaniel

Prince Hal
Hal Schumacher

Pudge
Gary Lavelle

Pug
Francis Griffin

Punkinhead
Len Gabrielson

Rabbi of Swat
Moses Solomon

Rabbit
Jim Miller

Rags
Ron Roenicke

Rajah
Rogers Hornsby

Rattlesnake
Tom Baker

Red
Leon Ames
Cecil Causey
John Davis
Francis Donahue
Charles Dooin
Francis Hardy
Wade Killefer
Ralph Kress
Charles Lucas
Japhet Lynn
John Murray
Albert Schoendienst
Patrick Shea
James Smith
Stephen Tramback
Thadford Treadway
John Waller
Samuel Webb
Al Worthington

Reddy
Oscar Foster
George McMillan

Red-Eye
Harvey Kuenn

Redford Bill
Bill Rariden

Rifle Jim
Jim Middleton

Roadblock
Sherman Jones

Rob
Robby Thompson

Rock
Rob Andrews

Rocky
Bobby Rhawn

Rosy
Wilfred Ryan

Rowdy Richard
Dick Bartell

Roxy
Roscoe Miller

R.T.
Robby Thompson

Rubberlegs
Roscoe Miller

Rube
John Benton
Reuben Fischer
Richard Marquard
Alexander Schauer

Sad Sam
Sam Jones

Sailor
Ralph Stroud

Sambo
Sam Leslie

Sandow
Sam Mertes

Sandy
Sandalio Consuegra
Tobias Griffin
Charles Piez

Sarge
Hank Gowdy

Say Hey
Willie Mays

Schnozz
Ernie Lombardi

Schoolboy
Waite Hoyt

Scoops
Jimmy Cooney

Scottie
Mike Garrelts
Elbert Slayback

Scow
Fay Thomas

Scrappy
Bill Joyce

Seldom Sam
Sam McDowell

Shad
John Barry

Shag
Leon Chagnon

Shakes
Walter Huntzinger

Shanty
Frank Hogan

Sheriff
Jim Constable
Jim Jones

Shorty
William Fuller
John Howe

Shotgun
Billy Gardner

Shucks
Hub Pruett

Shufflin' Phil
Phil Douglas

Silent Mike
Mike Tiernan

Silver
Charles King
Elmer Zacher

Silver Fox
Duke Snider

Sir Timothy
Tim Keefe

Skeeter
Frank Scalzi

Skip
Philip James
Lee Pitlock

Skitch
Ken Henderson

Slats
Ira Davis

Sleuth
Tom Fleming

Slick
Clydell Castleman
Grover Hartley

Slim
Bill Emmerich
Harry Sallee

Smiling Al
Al Maul

Smoky Joe
Joe Martin

Snake
Ray Sadecki

Sniffy
Ron Herbel

Snooker
Morrie Arnovich

Snooze
Ted Goulait

Snow
Fred Snodgrass

Specs
Carmen Hill
Bill Rigney

Spider
John Jorgensen

Spike
William Shannon

Spitball
Fred Anderson

Spook
Bob Speake

Steamboat
Clem Dreisewerd

Stonewall
Travis Jackson

Stormy
Roy Weatherly

Stretch
Willie McCovey

Stud
George Myatt

Stuffy
Frank Butler

Stump
George Weidman

Stumpy
Mel Ott

Sub
Carl Mayo

Sudden Sam
Sam McDowell

Suitcase
Bob Seeds

Sunny Jim
Jim Mallory

Swede
Andy Hansen

Sweetback
Tito Fuentes

Tacks
Clifford Latimer

Taco
Manny Perez

Tarzan
Roy Parmelee

Tex
Ernest Jeanes
John Kraus
Jesse Winters

The Arm
Tom Hafey

The Barber
Sal Maglie

The Blazer
Don Blasingame

The Bulldog
John Cumberland

The Count
John Montefusco

The Hoosier
Amos Rusie

The Old Perfessor
Casey Stengel

The Ripper
Jack Clark

Thin Man
Joe Moore

Thrill
Will Clark

Tillie
Arthur Shafer

Tiny
James Chaplin

Tip
James O'Neill
Johnny Tobin

Tito
Rigoberto Fuentes

Tommy
Fresco Thompson

Tookie
Harold Gilbert

Toothpick Sam
Sam Jones

Tornado Jake
Jacob Weimer

Tree Top
Ray Sadecki

Trout
Roger Metzger

Tuna
Dave Heaverlo

Tuny
Hub Andrews

Turkey Mike
Mike Donlin

Twig
Wayne Terwilliger

Ubbo Ubbo
Joe Hornung

Uncle Tom
Tom Bannon

Union Man
Walter Holke

Vee
Vida Blue

Victory
Charlie Faust

Watty
William Clark

Wee Willie
Willie Clark
Willie Keeler
Willie Mills

Wheat
Terry Whitfield

Whitey
Alex Konikowski
Carroll Lockman
Ken Miller
Burgess Whitehead

Whiz
Johnny Gee

Wild Bill
Bill Connolly
Bill Hunnefield

Win
George Mercer

Windy
John McCall

Wolfie
Jim Wohlford

Woody
Virgil Abernathy
Mike Woodward

Words
Ed Bailey

Zeke
Henry Bonura
George Wrigley

12

ALL-TIME GIANTS PLAYING ROSTER

1883-1986

NONPITCHERS

Player	Years with Giants	Position	Born	Died
Glenn Adams	1975-76	OF	10/4/47	
Ricky Adams	1985	3B/SS/3B	1/21/59	
Eddie Ainsmith	1924	C	2/4/90	9/6/81
Mike Aldrete	1986	1B/OF	1/29/61	
Gary Alexander	1975-77	C	3/27/53	
Ethan Allen	1930-32	OF	1/1/04	
Felipe Alou	1958-63	OF	5/12/35	
Jesus Alou	1963-68	OF	3/24/42	
Matty Alou	1960-65	OF	12/22/38	
Joe Amalfitano	1954-56	2B	1/23/34	
Rob Andrews	1977-79	2B	12/11/52	
Jack Aragon	1941	—	11/20/15	
Chris Arnold	1971-76	IF	11/6/47	
Morris Arnovich	1941	OF	11/20/10	7/20/59
Charley Babb	1903	SS	2/20/73	3/20/54
Charlie Babington	1915	OF	5/4/95	3/22/57
Ed Bailey	1961-63,65	C	4/15/31	
Al Baird	1917	IF	6/2/95	11/27/76
Doug Baird	1920	3B	9/27/91	6/13/67
Dusty Baker	1984	OF	6/15/49	
Howard Baker	1915	3B	3/1/88	1/16/64
Hal Bamberger	1948	OF	10/29/24	
Dave Bancroft	1920-23,30	SS	4/20/91	10/9/72
Tom Bannon	1895-96	OF	5/8/69	1/26/50
Herbert Barna	1943-41	OF	3/2/15	5/18/72

Player	Years with Giants	Position	Born	Died
Jose Barrios	1982-83	1B	6/26/57	
John Barry	1908	OF/IF	9/28/76	11/27/36
Dick Bartell	1935-38,41-43 1946	SS/3B	11/27/07	
Ed Barton	1965-69	C	7/30/41	
Charley Bassett	1890-92	IF	2/9/63	5/28/42
Larry Battam	1895	3B	5/1/78	1/27/38
Joe Bean	1902	SS	3/18/74	2/15/61
Des Beatty	1914	IF	4/7/93	10/4/69
Beals Becker	1910-12	OF	7/5/86	8/16/43
Marty Becker	1915	OF	12/25/89	9/25/57
Jake Beckley	1896-97	1B	8/4/67	6/25/18
Gene Begley	1886	C/OF	1863	N/A
Wally Berger	1937-38	OF	10/10/05	
Dave Bergman	1981-83	1B/OF	6/6/53	
Curt Bernard	1900-01	OF	2/18/79	4/10/55
Ray Berres	1912-15	C	8/21/08	
Joe Berry	1921-22	2B	12/21/94	4/29/76
Dick Bertell	1965	C	11/21/35	
Bob Bescher	1914	OF	2/25/84	11/29/42
Rae Blaemire	1941	C	2/8/11	
Damasco Blanco	1972-74	IF	12/11/41	
Don Blasingame	1960-61	2B	3/16/32	
Buddy Blattner	1946-48	IF	2/8/20	
Marv Blaylock	1950	1B	9/30/29	
John Boccabella	1974	C	6/29/41	
Carl Boles	1962	OF	10/31/34	
Bobby Bonds	1968-74	OF	3/15/46	
Zeke Bonura	1939	1B	9/20/08	
Ike Boone	1922	OF	2/17/97	8/1/58
Chick Bowen	1919	OF	7/26/97	8/9/48
Frank Bowerman	1900-07	C	12/5/68	11/30/48
Ernie Bowman	1961-63	IF	7/28/37	
Jack Boyle	1892	C,IF	3/22/66	1/7/13
Jim Boyle	1926	C	1/19/04	12/24/58
Vic Bradford	1943	OF	3/5/15	
Dave Brain	1908	IF	1/24/79	5/25/59
Fred Brainard	1914-16	IF	1/17/92	4/17/59
Jackie Brandt	1956,58-59	OF	4/28/34	
Bob Brenly	1981-86	C/1B/3B/OF	2/25/54	
Roger Bresnahan	1902-08	C/OF	6/11/79	12/4/44
Ed Bressoud	1956-57	SS	5/2/32	
Al Bridwell	1908-11	IF	1/4/84	6/24/69
Steve Brodie	1902	OF	9/11/68	10/30/35
Dan Brouthers	1904	1B	5/8/58	8/2/32
Chris Brown	1984-86	3B/SS	8/15/61	
Eddie Brown	1920-21	IF/OF	7/17/91	9/30/56
Jake Brown	1975	OF	3/22/46	
Ollie Brown	1965-68	OF	2/11/44	
Willard Brown	1887-89	C/1B	1866	12/20/97
George Browne	1902-07	OF	1/12/76	12/9/20
Dick Buckley	1890-91	C	9/21/58	12/12/29
Charlie Buelow	1901	IF	1/12/77	5/4/51

Player	Years with Giants	Position	Born	Died
Bob Burda	1965-66,69-70	1B/OF	7/16/38	
Eddie Burke	1892-95	OF	10/6/66	11/26/07
Frank Burke	1906	OF	2/16/80	9/17/46
John Burke	1902	OF/IF	1/2/77	8/4/50
Jesse Burkett	1890	OF	12/4/68	5/27/53
George Burns	1911-21	OF	11/24/89	8/15/66
Thomas Burns	1895	OF/IF	9/6/62	11/16/28
Frank Burrell	1891	C	12/8/66	5/8/62
Frank Butler	1895	OF	7/18/60	7/10/45
Enos Cabell	1981	3B/IF/OF	10/8/49	
Sam Calderone	1950	C	2/6/26	
Jose Cardenal	1963-64	OF	10/7/43	
Otis Carter	1925-26	OF	9/30/02	9/8/76
Dennis Casey	1887	OF	3/30/58	1/19/09
Ed Caskins	1883-84,86	IF	12/30/51	N/A
Foster Castleman	1954-57	IF	1/1/31	
Orlando Cepeda	1958-66	1B	9/17/37	
Hal Chase	1919	1B	2/13/83	5/18/47
Lou Chiozza	1937-39	IF/OF	5/11/10	2/28/71
Bill Cissell	1938	IF	1/3/04	3/15/49
John Clapp	1883	C/OF/IF	7/17/51	12/17/04
Archie Clark	1890-91	C/OF/IF	5/6/65	11/14/49
Jack Clark	1975-84	OF	11/10/55	
Royal Clark	1902	OF	5/11/74	11/1/25
Will Clark	1986	1B	3/13/64	
Willie Clark	1895-97	1B	8/16/72	11/13/32
William Clarke	1905	C	10/18/68	7/29/59
Elmer Cleveland	1888	3B	1862	10/8/13
Ty Cline	1967-68	OF	6/15/39	
Gil Coan	1955-56	OF	5/18/22	
Andy Cohen	1926,28-29	2B	10/25/04	
Jimmy Coker	1963	C	3/28/36	
Pete Compton	1918	OF	9/28/89	3/15/78
Frank Connaughton	1896	IF/OF	1/1/69	12/2/42
Joe Connell	1926	PH	1/16/02	9/21/77
Joe Connolly	1921	OF	6/4/96	3/30/60
Roger Connor	1883-89,91,93-94	1B	7/1/57	1/4/31
Jack Conway	1948	IF	7/30/19	
Jimmy Cooney	1919	SS	8/24/94	
Claude Cooper	1913	OF	4/1/93	1/21/78
Walker Cooper	1946-49	C	1/8/15	
Tommy Corcoran	1907	SS	1/4/69	6/25/60
Peter Cote	1926	PH	8/30/02	
Dick Cramer	1883	OF	N/A	8/12/85
Del Crandall	1964	C	3/5/30	
Sam Crane	1890	IF	1/2/54	6/26/25
Pat Crawford	1929-30	IF	1/28/02	
Pete Cregan	1899	OF	4/13/75	5/18/45
Hughie Critz	1930-35	2B	9/17/00	1/10/80
Arthur Crump	1924	OF	11/29/01	9/7/76
Hector Cruz	1978	OF/3B	4/2/53	
Al Cuccinello	1935	2B	11/26/14	
Tony Cuccinello	1940	IF	11/8/07	

Player	Years with Giants	Position	Born	Died
Dick Culler	1949	IF	1/25/15	6/16/64
Jack Cummings	1926-29	C	4/1/04	10/5/62
Bill Cunningham	1921-23	OF	7/30/95	9/26/53
Harry Curtis	1907	C	2/19/83	8/1/51
Bill Dahlen	1904-07	SS	1/5/70	12/5/50
Ed Daily	1890	OF/P	9/7/62	10/21/91
Harry Danning	1932-42	C	9/6/11	
Alvin Dark	1950-56	SS	1/7/22	
Jim Davenport	1958-70	3B	8/17/33	
Chili Davis	1981-86	OF	1/17/60	
George Davis	1893-1901,03	IF/OF	8/23/70	10/17/40
George Davis	1933,35-37	OF	2/12/02	2/4/83
Harry Davis	1895-96	1B	7/10/73	8/11/47
Ira Davis	1800	IF	7/8/70	12/21/43
John Davis	1041	?B	7/15/16	
Thomas Deauley	1885-87	C	11/17/57	4/1/43
Rob Deer	1984-85	OF	9/29/60	
Bill DeKoning	1945	C	12/19/19	7/26/79
Jim Delehanty	1902	IF/OF	6/20/79	10/17/53
Frank Demaree	1939-41	OF	6/10/10	8/30/58
Jerry Denny	1890-91	3B	3/16/59	8/16/27
William Devine	1925	C	5/9/92	10/1/37
Art Devlin	1904-11	3B	10/16/79	9/18/48
Josh Devore	1908-13	OF	11/13/87	10/5/54
Al DeVormer	1927	C	8/19/91	8/29/66
John Dickshot	1939	OF	1/24/10	
Charles Diering	1952	OF	2/5/23	
Dick Dietz	1966-71	C	9/18/41	
Vince DiMaggio	1946	OF	9/6/12	10/3/86
Albert Dolan	1922	OF	12/23/89	12/10/58
Jim Donely	1897	3B	7/19/65	3/5/15
Mike Donlin	1904-06,08,11	OF	5/30/78	9/24/33
Charles Dooin	1915-16	C	6/12/79	5/14/52
Mickey Doolan	1916	SS	5/7/80	11/1/51
Mike Dorgan	1883-87	OF	10/2/53	4/26/09
Jack Doyle	1892-95,98-1900,02	utility	10/25/69	12/31/58
Larry Doyle	1907-16,18-20	2B	7/31/86	3/1/74
Chuck Dressen	1933	3B	9/20/98	8/10/66
Dan Driessen	1985-86	1B	7/29/51	
Frank Duffy	1971	SS	10/14/46	
Jim Dwyer	1978	OF/1B	1/3/50	
Ben Dyer	1914-15	IF	2/13/93	8/7/59
Bob Elliott	1952	3B/OF	11/26/16	5/4/66
Randy Elliott	1977	OF	6/5/51	
Charlie English	1936	IF	4/8/10	
Gil English	1931-32	IF	7/2/09	
Thomas Esterbrook	1885-86,90	utility	6/20/60	4/30/01
Bobby Etheridge	1967	3B	11/25/43	
Darrell Evans	1976-83	3B/IB/OF	5/26/47	
Steve Evans	1908	OF	2/17/85	12/28/43
Walter Evers	1954	OF	2/8/21	
Joe Evers	1913	—	9/10/91	1/4/49
William Ewing	1883-89,91-92	C/IF/OF	10/17/59	10/20/06

Player	Years with Giants	Position	Born	Died
Bob Farley	1961	IB/OF	11/15/37	
Charles Farrell	1894-96	C/utility	8/31/66	2/15/25
Edward Farrell	1925-27,29	IF	12/26/01	12/20/66
Steve Filipowicz	1944-45	C	6/28/21	2/21/75
Jim Finigan	1958	IF	8/19/28	5/16/81
Bill Finley	1886	OF/C	10/4/63	10/6/12
Tom Fleming	1899	OF	11/20/73	12/26/57
Art Fletcher	1909-20	SS	1/5/85	2/6/50
Paul Florence	1926	C	4/22/00	5/28/86
Ray Foley	1928	PH	6/23/06	3/22/80
Tim Foli	1977	SS	12/8/50	
Clarence Foster	1898-1900	OF	4/8/78	4/16/44
Elmer Foster	1888-89	OF	8/15/61	7/22/46
George Foster	1969-71	OF	12/1/49	
Oscar Foster	1896	PH	1867	12/19/08
Charlie Fox	1942	C	10/7/21	
Herman Franks	1949	C	1/4/14	
Lonny Frey	1948	IF	8/23/10	
Charlie Frisbee	1900	OF	2/2/74	11/7/54
Frankie Frisch	1919-26	IF	9/9/98	3/12/73
Rigoberto Fuentes	1965-67,69-74	2B/IF	1/4/44	
William Fuller	1892-96	SS	10/10/67	4/11/04
Charles Fullis	1928-32	OF	2/27/04	3/28/46
Len Gabrielson	1965-66	OF/1B	2/14/40	
Augie Galan	1949	OF	5/25/12	
Alan Gallagher	1970-73	3B	10/19/45	
John Ganzel	1901	1B	4/7/75	1/14/59
Joe Garagiola	1954	C	2/12/26	
Al Gardella	1945	1B/OF	1/11/18	
Danny Gardella	1944-45	OF	2/26/20	
Art Gardner	1978	OF	9/21/52	
Billy Gardner	1954-55	IF	7/19/27	
Gil Garrido	1964	IF	6/26/41	
Alex Gaston	1920-23	C	3/12/93	2/8/76
Lloyd Gearhart	1947	OF	8/10/23	
Harvey Gentry	1954	PH	5/27/26	
Joe Gerhardt	1885-87	2B/IF	2/14/55	3/11/22
George Gibson	1917-18	C	7/22/80	1/25/67
Russ Gibson	1970-72	C	5/6/39	
Billy Gilbert	1903-06	2B	6/21/76	8/8/27
Harold Gilbert	1950,53	1B	4/4/29	6/23/67
Jack Gilbert	1898	OF	9/14/75	7/7/41
Pete Gillespie	1883-87	OF	11/30/51	5/5/10
Jim Gladd	1946	C	10/2/22	11/8/77
Dan Gladden	1983-86	OF	7/7/57	
Jack Glasscock	1890-91	SS	7/22/59	2/24/47
William Gleason	1896-1900	2B/P/utility	10/26/66	1/2/33
Ed Glenn	1898	OF	9/19/60	2/10/92
Alban Glossop	1939-40	IF	7/23/12	
Randy Gomez	1984	C	2/4/58	
Mike Gonzalez	1919-21	C	9/24/90	2/19/77
Ed Goodson	1970-75	1B/IF	1/25/48	
Sid Gordon	1941-43,46-49,55	OF/3B	8/13/17	6/17/75

Player	Years with Giants	Position	Born	Died
George Gore	1887-89,91-92	OF	5/3/52	9/16/33
Hank Gowdy	1910-11,23-25	C	8/24/89	8/1/66
Mike Grady	1898-1900	C/utility	12/23/69	12/3/43
Archibald Graham	1905	OF	11/9/79	8/25/65
Jack Graham	1946	1B/OF	12/24/16	
Eddie Grant	1913-15	IF	5/21/83	10/5/18
George Grantham	1934	utility	5/20/00	3/16/54
Mickey Grasso	1946	C	5/10/20	10/15/73
David Green	1985	1B/OF	12/4/60	
Francis Griffin	1920	1B/OF	4/24/96	10/12/51
Tobias Griffin	1884	OF	7/19/58	6/5/26
Roy Grimes	1920	2B	9/11/93	9/13/54
Dick Groat	1967	SS	11/4/30	
Henry Groh	1912-13,22-26	3B/2B	9/18/89	8/22/68
Brad Guldon	1986	O	6/10/56	
Oscar Gutierrez	1967	SS	1/26/43	
Bert Haas	1949	1B/3B/OF	2/8/14	
Bill Haeffner	1928	C	7/18/94	1/27/82
Tom Hafey	1939	3B	7/12/13	
Odell Hale	1941	IF	8/10/08	6/9/80
Bob Hall	1905	OF/IF	12/20/78	12/1/50
Tom Haller	1961-67	C	6/23/37	
Jim Hamby	1926-27	C	7/29/00	
Frank Hankinson	1883-84	3B/OF/IF	1854	4/5/11
Jack Hannifan	1906-08	IF	2/25/83	10/27/45
Scott Hardesty	1899	SS	1/26/70	10/29/44
George Harper	1927-28	OF	6/24/92	8/18/78
John Harrell	1969	C	11/27/47	
Gail Harris	1955-57	1B	10/15/31	
Vic Harris	1977-78	IF/OF	3/27/50	
Jim Hart	1963-73	3B/OF	10/30/41	
Grover Hartley	1911-13,24-26	C	7/2/88	10/19/64
Walter Hartley	1902	OF	8/22/80	7/18/48
Fred Hartman	1898-99	3B	4/25/68	11/11/38
Leo Hartnett	1941	C	12/20/00	12/20/72
Mickey Haslin	1937-38	IF	10/31/10	
Gil Hatfield	1887-89	IF	1/27/55	5/27/21
George Hausmann	1944-45,49	2B	2/11/16	
Ray Hayworth	1939	C	1/29/04	
Fran Healy	1971-72	C	9/6/46	
Francis Healy	1930-32	C	6/29/10	
Jim Hegan	1959	C	8/3/20	6/17/84
William Heine	1921	2B	9/22/00	9/2/76
Tom Heintzelman	1977-78	IF	11/3/46	
Bob Heise	1970-71	IF	5/12/47	
Ed Hemingway	1917	3B	5/8/93	7/5/69
Ken Henderson	1965-72	OF	6/15/46	
Jack Hendricks	1902	OF	4/9/75	5/13/43
Walter Henline	1921	C	12/20/94	10/9/57
John Henry	1890	OF	9/2/64	6/11/39
Larry Herndon	1976-81	OF	11/3/53	
Charles Herzog	1908-09,11-13,16-17	IF	7/9/85	9/4/53
Jack Hiatt	1965-69	C/1B	7/27/42	

Player	Years with Giants	Position	Born	Died
Charles Hickman	1900-01	1B/OF	3/4/76	4/19/34
Mahlon Higbee	1922	OF	8/16/01	4/7/68
Marc Hill	1975-78	C	2/18/52	
Chuck Hiller	1961-65	2B	10/1/35	
Bobby Hofman	1949,52-57	IF/C	10/5/25	
James Hogan	1928-32	C	3/21/06	4/7/67
Walter Holke	1914,16-18	1B	12/25/92	10/12/54
James Holmes	1897	OF	1/28/69	8/6/32
Rogers Hornsby	1927	2B	4/27/96	1/5/63
Joe Hornung	1890	OF	6/12/57	10/30/31
Jim Howarth	1971-74	OF	3/7/47	
John Howe	1890	2B	N/A	N/A
Bill Howerton	1952	OF	12/12/21	
Johnny Hudson	1945	IF	6/30/12	11/7/70
John Humphries	1883-84	C/OF	11/15/61	11/29/33
Randy Hundley	1964-65	C	6/1/42	
Bill Hunnefield	1931	IF	1/5/99	8/28/76
Ron Hunt	1968-70	IF	2/23/41	
Herb Hunter	1916	IF/OF	12/25/95	7/25/70
Monte Irvin	1949-55	OF/1B	2/25/19	
Mike Ivie	1978-81	1B/3B	8/8/52	
Ray Jablonski	1957-58	3B	12/17/26	
Jim Jackson	1902	OF	11/28/77	10/8/55
Travis Jackson	1922-36	SS/3B	11/2/03	
Mervin Jacobson	1915	OF	3/7/94	1/13/78
Art Jahn	1928	OF	12/2/97	1/9/48
Byrnie James	1933	IF	9/2/05	
Philip James	1977-78	1B	10/21/49	
Ernest Jeanes	1927	OF	12/19/00	4/5/73
Elmer Johnson	1914	C	6/12/84	10/31/66
Frank Johnson	1966-71	OF/IF	7/22/42	
Wallace Johnson	1983	2B	12/25/56	
Jimmy Johnston	1926	3B/OF	12/10/89	2/14/67
Chris Jones	1986	OF	7/13/57	
Jim Jones	1901-02	OF	12/25/78	5/6/53
Baxter Jordan	1927	1B	1/16/07	
John Jorgensen	1950-51	3B	11/3/19	
Von Joshua	1975-76	OF	5/1/48	
Bill Joyce	1896-98	3B/IF	9/21/65	5/8/41
Bill Jurges	1939-45	SS	5/9/08	
Alex Kampouris	1938-39	2B	11/13/12	
Ray Katt	1952-57	C	5/9/27	
Benny Kauff	1916-20	OF	1/5/90	11/17/61
Bob Kearney	1979	C	10/3/56	
Willie Keeler	1892-93,1910	OF	3/3/72	1/1/23
Albert Kelleher	1916	C	9/30/93	9/28/47
George Kelly	1915-17,19-26	1B/2B/OF	9/10/95	10/13/84
Michael Kelly	1893	OF/C/utility	12/30/57	11/8/94
John Kerr	1943-49	SS	11/6/22	
Pete Kilduff	1917	2B/IF	4/4/93	2/14/30
Wade Killefer	1916	OF/utility	4/13/84	9/4/58
Jim King	1958	OF	8/27/32	
Lee King	1919-22	OF	12/26/92	9/16/67

Player	Years with Giants	Position	Born	Died
Dave Kingman	1971-74	OF/1B	12/21/48	
Bob Kinsella	1919-20	OF	1/5/99	12/30/51
LaRue Kirby	1912	OF	12/30/89	6/10/61
Jay Kirke	1918	OF/IF	6/16/88	8/31/68
Willie Kirkland	1958-60	OF	2/17/34	
Joe Klinger	1927	C/1B	8/20/02	7/31/60
Clyde Kluttz	1945-46	C	12/12/17	5/12/79
Jim Knowles	1892	IF	1859	Feb. 1912
Brad Kocher	1915-16	C	1/16/88	2/13/65
Horace Koehler	1925	OF	1/16/02	
Len Koenecke	1932	OF	1/18/06	9/17/35
Mark Koenig	1935-36	IF	7/19/02	
Wally Kopf	1921	3B	7/10/99	4/30/79
Ralph Kress	1946	utility	1/2/07	11/29/62
Ernie Krueger	1917	C	12/27/00	4/22/76
Harvey Kuenn	1961-66	OF/SS	12/4/30	
Duane Kuiper	1982-85	2B	6/19/50	
Randy Kutcher	1986	OF/1B	4/20/60	
Joe Lafata	1947-49	1B/OF	8/3/21	
Dick Lajeski	1946	2B	1/8/26	8/15/76
Rick Lancellotti	1986	OF/1B	7/5/56	
Hobie Landrith	1959-61	C	3/16/30	
Don Landrum	1966	OF	2/16/36	
Hal Lanier	1964-71	IF	7/4/42	
Norm Larker	1963	1B/OF	12/27/30	
Arlie Latham	1909	3B	3/15/59	11/29/52
Clifford Latimer	1898	IF	10/22/88	7/26/71
Bill Lauder	1902-03	3B	2/23/74	5/20/33
Garland Lawing	1946	OF	8/26/19	
Les Layton	1948	OF	11/18/21	
Tony Lazzeri	1939	2B/IF	12/6/03	8/6/46
Freddy Leach	1929-31	OF	11/23/97	12/10/81
Fred Lear	1920	IF	4/7/94	10/13/55
Al LeFevre	1920	IF	9/16/98	1/21/82
Hank Leiber	1933-38,42	OF	1/17/11	
Johnny LeMaster	1975-85	SS	6/19/54	
Bob Lennon	1954	OF	9/15/28	
Jeff Leonard	1981-86	OF	9/22/55	
Sam Leslie	1929-33,36-38	1B	7/26/05	1/21/79
Fred Lindstrom	1924-32	3B/OF	11/21/05	10/4/81
Denny Littlejohn	1978-80	C	10/4/54	
Mickey Livingston	1947-49	C	11/15/14	4/3/83
Hans Lobert	1915-17	3B/SS	10/18/81	9/14/68
Carroll Lockman	1945,47-58	1B/OF	7/25/26	
Jack Lohrke	1947-51	3B/1F	2/25/24	
Ernie Lombardi	1943-47	C	4/6/08	9/26/77
Dale Long	1960	1B	2/6/26	
Hugh Luby	1944	IF	6/13/13	5/5/86
Denny Lyons	1892	3B	3/12/66	1/2/29
Harry Lyons	1889,92-93	OF	1866	6/30/12
Algie McBride	1901	OF	5/23/69	1/10/56
Roger McCardell	1959	C	8/29/32	
Johnny McCarthy	1936-41,48	1B	1/7/10	9/13/73

Player	Years with Giants	Position	Born	Died
Lew McCarty	1916-20	C	11/17/88	6/9/30
Harry McCormick	1904,08-09,12-13	OF	2/28/81	7/9/62
Mike McCormick	1950	OF	5/16/17	4/14/76
Willie McCovey	1959-73,77-80	1B/OF	1/10/38	
Tom McCreery	1897-98	OF/IF	10/19/74	7/3/41
Jim McDonald	1902	OF	N/A	N/A
Dan McGann	1902-07	1B	7/15/72	12/13/10
John McGraw	1902-06	3B/IF	4/7/73	2/25/34
Bill McKechnie	1916	3B/IF	8/7/86	10/29/65
Alex McKinnon	1884	1B	8/14/56	7/24/87
Art McLarney	1932	SS	12/20/08	
Larry McLean	1913-15	C	7/18/81	3/14/21
John McMahon	1892-93	1B/C	10/15/69	12/30/94
George McMillan	1890	OF	N/A	N/A
Hugh McMullen	1925-26	C	12/16/01	
Waddy MacPhee	1922	3B	12/23/99	1/20/80
Garry Maddox	1972-75	OF	9/1/49	
Ed Madjeski	1937	C	7/24/09	
Bill Madlock	1977-78	3B/IF	1/12/51	
Freddy Maguire	1922-23	2B	5/10/99	11/3/61
Jack Maguire	1950-51	OF	2/5/25	
Jim Mahady	1921	2B	4/22/01	8/9/36
Joe Malay	1933	1B	10/25/05	
Candy Maldonado	1986	OF/3B	9/5/60	
Jim Mallory	1945	OF	9/1/18	
Gus Mancuso	1933-38,42-44	C	12/5/05	10/26/84
Jim Mangan	1956	C	9/24/29	
Charlie Manlove	1884	C/OF	10/8/62	2/12/52
Les Mann	1927-28	OF	11/18/93	1/14/62
Dave Marshall	1967-69	OF	1/14/43	
Edward Marshall	1929-32	IF	6/4/06	
Jim Marshall	1960-61	1B	5/25/32	
Willard Marshall	1942,46-49	OF	2/8/21	
William Marshall	1904	C	9/22/75	12/11/59
Frank Martin	1899	N/A	N/A	
Joe Martin	1936	3B	8/28/11	9/28/60
Don Mason	1966-70	2B	12/20/44	
Gary Matthews	1972-76	OF	7/5/50	
Milt May	1980-83	C	8/1/50	
Jim Maynard	1940,42-43,46	OF/3B	3/25/13	9/7/77
Eddie Mayo	1936	3B/IF	4/15/10	
Willie Mays	1951-52,54-72	OF	5/6/31	
Charlie Mead	1943-45	OF	4/9/21	
Joe Medwick	1943-45	OF	11/24/11	3/21/75
Bob Melvin	1986	C/3B	10/28/61	
Fred Merkle	1907-16	1B	12/20/88	3/2/56
Howard Merritt	1913	OF	10/6/94	11/3/55
Sam Mertes	1903-06	OF/utility	8/6/72	3/11/45
Roger Metzger	1978-80	SS	10/10/47	
Emil Meusel	1921-26	OF	6/9/93	3/1/63
John Meyers	1909-15	C	7/29/80	7/25/71
Bruce Miller	1973-76	IF	3/3/49	
Jim Miller	1901	2B	10/2/80	2/8/37

Player	Years with Giants	Position	Born	Died
John Milligan	1893	C/1B	8/8/61	8/30/23
Pete Milne	1948-50	OF	4/10/25	
Johnny Mize	1942,46-49	1B	1/7/13	
Willie Montanez	1975-76	1B/OF	4/1/48	
Al Moore	1925-26	OF	8/4/02	11/29/74
Eddie Moore	1932	IF/OF	1/18/99	2/10/76
Joe Moore	1930-41	OF	12/25/08	
Joe Morgan	1981-82	2B	9/19/43	
Howie Moss	1942	OF/3B	10/17/18	
Manny Mota	1962	OF/IF	2/18/38	
Clarence Mueller	1926-27	OF	9/16/99	1/23/74
Don Mueller	1948-57	OF	4/14/27	
Ray Mueller	1949-50	C	3/8/12	
Fran Mullins	1984	3B/SS	5/14/57	
Bobby Murcer	1975-76	OF	5/20/46	
Danny Murphy	1900-01	2B/OF	8/11/76	11/22/55
Danny Murphy	1892	C	1864	12/14/15
Frank Murphy	1901	OF	1880	11/2/12
Pat Murphy	1887-90	C	1/2/57	5/19/27
Yale Murphy	1894-95,97	IF/OF	11/11/69	2/14/06
John Murray	1909-15,17	OF	3/4/84	12/4/58
George Myatt	1938-39	IF	6/14/14	
Glenn Myatt	1935	C	7/9/97	8/9/69
Theophilus Neal	1905	IF	6/5/76	4/11/50
Tom Needham	1908	C	4/7/79	12/13/26
Jack Nelson	1887	SS/OF	5/14/49	9/5/10
Ray Nelson	1901	2B	8/4/75	1/8/61
Charlie Newman	1892	OF	11/5/68	11/23/47
Roy Nichols	1944	IF	3/3/21	
Steve Nicosia	1983-84	C	8/6/55	
Bert Niehoff	1918	2B/IF	5/13/84	12/8/74
Bob Nieman	1962	OF	1/26/27	
Ray Noble	1951-53	C	3/15/22	
Matt Nokes	1985	C	10/31/63	
Bill North	1979-81	OF	5/14/48	
Tom O'Brien	1899	OF/IF	2/20/73	2/4/01
Danny O'Connell	1957-59	2B/IF	1/21/27	10/2/69
Jimmy O'Connell	1923-24	OF	2/11/01	11/11/76
Ken O'Dea	1939-41	C	3/16/13	12/17/85
Francis O'Doul	1928,1933-34	OF/P	3/4/97	12/7/69
Bob O'Farrell	1928-32	C	10/19/96	
Hal O'Hagan	1902	1B/OF	9/30/73	1/14/13
Bill O'Hara	1909	OF	12/19/75	12/1/54
Al Oliver	1984	1B	10/14/46	
Nate Oliver	1968	2B/IF	12/13/40	
Tom O'Malley	1982-84	IF	12/25/60	
James O'Neill	1883	OF/P	5/25/58	12/13/15
John O'Neill	1899	C	N/A	N/A
Mickey O'Neill	1927	C	4/12/98	4/8/64
Jack Onslow	1917	C	10/13/88	12/22/60
Steve Ontiveros	1973-76	3B	10/26/51	
Joe Orengo	1941	IF	11/29/14	
Jim O'Rourke	1885-89,91-92,1904	OF/utility	8/24/52	1/8/19

Player	Years with Giants	Position	Born	Died
Tom O'Rourke	1890	C	1863	7/19/29
Dave Orr	1883	1B	9/29/59	6/3/15
John Orsino	1961-62	C	4/22/38	
Mel Ott	1926-47	OF/3B	3/2/09	11/21/58
Phil Ouellette	1986	C	11/10/61	
Henry Oxley	1884	C	1/4/58	10/12/45
Jose Pagan	1959-65	SS/IF	5/5/35	
William Patterson	1921	3B/SS	1/29/01	10/1/77
Gene Paulette	1911	1B/utility	5/26/91	2/8/66
Grayson Pearce	1883	2B/OF	N/A	8/29/94
Homer Peel	1933-34	OF	10/10/02	
Marty Perez	1976	SS/2B	2/28/48	
Charles Peterson	1962-66	OF/IF	8/15/42	5/17/80
Joe Pettini	1980-83	IF	1/26/55	
Fred Pfeffer	1896	2b/utility	3/17/60	4/10/32
Monte Pfyl	1907	1B	5/11/84	10/18/45
Dave Philley	1960	OF/1B	5/16/20	
Dick Phillips	1962	1B	11/24/31	
Mike Phillips	1973-75	IF	8/19/50	
Charles Piez	1914	OF	10/13/92	12/29/30
Joe Pignatano	1962	C	8/4/29	
Jesse Pike	1946	OF	7/31/15	3/28/84
Joe Pittman	1984	3B/SS/2B	1/1/54	
Hugh Poland	1943	C	1/19/13	3/30/84
Les Powers	1938	1B	11/5/12	
Joe Price	1928	OF	4/10/97	1/15/61
Ron Pruitt	1982-83	C/OF	6/23/60	
John Puhl	1898-99	3B	1875	8/24/00
Luis Quinones	1986	SS/2B	4/28/62	
John Rabb	1982-84	C/OF	6/23/60	
Dave Rader	1971-76	C	12/26/48	
John Rainey	1887	OF/IF	7/26/64	11/11/12
Gary Rajsich	1985	1B	10/28/54	
Jeff Ransom	1981-83	C	11/11/60	
Earl Rapp	1951	OF	5/20/21	
Joseph Rapp	1921	3B	2/6/92	7/1/66
Bill Rariden	1916-18	C	2/5/88	8/28/42
Johnny Rawlings	1921-22	2B/IF	8/17/92	10/16/72
J. Reagan	1898	OF	N/A	N/A
Glenn Redmon	1974	2B	1/11/48	
Andy Reese	1927-30	OF/IF	2/7/04	1/10/66
Ken Reitz	1976	3B	6/24/51	
Napoleon Reyes	1943-45,50	3B/1B	11/24/19	
Bobby Rhawn	1947-48	IF	2/13/19	1984
James Rhodes	1952-59	OF	5/13/27	
Gene Richards	1984	OF	9/29/53	
Paul Richards	1933-35	C	11/21/08	5/4/86
Danny Richardson	1884-89,91	2B/SS	1/25/63	9/12/26
Hardy Richardson	1892	OF/IF/utility	4/21/55	1/14/31
Bill Rigney	1946-53	IF	1/29/19	
Jimmy Ripple	1936-39	OF	10/14/09	7/16/59
Dave Robertson	1912,14-17,19	OF	9/25/89	11/5/70
Craig Robinson	1975-76	SS/IF	8/21/48	

Player	Years with Giants	Position	Born	Died
John Robinson	1902	C	N/A	N/A
Andre Rodgers	1958-60	SS/IF	12/2/34	
Eric Rodin	1954	OF	2/5/30	
Jose Rodriguez	1916-18	IF	7/25/94	1/21/53
Ron Roenicke	1985	OF	8/19/56	
Wally Roettger	1930	OF	8/28/02	9/14/51
Jimmy Rosario	1971-72	OF	5/5/45	
Goody Rosen	1946	OF	8/28/12	
Harry Rosenberg	1930	OF	6/22/09	
Edd Roush	1916,27-29	OF	5/8/93	
Johnny Rucker	1940-41,43-46	OF	1/15/17	8/7/85
Ken Rudolph	1974,77	C	12/29/46	
Rudy Rufer	1949-50	SS	10/28/26	
John Ryan	1933-34,37-38	SS/IF	1/4/00	11/28/59
Connie Ryan	1942	2B/IF	2/27/20	
Mike Sadek	1973,75-78	C	5/30/46	
Ron Samford	1954	SS/IF	2/28/30	
Alejandro Sanchez	1984	OF	2/26/59	
Bill Sarni	1956	C	9/19/27	4/15/83
Hank Sauer	1958-59	OF	3/17/19	
Frank Scalzi	1939	IF	6/16/13	8/25/84
M. J. Scanlon	1890	1B	3/18/61	2/29/28
Ray Schalk	1929	C	8/13/92	5/19/70
Bobby Schang	1915	C	12/7/86	8/29/66
Mike Schemer	1945-46	1B	11/20/17	4/22/83
Hank Schenz	1951	IF	4/11/19	
George Schlei	1909-11	C	1/12/78	1/24/58
Bob Schmidt	1958-61	C	4/22/33	
Albert Schoendienst	1956-57	2B/utility	2/2/23	
Dick Schofield	1965-66	SS/IF	1/7/35	
Hank Schreiber	1921	IF	7/12/91	2/21/68
William Schriver	1895	C/utility	6/11/66	12/27/32
Bob Schroder	1965-68	IF	12/30/44	
Bob Seeds	1938-40	OF/IF	2/24/07	
Albert Selbach	1900-01	OF	3/24/72	2/17/56
James Seymour	1896-1900,06-10	OF/P	12/9/72	9/20/19
Arthur Shafer	1909-10,12-13	IF	3/22/89	1/10/62
William Shannon	1906-08	OF	2/7/78	5/16/40
Danny Shay	1907	IF	11/8/76	12/1/27
Dan Sheehan	1900	SS	12/18/72	N/A
Jim Sheehan	1936	C	6/3/13	
Ralph Shinners	1922-23	OF	10/4/95	7/23/62
Eddie Sicking	1918-20	IF	3/30/97	8/30/78
Mike Slattery	1888-89	OF	10/28/65	10/16/04
Elbert Slayback	1926	2B	10/5/01	11/30/79
Bruce Sloan	1944	OF	10/4/14	9/24/73
Alexander Smith	1901	utility	1871	7/9/19
Billy Smith	1981	IF	7/14/53	
Chris Smith	1983	OF/1B	7/18/57	
Earl Smith	1919-23	C	2/14/97	6/9/63
Elmer Smith	1900	OF/P	3/28/68	11/5/45
George Smith	1901-02	2B	10/24/71	6/25/39
Harry Smith	1914-15	C	5/15/90	4/1/22

Player	Years with Giants	Position	Born	Died
James Smith	1927	C	5/18/04	3/8/78
Jimmy Smith	1917	IF	5/15/95	1/1/74
Mike Smith	1926	OF	11/16/04	5/31/81
Reggie Smith	1982	OF/1B	4/2/45	
Edwin Snider	1964	OF	9/19/26	
Fred Snodgrass	1908-15	OF/1B	10/19/87	4/5/74
Frank Snyder	1919-26	C/1B	5/27/93	1/5/62
Moses Solomon	1923	OF	12/8/00	6/25/66
Pete Sommers	1890	C	10/26/66	7/22/08
Bill Sorrell	1967	3B/IF	10/14/40	
Billy Southworth	1924-26	OF	3/9/93	11/15/69
Bob Speake	1958-59	OF/1B	8/22/30	
Horace Speed	1975	OF	10/4/51	
Chris Speier	1971-77	SS	6/28/50	
Daryl Spencer	1958-59	IF	7/13/29	
Roy Spencer	1936	C	2/22/00	2/8/73
Vern Spencer	1920	OF	2/24/96	6/3/71
Harry Spilman	1986	Utility	7/18/54	
Al Spohrer	1928	C	12/3/02	7/12/72
Ebba St. Claire	1954	C	8/5/21	8/22/82
Bob Stafford	1893-97	OF/utility	N/A	N/A
Henry Stafford	1916	PH	11/1/91	7/29/72
Eddie Stanky	1950-51	2B	9/3/16	
Arnold Statz	1919-20	OF	10/20/97	
Charles Stengel	1921-23	OF	7/30/90	9/29/75
Joe Stephenson	1943	C	6/30/21	
Johnny Stephenson	1969-70	C	4/13/41	
Charles Stengel	1921-23	OF	7/30/90	9/29/75
Joe Stephenson	1943	C	6/30/21	
Johnny Stephenson	1969-70	C	4/13/41	
Glen Stewart	1940	IF	9/29/12	
Milt Stock	1913-14	3B/IF	7/11/93	7/16/77
Sammy Strang	1901,05-08	IF/OF	12/16/76	3/13/32
Bill Stuart	1899	IF	8/28/73	10/14/28
Guy Sularz	1980-83	IF	11/7/55	
Champ Summers	1982-83	1B/OF	6/15/48	
John Tamargo	1978	C	11/7/51	
Don Taussig	1958	OF	2/19/32	
Bob Taylor	1970	OF	3/20/44	
Bill Taylor	1954-57	OF	3/2/26	
Zack Taylor	1927	C	7/27/98	7/6/74
Fred Tenney	1908-09	1B/utility	11/26/71	7/3/52
Bill Terry	1923-36	1B	10/30/98	
Wayne Terwilliger	1955-56	IF	6/27/25	
Nick Testa	1958	C	6/29/28	
Derrel Thomas	1975-77	IF/OF	1/14/51	
Herb Thomas	1927	OF/IF	5/26/02	
Valmy Thomas	1957-58	C	10/21/30	
Gary Thomasson	1972-77	OF/1B	7/29/51	
Fresco Thompson	1926	IF	6/6/02	11/20/68
Henry Thompson	1949-56	IF/OF	12/8/25	9/30/69
Robby Thompson	1986	2B/SS	5/10/62	
Scot Thompson	1984-85	1B/OF	12/7/55	
Bobby Thomson	1946-53,57	OF/IF	10/25/23	

Player	Years with Giants	Position	Born	Died
Jim Thorpe	1913-15,17-19	OF	5/28/86	3/28/53
Mike Tiernan	1887-99	OF	1/21/67	11/9/18
Johnny Tobin	1932	PH	9/15/06	8/6/83
Stephen Tramback	1940	OF	11/1/15	12/28/79
Thadford Treadway	1944-45	OF	4/28/20	
Alex Trevino	1985	C/3B	8/26/56	
Manny Trillo	1984-85	2B/3B	12/25/50	
John Troy	1883	IF	5/8/56	3/30/38
Ty Tyson	1926-27	OF	6/1/92	8/16/53
George Ulrich	1896	utility	N/A	N/A
Jose Uribe	1985-86	SS/2B	1/21/60	
Mike Vail	1983	OF	11/10/51	
George Van Haltren	1894-1903	OF/utility	3/30/66	9/29/45
Ike Van Zandt	1901	OF	1877	9/14/00
Art Veltman	1928-29,32	O	3/24/00	10/1/80
Max Vonable	1979-81	C	6/6/57	
Johnny Vergez	1931-34	3B	7/9/06	
Ozzie Virgil	1956-57,66	utility	5/17/33	
Abraham Wade	1907	OF	12/20/80	7/21/68
Charles Wagner	1902	SS/IF	9/23/81	3/20/43
Leon Wagner	1958-59,69	OF	5/13/34	
Dick Wakefield	1952	OF	5/6/21	
Curt Walker	1920-21	OF	7/3/96	12/9/55
Frank Walker	1925	OF	9/22/94	9/16/74
Joe Wall	1901-02	C/OF	7/24/73	7/17/36
John Ward	1883-89,93-94	SS/P/utility	3/3/60	3/4/25
John Warner	1896-1901,03-04	C	8/15/72	12/21/43
Bennie Warren	1946-47	C	3/2/12	
Libe Washburn	1902	OF/P	6/16/74	3/22/40
George Watkins	1934	OF	6/4/02	6/1/70
Roy Weatherly	1950	OF	2/25/15	
Earl Webb	1925	OF	9/17/98	5/23/65
George Weidman	1887-88	OF/P	2/17/61	3/3/05
Phil Weintraub	1933-35,37,44-45	1B/OF	10/12/07	
Brad Wellman	1982-86	2B	8/17/59	
Jimmy Welsh	1928-29	OF	10/9/02	10/20/70
Lew Wendell	1915-16	C	3/22/92	7/11/53
Bill Werber	1942	3B/IF/OF	6/20/08	
Wes Westrum	1947-57	C	11/28/22	
Lew Whistler	1890-91	IF/OF	3/10/68	12/30/59
Steve Whitaker	1970	OF	5/7/43	
Albert White	1947	OF	6/27/18	
Bill White	1956	1B/OF	1/28/34	
Burgess Whitehead	1936-37,39-41	2B/IF	6/29/10	
Terry Whitfield	1977-80	OF	1/12/53	
Art Whitney	1888-89	3B/utility	1/16/58	8/17/43
Floyd Wicker	1971	OF	9/12/43	
Joe Wilhoit	1917-18	OF	12/20/91	9/25/30
Bernie Williams	1970-72	OF	10/8/48	
Davey Williams	1949,51-55	2B	11/2/27	
Walt Wilmot	1897-98	OF	10/18/63	2/1/29
Art Wilson	1908-13	C	12/11/85	6/12/60
Artie Wilson	1951	IF	10/28/20	

Player	Years with Giants	Position	Born	Died
Lewis Wilson	1923-25	OF	4/26/00	11/23/48
Neil Wilson	1960	C	6/14/35	
Parke Wilson	1893-99	C/IF/OF	10/26/67	12/20/34
Ted Wilson	1952-53,56	OF	8/30/25	10/29/74
Nick Witek	1940-43,46-47	2B/IF	12/19/15	
Pete Woodruff	1899	OF	N/A	N/A
Mike Woodard	1985-86	2B/3B/SS	3/2/60	
Russ Wrightstone	1928	IF/OF	3/18/93	3/1/69
George Wrigley	1899	IF/OF	1/18/73	9/28/52
George Yeager	1902	C	6/4/73	10/16/23
Norman Young	1936,39-42,46-47	1B/OF	7/1/15	12/25/83
Joel Youngblood	1983-86	OF/SS/1B	8/28/51	
Ross Youngs	1917-26	OF	4/10/97	10/22/27
Sal Yvars	1947-53	C	2/20/24	
Elmer Zacker	1910	OF	9/17/83	12/20/44
Dave Zearfoss	1896-98	C	1/1/68	9/12/45
Henry Zimmerman	1916-19	3B/IF	2/9/87	3/14/69
Roy Zimmerman	1945	1B	9/13/16	

PITCHERS

Pitcher	Years with Giants	Throw	Born	Died
Virgil Abernathy	1946-47	L	2/1/15	
Ace Adams	1941-46	R	3/2/12	
Vic Aldridge	1928	R	10/25/93	4/17/73
Johnny Allen	1943-44	R	9/30/04	3/29/59
Myron Allen	1883	R	3/22/54	3/8/24
Leon Ames	1903-13	R	8/2/82	10/8/36
Fred Anderson	1916-18	R	12/11/85	11/8/57
Hub Andrews	1947-48	R	8/31/22	
Nate Andrews	1946	R	9/30/13	
Johnny Antonelli	1954-60	L	4/12/30	
Bill Ayers	1947	R	9/27/19	9/24/80
Loren Bader	1912	R	4/27/88	6/2/73
Loren Bain	1945	R	7/4/22	
Tom Baker	1937-38	R	6/11/15	
Harry Baldwin	1924-25	R	6/30/00	1/23/58
Mark Baldwin	1893	R	10/29/65	11/10/29
George Bamberger	1951-52	R	8/1/25	
Steve Barber	1974	L	2/22/39	
Curt Barclay	1957-59	R	8/22/31	
Jesse Barnes	1918-23	R	8/26/92	9/9/61
Virgil Barnes	1919-20,22-28	R	3/5/97	7/24/58
Bob Barr	1891	N/A	1856	3/11/30
Jim Barr	1971-78,82-83	R	2/10/48	
Bill Bartley	1903	R	1/8/85	5/17/65
James Becannon	1887	N/A	8/22/59	11/5/23
Roy Beecher	1907-08	R	5/10/84	10/11/52
Joe Beggs	1947-48	R	11/4/10	7/19/83
Ed Begley	1884	N/A	1863	7/28/19
Hank Behrman	1949	R	6/27/21	
Herman Bell	1932-34	R	7/16/95	6/7/49
Jack Bentley	1923-27	L	3/8/95	10/24/69
Larry Benton	1927-30	R	11/20/97	4/3/53
John Benton	1915-21	L	6/27/87	12/12/37
Juan Berenguer	1986	R	11/30/54	
Jack Berly	1931	R	5/24/03	6/26/77
Bob Blewitt	1902	L	6/28/77	3/17/58
Vida Blue	1978-81,85-86	L	7/28/49	
Clint Blume	1922-23	R	10/17/00	6/12/73
Randy Bockus	1986	L	10/5/60	
Bob Bolin	1961-69	R	1/29/39	
Hank Boney	1927	R	10/28/03	
Bill Bordley	1980	L	1/9/58	
Andy Boswell	1895	N/A	9/5/74	2/3/36
Sutherland Bowen	1896	R	2/17/71	1/25/25
Bob Bowman	1941	R	10/3/10	9/4/72
Joe Bowman	1934	R	6/17/10	
Roger Bowman	1949-52	L	8/18/27	
Tom Bradley	1973-75	R	3/16/47	

Pitcher	Years with Giants	Throw	Born	Died
Don Brennan	1937	R	12/2/03	4/26/53
Jack Brewer	1944-46	R	7/21/19	
Ken Brondell	1944	R	10/17/21	
Jim Brown	1884	N/A	12/12/60	4/6/08
Walter Brown	1937-41	R	4/30/07	10/2/66
Ron Bryant	1967,1969-74	L	11/12/47	
Garland Buckeye	1928	L	10/16/97	11/14/75
Mike Budnick	1946-47	R	9/15/19	
Pete Burnside	1955,1957-58	L	7/2/30	
Joe Bush	1927	R	11/27/92	11/1/74
William Byerly	1959-60	R	10/26/20	
Leon Cadore	1924	R	10/20/91	3/16/58
Mike Caldwell	1974-76	L	1/22/49	
Mark Calvert	1983-84	R	8/29/56	
Sal Campfield	1896	N/A	2/19/68	5/16/52
Ben Cantwell	1927-28,1937	R	4/13/02	12/4/62
John Carden	1946	R	5/19/22	2/8/49
Steve Carlton	1986	L	12/22/44	
Bob Carpenter	1940-42,1946-47	R	12/12/17	
Bill Carrick	1898-1900	R	9/5/73	3/7/32
Don Carrithers	1970-73	R	9/15/49	
Wilfred Carsey	1899	R	10/22/70	3/29/60
Clydell Castleman	1934-39	R	9/18/13	
Cecil Causey	1918-19,1921-22	R	8/11/93	11/11/60
Leon Chagnon	1935	R	9/28/02	7/30/53
Jim Chaplin	1928,1930-31	R	7/13/05	3/25/39
Ken Chase	1943	L	10/6/13	
Nestor Chavez	1967	R	7/6/47	3/16/69
Virgil Cheeves	1927	R	2/12/01	
Don Choate	1960	R	7/2/38	
Mike Chris	1982-83	L	10/8/57	
William Clark	1933-34	L	5/16/02	3/4/72
William Clarke	1894-97	R	1/7/65	6/3/11
Bill Clarkson	1927-28	R	9/27/98	8/27/81
Arthur Clarkson	1891	R	8/31/66	2/6/11
Dick Coffman	1936-39	R	12/18/06	3/24/72
Dick Cogan	1900	R	12/5/71	5/2/48
Tom Colcolough	1899	R	10/8/70	12/10/19
Bill Connelly	1952-53	R	6/29/25	11/27/80
Jim Constable	1956-58	L	6/14/33	
Sandalio Consuegra	1957	R	9/3/20	
Bobby Coombs	1943	R	2/2/08	
Mort Cooper	1947	R	2/2/13	11/17/58
Larry Corcoran	1885-86	R	8/10/59	10/14/91
Jeff Cornell	1984	R	2/10/57	
Terry Cornutt	1977-78	R	10/2/52	
Al Corwin	1951-55	R	12/3/26	
Roscoe Coughlin	1891	R	2/25/66	3/20/51
James Crandall	1908-13	R	10/8/87	8/17/51
Ed Crane	1890	R	1862	9/19/96
Ray Crone	1957-58	R	8/7/31	
John Cronin	1902-03	R	5/26/74	7/13/29

Pitcher	Years with Giants	Throw	Born	Died
John Cumberland	1970-72	L	5/10/47	
John Curtis	1977-79	L	3/9/48	
Mike Cvengros	1922	L	12/1/01	8/2/70
John D'Acquisto	1973-76	R	12/24/51	
George Daly	1909	R	7/28/87	12/12/57
Claude Davenport	1920	R	5/28/98	6/13/76
Lloyd Davies	1925-26	L	3/6/92	9/5/73
George Davies	1893	N/A	2/22/68	9/22/06
Jim Davis	1957	L	9/15/24	
Mark Davis	1983-86	L	10/19/60	
Mike Davison	1969-70	L	8/4/45	
Paul Dean	1940-41	R	8/14/13	3/17/81
Wayland Dean	1924-26	R	6/20/03	4/10/30
John Doogan	1901	N/A	N/A	N/A
Al Demaree	1912-14,17-18	R	9/8/86	4/30/62
Mark Dempsey	1982-83	R	12/17/57	
Roger Denzer	1901	L	10/5/71	9/18/49
Jim Devine	1886	N/A	10/5/78	1/11/05
Jim Devlin	1886	L	1867	12/20/00
Walt Dickson	1910	R	1883	12/10/18
Ed Doheny	1895-1901	L	11/24/74	12/29/16
Francis Donahue	1893	R	1/23/73	8/25/13
Pete Donohue	1930-31	R	11/5/00	
Phil Douglas	1919-22	R	6/17/90	8/1/52
Kelly Downs	1986	R	10/25/60	
Clem Dreisewerd	1948	L	1/24/16	
Rob Dressler	1975-76	R	2/2/54	
Louis Drucke	1909-12	R	12/3/88	9/22/55
Jean Dubuc	1919	R	9/17/88	8/29/58
Jim Duffalo	1961-65	R	11/25/35	
Jack Dunn	1902,04	R	10/6/72	10/22/28
Andy Dunning	1891	R	8/12/71	6/21/52
Louis Durham	1908-09	R	6/27/77	6/28/60
Hugh East	1941-43	R	7/7/19	11/2/81
Claude Elliott	1904-05	R	11/17/79	6/21/23
Bill Emmerich	1945-46	R	9/29/19	
Eric Erickson	1914	R	5/13/92	5/19/65
Dick Estelle	1964-65	L	1/18/42	
Barry Evans	1978	L	3/3/55	
LeRoy Evans	1902	R	3/19/74	8/15/15
John Ewing	1891	R	6/1/63	4/23/95
Pete Falcone	1975	L	10/1/53	
Bill Paul	1970	R	4/21/40	
Jim Faulkner	1927-28	L	7/27/99	6/1/62
Charlie Faust	1911	N/A	10/9/80	6/18/15
Harry Feldman	1941-46	R	11/10/19	3/16/62
Harry Felix	1901	R	1877	10/18/61
George Ferguson	1906-07	N/A	8/19/86	9/5/43
Reuben Fischer	1941,43-46	R	9/19/16	
Leo Fishel	1899	R	12/13/87	5/19/60
Chauncey Fisher	1901	R	1/8/72	4/27/39
Don Fisher	1945	R	2/6/16	7/29/73

Pitcher	Years with Giants	Throw	Born	Died
Eddie Fisher	1959-61	R	7/16/36	
John Fitzgerald	1958	L	9/15/33	
Fred Fitzsimmons	1925-37	R	7/28/01	11/18/79
Cornelius Flynn	1896	L	1/23/75	2/10/47
Frank Foreman	1893	R	5/1/63	11/19/57
Alan Fowlkes	1982-83	R	8/8/58	
Art Fromme	1913-15	R	9/3/83	8/24/56
Frank Gabler	1935-37	R	11/6/11	11/1/67
Rich Gale	1982-83	R	1/19/54	
Scott Garrelts	1982-86	R	10/30/61	
Bob Garibaldi	1962-63,66,69	R	3/3/42	
Willie Garoni	1899	R	7/28/77	9/9/14
Dennis Gearin	1923-24	L	10/14/97	3/11/59
Johnny Gee	1944-46	L	12/7/15	
Joe Genewich	1928-30	R	1/15/97	
Bill George	1887-89	L	1/27/65	8/23/16
Oscar Georgy	1938	R	1/25/16	
Les German	1893-96	N/A	6/2/69	6/10/39
Jim Gott	1985-86	R	8/3/59	
Al Gettel	1951	R	9/17/17	
Charley Gettig	1896-99	N/A	1875	N/A
Joe Gibbon	1969	L	4/10/36	
Sam Gibson	1932	R	8/5/99	1/31/83
Paul Giel	1954-58	R	9/29/32	
Ruben Gomez	1953-58	R	7/13/27	
Tom Gorman	1939	L	3/16/16	8/12/86
Ted Goulait	1912	R	8/11/89	7/15/36
Mark Grant	1984-86	R	10/24/63	
Kent Greenfield	1924-27	R	7/1/02	3/14/78
Hal Gregg	1952	R	7/11/21	
Tom Griffin	1979-81	R	2/22/48	
Burleigh Grimes	1927	R	8/18/93	12/6/85
Marv Grissom	1946,53-58	R	3/31/18	
Tom Grubbs	1920	R	2/22/94	
Harry Gumbert	1935-41	R	11/5/09	
Irving Hadley	1941	R	7/5/04	2/15/63
Ed Halicki	1974-80	R	10/4/50	
Jack Hallett	1948	R	11/13/13	6/11/82
Steve Hamilton	1971	L	11/30/35	
Atlee Hammaker	1982-85	L	1/24/58	
Bill Hands	1965	R	5/6/40	
Andy Hansen	1944-45,47-50	R	11/12/24	
Francis Hardy	1951	R	1/6/23	
Alan Hargesheimer	1980-81	R	11/21/56	
Ray Harrell	1945	R	2/16/12	1/28/84
Jack Harshman	1948-50	L	7/12/27	
Clint Hartung	1947-52	R	8/10/22	
Emerson Hawley	1900	R	12/5/72	9/19/38
Bunn Hearn	1913	L	5/12/91	10/10/59
Jim Hearn	1950-56	R	4/11/21	
Dave Heaverlo	1975-77	R	8/25/50	
Bob Hendley	1964-65	L	4/30/39	

Pitcher	Years with Giants	Throw	Born	Died
Ed Hendricks	1910	L	6/20/86	11/28/30
Bill Henry	1965-68	L	10/15/27	
Frank Henry	1927-29	L	5/12/02	8/23/68
Chuck Hensley	1986	L	3/11/59	
Ron Herbel	1963-69	R	1/16/38	
Fred Herbert	1915	R	3/4/87	5/29/63
Larry Hesterfer	1901	N/A	6/20/78	9/22/43
Joe Heving	1930-31	R	9/2/00	4/11/70
Kirby Higbe	1949-50	R	4/8/15	5/6/85
Carmen Hill	1922	R	10/1/95	
Frank Hiller	1953	R	7/13/20	
Billy Hoeft	1963	L	5/17/32	
Al Holland	1979-82	L	8/16/52	
Howard Holland	1927	R	1/6/03	2/10/09
Waite Hoyt	1918	R	9/9/99	8/25/84
Bill Hubbell	1919-20	R	6/17/97	8/3/80
Carl Hubbell	1928-43	L	6/22/03	
Willis Hudlin	1940	R	5/23/06	
Al Huenke	1914	R	6/26/91	9/20/74
Walter Huntzinger	1923-25	R	2/6/99	8/11/81
Clarence Iott	1947	L	12/3/19	8/17/80
Larry Jansen	1947-54	R	7/16/20	
Ernest Jeanes	1927	R	12/19/00	4/5/73
Mike Jeffcoat	1985	L	8/3/59	
Art Johnson	1927	L	2/15/97	6/7/82
Don Johnson	1958	R	11/12/26	
Fred Johnson	1922-23	R	3/5/97	6/14/73
Jerry Johnson	1970-72	R	12/3/43	
Jim Johnson	1970	L	11/3/45	
Tom Johnson	1899	N/A	N/A	N/A
Roy Joiner	1940	L	10/30/06	
Charles Jones	1893	R	1/1/70	6/25/38
Gordon Jones	1957-59	R	4/2/30	
Johnny Jones	1919	R	8/25/94	6/5/80
Sam Jones	1959-61	R	12/14/25	11/5/71
Sheldon Jones	1946-51	R	2/2/22	
Sherman Jones	1960	R	2/10/35	
Claude Jonnard	1921-24	R	11/23/97	8/27/59
Bob Joyce	1946	R	1/14/15	12/10/81
Ralph Judd	1929-30	R	12/7/01	5/6/57
Tony Kaufman	1929	R	12/16/00	6/4/82
Tim Keefe	1885-89,91	R	1/1/56	4/23/33
Montia Kennedy	1946-53	L	5/11/22	
William Kennedy	1902	R	10/7/68	9/23/15
Charles King	1892-93	R	1/11/68	5/19/38
Brian Kingman	1983	R	7/27/54	
Al Klawitter	1909-10	R	4/12/88	5/2/50
Ron Kline	1969	R	3/9/32	
Frank Knauss	1895	N/A	1868	N/A
Bob Knepper	1976-80	L	5/25/54	
Alex Konikowski	1948, 1951	R	6/8/28	
Dave Koslo	1941-42,46-53	L	3/31/20	12/1/75

Pitcher	Years with Giants	Throw	Born	Died
Jack Kramer	1950-51	R	1/5/18	
John Kraus	1946	L	4/26/18	1/2/76
Mike Krukow	1983	R	1/21/52	
Bob Lacey	1984	L	8/25/53	
Mike LaCoss	1986	R	5/30/56	
Dave LaPoint	1985	L	7/29/59	
Max Lanier	1952-53	L	8/8/15	
Pat Larkin	1983	L	6/18/60	
Don Larsen	1962	R	8/7/29	
Bill Laskey	1981-86	R	12/20/57	
Gary Lavelle	1974-84	L	1/3/49	
Roy Lee	1945	L	9/28/17	
Thornton Lee	1948	L	9/13/06	
George Leitner	1901	R	6/19/71	2/20/60
Dick LeMay	1961-62	L	8/28/38	
Don Liddle	1954-56	L	5/25/25	
Frank Linzy	1963,65-70	R	9/15/40	
Dick Littlefield	1956	L	3/18/26	
Jake Livingstone	1901	N/A	1/1/86	3/22/49
Billy Loes	1960-61	R	12/13/29	
Bill Lohrman	1937-43	R	5/22/13	
Lou Lombardo	1948	L	11/18/28	
Charles Lucas	1923	R	4/28/02	
Ray Lucas	1929-31	R	10/2/08	10/9/69
Red Lucas	1923	R	4/28/02	7/9/86
Dolph Luque	1932-35	R	8/4/90	7/3/57
Mike Lynch	1907	L	6/28/80	4/2/27
Japhet Lynn	1939-40	R	12/27/13	10/27/77
Ken MacKenzie	1964	L	3/10/34	
John McCall	1954-57	L	7/18/25	
Mike McCormick	1956-62,67-70	L	9/29/38	
Lindy McDaniel	1966-68	R	12/13/35	
Sam McDowell	1972-73	L	9/21/42	
Andy McGaffigan	1982-83	R	10/25/56	
Bill McGee	1941-42	R	11/16/09	
Joe McGinnity	1902-08	R	3/19/71	11/14/29
Lynn McGlothen	1977-78	R	3/27/50	8/14/84
Tullis McGowan	1948	L	11/26/21	
Don McMahon	1969-74	R	1/4/30	
Tim McNamara	1926	R	11/20/98	
Frank McPartlin	1899	R	2/16/72	11/13/43
Hugh McQuillan	1922-27	R	9/15/97	8/26/47
Bill Magee	1901-02	R	1/11/68	8/15/22
Sal Maglie	1945,50-55	R	4/26/17	
Bill Malarkey	1908	R	5/10/72	12/12/56
Leo Mangum	1928	R	5/24/98	7/9/74
George Maranda	1960	R	1/15/32	
Fred Marberry	1936	R	11/30/98	6/30/76
Joe Margoneri	1956-57	L	1/13/30	
Juan Marichal	1960-73	R	10/24/37	
Richard Marquard	1908-15	L	10/9/89	6/1/80
Renie Martin	1982-84	R	8/30/55	

Pitcher	Years with Giants	Throw	Born	Died
Roger Mason	1985-86	R	9/18/58	
Christy Mathewson	1900-16	R	8/12/80	10/7/25
Henry Mathewson	1906-07	R	12/24/86	7/1/17
Mike Mattimore	1887	R	1859	4/29/31
Al Maul	1901	R	10/9/65	5/3/58
Ernie Maun	1924	R	2/3/01	
Bert Maxwell	1911	R	10/17/86	12/10/67
Carl Mays	1929	R	11/12/91	4/4/71
Jouett Meekin	1894-99	R	2/21/67	12/14/44
Cliff Melton	1937-44	L	1/3/12	
John Menefee	1898	R	1/16/68	3/11/53
George Mercer	1900	R	6/20/74	1/12/03
Clarence Metzger	1974	R	5/23/52	
Jim Middleton	1917	R	5/20/99	1/12/74
Ken Miller	1944	R	5/2/15	
Roscoe Miller	1902-03	N/A	12/2/76	12/18/13
Stu Miller	1957-62	R	12/26/27	
Bill Milligan	1904	L	1877	10/14/28
Willie Mills	1901	R	8/15/77	7/5/14
Greg Minton	1975-86	R	7/29/51	
Clarence Mitchell	1930-32	L	2/22/91	11/6/63
Randy Moffitt	1972-78	R	10/13/48	
Bill Monbouquette	1968	R	8/11/36	
John Montefusco	1974-78	R	5/25/50	
Ray Monzant	1954-58,60	R	1/4/33	
Jim Mooney	1931-32	L	9/4/06	4/27/79
Bobby Moore	1985	R	11/8/58	
Euel Moore	1935	R	5/27/08	
Bill Morrell	1930-31	R	4/9/00	8/15/75
John Morris	1972-74	L	8/23/41	
Billy Muffett	1959	R	9/21/30	
Terry Mulholland	1986	L	3/9/63	
Van Mungo	1942-43,45	R	6/8/11	2/13/85
Mansanori Murakami	1964-65	L	5/6/44	
Bob Murphy	1890	N/A	12/26/66	N/A
Art Nehf	1919-26	L	7/31/92	12/18/60
Louis Newsom	1948	R	8/11/07	12/7/62
Chet Nichols	1928	R	7/2/97	7/11/82
Walter Ockey	1944	R	7/4/20	12/4/71
Hank O'Day	1889	R	7/8/63	7/2/35
Billy O'Dell	1960-64	L	2/10/33	
Joe Oeschger	1919	R	5/24/91	7/28/86
Jack Ogden	1918	R	11/5/97	11/9/77
Marty O'Toole	1914	R	11/27/88	2/18/49
Emilio Palmero	1915-16	L	6/13/95	7/15/70
LeRoy Parmelee	1929-35	R	4/25/07	8/29/81
William Perritt	1915-21	R	8/30/92	10/15/47
Gaylord Perry	1962-71	R	9/15/38	
Charlie Petty	1893	R	6/28/68	N/A
John Phillips	1945	R	5/24/21	6/9/58
Bill Phyle	1901	R	6/25/75	8/7/53
Mario Picone	1947,52,54	R	7/5/26	

Pitcher	Years with Giants	Throw	Born	Died
Billy Pierce	1962-64	L	4/2/27	
Lee Pitlock	1970	L	11/6/47	
Emil Planeta	1931	R	1/13/09	2/2/62
Eddie Plank	1978-79	R	4/9/52	
Norman Plitt	1927	R	2/21/93	2/1/54
Ray Poat	1947-49	R	12/19/17	
Joe Poetz	1926	R	6/22/01	2/7/42
Lou Polli	1944	R	7/9/01	
Ned Porter	1926-27	R	5/6/05	6/30/68
John Pregenzer	1963-64	R	8/2/35	
Bob Priddy	1965-66	R	12/10/39	
Hub Pruett	1930	L	9/1/00	1/28/82
Miguel Puente	1970	R	5/8/48	
Ewald Pyle	1944-45	L	8/27/10	
Pat Ragan	1919	R	11/15/88	9/4/56
Arthur Raymond	1909-11	R	2/24/82	9/7/12
Frank Reberger	1970-72	R	6/7/44	
Bill Reidy	1896	R	10/9/73	10/14/15
Marshall Renfroe	1959	L	5/25/36	12/10/70
Frank Riccelli	1976	L	2/24/53	
Steve Ridzik	1956-57	R	4/29/29	
George Riley	1984	L	10/6/56	
Jimmy Ring	1926	R	2/15/95	7/6/65
William Ritter	1914-16	R	10/12/93	9/3/64
John Roach	1887	L	N/A	3/1/15
Rich Robertson	1966-71	R	10/14/44	
Jeff Robinson	1984-86	R	12/13/60	
Don Rose	1974	R	3/19/47	
George Ross	1918	L	6/28/93	4/22/35
Frank Rosso	1944	R	3/1/21	
Mike Rowland	1980-83	R	1/31/53	
Dick Rudolph	1910-11	R	8/25/87	10/20/49
Amos Rusie	1890-95,97-98	R	5/30/71	12/6/42
Wilfred Ryan	1919-24	R	3/15/98	12/10/80
Ray Sadecki	1966-69	L	12/26/40	
Harry Sallee	1916-18,20-21	L	2/3/85	3/22/50
Jack Salveson	1933-34	R	1/5/14	12/28/74
Manuel Salvo	1939	R	6/30/13	
Jack Sanford	1959-65	R	5/18/29	
Bill Sayles	1943	R	7/27/17	
Dan Schatzeder	1982-83	L	12/1/54	
Alexander Schauer	1913-16	R	3/19/91	4/15/57
Frederick Schmidt	1893	L	2/13/66	10/5/40
Hal Schumacher	1931-42,46	R	11/23/10	
Ferdie Schupp	1913-19	L	1/16/91	12/16/71
Jack Scott	1922-23,25-26	R	4/18/92	11/30/59
Theodore Sechrist	1899	R	2/10/76	4/2/50
Frank Seward	1943-44	R	4/7/21	
James Seymour	1896-1900	L	12/9/72	9/20/19
John Sharrott	1890-92	L	8/13/69	12/31/27
Bob Shaw	1964-66	R	6/29/33	
Patrick Shea	1921-22	R	11/29/98	

Pitcher	Years with Giants	Throw	Born	Died
Joe Shipley	1958-60	R	5/9/35	
Ernie Shore	1912	R	5/24/91	9/24/80
Bill Shores	1933	R	5/26/04	2/19/84
Seth Sigsby	1893	N/A	1874	N/A
Al Smith	1926	R	12/13/03	
Al Smith	1934-37	L	10/12/07	4/28/77
George Smith	1916-19	R	5/31/92	1/7/65
Colonel Snover	1919	L	5/16/95	4/30/69
Don Songer	1927	L	1/31/99	10/3/62
Elias Sosa	1972-74	R	6/10/50	
Warren Spahn	1965	L	4/23/21	
Tully Sparks	1902	R	4/18/77	7/15/37
George Spencer	1950-55	R	7/7/26	
Glenn Spencer	1933	R	9/11/05	12/30/58
Al Stanek	1960	L	12/24/43	
Ray Starr	1933	R	4/23/06	2/9/63
Bob Steele	1918-19	L	3/29/94	1/27/62
Steve Stone	1971-72	R	7/14/47	
Allyn Stout	1935	R	10/31/04	12/22/74
Ralph Stroud	1915-16	R	5/15/85	4/11/70
Mike Sullivan	1891,96-97	L	10/23/66	6/14/06
Tom Sunkel	1941-43	L	8/9/12	
Max Surkont	1956-57	R	6/16/22	10/8/86
Bill Swabach	1887	N/A	N/A	N/A
Ad Swigler	1917	R	9/21/95	2/5/75
Luther Taylor	1900-08	R	2/21/75	8/22/58
Jim Tennant	1929	R	3/3/08	4/16/67
Charles Tesreau	1912-18	R	3/5/89	9/24/46
Henry Thielman	1902	R	10/30/80	9/2/42
Fay Thomas	1927	R	10/10/04	
Gene Thompson	1946-47	R	6/7/17	
Ledell Titcomb	1887-89	L	8/21/65	6/9/50
Andy Tomasic	1949	R	12/10/19	
Tommy Toms	1975-77	R	10/15/51	
Fred Toney	1918-22	R	12/11/87	3/11/53
Ken Trinkle	1943,46-48	R	12/15/19	
Bob Tufts	1981	L	11/2/55	
George Uhle	1933	R	9/18/98	
Hy Vandenberg	1937-40	R	3/17/07	
Bill Voiselle	1942-47	R	1/29/19	
Bill Walker	1927-32	L	10/7/03	6/14/66
John Waller	1909	N/A	6/16/83	2/9/15
Colin Ward	1985	L	11/22/60	
Monte Ward	1883-89,83-94	R	3/3/60	3/4/25
John Watson	1923-24	R	10/15/96	8/25/49
Samuel Webb	1948-49	R	9/25/24	
George Weidman	1887-88	R	2/17/61	3/3/05
Jacob Weimer	1909	L	11/29/73	6/17/28
Michael Welch	1883-92	R	7/4/59	7/30/41
Huyler Westervelt	1894	N/A	10/1/70	N/A
Hoyt Wilhelm	1952-56	R	7/26/23	
Charlie Williams	1972-78	R	10/11/47	

Player	Years with Giants	Throw	Born	Died
Frank Williams	1984-1986	R	2/13/58	
Jim Willoughby	1971-74	R	1/31/49	
George Wiltse	1904-14	L	9/7/80	1/21/59
Jesse Winters	1919-20	R	12/22/93	6/5/86
John Wisner	1925-26	R	11/5/99	12/15/81
Johnny Wittig	1938-41,1943	R	6/16/14	
Al Worthington	1953-54,56-59	R	2/5/29	
Roy Wright	1956	R	9/26/33	
Adrian Zabala	1945-49	L	8/26/16	
Walt Zink	1921	R	11/21/99	6/12/64

INDEX
Selected Players and Events

ABOUT THE AUTHORS

Fred Stein's avid interest in the Giants goes back to the 1930's when he discovered the wonders of the Polo Grounds—and its on- and off-field inhabitants—from a right field bleacher seat (described in his *Under Coogan's Bluff—A Fan's Recollections of the New York Giants Under Terry and Ott*). He served appropriate periods of servitude in the infantry in World War 2, at Pennyslvania State University, and in the U.S. Departments of Agriculture and Commerce before his retirement in 1979. Since then he has been an environmental consultant and occasional contributor of articles on the long-departed New York Giants. He is a long-standing member of the Society for American Baseball Research (SABR) who roots for the Baltimore Orioles as well as the San Francisco Giants. A transplanted New York City native, he has resided in the Northern Virginia area, near Washington, D.C., for 35 years.

Nick Peters' scrutiny of the San Francisco Giants began in 1958 when he, as a San Jose State journalism major, watched the historic first game on the West Coast from the left field bleachers at Seals Stadium. He also attended the first game at Candlestick Park in 1960 and began his coverage of the team after he was graduated in 1961. He first worked as a baseball reporter for the *Berkeley Daily Gazette* and now covers the Giants for the *Oakland Tribune* and as a correspondent for the Associated Press and *The Sporting News*. A San Francisco native, Peters lived in Berkeley most of his professional career before recently moving to Reno, Nevada, where he resides with his wife, Lise. Peters also has authored *100 Years of Blue & Gold,* a 100-year history of University of California football. A collector of memorabilia, he enjoys writing on the history of sports and thanks his wife and daughter Lisa for relinquishing space for his hobby.